THE
CHILDREN'S
BUREAU

Shaping a Century of Child Welfare Practices, Programs, and Policies

KATHARINE BRIAR-LAWSON, MARY MCCARTHY, AND NANCY DICKINSON, Editors

NASW PRESS
National Association of Social Workers
Washington, DC

Jeane W. Anastas, PhD, LMSW, President
Angelo McClain, PhD, LICSW, Chief Executive Officer

Cheryl Y. Bradley, *Publisher*
Sarah Lowman, *Project Manager*
Amanda Morgan, *Copyeditor*
Juanita R. Doswell, *Proofreader*
Bernice Eisen, *Indexer*

Cover by Naylor Design, Inc.
Interior design and composition by Midatlantic Publishing Services
Printed and bound by Hamilton Printing Company

First impression: September 2013

Library of Congress Cataloging-in-Publication Data

The Children's Bureau : shaping a century of child welfare practices, programs, and policies / edited by Katharine Briar-Lawson, Mary McCarthy, and Nancy Dickinson.
   pages cm
 Includes bibliographical references and index.
 ISBN 978-0-87101-446-7
 1. United States. Children's Bureau. 2. Child welfare--United States. 3. Children--Services for--United States. I. Briar-Lawson, Katharine. II. National Association of Social workers.
 HV741.C5373 2013
 362.70973--dc23
                                                                          2013020017

Printed in the United States of America

TABLE OF CONTENTS

Brenda G. McGowan

PREFACE

A s we celebrate the 100-year anniversary of the Children's Bureau, we welcome this edited book on child welfare. By delineating some of the legacies and illustrating the ways that the work of the Children's Bureau has influenced modern-day child welfare practices, this book is a thought-provoking resource for practice and program improvements. We hope the reader will be inspired by the passionate commitment and a legacy of leadership of those serving in child welfare and will think carefully about new priorities and directions that will guide our work into our next century of service.

The social work profession has long identified child welfare as a core field of practice, as seen by the focus of the earliest social work agencies on "child and family welfare." Indeed, passionate and visionary social workers launched the Children's Bureau in 1912 to address the most critical issues affecting children and families. The Children's Bureau has a century-long history linked to the profession and looks forward to setting the stage as a leader for the next century of serving children and families.

Current Children's Bureau programs are designed to promote the safety, permanency, and well-being of all children—including those in foster care, available for adoption, recently adopted, abused, neglected, dependent, disabled, or homeless—and to prevent the neglect, abuse, and exploitation of children. These key goals of child welfare practice—and the organizational and workforce conditions needed to achieve them—are addressed in this book. The book focuses attention on the Children's Bureau's commitment to building and using evidence-informed and culturally relevant practice.

The historical policy and practice backdrop for child welfare innovations in the 21st century offers a fitting framework for linking some of the future work in child welfare to the origins of the Children's Bureau. Important issues are identified, such as unemployment and poverty and the need for more innovations involving poor, minority, and disenfranchised families, who often live in communities with few resources and are beset by complex social and economic challenges. By delineating the challenges and opportunities that lie ahead, we hope that this book will chart future agendas and innovations that may guide more effective practice, programming, and policies.

Joe Bock, MSW
Acting Associate Commissioner
Children's Bureau
Administration for Children and Families
U.S. Department of Health and Human Services

PREFACE

For generations, social workers have cared about children and their welfare. Many of the earliest social work and public health initiatives centered on the needs of children and how society could best care for and support them. At the forefront of these efforts has been the Children's Bureau.

The Children's Bureau grew out of the experiences of the settlement house movement and the first schools of social work, which took root at the turn of the last century. These early pioneers of social work were joined by leaders in the labor movement and other social activists who saw a federal role for protecting children and promoting their health and safety. Importantly, four of the first five heads of the Children's Bureau, covering its first 50 years, were social workers.

The first director, Julia Lathrop (1912–1921), launched studies to identify what services and interventions were needed. She stated in her first annual report that the Bureau was to serve all children, to try to work out standards of care and protection that would give every child a fair chance in the world (U.S. Department of Health, Education, and Welfare, 1962).

Grace Abbott, the second director, served during the years 1921–1934. She was a strong advocate for maternal and child health programs, overseeing the initiation of the Sheppard–Towner Act (P.L. 67-97), an early public commitment to community-based interventions for infants and their mothers, which led to the decline of infant mortality.

From 1934 to 1952, Katherine Lenroot served as head of the Children's Bureau, guiding its work through the Great Depression, the passage of the Social Security Act of 1935 (P.L. 74-271), and the second World War. Although she was involved in framing the Aid to Dependent Children program, only the child welfare provisions of the Social Security Act ended up in the Children's Bureau. The administration of the Aid to Dependent Children program was housed in the new Bureau of Public Assistance.

Following Lenroot was Martha Eliot, a pediatrician who had run the Emergency Maternal and Infant Care program during World War II. Katherine Oettinger, who came to the Children's Bureau after serving as dean of the Boston University School of Social Work, was the fifth head, serving from 1957 until 1968. She was a strong advocate for the Children's Bureau in Congress, successfully increasing the Bureau's budget and strengthening its programs (NASW Foundation, n.d.).

Many of the areas of focus in the early days of the Children's Bureau—juvenile justice, child labor, maternal and child health, prevention of disability, and elimination of infant mortality—eventually became major programs within different federal agencies. An important factor relating to the work of the Children's Bureau is that it has always been interdisciplinary, and from the start of federal child welfare services, there was support for the education and training of social workers and social work researchers.

The National Association of Social Workers (NASW) and the Children's Bureau also have a long and collaborative history. In the early 1960s, the social work research section of the newly formed NASW was called upon to work with the Child Welfare League of America to develop a research agenda for child welfare. The Children's Bureau has supported both individual field-initiated research studies and research centers over the years. This has led to the more recent implementation centers, quality improvement centers, and evidence-based home visiting programs.

The NASW Press is pleased to publish this book. It is one more indicator of the connections between NASW and the Children's Bureau and another reflection of the strong role that the social work profession has played from the beginning, both with and within the Children's Bureau. Organized and edited by Katharine Briar-Lawson, Mary McCarthy, and Nancy Dickinson, it showcases the continued social work commitment to the field. The 17 broad-ranging chapters, authored by current child welfare leaders, address the many practice and policy issues that make up child welfare service delivery. In doing so, they create a modern vision for family-driven and culturally congruent systems of care. *The Children's Bureau: Shaping a Century of Child Welfare Practices, Programs, and Policies* is a testament to the complexity of child welfare today, and it sets a stage for the work that the Children's Bureau can, and must, undertake in its second century.

Elizabeth J. Clark, PhD, ACSW, MPH
Executive Director
NASW

References

NASW Foundation. (n.d.). *Katherine Brownell Oettinger (1903–)*. Retrieved from http://www. naswfoundation.org/pioneers/o/oettinger.htm

Sheppard-Towner Maternity and Infancy Protection Act of 1921, P.L. 67-97 (1921).

Social Security Act of 1935, P.L. 74-271, 49 Stat. 620 (1935).

U.S. Department of Health, Education, and Welfare. (1962). *Five decades of action for children: A history of the Children's Bureau.* Washington, DC: Children's Bureau.

Chapter 1

LESSONS LEARNED AND THE WAY FORWARD

Nancy S. Dickinson and Richard P. Barth

The Children's Bureau began in 1912 as the first government agency in the world to focus solely on the problems of children and the first one in this country to be headed by a woman, years before women were allowed to vote. Among the Children's Bureau's many hard-fought battles and significant accomplishments, this chapter focuses on efforts that, in our opinion, require a renewed commitment by the bureau—child mortality, children's well-being, and rigorous research—and their implications for social work practice and education. The chapter calls attention to lessons from the past, which inform prospects for effective 21st century reforms.

Lessons from the Past

Child Mortality

As the first woman to head a federal agency, Julia Lathrop began her tenure as chief of the Children's Bureau in June 1912. The act establishing the Children's Bureau, in the Department of Commerce and Labor, mandated that it "investigate and report . . . upon all matters pertaining to the welfare of children and child life among all classes of our people" (Abbott, 1923, p. 190). With a broad mandate but limited funds—and the political savvy to choose her focus wisely—Julia Lathrop selected, as her first subject of investigation, the least controversial topic: infant mortality. This issue connected with families everywhere in the country and had the virtue of building on existing public interest. The U.S. Public Health Service had previously conducted limited studies of such contributors to infant mortality as contaminated milk but had not pursued more in-depth studies of why infants died (Lindenmeyer, 1995), leaving the way open for Lathrop's focus on the causes and prevention of infant mortality.

Only eight states in 1912 registered live births. Based on these limited data, the Children's Bureau estimated an infant mortality rate of 124 deaths per 1,000 live births (Bradbury, 1962). This placed the United States behind seven other countries that were then measuring infant mortality: New Zealand, Norway, Ireland, Sweden, Australia, Bulgaria, and Scotland (Phelps, 1908). The U.S. rate is currently down to six deaths per 1,000, but that places this country behind 33 other countries, according to the United Nations Population Division (2011). Many of these other industrialized countries took a different approach to dealing with infant mortality, implementing social remedies such as national health insurance, generous maternity benefits, and children's allowances.

As a protégé of Jane Addams of Hull House, Lathrop used a settlement house strategy to fight infant mortality that involved research, outreach, intervention, and political advocacy (Kemp, Almgren, Gilchrist, & Elsinger, 2001). The staff first concentrated their study of infant mortality in Johnstown, Pennsylvania, on 1,919 babies born during 1911. Of those babies' mothers, 81 percent were successfully interviewed about family, social, industrial, and civic factors pertaining to the baby's birth and, in some cases, death. Questions focused on income, ethnicity, mothers' maternal histories and ages, and environmental conditions (Lindenmeyer, 1995).

The Children's Bureau's Johnstown study (and subsequent field studies at seven other sites) documented factors related to infant mortality and showed the correlation between infant mortality and income, poor housing, and inadequate sanitation—demonstrating that poverty was as much a cause of babies' deaths as was poor health care. While the Bureau endorsed the position that high infant mortality could be lowered by community action to help eliminate poverty (Lindenmeyer, 1995), its political solution was to ignore its own research results and focus on maternal behavior rather than societal responsibilities. A series of instructional pamphlets on prenatal and infant care promoted a middle class approach to infant care and offered few solutions for helping poor families escape poverty. It could be argued that the country has continued to ignore poverty's impact on infant mortality.

Nonetheless, the Bureau's first pamphlet, *Infant Care*, became the federal government's best-selling publication, with over 12 million copies distributed between 1914 and 1940 (Kemp et al., 2001). Moreover, the Bureau's study of infant mortality supported progressive reform efforts that contributed to a significant decline in infant mortality rates, so that between 1912 and 1930, the national infant mortality rate was cut nearly in half, from 122 deaths per 1,000 births in 1910 to 66 per 1,000 by 1930 (Kemp et al., 2001).

The bureau's infant mortality research was key to the November 1921 passage of the Sheppard-Towner Maternity and Infancy Protection Act (1921). Considered one of Lathrop's greatest advocacy successes, the act extended matching funds from the Children's Bureau to states for maternal and child health promotion programs. States were encouraged to develop maternal and child health clinics, as well as to reach out to and educate more women in rural areas (Kemp et al., 2001). Because of opposition by the

American Medical Association, however, the act was allowed to lapse in 1929, ending the Children's Bureau's 15-year fight against infant mortality.

The bureau's legacy in the fight against infant mortality was also that of the emerging social work profession. As noted by Almgren, Kemp, and Eisinger (2000), "No single effort by the social work profession in the general domain of prevention has paralleled, in scope or popular support, the campaign to reduce infant mortality undertaken by the U.S. Children's Bureau between 1912 and 1930" (p. 1).

Promoting Children's Well-Being

These prevention efforts helped to increase the credibility of the Children's Bureau and allowed Lathrop to begin working on other projects, including advocating for playgrounds, establishing visiting nurse systems, promoting the registration of births, and opposing child labor. Childhood as a time of play and innocence was predominately a middle-class notion during this period; many poor children worked outside the home, in factories or elsewhere, receiving low wages and lacking access to education. The 1900 U.S. Census showed that one in six youths between 10 and 15 years of age was employed (Children's Bureau Express, 2011). Despite hard-fought efforts to eliminate child labor, the Children's Bureau was only successful in 1938 when the high adult unemployment rates changed political and legal attitudes toward child labor regulation (Lindenmeyer, 2011).

The early Children's Bureau did not officially look into issues of abuse or neglect. Lathrop's position, influenced by her work at Hull House, was that the brutal working conditions and terrible economic problems of the parents caused their abusive and neglectful behaviors (Tichi, 2007). She did not see that some parents abused their children because of factors unrelated to purely economic stress.

By the 1930s, much of the Children's Bureau's focus shifted to children's health. Title V of the 1935 Social Security Act provided states with maternal and child welfare grants, which were used to pay for physicians, dentists, medical social workers, and nutritionists, as well as home visits by public health nurses. These programs reached a racially and ethnically diverse population. "Thus the Children's Bureau provided pathbreaking ways of improving the health of historically underserved groups" (Helfand, Lazarus, & Theerman, 2000, p. 1703). The Social Security Act also enabled the Children's Bureau to support state and local child welfare services "for the protection and care of homeless, dependent, and neglected children, and children in danger of becoming delinquent" (Social Security Act, 1935, ch. 531, title V, § 521, 49 Stat. 633).

In 1946 the Children's Bureau was transferred to the Social Security Administration by an executive order of President Truman, which predicted that the transfer "will strengthen the child-care programs by bringing them in closer association with the health, welfare, and educational activities with which they are inextricably bound up"

(Social Security Online, n.d.). This move demonstrated the bureau's change in focus from infant mortality and child labor to other pressing child health and welfare issues.

By 1969, political and professional pressures caused most of the maternal and children's health programs to be moved out of the Children's Bureau to other parts of the Department of Health, Education, and Welfare, where the Bureau had moved in 1953. In the 1950s and 1960s, the Bureau also lost control of the mental health, child development, child care, and juvenile delinquency initiatives to other newly created departments (Parker, 1994) and focused more narrowly on child abuse and neglect.

During the 1960s and 1970s, there was an unprecedented expansion of government-supported child protection and foster care services. Increased public focus on child abuse and neglect (for example, Kempe, Silverman, Steele, Droegemueller, & Silver, 1962) turned the attention of the Children's Bureau to this issue. The government, rather than private or religious charitable groups, became the primary provider of these services (Davidson, 2008). Creating a federal research and policy framework for this work became essential and evolved into the central focus of the Children's Bureau. The Child Abuse Prevention and Treatment Act of 1974 (P.L. 93-247) became the first of three major child welfare policies passed from 1974 to 1980 for which the Bureau had implementation responsibilities; the other two were the Indian Child Welfare Act of 1978 (P.L. 95-608) and the Adoption Assistance and Child Welfare Act of 1980 (P.L. 96-272). The Child Abuse Prevention and Treatment Act is discussed in the section on prevention below and in more detail in chapter 7.

Research as a Driver of Practical Reform

From the beginning of the Children's Bureau, Julia Lathrop modeled her belief that research could buttress reform (Machtinger, 1999), a view she honed while she was the first head of the research department at the Chicago School of Civics and Philanthropy (later the School of Social Service Administration and one of the country's first schools of social work). Lathrop oversaw all research activities by the Bureau (Rodems, Shaefer, & Ybarra, 2011). In the infant mortality campaign, the Children's Bureau staff practiced on a national scale the integrated prevention strategies—applied research, multilevel outreach and intervention, and political advocacy—that they had learned and tested in the urban settlement houses (Kemp et al., 2001). In 1917 Lathrop initiated the Children's Bureau practice of collaborating with universities when she contracted with the Chicago School to do research on mothers' pensions (Machtinger, 1999).

Between 1912 and 1921, 46 evidence-informed documents on child and maternal health were published by the Children's Bureau, ranging from short pamphlets on care of infants and young children to reports on comprehensive field studies covering such subjects as state and federal infant health policies and visiting nurse programs (Rodems et al., 2011). In 1924 the Children's Bureau, in partnership with the Yale School of Medicine and the New Haven (Connecticut) Department of Health, conducted field research focused on the incidence and prevention of rickets in New Haven (Children's Bureau, 2012), a forerunner of the multidisciplinary research efforts supported by the Bureau today.

The methodological rigor of the field studies contributed to social science and social work scholarship. For example, in her field research on infant mortality, Lathrop was effective in using a cohort approach in which a birth cohort of infants was followed for a one-year period, a method that became standard in epidemiologic studies (Rodems et al., 2011) and, increasingly, child welfare studies (for example, Putnam-Hornstein, 2011).

The Children's Bureau also conducted cross-national comparisons of infant mortality and maternal health care, drawing attention to the fundamental role of government in other countries' support of maternal and child health and suggesting it as a model for the United States (Rodems et al., 2011). In 1917 the Bureau published a report on efforts in small towns and rural districts in New Zealand that produced low rates of infant mortality through the use of nurses who educated parents in their homes on infant care and home hygiene (Rodems et al., 2011). Now compiled by the United Nations (which was not established until nearly 30 years later) rather than the Children's Bureau, the international comparative listings of infant mortality rates have become a public health staple and now include 194 countries.

Research during the 1930s focused primarily on the effects of unemployment on families and children (Children's Bureau, 2012). In addition to looking at the living conditions of adolescents who were roaming the country and at the effects of the economy on families of railway workers, the Bureau compiled monthly national relief statistics from all U.S. cities with populations of 50,000 or more.

Children's Bureau researchers were not only interested in the epidemiology of health problems, but also studied the development of antisocial behavior. They studied the causes of juvenile delinquency during World Wars I and II and in 1927 began recording standardized juvenile court statistics on delinquency, dependency, and neglect (Children's Bureau, 2012).

Social Work and the Children's Bureau

Schools of social work were beginning to appear around the time the Children's Bureau was established. In 1904 the New York School of Applied Philanthropy (later the Columbia University School of Social Work) began as the country's first higher education program to train people in social work, including child development and youth work. As previously noted, the Chicago School of Civics and Philanthropy (later the School of Social Service Administration) was another early school of social work, opening its doors in 1908 and focusing on social science and social research.

Social Workers Lead the Children's Bureau. The first federal agency focused on children was headed by women whose careers were embedded in the settlement house movement and informed by schools of social work. As noted previously, Julia Lathrop, the first director of the Children's Bureau (1912–1921), lived and worked at Hull House and taught research at the Chicago School of Civics and Philanthropy.

The second director of the Children's Bureau, Grace Abbott, was also a resident at Hull House in 1908 and taught at the Chicago School of Civics and Philanthropy, where her sister, Edith Abbott, later became the dean of the newly created University of Chicago School of Social Service Administration in 1924, the first female dean of any graduate school in the country (School of Social Service Administration, University of Chicago, n.d.). Grace Abbott's greatest contribution to the Children's Bureau was helping to draft Title V of the Social Security Act, which included child welfare, services to children with disabilities, and maternal and child health provisions (Parker, 1994). After 13 exceptionally productive years as director, Grace Abbott resigned because of poor health.

In 1934, Katharine Lenroot assumed the bureau's helm, strongly supported by social workers connected to the New York School of Applied Philanthropy. Lenroot was thought to be an adequate administrator but to lack a vision for the future of the Bureau, a view shared by another social worker in the government, Harry Hopkins (Parker, 1994). Hopkins did not feel that Lenroot could successfully administer the program established under Title IV of the Social Security Act, Aid to Dependent Children, and so intervened to have a new agency, the Bureau of Public Assistance, assume responsibility for that program. At that point, the Children's Bureau lost an opportunity to support an integrated approach to serving families (Parker, 1994). Lenroot had more success in the international arena, creating the United Nations International Children's Emergency Fund (UNICEF), representing the United States at four Pan-American Child Congresses, and serving on the executive board of UNICEF from 1947 to 1951 (Children's Bureau, 2012).

Martha Eliot, a medical doctor, worked at the Children's Bureau as assistant and then associate chief to administer health-related Title V grants to states (Parker, 1994). Eliot was director of the Children's Bureau from 1952 to 1956. Among her accomplishments were helping to draft the child welfare portions of the Social Security Act and conceiving and implementing the Emergency Maternity and Infant Care program (Children's Bureau, 2012).

Katherine Oettinger was the next director of the Children's Bureau, the first who was formally trained as a social worker and a former dean of the Boston University School of Social Work. During her tenure (1957–1968), Oettinger presided over a sixfold increase in the Bureau's budget and was instrumental in focusing public attention on child abuse and neglect, child care, programs for children with disabilities and juvenile delinquency (Children's Bureau, 2012).

Social Work Plays a Central Role in Child Welfare. The rise in professional social work paralleled the beginning of the Children's Bureau and played an early role in the use of social casework in mothers' pensions programs between 1912 and 1930 (Machtinger,

1999). During Julia Lathrop's tenure at the Children's Bureau, there was strong advocacy for public provision of pensions to single mothers who had lost husbands to death, desertion, or imprisonment. Before becoming chief of the Children's Bureau, Lathrop had a prominent role in developing a mothers' pensions policy in Illinois. Her advocacy on this issue was based on her reading of the evidence that long-term public support for single mothers would help to eradicate female poverty, which contributed to infant mortality, and ease the burden of mothering and working for low wages (Machtinger, 1999). These settlement house reformers believed that poverty resulted not from personal shortcomings but from structural causes such as unemployment and low wages, and they advocated for state and federal governments to intervene to provide essential support for mothers and children.

Lathrop brought these convictions and policy successes into play at the Children's Bureau, where she advocated successfully for development of mothers' pensions laws in states, so that by 1920 there were such laws in 40 states (Machtinger, 1999). Problems with implementation of these laws led the Bureau to collect, analyze, and disseminate information about laws and standards of care of dependent children. Children's Bureau staff also wanted to ensure the quality of services by requiring delivery by trained social workers (Machtinger, 1999). The use of the newly developed social casework method became central to the work with mothers. Through its emphasis on investigation, diagnosis, and treatment, this individualized approach assumed social pathology on the part of recipients. It can be said that the use of social casework practice turned the focus of the mothers' pensions away from societal reform as necessary for the eradication of poverty, which the settlement house reformers had emphasized. As Machtinger (1999) stated, the social casework approach focused more on improving the individual mother and "was a step away from the bureau's original focus on mothers' pensions as a social and economic right" (p. 115).

Children's Bureau Plays a Lead Role in Social Work Education. With leadership from the Children's Bureau, agencies and universities collaborated to make social work education available to those wanting a career in child welfare (Ellett & Leighninger, 2007). Other chapters in this book discuss this collaboration in far more detail. This section summarizes policies that have supported these collaborations. The federal government began providing grants to states for child welfare in 1935 through the Child Welfare Services Program, Title IV-B of the Social Security Act (Child Welfare Information Gateway, 2011), and states were encouraged to use this funding to support educational leave for staff members seeking a social work degree. In 1962 the Title IV-B, Section 426 Discretionary Training Grant Program was created to provide financial support for social work education.

Since passage of the Adoption Assistance and Child Welfare Act of 1980 (P.L. 96-272), and more frequently since 1990, states have used Title IV-E funding to enable public universities to provide stipends for BSW and MSW education. There has also been a significant growth in IV-E-funded training academies that prepare child welfare workers for their roles. The country has, arguably, never had so many child welfare workers with specialized educational preparation and high-quality preservice training.

Despite this progress, there is no continuity across states in educational requirements for child welfare staff and no national data about educational backgrounds of current employees. Even counties within states vary in what they require—a substantial number of them now prefer a MSW for every child welfare worker, and many more require a MSW for every supervisor. These requirements are supported by research, which has shown that a social work degree, with an emphasis on child welfare practice, is a strong contributor to child welfare worker retention and improved worker competence (Fox, Miller, & Barbee, 2003; Jones & Okamura, 2000).

Prospects for Twenty-First Century Reforms: Policies, Programs, and Workforce Development

This chapter's first section dealt with selected issues and themes from the early decades of the Children's Bureau: child mortality and well-being, research, and the social work profession and practice. This section describes how these early themes were the seeds for 21st century reforms that we believe merit renewed attention. Topics discussed in this section are child abuse prevention (with an emphasis on preventing maltreatment fatalities), intervention research, and social work practice and education.

Child Abuse Prevention

Efforts by the Children's Bureau to prevent child abuse have increased in focus and intensity since the early 1960s. This section draws attention to policies and programs that are proving beneficial for preventing maltreatment fatalities, as well as physical and sexual abuse.

Maltreatment Fatalities. As described earlier, the Children's Bureau's first task was to study and work to prevent infant mortality, which was largely attributable to poverty, poor living conditions, and lack of health care. While infant mortality rates did decrease over time, concern has lately turned more specifically to fatalities resulting from abuse or neglect by a parent or a primary caregiver. Chapter 8 describes efforts over the last two decades to identify, count, and respond to fatal maltreatment.

Despite child protection programs, child maltreatment fatalities remain a serious problem, with an estimated 1,560 deaths a year, which translates to a rate of 2.07 deaths per 100,000 children and an average of four children—chiefly infants and toddlers—dying every day from abuse or neglect (Child Welfare Information Gateway, 2012). In the last few years, a growing number of states have been able to link birth records, child welfare services data, and mortality records to begin to develop a clearer picture of child mortality risk related to child maltreatment. Putnam-Hornstein (2011) has, for example, demonstrated that children in California who have ever had any contact (substantiated or not) with child welfare services have a five times greater likelihood of dying before the age of five than children in the general population. Such findings may help bring a public health perspective back to child welfare services.

Child Maltreatment Prevention. When addressing the issue of child maltreatment fatalities, prevention is a recurring theme. For example, the child fatality review process helps to identify risk factors, which is useful in developing strategies to prevent future fatalities.

In 1962 Henry Kempe coined the term "battered child syndrome" to describe children's physical and emotional trauma at the hands of family members and caretakers (Kempe et al., 1962). Between 1963 and 1967, all states and the District of Columbia passed child abuse reporting laws, and the Child Abuse Prevention and Treatment Act was passed in 1974. The act provided assistance to states, which developed their own definitions of child abuse and neglect; it was not until its reauthorization in 1996 that a minimum definition of child abuse was set for all states to follow (Child Welfare Information Gateway, 2009). This delay created some problems, which are discussed in more detail in chapter 7.

As a result of these policy efforts, the 1980s witnessed a significant expansion in public awareness of child maltreatment and the development and dissemination of both interventions and prevention strategies, with efforts to prevent sexual abuse diverging from efforts to prevent physical abuse and neglect (Daro, 1988). Most of the modest improvements reported in the 2006 Fourth Federal National Incidence Study on Child Maltreatment (Sedlak et al., 2010) were declines in sexual abuse. According to Daro (2010), these declines could be attributable to sexual abuse prevention efforts in schools, in youth-serving and religious organizations, and through broadly disseminated public safety messages designed to educate children and the general public that sexual abuse is unacceptable. Additionally, cases of sexual abuse are often aggressively prosecuted, with extended incarceration of offenders, and this could be having an effect (Daro, 2010).

Preventing physical child abuse and neglect, on the other hand, has been difficult. Recent prevention efforts focus on supporting parents during pregnancy and at birth, a key period for strengthening the parent-child relationship, which is essential to a child's healthy physical and emotional development. Prevention programs have usually included intensive home-based interventions, such as home visiting programs, but data show that these efforts have not brought about hoped-for results (Daro, 2010). Expanding these intensive services is imperative, and the Patient Protection and Affordable Care Act of 2010 (P.L. 111-148) is set to provide states $1.5 billion through 2016 to expand the provision of evidence-based home visitation programs to at-risk pregnant women and newborns (Child Welfare Information Gateway, 2011). These targeted programs may not be as effective as needed by the most challenged populations—those struggling with serious mental illness, domestic violence, and substance abuse, as well as those living in violent and chaotic neighborhoods. Prevention efforts that should be part of home visitation services include the following (Child Welfare Information Gateway, 2011; Daro, 2010):

- public awareness messages regarding child physical abuse and neglect that target specific parental behaviors that need to change (similar to successful past campaigns targeting sexual abuse)
- education efforts about abuse and neglect targeting all new parents, similar to the educational campaigns regarding "Back to Sleep" and shaken baby syndrome
- universal assessment of all new parents and linking of families with services according to their needs
- evidence-based parent education programs that teach positive parent–child interaction skills appropriate to the child's developmental level and that include skills demonstrations and practice
- child welfare systems with the capacity to work with parents who require mandatory intervention to ensure the safety of children, with staff who are willing to remove children from harm when parents are not willing or able to change

Future efforts by the Children's Bureau to advance prevention should include expanding current strategies that work, funding research to develop new strategies, and supporting the development of strategic partnerships for collective impact across communities (for example, Kania & Kramer, 2011). Challenges include the following (Child Welfare Information Gateway, 2011; see also Dubowitz, Feigelman, Lane, & Kim, 2009):

- improving the ability to reach all populations at risk, both those with severe and chronic challenges and those needing help on an emergency basis
- determining the best interventions for diverse ethnic and cultural groups
- identifying ways to use technology to expand contact and improve service access
- working with the expanding primary care workforce—under the Patient Protection and Affordable Care Act (2010)—to realize its potential for child abuse prevention

Research

As noted earlier, Julia Lathrop brought to the Children's Bureau her experience as head of the research department at the school now known as the University of Chicago's School of Social Service Administration. Lathrop personally oversaw all research activities at the Bureau and developed contracts with universities for specific research activities. Epidemiological research on infant mortality, rickets, juvenile delinquency, and other topics became a standard method for research at the Children's Bureau. Cohort analysis was a staple of this work as well.

State and National Data Collection, Analysis, and Reporting. Epidemiological research occurs today in the collection, analysis, and reporting of data on adoption and foster care, child abuse and neglect, and child welfare. Authorized in 1984, the Adoption and Foster Care Analysis and Reporting System collects and reports case-level information on all children in foster care and on children who are adopted under the auspices of the state's public child welfare agency. By 1993, the Children's Bureau was providing states with the opportunity to obtain 75 percent federal funding to plan, design, develop, and implement the automation systems needed to collect data on foster care and adoption. It has also provided support, beginning in the 1990s, for a National Resource Center on Child Welfare Data and Technology to assist states with their information technology needs. The Bureau has also developed an assessment review process to help states identify and solve problems with their automated information systems.

The National Child Abuse and Neglect Data System, a data collection and analysis system, was created in response to the requirements of the Child Abuse Prevention, Adoption, and Family Services Act of 1988 (P. L. 100-294), which authorized limited government research about child abuse prevention and treatment. In addition, the act created the National Clearinghouse on Child Abuse and Neglect Information and the National Center on Child Abuse and Neglect, which was charged with identifying issues and areas needing special focus in new research and demonstration projects (Child Welfare Information Gateway, 2009).

The act also broadened the scope of research to include the National Incidence Study of Child Abuse and Neglect, which started with much difficulty and has now been carried out four times. Early studies estimated overall incidence of moderate and severe child maltreatment. The latest (fourth) study had enough statistical power and measurement precision to test key hypotheses about populations at greatest risk for maltreatment (Sedlak et al., 2010).

Strengthening Research Infrastructure. In the early 1990s the Children's Bureau invested in strengthening the field's research infrastructure. Funding three National Child Welfare Research Centers for five years, the Bureau endeavored to develop research programs that could inspire child welfare researchers and provide instruction on research methods. Chapin Hall Center for Children at the University of Chicago began an ongoing summer administrative data analytics institute, and the University of California, Berkeley's Child Welfare Fellows Institute brought aspiring child welfare scholars in to learn about analysis of administrative data and other research matters.

Data from the Adoption and Foster Care Analysis and Reporting System and National Child Abuse and Neglect Data System are now drawn on to construct the annual Child

Welfare Outcomes report to Congress. The National Youth in Transition Database collects case-level information on youth currently in foster care and those who have aged out of care. In 1999, the Children's Bureau began the Child and Family Services Review, a process for assessing states' performance on seven outcomes and seven systemic factors supporting the achievement of outcomes related to safety, permanency, and well-being. This review system represents a departure from compliance-driven reviews under Titles IV-B and IV-E of the Social Security Act, which primarily ensured states' conformity to policies and procedures. The Child and Family Services Review makes it possible for states to learn important lessons from administrative data and, through a review of a small sample of cases, to understand service processes and outcomes for children, youths, and families.

Research funded by the Children's Bureau in collaboration with other federal offices and institutes includes the Longitudinal Study of Child Abuse and Neglect, on the causes and impact of child abuse and neglect, initiated in 1990 with grants from the National Center on Child Abuse and Neglect and composed of five collaborating longitudinal research projects. More recently, the National Survey of Child and Adolescent Well-Being has collected data that describe the child welfare system and the experiences of children and families who come in contact with it. Although managed by the Office of Planning, Research, and Evaluation, the National Survey of Child and Adolescent Well-Being follows the tradition of the Children's Bureau by tracking the life course of children to gather data about services received, measures of child well-being, and longer term results, information that will provide a clearer understanding of life outcomes for children and families involved with the child welfare system.

Promoting Investigator-Initiated Research. A possible negative consequence of funding these larger projects (especially the National Incidence Study and the National Survey of Child and Adolescent Well-Being) has been the contemporaneous decrease in field-initiated research by child welfare scholars. In contrast, the National Institutes of Health and the Institute of Education Science offer health and education scholars opportunities to apply for grants that reward innovative and rigorous research proposals through a peer-review grants mechanism. Strong proposals can be resubmitted, following painstaking and informative peer review, for reconsideration. No such mechanism for field-initiated research exists for child welfare scholars. Most Children's Bureau grant announcements are very narrowly defined, which arguably places significant limits on research.

Funding Intervention Research. In 2008, the Children's Bureau began awarding five-year cooperative agreements for Quality Improvement Centers to promote knowledge development to improve child welfare services in five areas of focus: nonresident fathers, privatization, differential response, early childhood, and the representation of children. Each Quality Improvement Center conducts a national needs assessment and gap analysis on its area of focus and funds demonstration projects to address identified gaps (Children's Bureau, 2012).

Unlike the historical approach of the Children's Bureau to collecting data for reports and general information, Quality Improvement Center demonstration projects are funded to develop robust evidence about specific interventions. This emerging research strategy is also evident in the recent funding announcements related to trauma-informed practice, permanency innovation initiatives, home visiting, and IV-E waiver demonstration projects, among others.

Evidence-Based Practices

The early leaders of the Children's Bureau promoted the use of research evidence to inform the bureau's practices and programs. They were committed to linking research to practice to improve the lives of infants and new mothers, homeless and delinquent children, and those with physical illnesses. That commitment to designing, implementing, and evaluating promising programs and practices to improve outcomes for children, youth, and families lost strength toward the end of the 20th century but appears to be gaining new impetus as the Children's Bureau enters its second century. Intervention testing and implementation tools that bring evidence to bear on outcomes are more available and effective than before. Whether they will have enduring use depends on the commitment of the child welfare system to creating evidence-based child welfare practices and ensuring their use.

Evidence-based practice (EBP) is a fairly new concept in child welfare, compared with fields such as medicine, public health, and mental health, which began broader discussions of EBP in the early 1990s. The California Evidence-Based Clearinghouse for Child Welfare (n.d.), one of several organizations that review and screen evidence-based interventions, defines evidence-based child welfare practice as based on a combination of best research evidence, best clinical experience, and consistency with family and client values. Identifying practices that are supported by strong scientific research ensures that the best possible interventions are available for use with child welfare populations.

The number of EBPs for child welfare is increasing, but slowly. On the Clearinghouse list, for example, 108 practices have a high child welfare relevance rating (possible ratings are high, medium, and low). Each practice listed by the Clearinghouse has been rated as (1) well supported by research evidence, (2) supported by research evidence, (3) having promising research evidence, (4) failing to demonstrate effect, (5) being a concerning practice, or (NR) not able to be rated. Searching the Clearinghouse for the highest scientific rating resulted in a list of 21 EBPs. Yet only two programs receive the highest rating for both level of evidence and child welfare relevance: Project SUPPORT, an in-home parenting education program for mothers who have left domestic violence shelters, and trauma-focused cognitive–behavioral therapy.

Implementing EBPs requires commitment and a host of supports, including expert practitioners to deliver or facilitate them, skilled supervisors to provide training and ongoing support, leadership to help overcome inertia and attachment to existing procedures, an organizational climate that encourages innovation, and adequate financial resources to build the necessary infrastructure. Once implemented, at least some EBPs have been highly endorsed by child welfare service providers (Aarons, Sommerfeld, Hecht, Silovsky, & Chaffin, 2009). When combined with experienced, intensive supervision, they help agencies to reduce the variability in the achievement of favorable outcomes so that families with greater problems are more likely to benefit (Chaffin, Hecht, Bard, Silovsky, & Beasley, 2012).

Child welfare agencies are beginning to demonstrate greater integration of some evidence-based parenting programs like Parent Child Interaction Therapy and SafeCare. Yet there is a long way to go before agencies routinely require and fund these interventions rather than training programs that are less intensive, do not have structured parenting practice, and are led by people without adequate training or coaching (Barth et al., 2005). The opportunity to increase the use of parenting programs and interventions to reduce the impact of trauma are two of the most promising additions to child welfare services. Far less developed are EBPs for reunification, case management, and post-adoption services.

Beyond the scope of this chapter is a discussion of the funding, organizational, community, professional, and practice challenges related to implementation of EBPs, as well as the role of the child welfare workforce in implementing EBPs. What should child welfare workers in different positions be able to do? Should they be able to assess which children need access to an EBP, refer children to the correct EBP based on assessment data they collect, ensure that contract workers are delivering an EBP, or deliver the EBP themselves? In order to be able to take any or all of these steps, child welfare workers must have knowledge about EBPs and the skills, motivation, and time to make appropriate referrals to them. Much has been learned about teaching EBPs so that they are used by the practitioners who learn them, but little is known about how to arrange for referrals to them (Barth, 2008).

Implications of Evidence-Based Practices for Social Work Education

Education of social workers on child welfare practice is beginning to adapt EBPs. A growing expertise in motivational interviewing, for example, is emerging. An innovative approach that engages the developers of EBPs in the training and ongoing coaching of field instructors and of MSW students has been tested in a cluster of schools of social work. This approach is reducing the gap between what is taught in the classroom and what is known by field instructors, and vice versa.

If given the chance, EBP can become a unifying framework for social work education, as it integrates cultural responsiveness, ethics, research, practice theory, skills, and macro and micro perspectives (Drake, Hovmand, Jonson-Reid, & Zayas, 2007). The response of social work programs—and the Children's Bureau—must be a commitment to preparing expert child welfare professionals (perhaps through a three-year MSW program), funding doctoral and postdoctoral child welfare research, and supporting social work faculty in developing evidence-based child welfare interventions.

Using Lessons Learned to Improve Prospects for Reform

In their article promoting a study of the past to reveal "good ideas that still deserve to be acted upon," Golden and Markel (2007, p. 445) assert that the founding of the Children's Bureau inspired hope that children would be in the forefront of U.S. domestic policy. That hope was energized by the passage of the Sheppard-Towner Maternity and Infancy Protection Act (1921), as a result of which more than 4 million infants and preschool children and approximately 700,000 pregnant women were served through state programs through 1929 (Lindenmeyer, 1995).

Following that achievement, as discussed earlier, the Children's Bureau's political compromises and loss of power resulted in a splintering of efforts to focus on the "whole child" (Kemp et al., 2001). The telling result of these political and professional setbacks is that today federal programs are organized by function rather than by constituency, so that services for children cut across multiple federal departments. For example, child health programs are under the U.S. Public Health Service and the Health Resources and Services Administration, the U.S. Department of Education oversees state grants for infants and toddlers, the economic well-being of children and families is the purview of the Temporary Assistance for Needy Families program in the U.S. Department of Health and Human Services (HHS), and the Substance Abuse and Mental Health Services Administration has funded women, children, and family treatment programs. This fractured approach to serving children, youth, and families wastes resources, including the financial and political resources required to keep the needs of the "whole child" (and the family) in the forefront of national interest and responsibility.

To counter this fractured approach, Golden and Markel (2007) envision a Department of Children's Affairs, a fully funded Cabinet-level agency responsible for raising standards of health, welfare, and education for children. All government agencies dealing with children, including the Department of Education and all HHS agencies serving children, would be brought under the leadership of the new department.

We propose consideration of an alternative approach that involves creation of a Cabinet-level Director for Children. The Director for Children would also be the director of the Children's Bureau and would have the responsibility to assist all Cabinet members to identify their children's portfolio and to recommend ways that their policies can most advantageously affect children. The Director for Children would also lead meetings of a Children's Cabinet, which would comprise designees from all Cabinet-level agencies who are responsible for children's interests. In leading the Children's Cabinet and participating in the national Cabinet, the Director for Children would assist all federal departments to make policy and program decisions in keeping with a unifying view of protecting children and improving children's outcomes.

However we might bring more attention and resources to bear on behalf of children, what should be certain is the commitment to see that a stronger Children's Bureau returns to its founding mandate to "investigate and report . . . upon all matters pertaining to the welfare of children and child life among all classes of our people" (Abbott, 1923, p. 190). "The achievements of the Children's Bureau in the opening decades of the twentieth century—when it faced political opposition, government infighting, and the economic strictures imposed by the Great Depression—should be regarded as an inspiration" (Golden & Markel, 2007, p. 449). Bringing action to inspiration will involve a lot of hard work. But the prospects for children who are increasingly living in poverty, failing to get a high-quality education, lacking medical care, dying unnecessarily in infancy, and suffering maltreatment are worth the effort.

References

Aarons, G. A., Sommerfeld, D. H., Hecht, D. B., Silovsky, J. F., & Chaffin, M. J. (2009). The impact of evidence-based practice implementation and fidelity monitoring on staff turnover: Evidence for a protective effect. *Journal of Consulting and Clinical Psychology, 77,* 270–280.

Adoption Assistance and Child Welfare Act, P.L. 96-272, 94 Stat. 500 (42 U.S.C. 1305) (1980).

Abbott, G. (1923). Ten years' work for children. *North American Review, 218,* 189–200.

Almgren, G., Kemp, S., & Eisinger, A. (2000). The legacy of Hull House and the Children's Bureau in the American mortality transition. *Social Service Review, 74,* 1–27.

Barth, R. P. (2008). The move to evidence-based practice: How well does it fit child welfare services? *Journal of Public Child Welfare, 2,* 145–172.

Barth, R. P., Landsverk, J., Chamberlain, P., Reid, J., Rolls, J., Hurlburt, M., & Kohl, P. L. (2005). Parent training in child welfare services: Planning for a more evidence based approach to serving biological parents. *Research on Social Work Practice, 15,* 353–371.

Bradbury, D. (1962). *Five decades of action for children: A history of the Children's Bureau.* Washington, DC: U.S. Department of Health, Education, and Welfare.

California Evidence-Based Clearinghouse for Child Welfare. (n.d.). *Welcome to the CEBC.* Retrieved from http://www.cebc4cw.org

Chaffin, M., Hecht, D., Bard, D., Silovsky, J. F., & Beasley, W. H. (2012). A statewide trial of the SafeCare home-based services model with parents in Child Protective Services. *Pediatrics, 129,* 509–515.

Child Abuse Prevention, Adoption, and Family Services Act, P. L. 100-294 , H.R. 1900, 102 Stat. 102 (Apr. 25, 1988).

Child Abuse Prevention and Treatment Act, P.L. 93-247, 88 Stat. 4 (42 U.S.C. 5101 et seq.) (Jan. 31, 1974).

Child Welfare Information Gateway. (2009). *Major federal legislation concerned with child protection, child welfare, and adoption.* Washington, DC: U.S. Department of Health and Human Services, Children's Bureau.

Child Welfare Information Gateway. (2011). *Child maltreatment prevention: Past, present, and future.* Washington, DC: U.S. Department of Health and Human Services, Children's Bureau.

Child Welfare Information Gateway. (2012). *Child abuse and neglect fatalities 2010: Statistics and interventions.* Retrieved from http://www.childwelfare.gov/pubs/factsheets/fatality.cfm

Children's Bureau. (2012). *The story of the Children's Bureau: 100 years of serving our nation's children and families.* Retrieved from https://cb100.acf.hhs.gov/Cb_ebrochure

Children's Bureau Express. (2011, May). Centennial series: An evolving view of childhood. *Children's Bureau Express, 12*(4). Retrieved from https://cbexpress.acf.hhs.gov/index.cfm?event=website.viewArticles&issueid=126&sectionid=1&articleid=3158

Daro, D. (1988). *Confronting child abuse: Research for effective program design.* New York: Free Press.

Daro, D. (2010). *Child abuse prevention: A job half done.* Chicago: Chapin Hall at the University of Chicago.

Davidson, H. (2008). Federal law and state intervention when parents fail: Has national guidance of our child welfare system been successful? *Family Law Quarterly, 42,* 481–510.

Drake, B., Hovmand, P., Jonson-Reid, M., & Zayas, L. H. (2007). Adopting and teaching evidence-based practice in master's level social work programs. *Journal of Social Work Education, 43,* 431–446.

Dubowitz, H., Feigelman, S., Lane, W., & Kim, J. (2009). Pediatric primary care to help prevent child maltreatment: The Safe Environment for Every Kid (SEEK) model. *Pediatrics, 123,* 858–864.

Ellett, A. J., & Leighninger, L. (2007). What happened? An historical analysis of the de-professionalization of child welfare with implications for policy and practice. *Journal of Public Child Welfare, 7*(1), 3–34.

Fox, S. R., Miller, V. P., & Barbee, A. P. (2003). Finding and keeping child welfare workers: Effective use of training and professional development. In K. Briar-Lawson & J. L. Zlotnik (Eds.), *Charting the impacts of university-child welfare collaboration* (pp. 67–81). New York: Haworth Press.

Golden, J., & Markel, H. (2007). A historically based thought experiment: Meeting new challenges for children's health and well-being. *Health Affairs, 26,* 445–449.

Helfand, W. G., Lazarus, J., & Theerman, P. (2000). Images of health: The Children's Bureau and public health at midcentury. *American Journal of Public Health, 90*(11), 1703.

Indian Child Welfare Act, P.L. 95-608, 92 Stat. 3069 (25 U.S.C. 1901 et seq.) (Nov. 8, 1978).

Jones, L. P., & Okamura, A. (2000). Reprofessionalizing child welfare services: An evaluation of a Title-IVE training program. *Research on Social Work Practice, 10,* 607–621.

Kania, J., & Kramer, M. (2011). Collective impact. *Stanford Social Innovation Review.* Retrieved from http://www.ssireview.org//articles/entry/collective_impact

Kemp, S., Almgren, G., Gilchrist, L., & Eisinger, A. (2001). Serving the "whole child": Prevention practice and the U.S. Children's Bureau. *Smith College Studies in Social Work, 71,* 475–499.

Kempe, C. H., Silverman, F., Steele, B., Droegemueller, W., & Silver, H. (1962). The battered child syndrome. *JAMA, 181,* 17–24.

Lindenmeyer, K. (1995). The U.S. Children's Bureau and infant mortality in the Progressive Era. *Journal of Education, 177*(3), 57–69.

Lindenmeyer, K. (2011, January 21). U.S. Children's Bureau. *The Social Welfare History Project.* Retrieved from http://www.socialwelfarehistory.com/organizations/u-s-children's-bureau

Machtinger, B. (1999). The U.S. Children's Bureau and Mothers' Pensions Administration, 1912–1930. *Social Service Review, 73,* 105–118.

Parker, J. K. (1994). Women at the helm: Succession politics at the Children's Bureau, 1912–1968. *Social Work, 39,* 551–559.

Patient Protection and Affordable Care Act, P.L. 111-148, 124 Stat. 119 (2010).

Phelps, E. B. (1908). A statistical study of infant mortality. *Quarterly Publications of the American Statistical Association, 11,* 233–272.

Putnam-Hornstein, E. (2011). Report of maltreatment as a risk factor for injury death: A prospective birth cohort study. *Child Maltreatment, 16,* 163–174.

Rodems, E. S., Shaefer, H. L., & Ybarra, M. (2011). The Children's Bureau and passage of the Sheppard-Towner Act of 1921: Early social work macro practice in action. *Families in Society, 92,* 358–362.

School of Social Service Administration, University of Chicago. (n.d.). *Our founding mothers.* Retrieved from http://www.ssa.uchicago.edu/our-founding-mothers

Sedlak, A. J., Mettenburg, J., Basena, M., Petta, I., McPherson, K., Greene, A., & Li, S. (2010). *Fourth national incidence study of child abuse and neglect (NIS-4): Report to Congress, executive summary.* Washington, DC: U.S. Department of Health and Human Services, Administration for Children and Families.

Sheppard-Towner Maternity and Infancy Protection Act, ch. 135, 42 Stat. 224 (Nov. 23, 1921).

Social Security Act, Section 721, acts Aug. 14, 1935, ch. 531, title V, § 521, 49 Stat. 633 (1935).

Social Security Online. (n.d.). *History: SSA-related topics: The Children's Bureau.* Retrieved from http://www.ssa.gov/history/childb1.html

Tichi, C. (2007, September). *Justice, not pity: Julia Lathrop, first chief of the U.S. Children's Bureau.* Presentation before the Office on Child Abuse and Neglect, Washington, DC.

United Nations Population Division. (2011). *World mortality 2011.* Retrieved from http://www.un.org/esa/population/publications/wmchart2011/wmchart2011.pdf

Chapter 2

FAMILY-DRIVEN AND COMMUNITY-BASED SYSTEMS OF CARE

William Bell and David Sanders

History of Child Welfare

The child welfare system in the United States was born out of historical currents that recognized the vulnerability of children. Its evolution is a reflection of how much government oversight, involvement, and intervention society believes is necessary to protect children from harm. This objective has been met in different ways over time—some good, and some that we now know to be harmful. As the child welfare system continues to evolve, it behooves us to remember its history. It was built upon a set of values that have historically considered "clients," whether they are children or families, as people who need to be rescued, changed, and resocialized to adhere to the standards of society at large. Even today, many of the elements that dictated the manner in which child welfare programs have historically been delivered are still with us.

The history of child welfare can be divided into three time periods: the eighteenth, nineteenth, and twentieth centuries. Although there was no public child welfare system prior to the nineteenth century, two groups of children became a common concern of early communities, due to the high emphasis on self-sufficiency and contributing to society: the orphaned and the poor (Hacsi, 1995; McGowan, 2005). Both groups were seen as vulnerable due to their inability to care for themselves. While early interventions did seek to protect and care for such children, this was not done to provide them with a safe and carefree childhood but rather to provide them with the necessary tools and training so that they could become productive members of society.

Children of the poor in particular were seen as requiring special attention so that they would not "acquire the 'bad habits' of their parents" (McGowan, 2005, p. 11). As a result of the growing population of orphaned and poor children and their need for a "proper" upbringing, children were placed in asylums, indentured, apprenticed, or bonded out to wealthy families, farmers, tradesmen, or small businesses to work in exchange for their care and the acquisition of a skill that would allow them to support themselves when they reached adulthood (Hacsi, 1995; Reef, 2005). These "arrangements were designed to ensure that children were taught the values of industriousness and hard work and received a strict religious upbringing" (McGowan, 2005, p. 12). Prior to the mid-1800s, these interventions were only provided to white children, as the majority of African American children were slaves and seen as property, to be provided for by their owners, and the majority of Native American children were outside of the realm of government control (Takaki, 1993).

The beginning of the nineteenth century saw the creation of poorhouses or almshouses—institutions that housed abandoned or orphaned children along with the infirm (the aged, the sick, and the mentally ill) who were unable to care for themselves. This time also saw the establishment of orphanages, specialized schools for children with blindness, deafness, or other special needs, and institutions for youth offenders (Reef, 2005). Many who entered these facilities were the children of immigrant parents who were unable to care for them due to poverty or other reasons (Charles & Garfat, 2009). Regardless of the reason, the main purpose of these institutions was for children to learn a trade and discipline.

At that time, mainstream society viewed idleness as the cause of poverty; therefore, the hope was that the work these children performed would prepare them for a life of independence and self-sufficiency (Iceland, 2006). By the mid-1800s, however, a backlash emerged against these facilities "as public officials and social professionals realized that such institutions did little to reduce poverty and sometimes even exacerbated family instability" (Iceland, 2006, p. 12). What would eventually become known as foster care emerged with the establishment of the Children's Aid Society in New York City, one of the first organizations dedicated to helping poor children.

The founder of the Children's Aid Society, Charles Loring Brace, shunned the charity-run orphanages, group homes, and special-needs boarding schools, believing that they fostered dependence on charity when they should be fostering independence. In fact, he believed institutional care had the potential to do more harm than good. Brace deemed that the only way to save these children was to place them in good Christian homes in rural areas, where they would receive a moral upbringing with a strong work ethic (McGowan, 2005). As a result, the New York Children's Aid Society placed tens of thousands of poor, homeless, and destitute children from New York on trains bound for small towns in the Midwest and South, to be placed with rural families (O'Connor, 2004).

The Society's "placing system was designed to 'protect' children from the urban environment and from their own parents, who were presumed to be unworthy individuals incapable of rearing children properly" (Hacsi, 1997, p. 167). Although Brace might appear paternalistic by today's standards, he did seem to be on the right track in that he believed that families did a better job of raising children than institutions. However, he failed in that he overlooked the importance of the child's birth family (Trattner, 1999).

The beginning of the twentieth century began to see a shift in how child development was viewed and, consequently, in how services for children were provided. Many institutions were replaced by foster homes; agencies like the New York Society for the Prevention of Cruelty to Children were created to protect children from abuse and neglect (Myers, 2008); social work professionals began to advocate for government to play a larger role in child welfare, and the concept that children needed to be removed from their family homes in order to be saved from poverty was rejected (Katz, 1996). In fact, "in 1909, the preservation of families ranked first among the recommendations of the White House Conference on Children" (Katz, 1996, p. 128).

In 1912, the first federal agency for children, the Children's Bureau, was created. The focus of child welfare shifted from rescuing children in poverty to protecting children from harm. Led by the Children's Bureau, a stronger emphasis was placed on providing services to the family and preserving the family unit (Katz, 1996). In response to this shift, federal and state governments took a stronger public policy response by enacting laws to prevent and respond to child abuse and neglect. For example, in 1935 the Social Security Act P.L. 74-271 provided federal funding for child welfare services for the first time. As a result, "by 1938 all but one state had submitted a plan for the coordinated delivery of child welfare services" (McGowan, 2005, p. 27).

Child advocacy and nonprofit organizations as well as the academic community also began to take a stronger role with the creation of social work organizations and schools of social work within universities. As federal and state governments expanded services, they began playing a larger role in the lives of children and families (McGowen, 2005). Despite the assertion that children should remain in their homes, child welfare practice, with its focus on child rescue, continued to remove children from their homes. The children being removed were no longer white children of immigrants, however, as most immigrants had now been absorbed into society (Jacobson, 1998), but rather children of color.

Starting in the mid-twentieth century, large numbers of African American and Native American children entered the child welfare system. Historically, African American communities had largely been excluded from the system; as a result, they had developed their own structure for taking care of their children, primarily through churches, community surveillance and discipline, kinship care, and formal and informal adoption (Jimenez, 2006). However, with the 1935 advent of Aid to Families with Dependent Children, a program designed to help children in families with little or no income, and the subsequent administrative Flemming Rule established by the Department of Health and Human Services, which dictated that the state must provide intervention services when a home was deemed unsuitable for a child, in the 1960s, more African American children began to enter foster care (Lawrence-Webb, 1997).

With no clear definition by the federal government as to what "suitable" meant, states (and by default social workers, who were often untrained) were left to their own interpretations (Lawrence-Webb, 1997). Native American children, whose families had historically been viewed as needing to be civilized and resocialized to adhere to Euro-centric values and standards (Takaki, 1993), also begin to enter the child welfare system in large numbers. Removal of Native American children from their communities was not new, however, as the United States had been forcibly placing them in federally run boarding schools since the mid-1800s (Margolis, 2004). The placement of Native children in foster care was simply an extension of this forced acculturation. For example, in 1958, the Bureau of Indian Affairs funded the Child Welfare League of America to implement the Indian Adoption Project, which sought to provide homes for Native American children "whose parents were deemed unable to provide a 'suitable' home" (Mannes, 1995, p. 267). As a result of this and other federally funded programs, it is estimated that about 35 percent of all Native American children were removed from their homes between 1969 and 1974 (Matheson, 1996).

By the 1960s, there was a growing recognition that there were too many children entering and lingering in the child welfare system and that policies needed to be better aligned with the intended purpose of child welfare services, which is to ensure child safety and to preserve families. Over the next several decades, the federal government passed legislation intended to address safety, as well as to increase the number of children exiting care:

- Child Abuse Prevention and Treatment Act of 1974, P.L. 93-247
- Indian Child Welfare Act of 1978, P.L. 95-608
- Adoption Assistance and Child Welfare Act of 1980, P.L. 96-272
- Family Preservation and Support Services Program of 1993, P.L. 103-66 (renamed the Promoting Safe and Stable Families Act in 1997)
- Multiethnic Placement Act and Interethnic Placement Act of 1994, P.L. 103-382
- Adoption and Safe Families Act of 1997, P.L 105-89
- Child Abuse Reform and Enforcement Act of 2000, P.L. 106-177
- Fostering Connection to Success and Increasing Adoptions Act of 2008, P.L. 110-351

These laws sought, in one form or another, to preserve families and prevent the need for foster care or reduce the length of time in care, by providing funding for prevention and intervention services and requiring states to achieve timely permanency for children in foster care. For example, the Adoption Assistance and Child Welfare Act "required states to establish programs and make procedural reforms to serve children in their own homes, prevent out-of-home placement, and facilitate family reunification following placement" (McGowan, 2005, p. 36). Similarly, the Adoption and Safe Families Act required states to make reasonable efforts to preserve and reunify families, but it also "shorten[ed] the time frame for making permanency planning decisions" (McGowan, 2005, p. 40). In some cases, the Adoption and Safe Families Act has been perceived as creating competing goals, as child welfare agencies work to both reunify families and achieve timely permanency through other avenues when reunification is not possible.

Some laws were created for specific populations in order to address historical differential treatment and realign practice with child welfare's intended purpose of safety and permanency for children. For instance, the Indian Child Welfare Act was the first law that attempted to rectify the United States' previous policy toward the Native American community, and it "mandated that state courts act to preserve the integrity and unity of Native American families" (McGowan, 2005, p. 36). It was also one of the first laws to recognize the importance of a child's culture and community. In 2001, the executive director of the Child Welfare League of America acknowledged the importance of the Indian Child Welfare Act at a meeting of the National Indian Child Welfare Association and formally apologized for the Indian Adoption Project.

What the above laws demonstrate is that the child welfare system began to make a philosophical shift from a system that viewed the child as needing to be rescued to one that viewed the child as needing a safe and permanent family, thanks primarily to the leadership and vision of the Children's Bureau. What these laws failed to do, however, was change the actual day-to-day practice of the child welfare system, and thus the system continued to view children in a disconnected manner rather than within the context of their family and community. The task of child welfare today is to realign practice with the intended purpose of the child welfare system: keeping children safe, ensuring their well-being, and keeping them with permanent families.

Child Welfare Today

As child welfare legislation sought to shift practice away from its rescue-based philosophy, changes in practice have led to decreasing numbers of children in foster care. These changes include a growing recognition

> that only those children who cannot be safely maintained in their homes should be placed in foster care; investment in prevention and [family support programs] that keep children safely in their homes whenever possible; and a commitment to involving families in decisions that affect the safety of the child. (Casey Family Programs, 2011a, p. 5)

The impact of these changes is reflected in the numbers: in 2010, there were 406,412 children in foster care in the United States, a 22 percent decrease from 2002. In 2011, there were just over 400,000 children in foster care in the United States, a 25 percent decrease from 2002. During this time there was also a large decline in children entering care (Adoption and Foster Care Analysis and Reporting System [AFCARS], 2011). Even as there are fewer children in foster care, the safety of children does not appear to be negatively impacted, as reflected in two federal measures of child safety: repeat maltreatment and rates of re-entry into foster care. Nationally, the percentage of repeat maltreatment has declined in recent years (U.S. Department of Health and Human Services, 2012 [HHS]), while the rate of re-entry has remained relatively steady since 2005, even as the number of children in foster care has decreased (AFCARS, 2011).

The trends reflected by these data are promising, but there is still a need for better awareness of the children who are in care and consideration of ways to more effectively meet their needs and ensure their well-being. Children up to age six and youths ages 16 to 18 make up an increasing proportion of children in care (AFCARS, 2011). Historically, child welfare policies, practices, and programs treated all children, regardless of age, in the same manner. But there is now increasing recognition that children of different ages have different developmental needs, and that children are affected differently based on the types of child abuse and neglect that they have experienced. For example, early-learning brain research has revealed that a child's early relationships can have a lifelong impact on outcomes such as emotional health, mechanisms for coping with stress, and even physical health such as the development of the immune system (National Scientific Council on the Developing Child, 2010).

Prior to their contact with the child welfare system, some children have had experiences that negatively affect their brain development, which can be exacerbated by removal from their parents and placement into foster care. Applying brain research to child welfare practices and policies can provide this vulnerable group of children ages six and under with improved opportunities for the best possible future. For example, decisions to move infants should reflect an understanding of the attachment process and the impact that moving can have on the infant's ability to develop a healthy attachment (Dicker & Gordon, 2004). Combining this knowledge with effective in-home interventions is one way to support both child safety and child well-being.

Three crucial points must be considered about children who are in the care of their parents. First, the vast majority of vulnerable children are not placed in foster care but instead receive services in their home. In fiscal year 2011, 869,000 children were receiving in-home services, more than twice the number of children in foster care (HHS, 2012). Second, the majority of children who exited foster care in fiscal year 2011 exited through reunification with their parents or permanency with other family members. Finally, about 20 percent of children who entered care in 2011 had been in foster care before (AFCARS, 2011). Together, these numbers point to the need to better support children in their homes, with their families, so that they do not enter care for the first time, much less re-enter for a second time—and so that when they do leave care, they can remain safely and permanently at home with their families. Evidence-based in-home services need to be made available to families before children are placed in foster care, as a preventative measure, as well as after children exit care, as a permanency support measure.

Homebuilders, for example, is an intensive family preservation services model that provides in-home crisis intervention and counseling to families with children at imminent risk of being placed in out-of-home care. When implemented with fidelity, the Homebuilders model can help to prevent the need for placement (Kirk & Griffith, 2004). However, "the major federal funding source for foster care, Title IV-E [of the Social Security Act], primarily pays for maintaining eligible children in licensed foster care" (Casey Family Programs, 2010a, p. 1). Title IV of the Social Security Act of 1935, P.L. 74-271 provides grants to states for aid and services to needy families with children and for child welfare services; subsections B and E are responsible for funding child welfare services. While Title IV-B funds are intended to provide for family support services and prevention services such as Homebuilders, the amount is insufficient to have national impact. As a comparison, in 2006 Title IV-E funds for foster care and adoption support exceeded $6 billion, while states spent only $637 million in Title IV-B funds (Casey Family Programs, 2010b). Unlike Title IV-B, Title IV-E does not provide services for families before and after contact with the child welfare system.

Despite the lack of federal funding, a growing number of child welfare agencies are changing their practice and implementing prevention-based approaches and in-home service delivery models. These approaches are sometimes funded by waiver programs that allow federal funds to be used flexibly, such as Title IV-E waivers and Medicaid waivers. We believe that comprehensive federal finance reform could support further practice changes and more successful approaches; child welfare agencies must be allowed to invest federal funds in programs that support improved safety, permanency, and well-being for children and families.

Los Angeles County, California, is an example of a child welfare system that changed its practice by implementing a promising approach known as the Prevention Initiative Demonstration Project (PIDP) (Casey Family Programs, 2010d). PIDP, funded primarily by a Title IV-E waiver, combines primary prevention approaches directed to the whole community and approaches directed to families already involved with the child welfare agency. The hypothesis behind PIDP is that child abuse and neglect can be reduced if families are less socially isolated and more economically stable, and if activities, resources, and support are integrated into the community and accessible to families. Evaluation results of PIDP are promising; for instance, children in PIDP's Family Reunification program were more likely to exit foster care to legal permanency; children in the Family Maintenance program were more likely to have their cases closed; and families who utilized the PIDP's Ask Seek Knock family support centers were about half as likely to be re-referred to the child welfare agency.

Another successful approach is the in-home program provided by Youth Villages, a Tennessee-based child welfare private agency (Casey Family Programs, 2010e; Grossman, Ross, & Foster, 2008). This program is funded by a Medicaid waiver. Youth Villages initially operated like many other private agencies, providing foster care and residential treatment. However, as they began tracking outcome data, they realized that many of the youths they were discharging were returning to care. They subsequently implemented a number of changes in order to improve outcomes by changing their practice and service delivery. In 1994, Youth Villages began providing multisystemic therapy, an evidence-based in-home program serving youths 12 to 17 years old with antisocial behavior. Rather than working with youths in isolation, multisystemic therapy "views the youth as embedded within multiple interconnected systems: family, peers, school, neighborhood, community/culture" (Multisystemic Therapy, 2010). Out of this experience, Youth Villages developed a second in-home model, Intercept, to serve a broader range of children with emotional and behavioral challenges. Their data now show that about 84 percent of the children who completed at least 60 days of service with Youth Villages were living successfully at home two years after leaving the program.

PIDP and Youth Villages are two examples of how practice and service delivery models are changing based on what we believe is better for children and families, and their outcomes are starting to build an evidence base indicating that it is indeed better for children to remain with their families and in their communities. Yet child welfare as a field needs to improve its ability to assess which services are most effective for each family. For example, after conducting in-depth assessments on a sample of children placed in foster care, Youth Villages determined that about two-thirds of those children could return home with appropriate in-home services. Child welfare agencies could learn from this example; by adequately assessing and tailoring services to individual families within their communities, they could serve more children without the need for foster care.

Another in-home intervention with a well-established history of improving safety and well-being for children and their mothers is the nurse-family partnership (NFP). NFP is a community health care program that partners nurse home visitors with low-income first-time mothers to empower them to improve their health, education, economic self-sufficiency, and parenting. Although NFP was not developed by or for the child welfare system, rigorous research has shown that NFP has a positive impact on child safety by reducing the rate of child abuse and neglect by almost 50 percent and the number of emergency room visits by over 50 percent (Olds et al., 1997). Child well-being is also positively affected. For example, NFP children through age 12 were less likely to use cigarettes, alcohol, or marijuana; reported fewer internalizing mental health problems; and achieved higher academic outcomes than their peers (Kitzman et al., 2010). NFP is one example of how effective in-home services can improve overall child safety, permanency, and well-being.

However, improving outcomes is more complex than simply implementing a program or a practice model. While there is growing recognition that no single solution exists, many jurisdictions have demonstrated improved outcomes through systemwide reform efforts. During site visits to jurisdictions that have significantly reduced the number of children in care, Casey Family Programs learned that they share some common elements (Casey Family Programs, n.d.):

- *Driver of reform:* In some jurisdictions, reform was driven by high-profile child injuries or deaths or consent decrees, combined with a general lack of public confidence in the system. In other jurisdictions, the driver was a proactive commitment resulting from evidence of poor outcomes for children, families, and the system itself.
- *Intentional change process:* The approach to managing the change process varied from grassroots community development to formal change management, but each jurisdiction had an intentional process with continuous quality improvement to increase the efficiency and effectiveness of the work.
- *Strong leadership:* Leaders were consistent in prioritizing the reform. They were mission- and values-driven and effective at building internal and external coalitions and strong management teams to sustain the effort, and they managed reform to produce clear and measurable outcomes.
- *Values:* The policies and practices were grounded in shared and articulated values.
- *Building support:* There was a strong commitment to building internal and external public support for the outcomes.
- *Data:* Jurisdictions made accurate and current data a priority. Desired outcomes were identified, measured, and reported, and the course was changed as needed, based on outcomes.
- *Financing:* Jurisdictions made upfront investments in reform efforts, which ultimately led to reduced caseloads and opportunities to capture savings for reinvestment; funding innovations and federal waivers were also strategies.
- *Maintaining and refocusing momentum:* Through strong alliances with the community and the support of internal staff, the reform efforts have been maintained and expanded in spite of crises, competing priorities, and leadership changes.

While no one of these elements is a "silver bullet" to improve the child welfare system, in combination they have led to improved outcomes in a number of jurisdictions. For instance, the appointment of strong executive leadership in 2004–2008 to Georgia's Division of Children and Family Services led to a climate of reform by establishing an agency value of "safe and thriving children with forever families" (Casey Family Programs, 2010c, p. 5). In keeping with this value, other systems changes were made, such as implementing a performance management approach known as G-force. G-force meetings began in 2004 and are held regularly at the state, regional, and county level; during these meetings, leadership and staff use data to examine trends and performance both overall and by region. As gaps in practice are revealed, staff brainstorm about possible causes, test different strategies, and ultimately implement the strategy that provides the best results. The G-force process and subsequent data-driven culture has been credited as the catalyst for system-level change in Georgia. It was instrumental in influencing practice change, holding all levels of staff accountable for improving outcomes, and stimulating creative, innovative thinking. The system changes made in Georgia led to a 42 percent reduction in the number of children in care from 2004 to 2009. At the same time, the percent of maltreatment recurrence decreased significantly, indicating that children in Georgia were as safe as or safer than they were before the changes were made.

Alachua County, Florida began its Foster Care Redesign System Project in 2007 with a different approach (Casey Family Programs, 2009). The goal was to safely reduce the number of children in the foster care system by preventing removal through improved practice and increased in-home services, accelerating permanency through practice change, and addressing disproportionality in the child welfare system. To build community support for these goals, the Florida Department of Children and Families (DCF) partnered with the lead agency in Alachua County's Circuit,[1] Partnership for Strong Families, to develop a strategic communications plan. Components of the plan included community meetings with nonprofit agencies, businesses, elected government officials, foster parents, relative caregivers, and the media; a quarterly newsletter that is distributed across the county; and a community steering committee to garner input from a cross-section of the local community. The public-private partnership in Florida has been critical to the success of the Redesign Project, as it allows for a more rapid and flexible response than a more traditional bureaucratic public system would.

Another way in which the child welfare system built public will and engaged the community was through the Library Partnership Neighborhood Resource Center, a model neighborhood center that is co-located with a public library. The Center provides supports and services to vulnerable families to help strengthen them before issues of child abuse or neglect arise. It is located in the area of Gainesville with the highest concentration of maltreatment cases, so that it is accessible and convenient for those families most in need. The Center is a partnership between the Florida Department of Children and Families, the Partnership for Strong Families, the Alachua County Library District, Casey Family Programs, and over 20 community organizations.

---

[1] Florida's DCF is organized by regions, which is made up of circuits and then counties. Alachua County is in Circuit 8, which is part of the Northeast Region.

Florida's Title IV-E waiver provides the financial support for the Center, in addition to many of the other reform efforts implemented by the Foster Care Redesign System Project. In fact, the IV-E waiver is cited as one of the key components of Alachua County's successful system redesign. It allows the Department of Children and Families and the Partnership for Strong Families to allocate resources in the way that they determine is best for the children of their county, rather than restricting use of federal funds to foster care. The IV-E waiver is primarily used to fund prevention and diversion services; between 2007 and 2009, Alachua County saw a 33 percent reduction in the number of children in foster care as well as a reduction in rates of re-entry into foster care.

Alachua County, Florida, and Georgia are just two examples, which can be replicated by other jurisdictions, of how the elements listed earlier can interact to promote reform. They also demonstrate that child welfare agencies cannot and should not do this work alone. Making practice changes that truly serve the best interest of the child and family can only be done in full partnership with the private sector, the public system, and the community. The changes that have already been carried out indicate that a focus on keeping children with their families can indeed lead to improved practice, which in turn leads to improved safety, permanency, and well-being. However, the time has come to move beyond episodic and often tragedy-driven systems improvement efforts. The examples identified in this chapter suggest that it is possible to implement and sustain system-wide transformation of how we approach the issue of child abuse and neglect.

Child Welfare in the Future

The original architects of this country's effort to ensure the safety and well-being of children thought that it was appropriate to isolate the child from the family. They thought it was acceptable to leave families in a poorhouse and take the children in order to change them so that they did not become like their parents. They believed in putting children on trains and sending them halfway across the country, far away from their communities. Many of today's intervention strategies continue to view children and families in an isolated manner, separate from their community. While some jurisdictions have made changes in their practice, many of these historical values continue to dictate the manner in which many jurisdictions approach the delivery of child welfare services (Figure 2-1).

Making a fundamental change in child welfare practice requires going beyond an isolated focus on the child and family to work within the community in which they reside. If communities are isolated and underresourced, the families living within them are most likely not going to be doing well, or only marginally so, and the children in those families will suffer the consequences. If this nation's vulnerable children and families are to succeed and thrive, we must consistently view children in the context of

Figure 2-1. Siloed Social Response Paradigm

their families, view families in the context of their communities, and design intervention strategies to address the needs of all three. We need to strengthen the community to strengthen the family, so that together they can safely care for the child. This is the key to keeping children safe and improving their well-being and that of their families.

In addition, child welfare services must move their focus from what to accomplish *for* children and families to what to accomplish *with* children, families, and communities. Children and families need to be asked and listened to. A study of the federal child and family service reviews conducted between fiscal years 2001 and 2004 indicated that not one state met the well-being criterion of "family involvement in case planning" (Altman, 2005, p. 75). We must improve the manner in which we engage families. Evidence indicates that when parents are involved in service planning, families have better outcomes (Dawson & Berry, 2002). Social workers must take the following into account in order to do a better job of engaging families:

- Unlike in other social service agencies, the majority of families working with the child welfare system are doing so involuntarily. These are parents who have come to the attention of the system because they have been deemed to be failing as caretakers (Altman, 2008). Too often, social workers forget this and see parents as uncooperative, when in reality resistance is a normal response when one's personal freedoms are threatened (Altman, 2005). Remembering this is crucial as it changes the way we view families and thus the way we engage them.
- While compliance with services is necessary, the primary goal of the engagement process should be to establish a truly collaborative relationship in which parents are active participants in both the development and implementation of their service plan (Dawson & Berry, 2002).
- We must consider parents as full partners with equal power, rights, and responsibilities (Pennell, 2011). We should not view families as dysfunctional, but rather as people who are undergoing a difficult situation at a particular moment in time who still have the right to be full participants in their service plan.

- We need to acknowledge families as experts in their own lives. While practitioners think they may know what services families need, in reality families know their situations best; thus, involving them early in the process and identifying collaborative goals is essential (Altman, 2008). For example, while social workers may be focused on having parents participate in parenting classes, they may be focused on getting a job in order to pay for transportation and for the class itself. Assisting them in achieving this goal "is important not only on its own terms, but also as a gateway to engagement" (Kemp, Marcenko, Hoagwood, & Vesneski, 2009, p. 112).
- An important step in providing culturally competent services is for social workers to be aware of their own cultural values, attitudes, and beliefs, as well as how these affect their work with families. Moreover, "knowing something about the client's worldview and having some useful strategies when attempting to engage them can help" (Altman, 2005, p. 77).
- Knowing about effective community-based services and connecting families to them can be a valuable way to engage parents, particularly with families "who may be unsure or distrustful of what workers can do for them" (Altman, 2005, p. 81). In addition to helping engage parents in services, connecting families to community-based services helps them develop and strengthen their own support network outside of the social worker–client relationship (Dawson & Berry, 2002).

As we shift the way we practice, however, we must ensure that the changes are based on research and data that support both promising and evidence-based practices that create a link between actions and improved outcomes.

As we move toward a vision of child welfare that considers children in the context of their families and communities, we have to be aware of what we know (or think we know) and what we have yet to learn. We must continue to refine our definition and understanding of the problem in order to avoid making false conclusions about the solution. For example, when we compare average reunification rates, it appears that African American children tend to exit to reunification more slowly than Caucasian children. The numbers however, are based on aggregate data. A recent study by Fred Wulczyn of Chapin Hall at the University of Chicago (Wulczyn, 2011) looked at permanency outcomes for African American and Caucasian children across 400 counties. Wulczyn's analysis revealed that African American children are reunified as fast as or faster than Caucasian children in many counties. Furthermore, when the model is expanded to include attributes of the counties where children live, the race effect at the individual level is greatly diminished. The data also revealed that children in poor counties are the ones who reunify more slowly—and since more African American children live in counties with elevated poverty rates, they tend to reunify at a lower rate. Analyzing the data at the local or community level yields more nuanced information about how to best serve children, families, and communities; in this case, the data tell us that if we want to increase rates of reunification, then we should focus on strengthening communities with high levels of structural disadvantage. What this information demonstrates is that place matters and that the community where a child lives can affect that child's outcomes.

Although the idea of engaging and strengthening communities is a fairly new concept in child welfare, other disciplines have a proven history of community-based work. For example, Communities that Care (CTC) uses a public health approach to strengthen the community through prevention efforts aimed at youths. CTC helps a coalition of stakeholders, the CTC community board, to assess risk and protective factors in their community through the CTC youth survey. Using the CTC Prevention Strategies Guide, the community board then selects and implements evidence-based programs that are known to reduce the elevated risk factors and promote the weak protective factors identified in their community. CTC is unique in that it does not dictate who should lead the community board or which programs should be implemented. It provides training and guidance, but decision-making is left to the community board. CTC has been rigorously evaluated. A randomized, controlled trial found that CTC youths were less likely than their peers to start smoking, start drinking alcohol, or engage in delinquent behavior at given points of time, leading to cumulatively lower rates of initiation in these behaviors over time (Hawkins et al., 2009; Hawkins et al., 2012). A conservative cost-benefit analysis of CTC, based only on the prevention of cigarette smoking and delinquency, estimated that the net benefit is $5,250 per youth, or $5.30 for every dollar invested in CTC (Kuklinski, Briney, Hawkins, & Catalano, 2011).

We must also begin to think differently about how the child welfare system is funded. In order to strengthen communities, we must move away from a system that pays for maintaining children in care and consider reallocating funds to provide more prevention services and neighborhood revitalization programs that are led by the community. These types of programs can help to improve overall child well-being by reducing the community's risk factors and strengthening its protective factors. While we wait for federal child welfare finance reform, we need to begin working with the community to build upon its strengths so that it can assist and strengthen the families within it, ensuring that families can safely care for their children.

Some public and private agencies have already started moving in this direction. For example, in Hawaii, the Department of Human Services noticed that there was a disproportionate number of Hawaiian children entering foster care and that these children stayed in care longer than other children. Instead of attempting to come up with a solution on its own, the Department reached out to the Hawaiian community, asking how it could partner with them to keep their children within their families and community. As a result of these conversations, Hawaiian community organizations began to organize among themselves, developing an array of culturally appropriate services for Hawaiian families. Thanks to these services, in combination with other system improvement efforts including an alternative response system focused on strengthening families, the rate of Hawaiian children entering care in Hawaii decreased by almost half between fiscal years 2005 and 2009 (personal communication with D. English, senior director for strategic consulting, Casey Family Programs, May 5, 2011).

In New York, five foundations joined to create a donors' collaborative, with the aim of developing a community-led and community-based child welfare social service model. As a result, 12 community agencies collaborated to create Bridge Builders in the Highbridge community in the Bronx. Over the years, the collaboration grew to 15 foundations and New York City's Administration for Children's Services. The agency focused on providing outreach and family support services to families in need within their community, as well as providing legal assistance to families involved with the child welfare system. Given the agency's community-based focus, Bridge Builders made it a priority to hire community members, including veteran parents,[2] so that the Highbridge community was both providing and benefiting from their services. Community members are also part of the governing board of Bridge Builders, so they are involved in the design and administration of the program, in addition to service delivery. The agency used data provided by the Administration for Children's Services to track child abuse and neglect trends block by block in the neighborhood and to effectively target their preventative outreach services. A 2006 evaluation by Chapin Hall at the University of Chicago indicated that the number of children placed into foster care dropped by 27 percent in the neighborhood between 2004 and 2005 as compared to the previous four years (personal communication with M. Baker, senior director for strategic consulting, Casey Family Programs, May 5, 2011).

In the Bushwick neighborhood in Brooklyn, the Coalition for Hispanic Family Services noticed that a large percentage of children were being placed in foster care outside their community. These children, who were predominately Latino and African American, did not have regular visitation with their families. Initially the coalition focused on attempting to recruit foster parents of color within the community so that children could stay in the neighborhood and have regular visitation with their families, but as they began to work with the community, they realized that there were other unmet needs. In response, the coalition developed a variety of additional services to address the well-being of the children and families in the community: They created an after-school program, formed a legal assistance program for families dealing with kinship care issues, and developed a partnership with a community hospital to provide adequate bilingual and bicultural mental health and primary health care services. The result was a community agency driven by the needs identified by the community, not the agency (personal communication with D. Rosario, executive director, Coalition for Hispanic Family Services, May 18, 2011).

---

[2] Veteran parents are parents who were previously involved with the child welfare system but were successfully reunited with their children.

The work these agencies have done has provided valuable lessons for how to engage communities, lessons that other child welfare systems should consider as they begin collaborating with communities:

- Child welfare agencies must not impose themselves upon the community by creating and establishing their own programs, but rather they should build upon resources that already exist within the community. If no effective programs exist, the community should be the leader in developing them, rather than the child welfare agency.
- Communities should be able to take responsibility for the safety and well-being of the children in their community. In Hawaii, once the community took full responsibility and was allowed to create and dictate its own services, community members began to see positive outcomes.
- Child welfare agencies need to engage community elders and leaders so that they can assist the agency in understanding what resources are available within the community as well as what issues the community is facing. Otherwise, the agencies run the risk of implementing programs that may be counter to traditional cultural practices.
- All three programs described earlier ensured that the leadership group was diverse and inclusive of all members within the community. This allowed not only greater inclusivity, but also more equal distribution of power.
- Child welfare agencies need to be willing to provide both material resources and expertise and technical assistance, and at the same time to defer decision-making power to the community.

The child welfare system cannot continue to simply focus on strengthening the child or the family, but must strengthen the community as a whole. As the work of engaging communities expands, it is imperative that child welfare agencies understand that every community has its own history and culture, that the families living within the communities have their own cultural norms, and that interventions must be informed by cultural competence.

Culturally congruent approaches cannot be generalized as a systemwide or statewide approach; they need to be adapted to each community. There also needs to be recognition that the child welfare system cannot come up with the solutions on its own. Transforming the way we approach the issue of child abuse and neglect will require the full participation of the community, including all levels of government, business, philanthropy, and all public systems that serve children and families (Figure 2-2).

If we continue to view child safety as the job of the child welfare system alone while viewing other government agencies as being fully responsible for other social welfare responses, we are likely to continue to fall short of our potential to demonstrate sustained improvements in outcomes for vulnerable children.

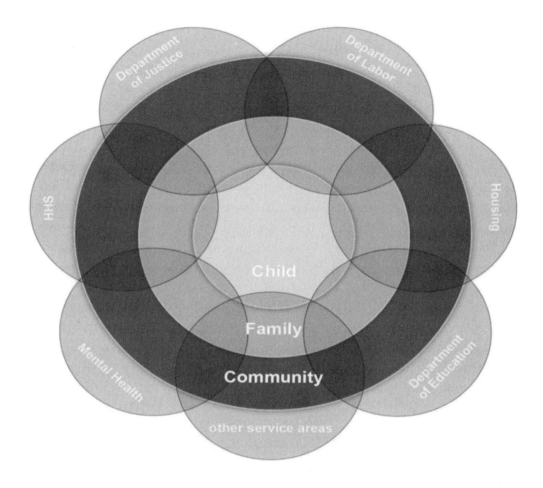

Figure 2-2. Integrated Social Response Paradigm

Implications for Social Work Education

Over the years, social work research and education have played an ever-increasing role in child welfare. Looking to the future, there are three key points to consider in the development of social work education and practice.

First, to effectively realign practice with the intended purpose of the child welfare system, we must create an environment in which decisions are based upon both practical experience and evidence. However, the evidence base is limited. Funding mechanisms need to be developed to "steadily increase the application of knowledge to practice, including federal support for intervention research, rigorous evaluation of promising practices and the dissemination of research-based practices" (Casey Family Programs, 2011b, p. 10). We must continue to expand the knowledge base of what works in child welfare, not just what we think works. It is imperative that schools of social work educate their students to think critically about the implications of research for effective practice within child welfare, so that students can continue to apply this evidence-based lens in their daily practice.

Second, as illustrated in Georgia, using data to inform and support decision-making can be an effective way of improving outcomes. However, we must carefully consider what we are trying to measure and therefore what data we need to collect, so that we are looking at the right information. Child welfare agencies should be responsible for ensuring that data are available to social workers and administrators, while schools of social work need to be responsible for ensuring that students are taught how to understand and apply data. Social workers often make decisions based on intuition; without discounting the importance of experience, it is imperative that they also understand the value of data and actively integrate it into their practice.

Third, assumptions need to change regarding expertise and the importance of engaging families, communities, and other agencies through an integrated response. The original architects of the U.S. child welfare system believed that they knew what was best for children. Many social workers today have been indoctrinated since early in their careers to view child welfare through this rescue-based paradigm. As social work has become more professionalized, there is a danger that social workers continue to see themselves as the only experts. The future of child welfare requires that the family and the community be treated as experts as well—they know their own strengths and their own needs. Child welfare professionals must also recognize that each family and community has its own culture, which must be respected by social workers. The role of social workers is to ask, listen, and learn so that they can effectively support families and communities. Families, social workers, and the community must be equal participants and partners as they work to keep their children safe.

To this end, both the academic and professional fields need to do a better job of teaching child welfare social workers how to engage families—not from a deficit-based approach but from a strengths-based approach. There is often a tendency in child welfare practice to focus on the negative circumstances that brought a family to the attention of child protection services, and while it is necessary to assess safety and risk factors, it is also necessary to identify and build upon the strengths of a family. Teaching individual social workers to recognize that all families have strengths and that all families experience difficult circumstances will allow them to engage families in a different and more effective manner. Working with families more effectively includes partnering with the community that surrounds them, as well as with the other agencies that are involved with the family. By teaching students how to practice social work through this integrated response approach, universities will enable social workers to more effectively engage communities and systems and therefore to better support families.

Schools of social work must also reflect upon the education of social work practitioners, by considering not just classroom teaching but also practicum instruction. University professors and practicum instructors must ensure that students have the opportunity to apply their classroom learning regarding evidence, data, expertise, and engagement in their field experience. This integrated learning will help social workers to develop the skills they need to be more effective partners with families. Teaching social workers to approach families differently and to work with families from an integrated standpoint will change not only the practice of individual social workers, but the practice of child welfare as a whole.

Conclusion

Child welfare is once again undergoing a shift in practice. We have moved from viewing the child in isolation to acknowledging that the best place for a child is with a permanent family within his or her own community and that each community has its own unique strengths and challenges. It is essential to recognize that the well-being of the child is dependent upon the well-being of the family, which is connected to the well-being of the community, and to address the needs of all three. We must strengthen the community in order to strengthen the family, so that together they can safely care for their own children. Embracing this vision means having a future in which all children are safe, all families are stable, and all communities are supported.

References

Adoption and Safe Families Act of 1997, P.L. 105-89, 111 Stat. 2115, codified as 42 USCA § 1305 note.

Adoption Assistance and Child Welfare Act of 1980, P.L. 96-272, 94 Stat. 500, codified as amended, 42 USCA § 670 et seq.

Adoption and Foster Care Analysis and Reporting System. (2011). Raw data originally collected by the Children's Bureau, Administration on Children, Youth and Families, and made available by the National Data Archive on Child Abuse and Neglect, Cornell University: http://www.ndacan.cornell.edu/ndacan/Datasets/Abstracts/DatasetAbstract_AFCARS_General.html

Altman, J. C. (2005). Engagement in children, youth, and family services: Current research and promising practices. In G. P. Mallon & P. M. Hess (Eds.), *Child welfare for the twenty-first century: A handbook of practices, policies, and programs* (pp. 72–86). New York: Columbia University Press.

Altman, J. C. (2008). Engaging families in child welfare services: Worker versus client perspectives. *Child Welfare, 87*(3), 41–61.

Casey Family Programs. (2009). *Alachua County common knowledge case study.* Seattle: Author.

Casey Family Programs. (2010a). *Ensuring safe, nurturing and permanent families for children: The need for federal finance reform.* Seattle: Author.

Casey Family Programs. (2010b). *Ensuring safe, nurturing and permanent families for children: The need to reauthorize and expand Title IV-E waivers.* Seattle: Author.

Casey Family Programs. (2010c). *Georgia common knowledge case study*. Seattle: Author.

Casey Family Programs. (2010d). *Executive summary*. In *Prevention Initiative Demonstration Project (PIDP): Year two evaluation report* (pp. 3–9). Seattle: Author.

Casey Family Programs. (2010e). *Tennessee and Youth Villages common knowledge case study*. Seattle: Author.

Casey Family Programs. (2011a). *Ensuring safe, nurturing and permanent families for children: Foster care reductions and child safety*. Seattle: Author.

Casey Family Programs. (2011b). *Ensuring safe, nurturing and permanent families for children: The role of accountability in child welfare finance reform*. Seattle: Author.

Casey Family Programs. (n.d.). *Common knowledge building blocks*. Seattle: Author.

Charles, G., & Garfat, T. (2009). Child and youth care practice in North America: Historical roots and current challenges. *Relational Child & Youth Care Practice, 22*(2), 17–28.

Child Abuse Prevention and Treatment Act of 1974, P.L. 93-247, 88 Stat. 4, codified as amended at 42 USC §§ 5101–5119.

Child Abuse Reform and Enforcement Act of 2000, P.L. 107-177, 113 Stat. 35, codified as 42 USCA § 3711 note.

Dawson, K., & Berry, M. (2002). Engaging families in child welfare services: An evidence-based approach to best practice. *Child Welfare, 81*(2), 293–317.

Dicker, S. & Gordon, E. (2004). *Ensuring the healthy development of infants in foster care: A guide for judges, advocates and child welfare professionals*. Retrieved from http://www.courts.state.ny.us/ip/justiceforchildren/PDF/Infant%20Booklet.pdf

Family Preservation and Support Services Act of 1993, P.L. 103-66, 107 Stat. 312 Part I § 13711, codified as amended, 42 USCA § 629 et seq.

Fostering Connection to Success and Increasing Adoptions Act of 2008, P.L. 110-351, 122 Stat. 3949, codified as 42 USCA § 1305 note.

Grossman, A., Ross, C., & Foster, W. (2008). *Youth villages* (N9-309-007). Boston: Harvard Business School.

Hacsi, T. (1995). From indenture to family foster care: A brief history of child placing. *Child Welfare, 74*(1), 162–180.

Hawkins, J. D., Oesterle, S., Brown, E. C., Arthur, M. W., Abbott, R. D., Fagan, A. A., et al. (2009). Results of a Type 2 translational research trial to prevent adolescent drug use and delinquency: A test of Communities That Care. *Archives of Pediatrics and Adolescent Medicine, 163*, 789–798.

Hawkins, J. D., Oesterle, S., Brown, E. C., Monahan, K. C., Abbott, R. D., Arthur, M.W., et al. (2012). Sustained decreases in risk exposure and youth problem behaviors after installation of the Communities That Care prevention system in a randomized trial. *Archives of Pediatrics and Adolescent Medicine, 166*,141–148.

Iceland, J. (2006). *Poverty in America: A handbook* (2nd ed.). Berkeley: University of California Press.

Indian Child Welfare Act of 1978, P.L. 95-608, 92 Stat. 3069, codified at 25 USC §§ 1901-1963.

Jacobson, M. F. (1998). *Whiteness of a different color: European immigrants and the alchemy of race*. Cambridge, MA: Harvard University Press.

Jimenez, J. (2006). The history of child protection in the African American community: Implications for current child welfare policies. *Children & Youth Services Review, 28,* 888–905.

Katz, M. B. (1996). *In the shadow of the poor house: A social history of welfare in America* (rev. ed.). New York: Basic Books.

Kemp, S. P., Marcenko, M. O., Hoagwood, K., & Vesneski, W. (2009). Engaging parents in child welfare services: Bridging family needs and child welfare mandates. *Child Welfare, 88*(1), 101–126.

Kirk, R. S., & Griffith, D. P. (2004). Intensive family preservation services: Demonstrating placement prevention using event history analysis. *Social Work Research, 28*(1), 5–15.

Kitzman, H. J., Olds, D. L., Cole, R. E., Hanks, C. A., Anson, E. A., Arcoleo, K. J., et al. (2010). Enduring effects of prenatal and infancy home visiting by nurses on children: Follow-up of a randomized trial among children at age 12 years. *Archives of Pediatrics & Adolescent Medicine, 164,* 412–418.

Kuklinski, M. R., Briney, J. S., Hawkins, J. D., & Catalano, R. F. (2011). Cost–benefit analysis of Communities That Care outcomes at eighth grade. *Prevention Science, 13*(2), 150–161.

Lawrence-Webb, C. (1997). African American children in the modern child welfare system: A legacy of the Flemming Rule. *Child Welfare, 76*(1), 9–30.

Mannes, M. (1995). Factors and events leading to the passage of the Indian Child Welfare Act. *Child Welfare, 74*(1), 264–282.

Margolis, E. (2004). Looking at discipline, looking at labor: Photographic representations of Indian boarding schools. *Visual Studies, 19*(1), 72–96.

Matheson, L. (1996). The politics of the Indian Child Welfare Act. *Social Work, 41,* 232–235.

McGowan, B. (2005). Historical evolution of child welfare services. In *Child welfare for the twenty-first century* (pp. 10–46). New York: Columbia University Press.

Multiethnic Placement Act of 1994, P.L. 103-382, 108 Stat. 4056 (1994), codified as amended, 42 USCA § 602, 1320A-2. The Interethnic Adoption Provisions of 1994, were approved as part of the Small Business Job Protection Act, P.L. 104-188 § 1808, 110 Stat. 1904 (1996), codified as 42 USCA § 671 (a)(18).

Multisystemic Therapy. (2010). *MST treatment model: Intensive family-focused therapy.* Retrieved from http://mstservices.com/index.php/what-is-mst/treatment-model

Myers, J. E. B. (2008). A short history of child protection in America. *Family Law Quarterly, 42,* 449–463.

National Scientific Council on the Developing Child. (2010). *The foundations of lifelong health are built in early childhood.* Boston: Harvard University, Center on the Developing Child. Retrieved from http://developingchild.harvard.edu/index.php/download_file/-/view/700/

O'Connor, S. (2004). *Orphan trains: The story of Charles Loring Brace and the children he saved and failed.* Chicago: University of Chicago Press.

Olds, D. L., Eckenrode, J., Henderson, C. R. Jr., Kitzman, H. J., Powers, J., Cole, R., et al. (1997). Long-term effects of home visitation on maternal life course and child abuse and neglect: Fifteen-year follow-up of a randomized trial. *JAMA, 278,* 637–643.

Pennell, J. (2011). Taking child and family rights seriously: Family engagement and its evidence in child welfare. *Child Welfare, 90*(4), 9–16.

Reef, C. (2005). *Alone in the world: Orphans and orphanages in America.* New York: Clarion Books.

Social Security Act of 1935, P.L. 74-271, 49 Stat. 620, codified as amended at 42 USC §§ 601-687.

Takaki, R. (1993). *A different mirror: A history of multicultural America.* Boston: Bay Back Books.

Trattner, W. I. (1999). *From poor law to welfare state: A history of social welfare in America* (6th ed.). New York: The Free Press.

U.S. Department of Health and Human Services, Administration for Children and Families, Administration on Children, Youth and Families, Children's Bureau. (2012). *Child maltreatment 2011.* Retrieved from http://www.acf.hhs.gov/programs/cb/resource/child-maltreatment-2011

Wulczyn, F. (2011). *Permanency, disparity and social context* [PowerPoint slides]. Retrieved from http://www.google.com/url?sa=t&rct=j&q=fred%20wulczyn%2C%20social%20context%20and%20permanency&source=web&cd=2&ved=0CDoQFjAB&url=http%3A%2F%2Fwww.law.harvard.edu%2Fprograms%2Fabout%2Fcap%2Fcap-conferences%2Frd-conference%2Frd-conference-papers%2Fcompatiblefinalrdconferenceppwulczyn.ppt&ei=1t4RUa_yN6S2iwKPooHACw&usg=AFQjCNF72uFHh5jPJhVzbBzSkUV0EkxT6w&bvm=bv.41934586,d.cGE

Chapter 3

ADDRESSING POVERTY AS A CHILD WELFARE STRATEGY

David Berns, Katharine Briar-Lawson, and Won Hee Kim

C hild welfare leaders and practitioners are continually required to reinvent their practices and demonstrate improved outcomes. Year after year, new blueprints for reform appear. Often their results are not apparent or known. Very frequently child welfare reforms fail to take into account the co-occurring challenges of poverty, homelessness, food insecurity, and unemployment.

In this chapter we argue that systematic attention to the needs of families who are poor may help to address some of the endemic crises that have engulfed child welfare systems. While the co-occurrence of poverty and child abuse and neglect (CAN) has long been documented (Gil, 1970; Lindsey, 1994; Pelton, 1978, 1994), attempts to systematically address poverty and child welfare have waxed and waned over the decades.

Not all families who are poor end up in the child welfare system. Although nearly 16 million children are poor (U.S. Census Bureau, 2011), fewer than 3.6 million are involved with the child welfare system each year (U.S. Department of Health and Human Services [HHS], 2007). Most poor children do not enter the child welfare system. However, the majority of children in the system come from families who are living in or near poverty (Barth, Wildfire, & Green, 2006; HHS, 2007). Poverty along with social and economic marginalization are also reflected in the prevalence of racial disproportionalities in child welfare systems, with a tendency toward overrepresentation of African American and Native American children and underrepresentation of white children (Child Welfare Information Gateway, 2011; Osterling, Andrade, & Austin, 2008).

This chapter identifies several reasons that dealing with poverty should be a centerpiece of child welfare policy and practice. It reviews a few of the poverty-related policies of the early years of the Children's Bureau, examines the programmatic separation of income supports from services and the consequences for families, and then describes two programs that show promise as more systematic approaches to serving poor and high-needs families and children. It concludes with observations about the role of social work, some key social work practice principles, the continued guidance and leadership provided by the Children's Bureau to child welfare, and collaborative approaches to addressing poverty in the United States.

Poverty's Pernicious Effects

The centennial of the Children's Bureau is a reminder of its historic leadership in serving the most vulnerable children and families. Since its inception, family impoverishment and its effects on parental capacities and child development have been a predominant focus for policy and practice. A review of the intersection of poverty and CAN may help inform more innovative and comprehensive approaches, including services, to impoverished and vulnerable children and families.

Poverty has long been recognized as one of the most frequently co-occurring risk factors for child abuse and especially neglect (Slack, Holl, McDaniel, Yoo, & Bolger, 2004). While the best way to measure poverty in the United States has long been debated, few would disagree that poverty may impede children's success in school, in psychosocial functioning, and in development. Correlates of poverty include parental risk factors such as depression, history of trauma, addiction, disabilities, domestic violence, and health problems (Herrenkohl, Sousa, Tajima, Herrenkohl, & Moylan, 2008). These risk factors are often prevalent in families in the child welfare system. Housing and other basic needs challenges are present as well (Cohen, Mulroy, Tull, White, & Crowley, 2004).

Children in poverty face more developmental and behavioral health challenges than their nonpoor counterparts. Duncan and Brooks-Gunn (1997, 2000) have shown that poor children have higher rates than nonpoor children of low birth weight, internalizing and externalizing behaviors, learning disabilities, and emotional and behavioral challenges. The National Institute of Child Health and Human Development Early Child Care Research Network (2005) has found that children in chronically impoverished families have lower cognitive and academic functioning and more behavior problems than their nonpoor counterparts.

Other research shows the effects of impoverished conditions on children's brain functioning, including brain lesions from lead (Stewart et al., 2006) and high cortisol levels from stress (Lupie, King, Meaney, & McEwen, 2001). One study showed that children who are poor may show more brain problems resembling those of a stroke than their nonpoor counterparts (Raizada & Kishiyama, 2010).

Nutrition also affects brain development. Poverty-induced nutritional shortfalls may impede children's learning as well as their behavioral and developmental functioning (Galler, Ramsay, Solimano, & Lowell, 1983; Tanner & Finn-Stevenson, 2002). Some of these developmental issues may increase parenting stress, heightening risks for CAN referrals. Compounding stressors may be derived from the intensive care required by children with disabilities, including those with trauma issues. Children with disabilities experience a disproportionally high rate of CAN (Sullivan & Knutson, 2000).

Housing instability and homelessness also place children at increased risk (Bassuk et al., 1997; Bassuk, Rubin, & Lauriat, 1986). In addition to the potential for diminished cognitive supports for children, housing instability may force mothers and children into makeshift living conditions that may introduce additional CAN risk factors, such as domestic violence or drug or alcohol abuse.

Chronic impoverishment (as opposed to one or more episodes of living in poverty) may have the most deleterious effects on children and their families (McLoyd, 1998). This is attributed to the compounding effects of negative life events and stressors. Such stress may add to the difficulties in effective parenting, increasing risks for problematic parent–child interactions and disciplinary behavior, resulting in CAN referrals.

Neighborhood poverty is also a risk factor for CAN (Coulton, Korbin, Su, & Chow, 1995; Freisthler, Merritt, & LaSacla, 2006). In fact, concentrated economic deprivation may be linked to more frequent rates of referrals for CAN (Coulton et al., 1995; Freisthler, 2004). Higher rates of referrals for CAN may also be an outgrowth of economic and employment-related exclusion among families who are African American or Native American. Along with poverty, high neighborhood rates of unemployment may also be linked to CAN (Deccio, Horner, & Wilson, 1994; Freisthler, 2004).

Although child neglect may more frequently lead a family into the child welfare system than physical or sexual abuse, many neglect cases also have poverty as a co-occurring risk factor. Slack et al. (2004) argued that when poverty and economic stress create risk factors for child neglect, parenting classes alone will not be successful unless the conditions that cause the stress (such as unemployment) or the material deprivation are simultaneously addressed. Many might have argued that parenting classes and skills alone might have prevented child protective services interventions. Slack et al.'s (2004) study underscores the need to ensure that poverty and correlates of economic hardship and joblessness are addressed explicitly in child welfare practice. Slack et al. (2004) also found that unemployment and material hardship are linked to more physical discipline than is found among employed parents.

The findings of the Fourth National Incidence Study of Child Abuse and Neglect (Sedlak et al., 2010) indicate that children with unemployed parents experienced higher rates of neglect than those with employed parents. This builds the case for more prevention-oriented innovations for Temporary Assistance for Needy Families (TANF) and related job and income supports for low-income families.

Effects of Job Loss

There are well-documented CAN risk factors associated with poverty and job loss (Gil, 1971). Longitudinal studies document stress and rising CAN with layoffs (Dooley & Catalano, 1980; Steinberg, Catalano, & Dooley, 1981). Sometimes the co-occurring conditions that accompany joblessness and a skid downward into poverty also may predispose a family to experience parental depression, interpersonal violence, and self-medication with drugs or alcohol along with other health risks (Briar, 1988). Parental job loss may also be linked to impediments in educational attainment, especially for black families (Kalil & Ziol-Guest, 2008). Like poverty, joblessness may affect the development of both children and youths (Oreopoulos, Page, & Stevens, 2008).

Moreover, the fact that the working poor, facing constant economic insecurity, comprise over 7 percent of the U.S. workforce adds to the challenges of escaping poverty through employment (U.S. Bureau of Labor Statistics, 2012 [BLS]). These challenges increase for black and Hispanic workers, whose percentages among the working poor are higher: 12.6 for black people and 14.1 percent for Hispanics (BLS, 2012). Moving from TANF to a minimum-wage job may provide a family with more cash, but this may still be insufficient to help them escape poverty. Programs and supports that allow family members to be employed while moving progressively to economic security may be the most effective intervention of all. This takes time and support from the entire community. Parents rarely progress directly from having no job, a spotty work history, and marginal education directly into jobs that bring their families economic self-sufficiency.

Given the long recognized links between poverty, unemployment, and risks for CAN, it is significant that the Children's Bureau has been an historic champion of more integrative practices and services that address the intersection of risk factors like poverty and CAN. Poverty and unemployment programs for the latter half of the 20th century were not overseen by the Children's Bureau, but its integrative policy advocacy and leadership role has been essential to families through the decades.

Emergence of the Children's Bureau

The Children's Bureau, initially introduced as a new unit in the U.S. Department of Labor in 1912, focused on poverty and child and maternal labor. Family poverty, sometimes resulting from the death of the breadwinner, drove mothers to work. This often left children without child care and sometimes resulted in their removal from their families. In other cases, children were forced to go to work. At times, the entire family had to move into the workhouse.

In Cook County, Illinois, in 1911 the first mother's pension program was developed as a prototype. Using military pensions as a model, women leaders argued that a pension was warranted for a similar public good, namely, child rearing (Machtinger, 1999). The enactment of mother's pensions nationwide, a cash assistance program for poor families, was spearheaded by the Children's Bureau. The first models were developed selectively and often on racial lines, excluding families of color. Such pensions reduced family poverty and institutionalization for some children. Mother's pensions were, in fact, a beginning step for child welfare programs recognizing the role poverty played in out-of-home placement for children.

States and counties enacted fitness criteria for mother's pensions that excluded African American mothers who were seen as work capable (Machtinger, 1999). After the repeal of slavery, unemployment was widespread among African American families. Thus, for African American mothers who were seen as employable, discrimination and racial disparities in both mother's pensions and employment opportunities prevailed.

The Children's Bureau was a primary national advocate for pensions for mothers; it also emphasized the need for casework. Its leadership on mother's pensions helped it to champion the Aid to Dependent Children (ADC) program as part of the Social Security Act of 1935 (P.L. 74-271)

When ADC was enacted in 1935, the intent was to support children and families who had lost a breadwinner. Even so, many low-income women always worked. This legislation, like mother's pensions, helped to reduce the instances in which poverty drove children into institutions or foster homes. Eligibility and supports gradually expanded so that by the 1960s, income maintenance workers were often trained social workers. Moreover, they were able to offer special-need grants to families whose children were at risk of being moved into foster care. These grants complemented basic counseling and related services and supports for vulnerable families and helped to divert out-of-home placements through early intervention.

Services at the time were also seen to be the key to self-sufficiency, as social workers would address the "personal pathologies" that caused poverty (Piliavin & Gross, 1977). Integrative practices in which income maintenance workers provided supportive and casework services persisted until the late 1960s. Since that time, most states have separated the functions of eligibility and specialized services such as employment or targeted interventions.

Separation of Income Supports from Services

In the 1960s, it was argued in the Department of Health, Education and Welfare by poverty lawyers, social workers, and others that a welfare grant should not be offered contingently, as it was in some states. This was to ensure that income eligibility decisions were made strictly on the basis of entitlement rights, regardless of social service needs. In effect, those who were income eligible could access funds without service requisites, since services could no longer be required. When the services were no longer mandatory, many states reduced or eliminated them entirely. For some chronically vulnerable families, this meant the end of critical social services. In the past, an income maintenance caseworker might see a family for years as they relied on income supports as well as casework services. Elimination of the integrative function of income supports and casework deprived some chronically vulnerable families of supports that may have helped them to remain intact.

Acting as long-term-care family support workers, some income maintenance caseworkers were able to follow a family until the children reached adulthood. In some cases, they provided crisis services along with social supports. Such families were seen as "multi-problem" families because they often had co-occurring issues such as disability, mental health challenges, substance abuse, domestic violence, and possible CAN risk factors (Geismar, 1964).

With the dismantling of services for impoverished families, some of the basic holistic and preventive approaches involving early detection, intervention, and placement prevention were simultaneously removed. From the early 1970s on, separate systems of income supports and child welfare emerged in every state. Separation was for the most part supported by social workers, who believed that services could be provided in a less stigmatizing, nonadversarial manner.

In most states, this separation also brought with it the declassification and deprofessionalization of staff. Income maintenance caseworker roles, which once often involved trained social workers, were sharply reduced. These roles were viewed as technical as eligibility determination became their primary function. Devoid of casework skills, a clerk in the income maintenance role might not recognize risk factors for abuse and neglect. Parallel systems of investigatory-based Child Protection Services (CPS) emerged nationally. Casework staff were often located in a separate building under a separate organizational structure that reflected the separation of services and income maintenance.

A needs assessment framework for impoverished families was replaced with a risk framework and assessment process that focused on probabilistic and actuarial approaches. Instead of addressing income support and related basic family needs, such risk assessment tools offered a probability framework for determining child protection needs. Rather than focusing on relationship building around resource needs that may have had implications for CAN and even out-of-home placement, the newly evolving CPS caseworker became primarily an investigator and fact finder. Such investigatory functions were seen by some as so adversarial that arguments were offered in favor of having the police replace caseworkers in doing CPS investigations (Pelton, 2008).

Family Preservation, Family Support, and Cash Assistance

A few exceptions in policy and practice emerged in the intervening decades. The Adoption Assistance and Child Welfare Act of 1980 (P.L. 96-272) and the Indian Child Welfare Act of 1978 (PL 95-608) called for significant efforts to prevent out-of-home place-ment. Led by innovations in the Children's Bureau, such service enhancements not only diverted many unnecessary placements but also demonstrated the capacity of families to benefit from intensive services and to alter problem behaviors and conditions.

One innovation involved intensive family preservation services that provided for some families a 24/7 crisis response team. In some counties and states, small cash grants to families to address resource needs were provided by family preservation workers. Such a resource focus also became a relationship-building tool, as families might be less likely to engage in mental health or substance abuse treatment until their fundamental resource needs, like repair of a car used to get to work, were addressed. Homebuild-ers, the leader in intensive family preservation services, found that when these services were initiated for a family at risk of having a child placed out of the home, addressing resource needs was essential to relationship building and to later use of more intensive services or mental health treatment (personal communication with D. Hapala, Tacoma, WA, 1987). Cash assistance was a key resource in some of the more successful intensive family preservation service models such as Homebuilders (Berry, Cash, & Brook, 2000).

More recently, again supported by the Children's Bureau, states and counties have implemented dual-track or alternative-response systems. These enable families with low and moderate risk factors at intake to receive services rather than a CPS investiga-tion. Dual-track (sometimes called family assessment response) services offer some of the attributes of integrative income maintenance services that were offered before the separation of services and cash assistance. A family assessment rather than a CPS inves-tigation ensues. Although the assessment may be more service than income focused (because few child welfare agencies undertaking dual-track assessments have income, employment, or educational resources), the assessment is nonetheless more holis-tic, strength based and prevention oriented than the deficit-based, investigatory, risk approach. The dual-track strategy also enables service providers to examine CAN corre-lates or root causes such as poverty, joblessness, and underemployment to potentially provide referrals to services that address these (HHS, 2003).

As desirable as the reintegration of income support and services might seem to some, few states or counties have seen such reintegration as an opportunity to rebuild supports for impoverished and vulnerable families. While a few states began to rehire social workers to address the needs of welfare families with the advent of TANF, this short-term income support program does not explicitly provide the resources or incen-tives to states to address family or child well-being beyond income support.

New Models for Addressing Poverty and Child Welfare

Despite the separation of income and services, most child welfare and welfare agen-cies try to work together. It would be difficult to find a social service system that does not have coordination committees, referral processes, and innovative approaches for blending welfare and child welfare resources and services. Some have merged agencies under a common director. Some have dismantled umbrella agencies to give more attention to each component. In some states, TANF funds support child welfare services (Geen, 2002). Unfortunately, we were unable to identify a single model that has demonstrated a substantial difference in poverty-related outcomes for families in the child welfare system, and no administrative structure has emerged as superior to others.

Despite this, a few models have moved to the forefront that may provide guidance for further innovations. They are based on a common philosophical framework and a few core concepts. Most of the remainder of this chapter will describe this framework and give examples, based on the authors' personal experiences and familiarity, of how it has developed or is developing in two jurisdictions.

Redefining Prevention

The new philosophy starts with the premise that every social agency has a prevention aspect. Healthy communities and good schools help prevent the need for TANF. Economic supports help prevent the need for intervention by child welfare and juvenile justice agencies. Good child welfare programs prevent criminal justice problems and homelessness. But if agencies do not creatively and comprehensively define the business they are in, approaches become siloed and agency-centered.

The TANF agency's mission must be defined as extending beyond running a good welfare program to serving as the primary prevention component of the child welfare system. Success should be measured not by how many people leave the welfare or TANF rolls but by how many children and families are safe and economically secure.

Becoming Truly Family Centered

A second principle is striving to make services truly family centered. Virtually all agency leaders try to make their operations responsive to the needs of families, but they often have not fully defined what it means to be family centered. Traditionally, human services organizations have taken an agency-centered view of the services they provide. They may concentrate on what families are eligible for and forget to ask what they need. They may reach out to other agencies to assist in their mission and fail to understand how all their efforts should fit together or how the family relates to all the agencies. As an example, families may be eligible for a variety of substance abuse programs but be unable to access any of them because no one will pay for transportation to get there.

In a family-centered approach, success is defined in terms of what has improved for children and families. Process indicators such as level of service or frequency of contact are replaced with changes in safety, permanence, and well-being. The Children's Bureau under the leadership of Carol Williams-Spigner, a social work educator and leader, led the way in emphasizing these changes in the mid-1990s. Process indicators are still widely used in both TANF and child welfare systems.

Listening to Clients

TANF agencies need to ask more questions such as "How did you make it this long without us? What is different now? What do you want to accomplish? What have you already tried? What has helped in the past and what got in your way? What can we do to help you get more of what works and to avoid doing things that interfere with your progress?" Clients' input is essential not only in designing their own plans but also in guiding systemic change.

Fostering a Sense of Hope and Abundance

Little progress comes from dwelling on what agencies do not have. They need to look at the strengths not only of their clients but of their staff, other agencies, and communities. The problem is not just a lack of resources. Currently, all human service systems have huge expenditures, but the present way of doing business can too often lead to very bad outcomes. A sense of abundance gives hope and excites passion. In the long run, good outcomes are cheaper than bad outcomes. Communities are resilient and thriving despite economic downturns. Instead of focusing entirely on scarcity, agencies need to look at abundance of resources including compassionate caseworkers, dedicated volunteers, and family members who are experts in their own unique circumstances.

Doing the Right Thing as Well as Doing Things Right

Doing things right means meeting regulatory requirements and working effectively and efficiently. It includes timeliness, accuracy, respect, and effective use of technology. These are all essential but will not get families all the way to where they need to go.

A TANF program can be highly effective and efficient according to the rules but still fail if many families end up in intrusive, costly, and unpopular child welfare and juvenile justice services. How can agencies prevent families' slide into those systems? Strict enforcement of time limits and work requirements easily reduces the number of people receiving TANF. But if those families end up homeless, hungry, and unemployed, the agencies have neglected the most vital part of their job. Some jurisdictions are beginning to tell their staff that it is half the agency's fault if any clients leave TANF due to sanctions or time limits. All should leave because they have better ways to support their families.

Maintaining a Sense of Urgency

Earlier in this chapter, some of the consequences of poverty for children and families were listed and documented. This alone should provide a sense of urgency, but often systems proceed along bureaucratic and procedural time frames. Every community needs a philosophy that no one deserves to be living on TANF; families deserve much more. A family whose only income is TANF is generally living at about 40 percent of the poverty level. This would not be viewed as good enough for the authors' families or for the readers' families, and it should not be viewed as good enough for any family. Every day a child remains in poverty should be seen as a day of lost opportunity.

Principles in Action

The above principles were originally articulated for integration of TANF and child welfare in El Paso County, Colorado. Beginning in Colorado Springs in the late 1990s, TANF was tested as an integrative model serving as the family preservation arm of the child welfare system. Trained master's-level child welfare workers were transferred into the TANF section to provide comprehensive services to families. Units provided specialized services to high-need TANF families and to lower risk families who otherwise would have been served in the child welfare system. Flexible funding through TANF allowed for families and individuals to receive tailored or wrap-around approaches giving them what they needed that was not based on strict programmatic design or eligibility. Families designed their own plans with the help and guidance of their caseworkers.

The law provided for a full sanction (often termination) of their family benefits for noncompliance with the work plan, and a five-year time limit. These requirements were used to emphasize a sense of urgency for families, staff, and the community. Workers and families were held accountable for assuring that the families developed realistic plans and had the resources and supports required for implementation. Noncompliance was met with renegotiation of the plan to better meet the real needs of the family. In the first six years of the program, none of the families reached the point requiring a full family sanction, and only a dozen or so of the initial 3,800 families remained on assistance after five years. All of those were assisted into more appropriate programs such as Supplemental Security Income (SSI).

Over a dozen community and governmental services were collocated into the TANF office, all sharing information as liberally authorized by the clients. Innovations included a family-centered approach to TANF recipients and a strength- and asset-enhancing practice orientation. Service users were hired as consultants as well as staff supports to help ensure that services were provided with a high quality of treatment. Other innovations included a family needs assessment, which resulted in holistic casework supports to meet family needs and to address parental employment goals. At the same time, institutional placements of children in the child welfare system were reduced by more than 50 percent, and foster care placements were reduced by about 40 percent.

The approach was fully described by the Center for Law and Social Policy (Hutson, 2003) and in a case study jointly conducted by the Kennedy School of Government at

Harvard University and the Muskie Center at the University of Southern Maine. Several articles (Berns, 2001, 2011; Briar-Lawson, 2001) also address the benefits of using TANF as the primary prevention arm of the child welfare system.

In 2011, similar innovations were introduced into income maintenance services in Washington, DC. In this model, programs like TANF, Supplemental Nutrition Assistance Program, Medicaid, social service block grants, and community development block grants all are being refined and reconceptualized. Thus, TANF and related programs are seen as preventive services (Berns, 2011). This innovative strategy reintegrates income supports and services and helps to advance assessment of families' needs and not just their income eligibility. In fact, in this model it is argued that the overriding focus should be the preventive strategies that can be employed along with the promotion of self-sufficiency.

Bringing holistic services back to TANF in Washington, DC, involves a family-centered strategy. Casework staff in TANF are expected to be resource developers based on a family needs assessment and not just deployers of programs for which the family is eligible. Such needs assessments are strength based and probe what life would look like if a "miracle" occurred. From such a vision of how families would like things to be better and different, service providers in TANF are expected to mobilize relevant supports.

Led by the client voice, such holistic and family centered planning by casework staff involves probes to identify what has worked in the past. Tailoring such responses to the unique needs of each family involves mobilization of local neighborhood resources from churches, adult education programs, and local employers. If TANF time limits are driving families into the child welfare or juvenile justice system, this is seen as a poor TANF outcome. If families hit their TANF time limits or need to be sanctioned for noncompliance, this is a sign of systems and structural failure rather than family deficits. Workers are expected to help families attain a better set of material and economic conditions. Case plans are in part led by families themselves, as they identify what would give them skills, related supports, and occupational paths. Families can "fire" their case manager if they are not getting their needs met. Drawing on some of the wrap-around practices and successes of family prevention services, this integrated service delivery promotes the worker as a case manager for strength-based supports. Moreover, a case plan for a family in child welfare becomes the case plan for the TANF worker. In essence, all work toward the same outcomes, and professional collaboration is expected.

While introduced successfully in two regions of the nation, this policy pilot might help to inform more integration between TANF and child welfare. Children's Bureau grantees in the past have examined such integrative opportunities, but the lessons derived have yet to become models for best practices and public policy reforms (Berns, 2011; Briar-Lawson, 2001). Thus, the challenge that lies ahead is one of systematic lessons, drawing from promising models that address poverty along with family supports and preservation.

Integrative practices are warranted given the evidence that services such as parenting classes for CAN families will be less effective unless there is simultaneous attention to their material needs. Poverty may be masked by overriding CAN issues. However, more recent attention to child well-being, called for by the HHS Commissioner of Children, Youth and Families, Bryan Samuels (HHS, 2012), creates the platform for new accountability for child outcomes. Safety and permanency are no longer seen as sufficient child outcomes. Thus, given the need for systematic attention to well-being, promoting successive steps up the income ladder with employment-related services and job mobility at increasing rates of pay, become key challenges for 21st-century systems and their practitioners.

Social workers have long demonstrated that such integrative practices are within their repertoire. This is despite the fact that many are seen to have abandoned a focus on the poverty-related needs of families who depend on public sector services such as TANF, child welfare, SSI, Medicaid, and so forth (Specht & Courtney, 1994). Even so, the service and practice innovations within the El Paso County, Colorado, and Washington, DC, systems of income maintenance warrant symmetrical innovations in child welfare. Child well-being requirements invite new syntheses of service approaches, resources, and integrative practices. Moreover, given that families of color make up a disproportionate amount of child welfare families with poverty and joblessness concerns, access to jobs, financial literacy, and income ladders need to be paramount concerns.

Roles for Schools of Social Work

Although social work education has always included a focus on poverty, attention to new models for assisting the poor has fluctuated over the decades (Specht & Courtney, 1994). In the midst of the current recession, however, some innovative work has been undertaken. This includes new course work on financial and economic literacy in schools of social work in New York City. Led by the Hunter School of Social Work, competency-based curriculums in financial literacy have been developed at the master's level.

Similarly, at the School of Social Welfare at the University at Albany, a faculty member's research on the needs of Earned Income Tax Credit filers determined that up to 10 percent wanted to start a small business. This led to the development of character-based micro-lending. An adaptation of the Grameen Bank has been implemented by the School of Social Welfare, the School of Business and its Small Business Development Center, and the State Employees Federal Credit Union, as well as the state. This micro-lending program for low-income applicants, called Small Enterprise Economic Development (SEED), tests new models of character-based lending in lieu of traditional cash, credit, and collateral criteria for loans. SEED has funded over $825,000 in loans, creating more than 92 jobs and serving 23 microbusinesses. In addition, through the Center for Excellence in Aging Services and Community Wellness at the School of Social Welfare, partnerships have been developed with several banks to address financial abuse and fraud and to promote an online financial literacy toolkit.

The recession and its grave human costs, along with retrenchments in the nation, invite more research and practice innovations by schools of social work and institutions that can address financial needs and entitlements. Financial literacy along with increased access to lending organizations are among the keys to social and economic support for the poor, including the working poor.

Conclusion

Child welfare agencies and schools of social work have opportunities to address poverty head-on in the twenty-first century by working to reduce the social and economic marginalization of parents and older youths in the child welfare system. By partnering with TANF agencies in new roles, and by generating new income supports and related resources, some child welfare system parents can become family experts or parent aides and provide peer services. The twin goals of eliminating poverty and promoting child safety and well-being should inspire and compel nothing less for America's most vulnerable and marginalized families.

References

Adoption Assistance and Child Welfare Act of 1980, P.L. 96-272, 94 Stat. 500 (1980).

Barth, R. P., Wildfire, J., & Green, R. L. (2006). Placement into foster care and the interplay of urbanicity, child behavior problems, and poverty. *American Journal of Orthopsychiatry, 76,* 358–366.

Bassuk, E. L., Buckner, J. C., Weinraub, L. F., Broen, A., Bassuk, S. S., Dawson, R., et al. (1997). Homelessness in female headed families: Childhood and adult risk and protective factors. *American Journal of Public Health, 87,* 241–248.

Bassuk, E. L., Rubin, L., & Lauriat, A. (1986). Characteristics of sheltered homeless families. *American Journal of Public Health, 76,* 1097–1101.

Berns, D. (2001). Addressing poverty issues in child welfare: Effective use of TANF as a prevention resource. In A. Sallee, H. Lawson, & K. Briar-Lawson (Eds.), *Innovative practices with vulnerable children and families* (pp. 33–51). Peosta, IA: Eddie Bowers.

Berns, D. (2011). Is our business family-centered? *Journal of Family Strengths, 11*(1), article 3. Retrieved from http://digitalcommons.library.tmc.edu/jfs/vol11/iss1/3

Berry, M., Cash, S. J., & Brook, J. P. (2000). Intensive family preservation services: An examination of critical service components. *Child & Family Social Work, 5*(3), 191–203.

Briar, K. (1988). *Social work with the unemployed.* Silver Spring, MD: NASW Press.

Briar-Lawson, K. (2001). Integrating employment, economic supports, and family capacity building. In A. Sallee, H. Lawson, & K. Briar-Lawson (Eds.), *Innovative practices with vulnerable children and families* (pp. 13–31). Peosta, IA: Eddie Bowers.

Child Welfare Information Gateway. (2011). *Addressing racial disproportionality in child welfare.* Washington, DC: U.S. Department of Health and Human Services, Children's Bureau.

Cohen, C. S., Mulroy, E., Tull, T., White, C., & Crowley, S. (2004). Housing plus services: Supporting vulnerable families in permanent housing. *Child Welfare, 83,* 509–528.

Coulton, C. J., Korbin, J. E., Su, M., & Chow, J. (1995). Community level factors and child maltreatment rates. *Child Development, 66,* 1262–1276.

Deccio, G., Horner, W. C., & Wilson, D. (1994). High-risk neighborhoods and high-risk families: Replication research related to the human ecology of child maltreatment. *Journal of Social Services Research, 18,* 123–137.

Dooley, D., & Catalano, R. (1980). Economic change as a cause of behavioral disorder. *Psychological Bulletin, 87,* 450–468.

Duncan, G. J., & Brooks-Gunn, J. (1997). Income effects across the life span: Integration and interpretation. In G. J. Duncan & J. Brooks-Gunn (Eds.), *Consequences of growing up poor* (pp. 596–610). New York: Russell Sage.

Duncan, J. G., & Brooks-Gunn, J. (2000). Family poverty, welfare reform, and child development. *Child Development, 71,* 188–196.

Freisthler, B. (2004). A spatial analysis of social disorganization, alcohol access, and rates of child maltreatment in neighborhoods. *Children and Youth Services Review, 26,* 307–319.

Freisthler, B., Merritt, D. H., & LaSacla, E. A. (2006). Understanding the ecology of child maltreatment: A review of the literature and directions for future research. *Child Maltreatment, 11,* 263–280.

Galler, J. R., Ramsay, F., Solimano, G., & Lowell, W. (1983). The influence of early malnutrition on subsequent behavioral development: II. Classroom behavior. *Journal of the American Academy of Child Psychiatry, 22,* 16–22.

Geen, R. (2002). *Shoring up the child welfare–TANF link.* Washington, DC: Urban Institute.

Geismar, L. (1964). *Understanding the multi-problem family: A conceptual analysis and exploration in early identification.* New York: Association Press.

Gil, D. G. (1970). *Violence against children: Physical child abuse in the United States.* Boston: Harvard University Press.

Gil, D. G. (1971). Violence against children. *Journal of Marriage and Family, 33,* 637–648.

Herrenkohl, T. I., Sousa, C., Tajima, E. A., Herrenkohl, R. C., & Moylan, C. A. (2008). Intersection of child abuse and children's exposure to domestic violence. *Trauma, Violence, & Abuse, 9,* 84–99.

Hutson, R. Q. (2003). *A vision for eliminating poverty and family violence: Transforming child welfare and TANF in El Paso County, Colorado.* Washington, DC: Center for Law and Social Policy.

Indian Child Welfare Act of 1978, P.L. 95-608, 92 Stat. 3069 (1978).

Kalil, A., & Ziol-Guest, K. (2008). Parental job loss and children's academic progress in two-parent families. *Social Science Research, 37,* 500–515.

Lindsey, D. (1994). *The welfare of children.* New York: Oxford University Press.

Lupie, S. J., King, S., Meaney, M. J., & McEwen, B. S. (2001). Can poverty get under your skin? Basal cortisol levels and cognitive function in children from low and high socioeconomic status. *Developmental Psychopathology, 13,* 653–676.

Machtinger, B. (1999). The U.S. Children's Bureau and Mothers' Pensions Administration, 1912–1930. *Social Service Review, 73,* 105–118.

McLoyd, V. C. (1998). Socioeconomic disadvantage and child development. *American Psychologist, 53,*185–205.

National Institute of Child Health Human Development Early Child Care Research Network. (2005). Duration and developmental timing of poverty and children's cognitive and social development from birth through third grade. *Child Development, 76,* 795–810.

Oreopoulos, P. M, Page, M., & Stevens, A. (2008). The intergenerational effect of worker displacement. *Journal of Labor Economics, 26,* 455–483.

Osterling, L. K., Andrade, D. A., & Austin, J. M. (2008). Understanding and addressing racial/ethnic disproportionality in the front end of the child welfare system. *Journal of Evidence-Based Social Work, 5*(1/2), 9–30.

Pelton, L. H. (1978). Child abuse and neglect: The myth of classlessness. *American Journal of Orthopsychiatry, 48,* 608–617.

Pelton, L. H. (1994). The role of material factors in child abuse and neglect. In G. Melton & F. D. Barry (Eds.), *Protecting from abuse and neglect* (pp. 131–181). New York: Guilford Press.

Pelton, L. H. (2008). Informing child welfare: The promise and limits of empirical research. In D. Lindsey & A. Shlonsk (Eds.), *Child welfare research: Advances for practice and policy* (pp. 25–48). New York: Oxford University Press.

Piliavin, I., & Gross, A. E. (1977). The effects of separation of services and income maintenance on AFDC recipients. *Social Service Review, 51,* 389–406.

Raizada, R. D., & Kishiyama, M. M. (2010). Effects of socioeconomic status on brain development, and how cognitive neuroscience may contribute to leveling the playing field. *Frontiers in Human Neuroscience, 5,* 1–18.

Sedlak, A. J., Mettenburg, J., Basena, M., Petta, I., McPherson, K., & Greene, A. (2010). *Fourth national incidence study of child abuse and neglect* (NIS-4). Washington, DC: U.S. Department of Health and Human Services.

Slack, S. K., Holl, L. J., McDaniel, M., Yoo, J., & Bolger, K. (2004).Understanding the risks of child neglect: An exploration of poverty and parenting characteristics. *Child Maltreatment, 9,* 395–408.

Social Security Act of 1935, P.L. 74-271, ch. 531, 49 Stat. 620 (1935).

Specht, H., & Courtney, M. E. (1994) *Unfaithful angels*. New York: Free Press.

Steinberg, L. D., Catalano, R., & Dooley, D. (1981). Economic antecedents of child abuse and neglect. *Child Development, 52,* 975–985.

Stewart, W. F., Schwartz, B. S., Davatzikos, C., Shen, L. D., Wu, X., Todd, A. C., et al. (2006). Past adult lead exposure is linked to neurodegeneration measured by brain MRI. *Neurology, 66,* 1476–1484.

Sullivan, P. M., & Knutson, J. F. (2000). Maltreatment and disabilities: A population-based epidemiological study. *Child Abuse & Neglect, 24,* 1257–1273.

Tanner, E. M., & Finn-Stevenson, M. (2002). Nutrition and brain development: Social policy implications. *American Journal of Orthopsychiatry, 72,* 182–193.

U.S. Bureau of Labor Statistics. (2012). *A profile of the working poor, 2010.* Washington, DC: U.S. Department of Labor.

U.S. Census Bureau. (2011). *A profile of the working poor, 2010.* Washington, DC: U.S. Department of Labor.U.S.

U.S. Department of Health and Human Services. (2003). *Children of color in the child welfare system: Perspectives from the child welfare community.* Washington, DC: Author.

U.S. Department of Health and Human Services, Administration for Children and Families, Administration on Children, Youth and Families, Children's Bureau. (2012). *Promoting social and emotional well-being for children and youth receiving child welfare services* (ACYF-CB-IM-12-04). Washington, DC: Author.

U.S. Department of Health and Human Services, Administration on Children Youth and Families. (2007). *Child maltreatment 2007.* Washington, DC: US Government Printing Office.

Chapter 4

FAMILY-CENTERED PRACTICE

Miriam J. Landsman

F amily-centered practice is an approach to working with families built on a clear set of values and principles that can be actualized in different ways. The concept has emerged in professions as varied as social work, education, medicine, and nursing, as well as practice fields such as child welfare, developmental disabilities, and aging.

Even within the specialized field of child welfare, family-centered practice cannot be restricted to a specific service or model; it demands flexibility in order to respond to families' diverse needs and situations. Broadly defined, family-centered practice in child welfare seeks to strengthen and support families' ability to provide for their children's welfare. This can involve providing services such as skill-building, therapy, or assistance with concrete needs. Since many constraints on family and child well-being involve external systems and social structural problems, family-centered practice can also involve interventions at the neighborhood, community, or state level through collaboration, mediation, and/or advocacy for social change.

Family-centered practice spans a continuum from community-based services for those who may be at risk of experiencing more serious problems to intensive and focused in-home services directed at preventing family disruption, to family involvement and guidance when a period of out-of-home placement is necessary, to strong family support following adoption in order to prevent subsequent disruptions and further trauma.

Child welfare has long struggled with the dual roles of agent of social control and helper or change agent. This tension plays out in many ways but is fundamental to understanding how family-centered practice is actualized in the context of public child welfare services. Dunst et al. (2002) described four models of family oriented service provision based on different assumptions about the capacities and roles of the professional and the family: (1) the *professional-centered* model, in which profession-als are seen as experts and key decision-makers about courses of action families will take; (2) the *family-allied* model, in which families are believed to have some capacity to carry out professionally prescribed courses of action; (3) the *family-focused* model, in which families choose among options recommended by professionals; and (4) the *family-centered* model, which views families as having the capacity to make informed decisions and act on them. In the family-centered model, the professional serves as the agent for the family, helping to strengthen the family's capacity. In child welfare, family-centered language is often used while implementing a professional-centered model.

Theory and Values

Walton (2001) offered a useful analysis of the theoretical orientations underlying family-centered practice, which include ecological, family systems, attachment, strength-based, and empowerment theories. *Ecological* theory emphasizes a holistic approach to individual and family developmental processes as well as the interplay between per-son and environment (Bronfenbrenner, 1979; Garbarino, 1982; Germain & Gitterman, 1980; Walton, 2001). *Family systems* theory, the foundation of family therapy, views the family as a dynamic system comprised of individuals who are interconnected while constantly changing (Walton, 2001). *Attachment* theory, articulated by Bowlby (1982), stresses the importance of early attachment and the effects of attachment disruptions on child development. The *strength-based* perspective (Saleebey, 1992) highlights the importance of building on the strengths and capacities of clients themselves to effect meaningful changes. Finally, *empowerment* theory focuses on the ways that barriers child welfare clients face are rooted in oppression by social class, gender, race, ethnicity, ability, age, and national origin (Lee, 1996). Family-centered practice is not solely about helping clients change, but also about advocating for needed social change.

Walton (2001) also noted several social work models that inform family-centered practice, including *crisis intervention*, which views a crisis as an event that challenges individual and family functioning but can also serve as an opportunity for change; *brief solution-focused therapy*, which focuses on solving immediate problems and builds competence as individuals experience success (Berg, 1994); and *cognitive-behavioral therapy*, which helps clients to understand how thoughts influence behavior and to implement more successful patterns (Carlson, Sperry, & Lewis, 1991). These social work models are apparent in some of the evidence-supported interventions discussed later in this chapter.

Cultural competence and *trauma-informed* perspectives are also critical to family-centered practice. A cultural competence perspective keeps an understanding of the family's cultural norms, values, and beliefs at the forefront of practice rather than treating it as an afterthought. Culture plays an important role in the lives of family members and networks, and family-centered practice demands respect for cultural differences among individuals and families. Family-centered practice acknowledges the diversity in family structure, traditions, beliefs, behaviors, and experiences, and the various dimensions of culture (race and ethnicity, social class, age, gender and gender identity, religion, and national origin). While there is no single approach to "culturally competent" practice, family-centered work requires practitioners to suspend assumptions based on their own experiences and be open to hearing the cultural understandings and experiences of their clients. A *trauma-informed* perspective keeps the family-centered practitioner cognizant of the impact of various traumas—such as abuse, poverty, and family separation—on individuals and families, and the role of resiliency in mediating that impact.

The values underlying family-centered practice have been articulated previously (see, for example, Maluccio, 1990; Nelson & Landsman, 1992; Ronnau, 2001). Family-centered practice starts with the family as the fundamental social unit to be maintained and supported (Hartman, 1981). Next, it recognizes that children need continuity and stability in their lives in order to thrive and should grow up in their families whenever possible. While some children cannot remain safe and well within their families in the short or long term, these cases represent a small segment of those that come to the attention of child welfare. In most situations, society should invest at least as much in supporting and strengthening families to help solve problems as in placing children with alternative families (Nelson, Walters, Schweitzer, Blythe, & Pecora, 2009).

Engaging with family members to understand their lives, goals, strengths, and challenges is essential; without developing a relationship, the role of social control agent almost always prevails. Central to family-centered practice is a belief that individuals have the capacity to grow and develop new skills which can be facilitated through a strong partnership between family and practitioner. Family-centered practitioners treat family members with dignity and respect and seek to empower them to make decisions about their goals, priorities, and needs. Identifying and building on strengths are key to supporting families in the change process. Interventions need to be tailored to the family members' individual needs and use approaches that are based on the best available evidence.

Family-centered practice recognizes families as social systems that can take many forms, with membership defined by the family rather than imposed by social norms or external authorities. "Family" is not limited to the traditional nuclear family but may include multiple generations, extended family, fictive kin, and others. Strengthening the family's capacity to keep children safe and well may involve this broader family network. As interdependent social systems, families exist in a social world, interacting with a variety of formal and informal external systems. Community systems can be supportive or non-supportive, and an important part of family-centered practice involves helping families learn to negotiate these systems. Family-centered practitioners also need to be prepared to advocate on behalf of families for changes at organizational, neighborhood, and state levels.

History of Family-Centered Practice

Role of the Children's Bureau

The U.S. Children's Bureau was established within the Department of Commerce and Labor in 1912 as the first federal agency dedicated to all aspects pertaining to children (Kemp, Almgren, Gilchrist, & Eisinger, 2001). The first two bureau chiefs, Julia Lathrop and Grace Abbott, brought their experiences from Hull House and the Progressive movement to their leadership of the Bureau, focusing on prevention and the importance of addressing social conditions to improve child well-being. The Children's Bureau's attention to the whole child (Kemp et al., 2001) was an early precursor to, and consistent with, the family systems and ecological approaches of family-centered practice.

The Children's Bureau's first initiative was reducing infant mortality, a formidable problem at the time of the Bureau's founding and one that would require attention to a host of social issues involving health, education, employment, and poverty. The Bureau approached the infant mortality initiative through empirical field research, prevention strategies at multiple levels, and legislative advocacy (Almgren, Kemp, & Eisinger, 2000). This combination of research, preventive intervention, and advocacy can also be seen in its later efforts to promote family-centered practice. Through specifically defined priority areas and field-initiated research, the Bureau has funded projects to develop and test different approaches to family-centered practice.

The Bureau funded the first of its national resource centers, the National Resource Center for Family Based Services at the University of Iowa, after enactment of the Adoption Assistance and Child Welfare Act of 1980 (P.L. 96-272) (AACWA). The Center's purpose was to provide training, technical assistance, and information services to state child welfare agencies as they implemented the requirements of AACWA, especially the requirement for reasonable efforts to prevent placement and expedite reunification. The Children's Bureau's family-centered orientation continues today, with the University of Iowa serving as the National Resource Center for In-Home Services, working collaboratively within a larger network of resource centers and implementation centers to help states and tribes improve outcomes for children who are living at home.

Federal Legislation Shaping Family-Centered Practice

Contemporary family-centered practice in child welfare has been strongly influenced by AACWA, created to address the increasing numbers of children in foster care, the length and stability of those placements, and inadequate efforts and resources directed toward reunification or adoption. Prior to AACWA, the Child Abuse Prevention and

Treatment Act (P.L. 93-247) had resulted in increasing child welfare caseloads through investigations and placements. Despite that law's profound impact on families, however, its original version did not even mention families (Sandau-Beckler, Salcido, Beckler, Mannes, & Beck, 2002).

Under AACWA, in order to receive matching federal funds for foster care, states had to make "reasonable efforts" to prevent placement and expedite reunification. To receive maximum funding, states had to provide a comprehensive array of preplacement prevention and reunification services. This legislation established the principles of least restrictive setting, most family-like setting, and placement as close to home as possible (unless this would not be beneficial to the child). AACWA also strengthened adoption by requiring states to develop adoption subsidy programs and partially subsidizing special-needs adoptions. Finally, the legislation mandated case reviews by the court every six months and a dispositional hearing within 18 months after placement.

The Indian Child Welfare Act of 1978 (P.L. 95-608) (ICWA), which preceded AACWA, had addressed the destructive, long-standing practice of removing Indian children from their families, tribes, and communities and placing them in boarding schools and with non-Indian families. ICWA established more stringent criteria when placing Indian children and terminating parental rights than those applied to non-Indian children (Pecora et al., 2010). When child placement was necessary, ICWA articulated a clear preference for the child's extended family, then foster families approved by the child's tribe, and then other Indian foster homes or alternative settings (Pecora et al., 2010). Despite problems in implementation, notably inadequate compliance by state child welfare agencies, ICWA strengthened the roles of family and tribe in making decisions regarding the well-being of Indian children and affirmed the importance of culture in child welfare decision-making.

The Family Preservation and Support Services Program (FPSSP), established through the Omnibus Budget Reconciliation Act of 1993 (P.L. 103-66), was a limited, capped entitlement program that expanded funding for prevention and family support services. With an initial year for extensive state and local collaborative planning, there were high hopes that states would use the new funding creatively and strategically to fill gaps in categorical programs (those funded through legislation with a specific intent and associated policies) and fragmented service systems and to advance broader system reforms. In contrast to AACWA's narrower focus on services, FPSSP recognized the importance of community and cross-system collaboration (Maluccio, Abramczyk, & Thomlison, 1996). With the later passage of the Adoption and Safe Families Act of 1997, FPSSP was renamed Promoting Safe and Stable Families and added time-limited reunification and adoption promotion to its previous scope of family preservation and support. The grand vision of FPSSP as a mechanism for integrating services and furthering system reform has not been fully realized.

The Adoption and Safe Families Act modified provisions of AACWA in significant ways. It established time frames for pursuing termination of parental rights and (with some exceptions) required states to seek termination if a child had been placed out of the home for 15 of the previous 22 months. It waived the requirements for "reasonable efforts" to prevent placement or to reunify families under certain circumstances and shortened the time frames for the permanency hearing. Finally, it established three key outcomes—safety, permanency, and child well-being—elevating safety as the first priority of child welfare services. These provisions were enacted to expedite permanency and reduce long-term foster care. The shorter time frames, however, pose challenges when families are making progress, albeit at a slower pace than the system would prefer.

The newest federal law affecting family-centered practice is the Fostering Connections to Success and Increasing Adoptions Act of 2008 (P.L. 110-251). Although focused on youths in foster care, it emphasizes making connections with and supporting caregivers from the extended family and avoiding institutional or nonfamilial placements. Fostering Connections supports the child's right to maintain connections to his or her family and the rights of parents and relatives to be involved in the child's life. The act acknowledges the impact of family connections on child well-being by increasing efforts to seek out and engage immediate and extended family members and requiring the state to notify all adult relatives within 30 days of a child's removal from the home and explain their options to be involved in the child's care. States must now make reasonable efforts to place siblings together or, if this is not feasible, to provide for frequent visitation or ongoing sibling interaction (unless contrary to the children's welfare). In short, this most recent federal law affirms the importance of a family-centered approach across the continuum of child welfare services.

Evidence Base for Family-Centered Practice

Establishing a clear evidence base for family-centered practice is a daunting challenge. Despite a widespread desire for practice methods with strong evidence behind them, the circumstances in which child welfare services are delivered make this an elusive goal. Gambrill (2006) noted that evidence-based practice (EBP) was designed to reduce gaps between research and practice and to provide the greatest help and avoid harm to clients (see also Gray, 2001; Sackett, Straus, Richardson, Rosenberg, & Haynes, 2000). Combining the best available research evidence, clinical judgment, and a client-centered approach, EBP emphasizes researchers' ethical responsibilities in designing, implementing, and interpreting research results, and administrators' and practitioners' responsibilities in integrating research into practice. EBP honors ethical responsibilities to clients through informed participation, rejecting ineffective or harmful services and promoting services "critically tested and found to help clients attain the outcomes they value" (Gambrill, 2006, p. 351). Mullen, Bledsoe, and Bellamy (2008) distinguished between *evidence-based practice*—the process of examining the evidence underlying different interventions or treatment approaches in light of the individual circumstances, values, and preferences of the clients—and *evidence-supported interventions*, the specific interventions identified through this process.

EBP is highly consistent with family-centered practice, maximizing the family's decision-making role and providing interventions with a strong track record in achieving the client's desired and relevant outcomes. But there are clear gaps between EBP and child welfare service delivery. Child welfare clients may not be in the position of choosing their services because whether by formal mandate (court order) or less formalized methods of coercion, services are often involuntary. Child welfare agencies operate under stringent budgets that may not permit the selection of evidence-supported interventions. Thus, ethical responsibilities to clients—involving clients as informed participants with choices, and providing interventions with the greatest likelihood of achieving the client's desired outcomes—may be compromised.

Another gap is the legitimate concern about the integrity of the knowledge base for interventions that comprise child welfare services. Barth (2008) has pointed out that interventions with the strongest evidence base are generally found for specific diagnostic groups, in contrast with child welfare services, which tend to consist of varied interventions applied to a diverse range of families and situations. Furthermore, evidence is considered to be strongest if it is based on a rigorous design, with a preference for randomized designs implemented under well-controlled conditions, which are difficult to execute in child welfare settings. As a result, many evidence-supported interventions have not been validated with child welfare populations. Complicating matters are the inability to control for multiple interventions different family members may be receiving from varied service providers, and difficulties in ensuring that evidence-supported interventions, even when used, are implemented with fidelity.

Within these limitations, we identify some system reform efforts and evidence-supported interventions that reflect the theoretical foundations of a holistic family-centered approach. This is not exhaustive; for example, we do not discuss parent training interventions because, while some have empirical support, parent training is one component of a family-centered approach rather than a comprehensive approach in its own right. In addition, since research is an ongoing process of generating hypotheses and testing them in light of new information and under different conditions, the evidence base is constantly evolving.

System Reforms

Two system reform efforts have enhanced child welfare agencies' ability to provide family-centered services. Both are models of practice that can be integrated into child welfare systems and that can take different forms.

Alternative response, or differential response, is an approach to handling child maltreatment intake reports that establishes different mechanisms to respond to more and less serious allegations. States that have implemented alternative response systems handle the most serious situations (such as sexual abuse or serious physical injury) through the traditional forensic child abuse investigative process. An alternative, nonadversarial family assessment track is used for low- to moderate-risk cases; in this track, workers assess family strengths and needs and approach the family with an eye toward ensuring that children are safe while solving problems that precipitated the maltreatment referral.

Alternative response is designed to focus on the whole family, identifying and building on family strengths while addressing a variety of family needs that may be involved in child maltreatment. The traditional child protective focus on substantiating a caregiver's negligence or abuse creates animosity between the parent and child welfare worker. An alternative response allows for the development of a helping relationship that can begin immediately upon referral and lead to a more expeditious mobilization of community resources.

States that have implemented differential response have varied the number of tracks (all have at least two tracks, while some have three or four); criteria for eligibility, such as child's age and prior maltreatment reports; and statewide versus local implementation (Merkel-Holguin, Kaplan, & Kwak, 2006). Due to these variations, differential response is best regarded as an approach rather than a specific intervention. The strongest empirical evidence for alternative response is an experimental study in 14 Minnesota counties in which families were randomly assigned to an alternative response or standard child protective services intervention after a child maltreatment allegation. Families receiving alternative response improved significantly more in safety, did not experience higher recidivism, and expressed greater satisfaction with services than those in the control group (Johnson, Sutton & Thompson, 2005; Loman & Siegel, 2005).

Family group conferencing, which originated in New Zealand in the late 1980s, engages extended family members in planning and making decisions to ensure child and family well-being (Walton, Roby, Frandsen, & Davidson, 2003). It positions the family at the helm of decision-making and action planning. The model is premised on the assumption that the family has a stronger interest than the state in the child's well-being and can provide long-term support to remedy the problems precipitating child welfare involvement. Family group conferencing originated in response to indigenous peoples' concerns about discriminatory practices and has been used with families of diverse cultures and situations (Crampton & Jackson, 2007; Sheets et al., 2009; Waites, Macgowan, Pennell, Carlton-LaNey, & Weil, 2004).

Various forms of family group conferencing have emerged, and different terms are used to describe the approach, but certain attributes appear to be common. The meeting gives primary voice to the family; it focuses first on strengths; and in many variations, families have their own time apart from the professionals to talk and to present a plan. Family conferences are coordinated by a neutral individual who does not have formal authority over the family; they may include relatives and other supportive individuals identified by the family. Meetings are used to make decisions and create action plans that are mutually agreeable to all participants.

Family group decision-making is now widely used in child welfare agencies. In a review of the first round of federally mandated child and family service reviews and states' plans to make improvements based on deficiencies noted by the federal review, 45 states described some type of family conferencing as their approach to family engagement (Munson & Freundlich, 2008). More is known about the process of family conferencing than about the impact on case outcomes, in part due to difficulties in implementing controlled studies and in articulating a clear theory of change to test (Crampton, 2007), as well as considerable variation in model implementation (Crea, Crampton, Abramson-Madden, & Usher, 2008). Nonetheless, studies to date have documented promising findings, including greater family unity and safety (Pennell & Burford, 2000), family satisfaction (Sieppert, Hudson, & Unrau, 2000), a greater likelihood of kinship placement (Landsman & Boel-Studt, 2011; Pennell, Edwards, & Burford, 2010), and reduced likelihood of entering care (Crea et al., 2008). Some studies, however, have not found a positive effect of family team meetings on safety and permanency (Berzin, 2006; Sundell & Vinnerljung, 2004).

Family-Centered Interventions with Child Welfare Populations

Solution-based casework is a practice model developed at the University of Louisville and implemented in Kentucky's child welfare system (Christensen & Todahl, 1999). It is based on three key elements: striving for full partnership with the family, focusing on the family's everyday life, and developing solutions focused on skills for the day-to-day situations with which the family struggles (Antle, Barbee, Christensen, & Sullivan, 2009). The solution focus keeps the work oriented toward problem-solving, framing needs as situational rather than pathological, and reinforcing what is working well while preventing a return to ineffective or harmful patterns of behavior.

Solution-based casework combines a strong family-centered theoretical orientation with casework, an essential function of public child welfare agencies that usually lacks a theoretical basis and clearly articulated practice method. It is grounded in solution-focused therapy in which the therapist supports the client in working toward a preferred future (Berg, 1994). The model is also based on family life cycle theory, which acknowledges different stages of family development (Carter & McGoldrick, 1980) and asserts that problems in everyday life are best understood in context of these developmental stages. Solution-based casework also draws from relapse prevention; workers can help family members understand patterns of behavior and practice the skills to prevent the recurrence of harmful behaviors (Antle, Barbee, Christensen, & Martin, 2008).

Quasi-experimental studies of solution-based casework have found that participants experienced fewer re-referrals for child maltreatment over a six-month follow-up period (Antle et al., 2009), that caseworkers using solution-based casework were less likely to initiate early legal actions or to remove children from their homes (Antle et al., 2008), and that goal achievement and participation were stronger for those receiving solution-based casework (Antle et al., 2008). The evidence is promising, but to date there are no published studies involving randomized controls. The existing research has also not addressed issues related to diverse populations, an area in need of further exploration.

Family preservation, or placement prevention services, proliferated after passage of AACWA and remained a prominent service component in child welfare until the mid-1990s. Although a variety of models were implemented in public and voluntary child welfare agencies (Nelson, Landsman, & Deutelbaum, 1990), intensive family preservation services (IFPS), especially the Homebuilders model (Kinney, Haapala, & Booth, 1991), received the most attention. IFPS works with families in their homes and communities when out-of-home placement of a child is believed to be imminent due to child maltreatment, child behavioral problems, or severe family conflict. It provides brief but intensive services (four to six weeks, with at least 12 to 15 hours of face-to-face contact weekly), with providers working in teams, available around the clock, and carrying very low caseloads. IFPS focuses on immediate response, assessment, and engagement, concrete services, skill building, behavioral change, connecting families with community resources, and advocacy.

In the 1990s, public support for IFPS began to wane in the face of increases in the number and complexity of child welfare caseloads. Experimental studies failed to document superior outcomes for children receiving IFPS compared with standard child welfare services. These studies were complicated by problems of targeting (identifying children at imminent placement risk); inconsistent model implementation; and relying on outcome measures controlled by child welfare agencies, especially placement. More recent meta-analyses have concluded that IFPS programs that adhere to Homebuilders standards effectively achieve their intended outcomes (Nelson, Walters, Schweitzer, Blythe, & Pecora, 2009; Washington State Institute for Public Policy, 2006). Nelson et al. (2009) found a range of effect sizes across IFPS studies in a variety of outcome measures including repeat maltreatment, placement avoidance, and improvement in social support, and concluded that continued research is needed to identify the program components most effective for various subgroups and populations including racial and ethnic minorities, different age groups, and different presenting problems.

Prevention-Focused Family-Centered Interventions

Family Connections, a Children's Bureau–funded demonstration project designed to prevent child neglect, was first implemented in a high-poverty area in Baltimore serving a large percentage of African American families, referred with child neglect concerns but no active child protection involvement. The project was subsequently replicated in eight geographically diverse sites representing diverse racial and ethnic populations (American Humane Association, 2009). It is based on Bronfenbrenner's (1979) social ecology framework; child neglect is believed to develop "when risk factors related to the child, caregivers, family system, and environment challenge the capacity of caregivers and broader systems to meet the basic needs of children" (DePanfilis & Dubowitz, 2005, p. 110).

Family Connections includes home-based services that are individually tailored and outcome-driven, emergency assistance, service coordination directed at enhancing protective factors and reducing risks, and recreational activities involving multiple families. Its underpinnings—strength-based, empowerment, and cultural competence perspectives; assessment and intervention plans that are outcome driven and developmentally focused; community outreach; and helping alliances—are all consistent with family-centered practice.

The current evidence base for Family Connections is limited to analyses based on randomization of groups to three or nine months of service (DePanfilis & Dubowitz, 2005), predictors of program completion (Girvin, DePanfilis, & Daining, 2007), and cost-effectiveness of three versus nine months (DePanfilis, Dubowitz, & Kunz, 2008). Some improvements in protective factors and child safety and reductions in risk factors have been noted. To date there are no published studies comparing this program with an alternative program or no intervention.

Nurse-family partnership is an in-home program that uses trained registered nurses as educators and supportive helpers for low-income first-time mothers. The program begins before the child's birth and extends through the child's second birthday, providing an extended period of support. It has three goals: to improve pregnancy outcomes through prenatal care, to improve child health and development by teaching parents how to provide care, and to improve parents' overall life trajectories through family planning and support for completing an education and obtaining employment (Olds, 2006).

Three integrated theoretical frameworks form the foundation of nurse–family partnership: Bronfenbrenner's (1979) social ecology, Bandura's (1977) self-efficacy, and Bowlby's (1982) work on human attachment. Social ecology suggests that children's development is affected by how they are cared for by their parents in the context of their social environment. Through in-home work, nurses help to connect families with their social networks and community services. Self-efficacy theory suggests that women's perceptions of their available choices affect their decisions and that experiencing success in achieving goals leads to improved life circumstances. Human attachment theory emphasizes that children's healthy development is based on forming an attachment with a caring adult; nurses teach and model sensitive and responsive caregiving toward this end.

Nurse–family partnership has been the subject of multiple studies over an extensive period of time with positive results (see, for example, Eckenrode et al., 2010; Olds et al., 1997; Olds et al., 2002). Most of the randomized studies have included predominantly Caucasian populations, though some have large proportions of African American or Hispanic participants.

Family-Centered Interventions Addressing Child Behavior

Multidimensional family therapy is a family-centered intervention targeted to adolescents with substance abuse and related behavioral problems (Liddle et al., 2000). The program is based on the premise that change in multiple behavioral domains can improve developmental functioning and reduce negative symptoms. It includes four interdependent areas of treatment: interventions with the adolescent, interventions with the parent and/or other family members, interactional work with joint adolescent–parent sessions, and extrafamilial work involving collaboration with other entities with which the adolescent is involved (Hogue, Dauber, Samuolis, & Liddle, 2006). A key aspect is development of a therapeutic alliance between youths and therapists that differs from the alliance developed with parents and other family members.

Research—including randomized studies comparing multidimensional family therapy with different programs such as group therapy, multifamily educational interventions, alternative outpatient programs, peer group therapy, and cognitive behavioral therapy—has found decreases in substance use and behavioral problems and improvement in family functioning and school performance for those receiving multidimensional family therapy (that is, Dennis et al., 2004; Liddle et al., 2001; Liddle et al., 2004; Liddle, Dakof, Turner, Henderson, & Greenbaum, 2008; Liddle, Rowe, Dakof, Henderson, & Greenbaum, 2009). Earlier studies were conducted primarily with Caucasians, but more recent studies include larger proportions of Hispanic and African American youths; female participants comprise about 20 percent of the study samples.

Multisystemic therapy is an intensive, home-based program developed for adolescents who exhibit serious antisocial behavior that puts them at risk for placement in psychiatric or juvenile detention facilities (Henggeler, Melton, Brondino, Scherer, & Hanley, 1997), but it has also been tested with child maltreatment populations (Swenson, Schaeffer, Henggeler, Faldowski, & Mayhew, 2010). It ranges in duration from three to five months. Multisystemic therapists work in teams with a clinical supervisor and carry very low caseloads. The team is available 24 hours a day, seven days a week for family crises, and may provide services as frequently as needed (Schoenwald, Sheidow, & Letourneau, 2004). Multisystemic therapy is grounded in ecological theory, which examines behavior in the context of reciprocal relationships between youths and their social systems such as school, peer group, neighborhood, and community. Interventions are individualized to meet the unique strengths and needs of youths and families and must be flexible and comprehensive to address all aspects of youths' social networks that contribute to problematic behaviors (Henggeler, 1996).

A considerable amount of research has been conducted on multisystemic therapy, with randomized trials finding the intervention more effective than standard juvenile justice services or alternative programs in such areas as improved family and peer relationships and decreased recidivism and incarceration (Borduin et al., 1995; Borduin, Schaeffer, & Heiblum, 2009; Henggeler, Melton, & Smith, 1992; Henggeler et al., 1997; Timmons-Mitchell, Bender, Kishna, & Mitchell, 2006). It has been studied primarily with African American and Caucasian populations. Many of the studies do not identify the gender composition.

Summary

This brief review is intended to highlight the current state of knowledge regarding several evidence-supported interventions and practice approaches that are consistent with the theoretical foundations of family-centered child welfare practice. The interventions described here also are clearly defined, with training protocols and manuals and practice and supervision standards. This is not an exhaustive compilation but suggestive of approaches that in some cases have a credible research base and in other cases have the potential for developing a stronger base.

Implications for Social Work Education

Social work educators are charged with preparing future practitioners, supervisors, administrators, and scholars to meet professional expectations while functioning within the constraints of real-world settings. This section discusses ways that educators can address some of the challenges to providing family-centered child welfare services.

Preparing Students as Family-Centered Practitioners

The term "family-centered" is used casually and ubiquitously in social work education and practice. To prepare students as family-centered practitioners, educators must help them to think critically about this construct and to learn to differentiate what is family-centered in name only from truly collaborative work that engages families as partners. Through field placements and classroom learning, educators can help students to anticipate the challenges they may face in striving to be family-centered practitioners in agency settings that do not fully embrace this approach, and to learn strategies for becoming agents of organizational change.

Child welfare practitioners face tensions in fulfilling the dual role of state agent and helping agent. Future child welfare practitioners should be prepared in practice-focused courses, beginning with a focus on language. The prevailing strategy of teaching students how to deal with "involuntary clients" or "resistant clients" should be transformed to that of engaging clients who are directed to involuntary services. The service, not the client, is involuntary; and when services are involuntary, the onus for engagement is on the practitioner, not the recipient. Educators should not be teaching students how to write a case plan *for* a client, but how to co-create a case plan *with* the client that reflects the client's strengths and goals while addressing problems that are impeding success. We tend to focus on the technical merits of behaviorally specific indicators and measurable outcomes while missing the bigger picture of just whose plan it is.

Preparing Students as Evidence-Based Practitioners

With increasing demand for interventions with a strong evidence base, future practitioners need to hone their skills in evaluating the credibility of research findings and interpreting results in light of the study design, analytic methods, and populations included. The search for the best evidence is ongoing and constantly changing. Social work educators need to prepare future practitioners to use research and contribute to knowledge through their own practice. Increasing opportunities for students to actively participate in research through classroom and field experiences are useful strategies for reinforcing these skills. Practice courses must include a critical analysis of the evidence behind the techniques and skills taught. The days in which research and practice were taught as mutually exclusive activities are long past; evidence-based practice demands that researchers understand practice and that practitioners understand research.

Preparing Students as Future Leaders

Child welfare is well known as a field undergoing constant change. Preparing students as future leaders requires them to develop skills as critical thinkers and problem-solvers, capable of working collaboratively within agencies and communities, and able to negotiate complex adaptive challenges in addition to the technical challenges of child welfare work. Social work education has paid scant attention to leadership development, but this is emerging as an important component of professional practice.

Future Directions

Interest in the construct of family-centered practice continues to expand, and the language of family-centered practice has permeated the continuum of child welfare services from prevention through post-adoption. One question for the future is whether child welfare practice will become family centered as the term was defined by Dunst et al. (2002). Will practitioners become agents for families, regarding families as capable of making informed decisions and acting upon them? Will families be treated as partners and viewed as the experts, or will the dichotomy between "professionals" and "clients" continue to prevent meaningful progress (Briar-Lawson, Lawson, Hennon, & Jones 2001)? How can the full potential of family-centered practice be realized in the context of state-controlled involuntary services?

A combination of system reforms and evidence-supported interventions could conceivably generate a more efficient, effective, and family-centered system. Alternative response systems divert large numbers of families from formal system involvement, offering prompt and accessible supportive services based on families' strengths and goals. Child welfare agencies are recognizing that the disproportionate effort expended on substantiating child maltreatment can often be redirected toward more constructive ends. The widespread use of family group conferencing indicates a growing recognition of family members as assets in ensuring safety, permanency, and well-being for children. Our conceptualization of "family" is continuing to expand as we look beyond the nuclear family unit to extended family, fictive kin, natural supports, long forsaken paternal relatives, and former family connections. Working with families to strengthen their support systems holds promise for child and family well-being in the long term. These strategies may also help to reduce the racial disproportionality that continues to permeate child welfare services.

We have identified a number of evidence-supported interventions that use a holistic family-centered approach but that are currently not accessible to the majority of families involved with child welfare services. Interventions that have been carefully developed, tested, and found to have positive results have the potential to improve the effectiveness of child welfare services. Simultaneously, ongoing work is needed to understand which interventions produce the best outcomes, the conditions under which they are most effective, and for whom they are most and least effective. Much of the effort in assessing program effectiveness is directed at comparing treatment and control groups, but examinations of subgroup differences are needed in order to better apply research to practice.

We must also consider how outcomes can be defined and measured in terms of whether they are desired by families and address meaningful changes in family and child well-being. Child welfare outcomes tend to be defined by the state and service providers, and as such these are usually indicators of importance to the child welfare system; in a truly family-centered service system, families would also have a voice in defining those outcomes. Current efforts to involve family members and service consumers as key stakeholders in state and local planning and as parent mentors and advocates may help to bridge the gap between professional and client.

There is an increasing awareness of the role of child welfare organizations and leadership in developing and supporting family-centered service systems, and this recognition holds promise for the future. Recent Children's Bureau efforts to improve recruitment and retention of child welfare workers, to provide leadership training for supervisors and managers, and to support comprehensive workforce reforms have the potential to strengthen the capacity of child welfare agencies to provide services that are family-centered, culturally responsive, and evidence-based.

References

Adoption and Safe Families Act of 1997, P.L. 105-89, 111 Stat. 2115 (1997).

Adoption Assistance and Child Welfare Act of 1980, P.L. 96-272, 94 Stat. 500 (1980).

Almgren, G., Kemp, S. P., & Eisinger, A. (2000). The legacy of Hull House and the Children's Bureau in the American mortality transition. *Social Service Review, 74*(1), 1–27.

American Humane Association. (2009). Replicating the Family Connections program: Lessons learned. *Protecting Children, 24,* 1–88.

Antle, B. F., Barbee, A. P., Christensen, D. N., & Martin, M. H. (2008). Solution-based casework in child welfare: Preliminary evaluation research. *Journal of Public Child Welfare, 2,* 197–227.

Antle, B. F., Barbee, A. P., Christensen, D. N., & Sullivan, D. J. (2009). The prevention of child maltreatment recidivism through the solution-based casework model of child welfare practice. *Children and Youth Services Review, 31,* 1346–1351.

Bandura, A. (1977). Self-efficacy: Toward a unifying theory of behavioral change. *Psychological Review, 84,* 191–215.

Barth, R. P. (2008). The move to evidence-based practice: How well does it fit child welfare services? *Journal of Public Child Welfare, 2,* 145–172.

Berg, I. K. (1994). *Family-based services: A solution-focused approach.* New York: Springer.

Berzin, S. C. (2006). Using sibling data to understand the impact of family group decision-making on child welfare outcomes. *Children and Youth Services Review, 28,* 1449–1458.

Borduin, C. M., Mann, B. J., Cone, L. T., Henggeler, S. W., Fucci, B. R., Blaske, D. M., et al. (1995). Multisystemic treatment of serious juvenile offenders: Long-term prevention of criminality and violence. *Journal of Consulting and Clinical Psychology, 63,* 569–578.

Borduin, C. M., Schaeffer, C. M., & Heiblum, N. (2009). A randomized clinical trial of multisystemic therapy with juvenile sexual offenders: Effects on youth social ecology and criminal activity. *Journal of Consulting and Clinical Psychology, 77,* 26–37.

Bowlby, J. (1982). *Attachment and loss: Vol. 1. Attachment.* New York: Basic Books.

Briar-Lawson, K., Lawson, H. A., Hennon, C. B, & Jones, A. R. (2001). Introduction. In K. Briar-Lawson, H. A. Lawson, C. B Hennon, & A. R. Jones (Eds.), *Family-centered policies & practices: International implications* (pp. 1-19). New York: Columbia University Press.

Bronfenbrenner, U. (1979). *The ecology of human development: Experiments by design and nature.* Cambridge, MA: Harvard University Press.

Carlson, J., Sperry, L., & Lewis, J. (1991). *Family therapy: Ensuring treatment efficacy.* Pacific Grove, CA: Brooks/Cole.

Carter, B., & McGoldrick, M. (1980). *The family life cycle*. New York: Gardner.

Child Abuse Prevention and Treatment Act, P.L. 93-247, 88 Stat. 4 (1974).

Christensen, D.N., & Todahl, J. (1999). Solution-based casework: Case planning to reduce risk. *Journal of Family Social Work, 3*(4), 3–24.

Crampton, D. (2007). Research review: Family group decision-making: A promising practice in need of more programme theory and research. *Child and Family Social Work, 12,* 202–209.

Crampton, D., & Jackson, W. L. (2007). Family group decision making and disproportionality in foster care: A case study. *Child Welfare, 86*(3), 51–69.

Crea, T. M., Crampton, D. S., Abramson-Madden, A., & Usher, C. L. (2008). Variability in the implementation of Team Decisionmaking (TDM): Scope and compliance with the Family to Family practice model. *Children and Youth Services Review, 39,* 1221–1232.

DePanfilis, D., & Dubowitz, H. (2005). Family Connections: A program for preventing child neglect. *Child Maltreatment, 10,* 108–123.

DePanfilis, D., Dubowitz, H., & Kunz, J. (2008). Assessing the cost-effectiveness of Family Connections. *Child Abuse & Neglect, 32,* 335–351.

Dennis, M. L., Godley, S. H., Diamond, G. S., Tims, F. M., Babor, T., Donaldson, J., & Funk, R. R. (2004). The Cannabis Youth Treatment (CYT) study: Main findings from two randomized trials. *Journal of Substance Abuse Treatment, 27,* 197–213.

Dunst, C. J., Boyd, K., Trivette, C. M., & Hamby, D. W. (2002). Family-oriented program models and professional helpgiving practices. *Family Relations, 51*(3), 221–229.

Eckenrode, J., Campa, M., Luckey, D. W., Henderson, C. R., Cole, R., Kitzman, H., et al. (2010). Long-term effects of prenatal and infancy nurse home visitation on the life course of youths: 19 year follow-up of a randomized trial. *Archives of Pediatrics & Adolescent Medicine, 164*(1), 9–16.

Fostering Connections to Success and Increasing Adoptions Act of 2008, P.L. 110-351, 122 Stat. 3949 (2008).

Gambrill, E. (2006). Evidence-based practice and policy: Choices ahead. *Research on Social Work Practice, 16,* 338–357.

Garbarino, J. (1982). *Children and families in the social environment*. Hawthorne, NY: Aldine de Gruyter.

Germain, C., & Gitterman, A. (1980). *The life model of social work practice*. New York: Columbia University Press.

Girvin, H., DePanfilis, D., & Daining, C. (2007). Predicting program completion among families enrolled in a child neglect prevention intervention. *Research on Social Work Practice, 17,* 674–685.

Gray, J.A.M. (2001). *Evidence-based health care: How to make health policy and management decisions* (2nd ed.). New York: Churchill Livingstone.

Hartman, A. (1981). The family: A central focus for practice. *Social Work, 26,* 7–13.

Henggeler, S. W. (1996). Treatment of violent juvenile offenders—We have the knowledge: Comment on Gorman-Smith et al. *Journal of Family Psychology, 10*(2), 137–141.

Henggeler, S. W., Melton, G. B., Brondino, M. J., Scherer, D. G., & Hanley, J. H. (1997). Multisystemic therapy with violent and chronic juvenile offenders and their families: The role of treatment fidelity. *Journal of Consulting and Clinical Psychology, 65,* 821–833.

Henggeler, S. W., Melton, G. B., & Smith, L. A. (1992). Family preservation using Multisystemic Therapy: An effective alternative to incarcerating serious juvenile offenders. *Journal of Consulting and Clinical Psychology, 60,* 953–961.

Hogue, A., Dauber, S., Samuolis, J., & Liddle, H. A. (2006). Treatment techniques and outcomes in Multidimensional Family Therapy for adolescent behavior problems. *Journal of Family Psychology, 20,* 535–543.

Indian Child Welfare Act of 1978, P.L. 95-608, 92 Stat. 3069 (1978).

Johnson, C., Sutton, E. S., & Thompson, D. (2005). Child welfare reform in Minnesota. *Protecting Children, 20*(2/3), 55–60.

Kemp, S., Almgren, G., Gilchrist, L., & Eisinger, A. (2001). Serving the "whole child": Prevention practice and the U.S. Children's Bureau. *Smith College Studies in Social Work, 71,* 475–499.

Kinney, J., Haapala, D., & Booth, C. (1991). *Keeping Families Together: The homebuilders model.* New Brunswick, NJ: Transaction.

Landsman, M. J., & Boel-Studt, S. (2012). Fostering families' and children's rights to family connections. *Child Welfare, 90*(4), 19–40.

Lee, J.A.B. (1996). The empowerment approach to social work practice. In F. J. Turner (Ed.), *Social work treatment: Interlocking theoretical approaches* (4th ed., pp. 218–249). New York: Free Press.

Liddle, H. A., Dakof, G. A., Parker, K., Diamond, G. S., Barrett, K., & Tejeda, M. (2001). Multidimensional family therapy for adolescent drug abuse: Results of a randomized clinical trial. *American Journal of Drug & Alcohol Abuse, 27,* 651–688.

Liddle, H., Dakof, G., Turner, R. , Henderson, C., & Greenbaum, P. (2008). Treating adolescent drug abuse: A randomized trial comparing multidimensional family therapy and cognitive behavior therapy. *Addiction, 103,* 1660–1670.

Liddle, H., Rowe, C., Dakof, G., Henderson, C., & Greenbaum, P. (2009). Multidimensional family therapy for young adolescent substance abuse: Twelve-month outcomes of a randomized controlled trial. *Journal of Consulting and Clinical Psychology, 77,* 12–25.

Liddle, H. A., Rowe, C. L., Ungaro, R. A., Dakof, G. A., & Henderson, C. (2004). Early intervention for adolescent substance abuse: Pretreatment to posttreatment outcomes of a randomized control trial comparing multidimensional family therapy and peer group treatment. *Journal of Psychoactive Drugs, 36*(1), 49–63.

Loman, L. A., & Siegel, G. L. (2005). Alternative response in Minnesota: Findings of the program evaluation. *Protecting Children, 20*(2/3), 78–92.

Maluccio, A. N. (1990). Family preservation services and the social work practice sequence. In J. K. Whitaker, J. Kinney, E. M. Tracy, & C. Booth (Eds.), *Reaching high-risk families* (pp. 113–126). New York: Walter de Gruyter.

Maluccio, A. N., Abramczyk, L. W., & Thomlison, B. (1996). Family reunification of children in out-of-home care: Research perspectives. *Children and Youth Services Review, 18,* 287–305.

Merkel-Holguin, L., Kaplan, C., & Kwak, A. (2006). *National study on Differential Response in child welfare.* Retrieved from www.americanhumane.org/assets/pdfs/children/pc-2006-national-study-differential-response.pdf

Mullen, J., Bledsoe, S. E., & Bellamy, J. L. (2008). Implementing evidence-based social work practice. *Research on Social Work Practice, 18,* 325–338.

Munson, S., & Freundlich, M. (2008*). Families gaining their seat at the table: Family engagement strategies in the first round of Child and Family Services reviews and program improvement plans.* Retrieved from http://www.americanhumane.org/assets/docs/protecting-children/PC-fgdm-CFSR-PIP-review.pdf

Nelson, K. E., & Landsman, M. J. (1992). *Alternative models of family preservation: Family-based services in context.* Springfield, IL: Charles C Thomas.

Nelson, K. E., Landsman, M. J., & Deutelbaum, W. (1990). Three models of family-centered placement prevention services. *Child Welfare, 69,* 3–21.

Nelson, K., Walters, B., Schweitzer, D., Blythe, B. J., & Pecora P. J. (2009). *A ten-year review of family preservation research: Building the evidence base.* Retrieved from http://www.nxtbook.com/nxtbooks/casey/tenyearreviewfamilypreservation/#/4

Olds, D. L. (2006).The nurse–family partnership: An evidence-based preventive intervention. *Infant Mental Health Journal, 27*(1), 5–25.

Olds, D. L., Eckenrode, J., Henderson, C. R. Jr., Kitzman, H., Powers, J., Cole, R., et al. (1997). Long-term effects of home visitation on maternal life course and child abuse and neglect: Fifteen-year follow-up of a randomized trial. *JAMA, 278,* 637–643.

Olds, D. L., Robinson, J., O'Brien, R., Luckey, D. W., Pettitt, L. M., Henderson, C. R., et al. (2002). Home visiting by paraprofessionals and by nurses: A randomized control trial. *Pediatrics, 110,* 486–496.

Omnibus Budget Reconciliation Act of 1993, P.L. 103-66, 107 Stat. 312 (1993).

Pecora, P. J., Whittaker, J. K., Maluccio, A. N., Barth, R. P., DePanfilis, D., & Plotnick, R. D. (2010). *The child welfare challenge: Policy, practice, and research* (3rd ed.). Piscataway, NJ: Aldine Transaction.

Pennell, J., & Burford, G. (2000). Family group decision making: Protecting children and women. *Child Welfare, 79*(2), 131–158.

Pennell, J., Edwards, M., & Burford, G. (2010). Expedited family group engagement and child permanency. *Children and Youth Services Review, 32,* 1012–1017.

Ronnau, J. (2001). Values and ethics for family-centered practice. In E. Walton, P. Sandau-Beckler, & M. Mannes (Eds.), *Balancing family-centered services and child well-being* (pp. 34–54). New York: Columbia University Press.

Sackett, D. L., Straus, S. E., Richardson, W. C., Rosenberg, W., & Haynes, R. M. (2000). *Evidence-based medicine: How to practice and teach EBM* (2nd ed.). New York: Churchill Livingstone.

Saleebey, D. (1992). *The strengths perspective in social work practice*. White Plains, NY: Longman.

Sandau-Beckler, P., Salcido, R., Beckler, M. J., Mannes, M., & Beck, M. (2002). Infusing family-centered values into child protection practice. *Children and Youth Services Review, 24,* 719–741.

Schoenwald, S. K., Sheidow, A. J., & Letourneau, E. J. (2004). Toward effective quality assurance in evidence-based practice: Links between expert consultation, therapist fidelity, and child outcomes. *Journal of Clinical and Adolescent Psychology, 33,* 94–104.

Sheets, J., Wittenstrom, K., Fong, R., James, J., Tecci, M., Baumann, D. J., & Rodriguez, C. (2009). Evidence-based practice in family group decision-making for Anglo, African American and Hispanic families. *Children and Youth Services Review, 31,* 1187–1191.

Sieppert, J. D., Hudson, J., & Unrau, Y. (2000). Family group conferencing in child welfare: Lessons from a demonstration project. *Families in Society, 8,* 382–391.

Sundell, K., & Vinnerljung, B. (2004). Outcomes of family group conferencing in Sweden: A 3-year follow-up. *Child Abuse & Neglect, 28,* 267–287.

Swenson, C. C., Schaeffer, C. M., Henggeler, S. W., Faldowski, R., & Mayhew, A. M. (2010). Multisystemic therapy for child abuse and neglect: A randomized effectiveness trial. *Journal of Family Psychology, 24,* 497–507.

Timmons-Mitchell, J., Bender, M. B., Kishna, M. A., & Mitchell, C. C. (2006). An independent effectiveness trial of multisystemic therapy with juvenile justice youth. *Journal of Clinical Child and Adolescent Psychology, 35,* 227–236.

Waites, C., Macgowan, M. J., Pennell, J., Carlton-LaNey, I., & Weil, M. (2004). Increasing the cultural responsiveness of family group conferencing. *Social Work, 49,* 291–300.

Walton, E. (2001). A Conceptual framework for family-centered services. In In E. Walton, P. Sandau-Beckler, & M. Mannes (Eds.), *Balancing family-centered services and child well-being* (pp. 69–92). New York: Columbia University Press.

Walton, E., Roby, J., Frandsen, A., & Davidson, R. (2003). Strengthening at-risk families by involving the extended family. *Journal of Family Social Work, 7*(4), 1–21.

Washington State Institute for Public Policy. (2006). *Intensive family preservation programs: Program fidelity influences effectiveness.* Olympia, WA: Author. Retrieved from http://wwwf.wsipp.wa.gov/rptfiles/06-02-3901.pdf

Chapter 5

NOTHING ABOUT US, WITHOUT US: MEANINGFUL YOUTH AND FAMILY ENGAGEMENT IN CHILD WELFARE

Nicole Bossard, Sara Munson, Angela Braxton, Debra Conway, Benjamin Muhammad, and Gerald P. Mallon

In my agency they always said that they engaged young people, but it was superficial—we were asked to comment on some small things, but on the bigger things, they left us out. Our opinions matter.

—youth in foster care

Engaging families and youth is a foundational principle of good social work practice in the child welfare field (ACT for Youth, 2011; Child Welfare League of America, 2003, 2005; Council on Accreditation, 2008; DePanfilis & Salus, 2003; National Association of Social Workers, 2005), and an essential element in the promotion of positive case outcomes such as safety, permanency, and well-being (Cheng, 2010; Child Welfare Information Gateway, 2011; Kemp, Marcenko, Hoagwood, & Vesneski, 2009; Munson & Freundlich, 2008; National Conference of State Legislatures, 2010; U.S. Department of Health and Human Services, 2009). Good practice necessitates a service delivery model emphasizing authentic and meaningful youth and family engagement at every phase along the service continuum—from the initial investigation, intake, and assessment, to case planning, case management, and service provision, all the way through to the achievement of permanency and in post-permanency work (Child Welfare Information Gateway, 2011). The successful implementation of this effective practice model requires ongoing organizational support—including agency policy development, service design, training, and evaluation—that reflects a culture of family and youth engagement (Child Welfare Information Gateway, 2010).

Across child- and family-serving systems, there has been increasing attention to moving beyond the traditional professional-as-expert hierarchical model toward an evidence-informed model that stresses authentic, meaningful, and ongoing engagement between professional service providers, agency administrators, and policymakers with the youth and families they serve (Hornberger, Gardner, Young, Gannon, & Osher, 2005; Morse, Markowitz, Zanghi, & Burns, 2003). Partnerships between agencies, youths, and families are changing the form, function, and outcomes of these human service systems. Moreover, the push toward collaborative and empowering practices is creating new space at the table for families and youths in child- and family-serving systems (Lohrback & Sawyer, 2004; Zeldin, McDaniel, Topitzes, & Lorens, 2001).

As a result, families and youths are emerging as a powerful resource driving programming, policy development, and practice in numerous service delivery systems across the human services spectrum (Bossard, 2011), including children's mental health (Adams, Biss, Burrell-Mohammed, Meyers, & Slaton, 2000; Osher, 2005; Osher, deFur, Nava, Spencer, & Toth-Dennis, 1999); public education (Corbett & Wilson, 2000; Henderson, Jacob, Kernan-Schloss, & Raimondo, 2004; Weiss & Stephen, 2009); behavioral health (Daniels et al., 2010); child abuse prevention (FRIENDS National Resource Center for Community-Based Child Abuse Prevention, 2007; Jennings, 2002; Jeppson et al., 1997; Parents Anonymous, 2005; Polinsky & Polin-Berlin, 2001); and, as discussed in this chapter, child protection and child welfare (Altman, 2008a, 2008b; Anthony, Berrick, Cohen, & Wilder, 2009; Burford, Pennell & Edwards, 2011; Cohen & Canan, 2006; Frame, Berrick, & Knittel, 2010; Frame, Conley, & Berrick, 2006; Kemp et al, 2009; Larsen-Rife & Brooks, 2009; Nilsen, Affronti, & Coombes, 2009; Rauber, 2009, 2010).

Although there have been marked improvements over the last 15 years, engaging families and youths continues to challenge public child welfare systems across the country. Substantive partnerships with families and youths beyond the development of a case plan present a range of issues for child welfare systems to address as they strive to make the transition from an expert-based model of practice to a more collaborative one. Meaningful engagement with certain populations has proven difficult as well, particularly youths transitioning from foster care to adulthood without lifelong family connections, birth fathers, incarcerated parents, and families affected by substance abuse (Ansell et al., 2007; Collins, in press; Morse et al., 2003; National Conference of State Legislatures, 2010). Without careful attention to both frontline casework and organizational climate and culture, the gravitational pull of doing things "the way they have always been done" often drags efforts back to the status quo. All too often youths and families continue to be disempowered and disenfranchised by the hierarchical relationships implicit in traditional child welfare approaches (Merkel-Holguin, 2003).

This chapter focuses attention on both frontline casework and organizational levels of engagement in order to build capacity within child welfare agencies to establish and strengthen ongoing partnerships with families and youths. It provides a brief history and overview of meaningful youth and family engagement, including the role of the social work profession and the federal Children's Bureau in supporting this shift in child welfare from the traditional professional-as-expert model to emerging evidence-informed practices of authentic collaboration and engagement with youths and families. It offers a summary of the benefits associated with improving youth and family engagement in child welfare services, including personal reflections from parents and youth who have been involved in the child welfare system. The authors—two birth parents and a former foster youth who have received child welfare services and three child welfare professionals—highlight the organizational and casework practice elements necessary for improved youth and family engagement; identify specific evidence-informed engagement strategies at the case, peer, and system levels; and offer recommendations for further study and exploration.

Overview of Youth and Family Engagement

Definition

Meaningful family and youth engagement means seeing families and youths as essential partners and experts, not only on their particular case but also on the child welfare system as a whole. Consequently, meaningfully engaging youths and families means providing real opportunities for collaborative and authentic inclusion of their voices in decision making about services, supports, policies, training, evaluation, and other systemic issues (Adams et al., 2000). At its core, engagement moves well beyond involvement, reflecting deep and sustained partnership at both the casework and organizational and system levels.

> #### Casework level:
>
> Involvement of families in child welfare services is important, but real engagement goes beyond that. Families can be involved and compliant without being engaged. Engagement is about motivating and empowering families to recognize their own needs, strengths, and resources and to take an active role in changing things for the better. Engagement is what keeps families working in the long and sometimes slow process of positive change. (Steib, 2004, p. 14)

> #### Organizational and system level:
>
> This framework suggests that families are already critical participants in the ecosystem that raises and serves children. The task is not to bring families into an arena that they've not previously belonged to. The task is to fully recognize and honor the membership they already have—a membership that is abso-

lutely central to the life of the child . . . creating linkages between all the members of the system—between the professionals and the families. Linkages, or "feedback loops," are basic to the process of optimizing the role of every member of the system. (Adams et al., 2000, p. 3)

Benefits

Publically and privately funded system reform initiatives have expanded in recent years, and nearly all of them have explicitly identified consumer involvement in decision making as an essential component (Horwath & Morrison, 2007; Pitchal, 2012). There is an extensive literature suggesting that family engagement affords numerous benefits for professionals, youths, and families (Chrislip & Larson, 1994; Jennings, 2002; Milner, 2003; Parents Anonymous, 2005; Pennell, Burford, Connolly, & Morris, 2011; Whipple & Zalenski, 2006). Authentic engagement yields the following benefits:

- *It enhances the helping relationship.* Youths and families feel respected and see that their perspectives are heard, which strengthens their relationship with their caseworker and can increase the chances for successful intervention (Child Welfare Information Gateway, 2010).
- *It promotes family "buy-in."* Family members who have a say in decision making and planning are more likely to be invested in the process and more likely to commit to achieving objectives and complying with treatment (U.S. Department of Health and Human Services Children's Bureau,, 2009).
- *It expands options.* Including family members early in a case provides more opportunities to explore the possibility of relatives serving as temporary or permanent placement options for children (Child Welfare Information Gateway, 2010).
- *It improves the quality and focus of visits.* Caseworker–family partnerships strengthen assessments and lead to more appropriate service provision (Child Welfare Information Gateway, 2010).
- *It increases placement stability and timeliness of permanency decisions.* Greater family involvement in decision making and planning can lead to improvements in stability and family continuity and quicker reunification or other form of permanency (Merkel-Holguin, Nixon, & Burford, 2003; Pennell, Edwards, & Burford, 2010; Tam & Ho, 1996; U.S. Department of Health and Human Services, 2004).
- *It builds family decision-making skills.* Being involved in strength-based decision-making processes and having appropriate problem-solving approaches modeled, families are more comfortable communicating their own problem-solving strategies and exploring new strategies that may benefit them and their children (Child Welfare Information Gateway, 2010).
- *It enhances the fit between family needs and services.* Collaboration between caseworkers and families allows for better identification of family needs and devel-

opment of relevant and culturally appropriate service plans that address needs, build on strengths, and draw on community supports (Child Welfare Information Gateway, 2010; Doolan, 2005).

- *It reduces racial disparity and disproportionality.* Preliminary evidence suggests that early and consistent engagement including opportunities for shared decision making particularly with youths and families of color supports increased involvement of immediate, extended, and fictive kin in case planning and has contributed to a reduction in the numbers of children of color entering foster care (Lemon, D'Andrade, & Austin, 2005; Marts, Eun-Kyoung, McRoy, & McCroskey, 2008), greater identification of family strengths by caseworkers (Richardson, 2008), higher reunification rates and placement with kin (James, Green, Rodriguez, & Fong, 2008), and improved stability and longevity of guardianship placement (Crampton & Jackson, 2007).

Context

Youth and family engagement in child welfare has its roots in direct social work practice. A family-centered, youth-positive, strengths-based, partnership-driven approach to service planning and delivery reflects ethical and philosophical assumptions consistent with long-held social work values, such as collaboration, mutuality, self-determination, advocacy, and shared power (Altman, 2005; Pecora, Reed-Ashcraft, & Kirk, 2001). These core beliefs are reflected in a number of the standards for social work practice in the child welfare field, in particular those put forth by the National Association of Social Workers (2005):

Standard 11. Engagement—Social workers in child welfare shall engage families as partners in the process of assessment and intervention. . . . Engagement requires social workers in child welfare to be clear about the reasons for the family intervention, whether it is an investigation or services following an investigation. The social worker shall seek to understand and incorporate, as appropriate, the family's perspective and definition of the problem and potential solutions. It is important that the social worker be able to convey an understanding and empathy for the family's situation or difficulties. Engagement involves "contracting" for services and assisting the family to look forward to a better future, with no need for services.

Standard 12. Comprehensive Service Planning—Social workers in child welfare shall develop, in collaboration with the family, a comprehensive service plan to strengthen the family's ability to care for their children, with specific attention to their developmental needs, and to enhance the overall functioning of its members. It must include a system for documenting progress and case closings. . . . The social worker shall seek the family and child's participation, input, and feedback to ensure that service is a mutual undertaking between social worker, family, and child. (p. 22)

These standards are supported through social work education, as courses on social work practice often include a brief overview of strategies to engage families in accepting treatment, and some administration courses address ways to involve clients by collecting consumer satisfaction and other information, conducting focus groups, and other methods. However, while certain strategies or legislation may be reviewed (such as family team meetings or the Foster Care Independence Act of 1999), most social work programs do not teach students how to implement the strategies or ensure their practice reflects the legislation.

The traditional child welfare service model, in which youths and families are seen as having issues that need to be resolved by a trained professional with the presumed expertise and knowledge to create a case plan *for* them, focused on deficits and imposed a hierarchical structure on the helping process. The professional diagnosed the problem and prescribed a solution, and the youth or family did what was expected of them to ensure progress (Ronnau, 2001). This "power over" model was reinforced by professionals acting as gatekeepers for access to needed services; laws that assigned legal authority to social workers—for example, the right to remove children at risk from their parents' custody; the respect and deference given to those in authority and to those who are educated and can use language well; and recognition of professional status (Diorio, 1992; Juhila, Pösö, Hall, & Parton 2003; Webb, 2000). As a result, professional and systemic knowledge has generally been prioritized over the youth's or family's knowledge, resulting in a process that reinforced responses of compliance and deception rather than mutuality, collaboration, and positive change.

This professional-as-expert model has been giving way to a more cooperative relationship between professionals and the youths and families with whom they work (Berg & De Jong, 2004; Collins, in press, DePanfilis & Salus, 2003). Over the last 15 years, the field of child welfare has seen a shift toward greater commitment to engaging families, children, and youths as active decision makers in all stages of the case planning process. A number of laws and regulations have provided solid footing for increased family and youth engagement. The Adoption and Safe Families Act of 1997 (P.L. 105-89), the Foster Care Independence Act of 1999 (P.L. 106-169), and the Fostering Connections to Success and Increasing Adoptions Act of 2008 (P.L. 110-351) have all supported the full engagement of those served by child welfare systems (National Resource Center for Permanency and Family Connections, 2009).

Table 5-1. Child Welfare Caseworkers: Values, Knowledge, and Skills

Belief that all people have a reservoir of untapped, renewable, and expandable abilities (mental, physical, emotional, social, and spiritual) that can be used to facilitate change.... Each child and family member should be empowered to work toward his or her own needs and goals.
Respect for each person's dignity, individuality, and right to self-determination.
Understanding of family systems, the family's environment, the family in a historical context, diverse family structures, and concepts of family empowerment.
Ability to identify strengths and needs and engage the family in a strengths-based assessment process.... Assess a family's readiness to change and employ appropriate strategies for increasing motivation and building the helping alliance.
Aptitude for empowering the child and family to sustain gains and use family and community supports.
Expertise in negotiating, implementing, and evaluating the case plan with the family.... Work with the family and key supports to accomplish the service agreement goals.

Source: Depanfilis & Salus, 2003, pp. 12–14.

The Children's Bureau has also played a key role in supporting the shift toward greater engagement. It has championed youth and family engagement through its articulation of core values, knowledge, and skills for child welfare caseworkers.

The Children's Bureau has also promoted child welfare agencies' attention to improving outcomes and fostering a results-oriented culture in which timely information drives decision making at all levels of the organization (Moore, 2002). As a result, agencies have had to think more strategically about their stakeholders and have an open dialogue with them about the services, supports, and helping relationships that work best for them.

Since 2000, the Children's Bureau has conducted Child and Family Services Reviews (CFSRs) in every state and territory to ensure conformity with federal child welfare requirements and to determine what is happening to children and families involved in child welfare services (Children's Bureau, n.d; Milner, Mitchell, & Hornsby, 2005). States found not to have achieved substantial conformity in areas assessed in the CFSR are required to develop and implement Program Improvement Plans (PIPs). The current CFSR assessment tool has two indicators that specifically address youth and family engagement: Well-Being Outcome 1, Item 18, asks, "How effective is the agency in involving parents and children in the case planning process?" and Systemic Factors, Case Review System, Item 25 asks, "Does the state provide a process that ensures that each child has a written case plan to be developed jointly with the child, when appropriate, and the child's parent(s), that includes the required provisions?" (U.S. Department of Health and Human Services, 2006, p. 58).

The first round of CFSRs identified a need for state child welfare systems to more effectively engage family groups—as meaningful participants in assessment, case planning, and service delivery—in ensuring positive outcomes for children (Munson & Freundlich, 2008). Although many states noted some type of formal engagement mechanism, the full utilization of these strategies was frequently not evident, as many states did not excel at engaging families and involving parents and children in the case planning process (Munson & Freundlich, 2008). In response to the first round of the CFSRs, 45 states identified the exploration, development, implementation, and/or expansion of specific family engagement strategies as action steps in their PIPs (Munson & Freundlich, 2008). This trend has continued with the second round of CFSRs and PIPs (Mitchell, Lynch-Thomas, & Parker, in press).

The Children's Bureau has also provided funding support for special initiatives aimed at increasing youth and family engagement. In 2003, the Children's Bureau funded nine demonstration grants to test a systems-of-care[1] approach for children and families involved in the child welfare system and to address policy, practice, and cross-system collaboration issues raised by the CFSRs (National Technical Assistance and Evaluation Center for Systems of Care, 2010). Family involvement is one of the six principles of child welfare–driven systems of care, and these grant projects confirmed that processes, services, and outcomes do improve when authentic youth and family engagement is sought and sustained at all levels of the system.

Through its Training and Technical Assistance Network, the Children's Bureau currently supports six resource centers and technical assistance partnerships that help states and territories increase engagement of youths and families (Children's Bureau, 2012):

1. the National Resource Center for Permanency and Family Connections, to "support practice to engage youth and families at all levels of the system" (p. 7)
2. the National Resource Center for Adoption, to "promote stakeholder involvement" (p. 8)
3. the National Resource Center for Youth Development, to "engage youth in all aspects of program planning, delivery, and evaluation" (p. 8)
4. the National Resource Center for Community-Based Child Abuse Prevention, to "promote parent leadership, especially for parents of children with disabilities, racial and ethnic minorities, and other groups" (p. 15)
5. the National Center on Substance Abuse and Child Welfare, to "advise on screening and assessment for family engagement, retention, and recovery" (p. 18)

---

[1] Systems of care is a service delivery approach that builds partnerships to create a broad, integrated process for meeting families' multiple needs (Child Welfare Information Gateway, 2008).

6. the Technical Assistance Partnership for Child and Family Mental Health, to "implement technical assistance strategies that promote family–professional partnerships" (p. 19).

Taken together, the Children's Bureau's varied supports and funding priorities have undoubtedly served to underscore the importance of increasing youth and family engagement in child welfare case planning, service delivery, policy development, and system reform.

Key Practice and Organizational Elements that Support Engagement

As previously noted, meaningful engagement goes beyond cursory involvement and compliance, requiring professionals and organizations to employ a different set of skills, values, and approaches for successful achievement (Hartling & Sparks, 2008; Smith, 2008). In order for meaningful engagement of youths and families to be fully realized, a number of casework and systems elements must be put into place. Although there is often great enthusiasm for youth and family participation, there is not always sufficient planning and infrastructure for authentic engagement. Practices, policies, and procedures must support these sorts of mutual, collaborative partnerships.

Family and youth engagement begins with a model of family-centered practice that has four essential components: (1) The family unit is the focus of attention; (2) strengthening the capacity of families to function effectively is emphasized; (3) families are engaged in designing all aspects of the policies, services, and program evaluations; and (4) families are linked with more comprehensive, diverse, and community-based networks of supports and services (Goldman, Salus, Wolcott, & Kennedy, 2003; National Child Welfare Resource Center for Family-Centered Practice, 2000).

Meaningful engagement in frontline practice is complicated by the fact that though some families and youths are voluntarily involved, most are not (Shireman, 2003; Yatchmenoff, 2005). The anger, guilt, and shame that often accompany a youth's or family's experience of child welfare involvement can greatly impede efforts toward authentic engagement (Braxton, 2006; Whipple & Zalenski, 2006) and raise important concerns about how to foster an effective helping process that supports shared power and decision making (Birrell & Freyd, 2006).

There is a robust and expansive literature on improving professional–youth–family engagement (de Boer & Coady, 2007; Drake, 1996; Gockel, Russell, & Harris, 2008; Saint-Jacques, Drapeau, Lessard, & Beaudoin, 2006; Smith, 2006; Williams, Malm, Allen, & Ellis, 2011; Williamson & Gray, 2011), and a number of casework skills have been identified to foster a supportive, trusting relationship between youths and families and professionals. Some of the key casework elements for engagement, along with first-person reflections from birth parents and youths and some practice tips for professionals, are presented in Table 5-2.

Table 5-2. Key Casework Elements for Engagement

Stakeholder Reflections	Key Casework Elements[a]	Tips for Professionals
"The best social workers (especially the ones that I had in my life) are those who take the time to build a trusting relationship, to explain the situation, to ask the youth what they want, but also notify them of their options. If something couldn't be done then the reasons are explained in full detail. . . . It's important that the young person is constantly kept in the loop, this keeps communication strong and makes the youth feel actively engaged with their case plan"—youth in foster care.	Clear, honest, and respectful communication with families, which helps set a foundation for building trust	Be honest; use full and open disclosure without being cruel. Take the time to explain things clearly without sugar-coating to youth and parents so that they can be informed consumers and decision makers regarding their family. For example, don't assume that youth and families understand all the spoken and unspoken expectations of them related to court-ordered services.
"It doesn't matter what we look like on paper, or how bad our addiction is, it's not that we don't love our kids. For some of us parents, it's not that we are trying to be noncompliant. . . . I just want social workers to remember that no matter what's in the record it has nothing to do with how much we love our kids"—birth parent.	Commitment to family-centered practice and its underlying philosophy and values	Learn more about grief and loss in the change process. Don't underestimate the power of shame, grief, and hopelessness to impede or halt altogether the youth's and family's engagement with the social worker and the case plan objectives. Likewise, expanding social worker knowledge of the impact of substance abuse disorders is also crucial to effective engagement with substance-abuse-affected families.
"What I would say to social workers is sometimes it's the simple things. . . . So, when you get a phone call from that Mom or Dad,	Sufficient frequency and length of contact with families and their identified formal and informal supports	Follow up and follow through. Do what you say you will, and communicate honestly with the youth and family when you can't.

The Children's Bureau

Table 5-2. Key Casework Elements for Engagement (*Continued*)

Stakeholder Reflections	Key Casework Elements[a]	Tips for Professionals
or you said you would do something, follow through. And, when you can't, let the parent know what's happening. Basically, treat that parent how you would want to be treated if you were on the other side trying to put your life back together."—birth parent		This is an important modeling behavior for families, but it also helps to equalize accountability within the helping relationship—the social worker explicitly embraces accountability for her/his part of the case plan, just as the youth or family is expected to do.
"I want social workers to remember to meet [the parent] where they are at, and not put us off until we cool down. Don't stop engaging (because I'm angry)."—birth parent	A strengths-based approach that recognizes and reinforces families' capabilities and not just their needs and problems	Make time for families to vent their frustrations. Families and youth will experience and enact a range of emotions throughout their involvement with child welfare. Understanding that families and youth will just need to blow off steam recognizes the normalcy of varying emotional responses to the trauma of child welfare involvement, and establishes the foundation of trust necessary for engagement.
"The other thing I want social workers to know is that when I do cool down, don't put a case plan in front of me to sign when you haven't engaged me. That's not my case plan. That's your case plan for me . . . most parents are not going to tell you that they are scared or overwhelmed . . . we will just keep noddin' and sighin'	Shared decision making and participatory planning, which results in mutually agreed-upon goals and plans reflecting both the caseworker's professional training and the family's knowledge of their own situation	Investing in participatory planning may mean spending a considerable amount of time preparing youth and families before meetings, offering respectful support during meetings, and debriefing with them after a meeting has ended. Everyone will need to understand that it takes time to achieve true, meaningful partnerships—

(Continued)

Table 5-2. Key Casework Elements for Engagement (*Continued*)

Stakeholder Reflections	Key Casework Elements[a]	Tips for Professionals
because we'll do anything to get our kids back."—birth parent		time to feel comfortable with one another, to agree on areas of importance, and to come to decisions that are agreed on by both the youth or family and the caseworker. A common language must also be developed so that everyone can understand what is being discussed.
"I am frequently asked to be a part of committees with social workers but it seems like there isn't any forethought. It's like I'm an add-on. And nobody ever thinks about what it takes for me to get to those meetings. Sometimes I have to drive three hours each way just to get to the meeting. Let alone how exhausting it can be trying to figure everything out on the fly when I get there."—birth parent	Broad-based involvement by both parents, extended family members, informal networks, and community representatives who create a web of support that promotes safety, increases permanency options, and provides links to needed services	Be prepared to have families and youth at decision-making tables. Have some form of compensation in place for families— a stipend or gift card can help to offset travel expenses and time away from work. Always invite more than one youth or family member to large meetings. Being the lone voice at the table can be intimidating. Make sure to prepare families and youth to participate in meetings. Let them know what will be expected of them at the meeting, including appropriate dress; what items are on the agenda; and meeting location, start time, and expected length. Sharing their story can be very emotional for families and youth. Support and coaching on how and what to share are often welcome.

Table 5-2. Key Casework Elements for Engagement (*Continued*)

Stakeholder Reflections	Key Casework Elements[a]	Tips for Professionals
"Make sure to explain things in as much detail as possible, and ask the parents if they have questions a lot because it can take a long time to have the trust where the parent will ask something they don't know. One thing with that trust piece, be real honest and up front about what will be in the case record before you get in front of the judge. A parent can feel so betrayed when they haven't heard something from their social worker, especially something that's bad, until they are in court."—birth parent	Understanding of the role of confidentiality and how to involve partners in case planning in a manner which is respectful of the family, but which also enables partners to plan realistically to protect the child and work toward permanency	Be forthright and consistent about information regarding the case, and repeat the most important details of the case plan—timelines, strengths, concurrent planning requirements, achieved goals, and compliance criteria—as often as possible. Probe frequently for understanding, and constantly make families and youth aware that their questions are welcome and valuable.
"One of the greatest supports I had going through the child welfare system was my kids' foster mom. She was a mentor to me and really believed I could get my kids back home. I never felt like she was against me. She was always in my corner."—birth parent	Recognition of foster and adoptive parents as resources not only for the children in their care, but for the entire birth family	Look for ways to widen the circle of support to include foster and adoptive parents as supportive resources for the birth parent, not just for the child or youth.
"Youth need their social workers to first and foremost serve as an advocate. Far too often there is a schism between the needs and the wants of the young person and the direction the social worker goes for. Foster youth	Individualized service plans that go beyond traditional preset service packages (e.g., parenting classes and counseling) and respond to parents' identified needs, specific circumstances, and available supports	Work closely with youth to collaboratively create service plans that are built around their goals and to remove barriers to resources youth need to achieve their goals.

(*Continued*)

Table 5-2. Key Casework Elements for Engagement (*Continued*)

Stakeholder Reflections	Key Casework Elements[a]	Tips for Professionals
need to know that they are being listened to and that their voice really matters and will be considered and acted upon! It's not just enough to have a youth express their wants and/or concerns if there is no use of the knowledge afterward with a follow up."— youth in foster care		
"I remember getting a case plan that was two inches thick with all kinds of stuff in there. I had no idea where to start. It said I had to get a job, find housing, go to counseling, attend parenting classes, anger management. My addiction was the reason my kids entered care, but I had to wait for a bed in substance abuse treatment for a long time. If I was going to get my kids back I needed help with my substance abuse. I needed help figuring out how to work through that thick case plan. I was totally overwhelmed."—birth parent	Concrete services that meet immediate needs for food, housing, transportation, and other costs, and help communicate to families a sincere desire to help	Work closely with the family or youth to create a prioritized approach to completing the case plan goals and objectives. If substance abuse is the central issue, substance abuse treatment has to be on the top of the list, because all other services are in jeopardy if the substance abuse is not addressed. Consider what are the basic needs that need to be addressed for the plan to succeed— for example, housing, employment supports, and food.
"Do random acts of affirmation and acknowledgement for parents. Those words and acts of encouragement go a long way as we move through all the services and do our healing. In my own case,	Praise for and recognition of parents who are making life changes that enable safe and permanent living situations for their children (including reunification, adoption, kinship placement, or guardianship)	The simplest things can have the greatest impact. Acknowledgements that are both respectful and authentic can provide a needed boost of confidence or a glimmer of hope that things can get

The Children's Bureau

Table 5-2. Key Casework Elements for Engagement (*Continued*)

Stakeholder Reflections	Key Casework Elements[a]	Tips for Professionals
my social worker attended my one-year anniversary of being clean and sober. That meant a lot to me and to her to see my progress in such a positive way."— birth parent	Praise for and recognition of parents who are making life changes that enable safe and permanent living situations for their children (including reunification, adoption, kinship placement, or guardianship)	better and that Mom or Dad is on the right track. The system is full of unknowns for most youth and families, and knowing that they are moving in the right direction can be of great encouragement and reassurance.

[a]*Source:* Child Welfare Information Gateway, 2010, pp. 5–6.

At the organizational level, the following elements are necessary to support family-centered practice and increased engagement (Child Welfare Information Gateway, 2010):

- agency leadership that demonstrates a strong commitment to family-centered practice and champions family engagement as a priority
- organizational culture that models desired behaviors, actions, and communication among managers, supervisors, and frontline caseworkers
- systems change initiatives and Program Improvement Plans with detailed strategies for achieving family and youth involvement
- policies and standards that clearly define expectations, identify requirements, and reinforce family engagement in case practice
- trained supervisors who explain agency policies that apply to family engagement, offer coaching to caseworkers, and provide support and feedback
- manageable caseloads and workloads allowing caseworkers to attend to the time-consuming efforts of building rapport, engaging families, actively participating in team decision-making meetings, and maintaining frequent, meaningful contact with children and families
- defined roles for planning and facilitation of team decision-making meetings to ensure that the meetings are timely (with reasonable notice to all parties), well facilitated, focused on the family and children's strengths and needs, goal directed, and inclusive of all team members
- skillful facilitation, which in some agencies is carried out by external facilitators or coordinators who guide engagement activities such as family group conferences and make sure that all points of view are heard
- availability and accessibility of diverse services that can respond specifically to the family's identified needs and conditions

- identification of service gaps and new ways to develop the community services that families need
- training and coaching to build family engagement skills among child welfare caseworkers and supervisors, and to help birth families, foster families, caseworkers, administrators, and other helping professionals work together effectively
- systematic documentation of caseworker–family interaction and communication and family involvement
- individualized performance review systems that reward staff for family engagement efforts and provide ongoing feedback regarding performance
- quality assurance and case review processes that monitor effective implementation of family engagement and measure its effects on safety, permanency, and well-being
- external assistance in the form of training, consultation, and technical assistance from recognized family engagement experts
- monitoring of family engagement activities and family progress toward mutually agreed-upon goals (pp. 4–5).

Engagement Strategies at the Casework, Peer, and System Levels

The National Technical Assistance and Evaluation Center for Systems of Care (2010) identified three primary domains of youth and family engagement: the individual case, peer-to-peer supports, and the system. These serve as a comprehensive conceptual framework for promoting meaningful youth and family engagement within and beyond the case plan.

Casework Level

Meaningful engagement at the casework level is accomplished through individualized, strengths-based, family-driven work. The use of various models of practice can implicitly and explicitly assert the equal and interdependent voices of youths and families within the context of the case plan in ways that shift the power dynamic to a distributed, shared leadership paradigm (Marcenko, Brown, DeVoy, & Conway, 2010; Merkel-Holguin, 2003).

Family meetings—variously referred to as family group conferences, family unity meetings, or family decision meetings (all forms of the Family Group Decision Making model proposed by the American Humane Association); team decision-making meetings and family team meetings (both components of the Annie E. Casey Foundation's Family-to-Family Initiative); and family team conferences (an element of the Community Partnerships for Protecting Children program, Iowa Department of Human Services)—are designed to maximize a family's strengths and give voice to its perspectives.

Prior to the advent of family meetings, child welfare agencies often made decisions about children and families with little or no input from the families. However, when key family and community members, formal and informal supports, and child welfare agency representatives join together in mutual respect, better decisions and integrated plans for families result. (Center for the Study of Social Policy, 2002, p. 1)

Although these evidence-informed processes may vary in terms of format and timing, all of them bring families together with agency staff and community representatives in order to make decisions and develop plans for care and services (Child Welfare Information Gateway, 2010; Crampton, Usher, Wildfire, Webster, & Cuccaro-Alamin, 2011; Olson, 2009; Sheets et al., 2009).

Another strategy to increase youth and family engagement is ensuring more frequent and meaningful caseworker visitation. Caseworkers who have regular and substantive contact with youths and families are able to improve engagement by ensuring better client–worker relationships and the achievement of timely permanency goals such as reunification, guardianship, or permanent placement with relatives (Child Welfare Information Gateway, 2010; Lee & Ayón, 2004; U.S. Department of Health and Human Services Children's Bureau, 2004).

Motivational interviewing is an evidence-based engagement technique drawn from motivational psychology that uses reflective listening and directive questioning to enhance motivation for behavior change by exploring and resolving ambivalence (California Evidence-Based Clearinghouse for Child Welfare, 2011a). When used by child welfare caseworkers, this approach has shown positive results for clients with substance abuse issues (Hohman, 1998).

The solution-focused casework model is an evidence-based approach to assessment, case planning, and ongoing case management that focuses on specific everyday events in the life of a family that have caused the family difficulty and situations in which at least one family member cannot reliably maintain the behavior that the family needs to accomplish its goals (California Evidence-Based Clearinghouse on Child Welfare, 2011b). This model combines solution-focused models that developed from family systems casework and therapy with problem-focused relapse prevention approaches that evolved from work with addiction, violence, and helplessness. In this model, partnerships between family, caseworker, and service providers are developed to address basic needs and restore the family's pride and sense of competence (Antle, Barbee, Christensen, & Martin, 2008; Berg & De Jong, 2004; California Evidence-Based Clearinghouse on Child Welfare, 2011b).

While the term "family engagement" presumably encompasses fathers and paternal relatives, child welfare systems and interventions have historically focused on mothers and maternal relatives (Huebner, Werner, Hartwig, White, & Shewa, 2008; Malm, Murray, & Geen, 2006). Recently, however, greater attention has been paid to the importance of fathers in the healthy development of children, and as a result, a variety of child welfare initiatives have been developed to increase fathers' involvement with their children. Casework efforts are being expanded to include greater outreach to fathers and paternal relatives during assessment and case planning, as well as the provision of services to help engage fathers and address the stressors or behaviors that affect their ability to care for or support their children (Child Welfare Information Gateway, 2010; Malm et al., 2006).

Family search and engagement or family finding supports youth and family engagement by encouraging broad participation in collaborative efforts to locate and leverage kinship connections to increase permanency options for youths in foster care (Allen, Malm, Williams, & Ellis, 2011; Child Welfare Information Gateway, 2010; Malm & Allen, 2011). This is a youth-driven process in which family and fictive kin help develop, plan, and achieve the youth's permanence (Louisell, 2006). Preliminary findings suggest that it increases the number of family members involved and the likelihood of family reunification or kinship care (Landsman & Boel-Studt, 2011).

Finally, foster family–birth family collaborations, such as icebreaker meetings (stand-alone meetings designed to build a critical connection between birth parents and the foster parents who are caring for a child), mentoring relationships between foster and birth families, and shared family care, encourage birth families and foster families to share information, parenting tips and skills, and commitment to reunification planning (Biehle & Goodman, 2012; Child Welfare Information Gateway, 2010; National Resource Center for Permanency and Family Connections, 2009).

Peer Level

At the peer level, former service recipients with their own firsthand experience of the child welfare system can be engaged to help other youths and families successfully navigate the system. Expanding child welfare services to include parent mentors and youth leaders in the helping process alongside caseworkers reflects the values of mutuality, empowerment, and collaborative practice. Seeing youth leaders and parent mentors work in this capacity inspires and rejuvenates not only youths and families, but also agency staff (National Technical Assistance and Evaluation Center for Systems of Care, 2007).

There are emerging models in which birth parents or youths fulfill paraprofessional roles as leaders, mentors, advocates, navigators, and networkers (Berrick, Young, Cohen, & Anthony, 2011; Bossard, 2011; Corwin, 2012; Child Welfare Organizing Project, 2006; Frame et al., 2010; Morse et al., 2003; National Technical Assistance and Evaluation Center for Systems of Care, 2010; Nilsen et al., 2009; Rauber, 2009). Programs have included Family Coaches (National Technical Assistance and Evaluation Center for Systems of Care, 2010); Parent Partners (Anthony et al., 2009); Parent Advocates (Casey Family Programs, 2012; National Resource Center for Permanency and Family Connections, 2011); Parent Mentors (Taylor et al., 2010); The Power of Youth and Adult Partnerships (Search Institute, 2005); Veteran Parents (Nilsen et al., 2009); Family Leaders (National Technical Assistance and Evaluation Center for Systems of Care, 2010); and Parent Leaders (Bossard, 2011; McGlade & Ackerman, 2006).

These programs are based on the principle that "having walked in someone else's shoes makes a person uniquely able to connect, support, and inspire" (Taylor et al., 2010, p. 20). They involve a focus on the helping and healing capacity of the life experience of someone "who's been there" (Cohen & Canan, 2006) and the use of one's lived personal experience to engage youths and families and to inspire hope and change (Bossard, 2011). The essential thread that connects these approaches is that the youth leader or parent mentor has had his or her own experience within the child welfare system and has learned how to use that experience to help other youths and families successfully navigate the complexities of the child welfare system (Rauber, 2009, 2010; Taylor et al., 2010).

In addition to helping youths and family understand the process, parent mentors and youth leaders may also work closely with caseworkers to provide greater insight into the ways that their clients may be experiencing the system as well as how they might be inclined to handle it (for example, not following through on case plan goals and objectives, relapsing, or using ineffective coping or communication strategies). Consequently, parent mentors and youth leaders can help to establish crucial bridges of understanding between a family or youth, the caseworker, court staff, and other service providers (Bossard, 2011; Virginia Department of Social Services, Child Protection Unit, 2011).

System Level

Meaningful family and youth engagement at the system level includes youths and families as active and authentic participants in system improvement activities (National Technical Assistance and Evaluation Center for Systems of Care, 2010). Families and youths may conduct or co-facilitate orientation and other training for new foster or adoptive families, new staff, and new social work students; participate in program and policy reviews; engage in cross-system partnerships such as systems of care; or facilitate or participate in collaborative workgroups, such as CFSR stakeholder groups or advisory boards that provide ongoing input into program and policy development, service design, and program evaluation (Child Welfare Information Gateway, 2010; National Resource Center for Permanency and Family Connections, 2009).

There are a number of ways to help bring these casework-, peer-, and system-level strategies to fruition . Implementation supports are illustrated in Table 5-3.

Table 5-3. Implementation Supports at Casework, Peer, and Systems Levels

Level of Approach	Implementation Tips
Casework	• When entering into collaborative partnerships, be aware of any personal or professional assumptions (your own or others') that may negatively impact partners' ability to work together. For example, defining families based on their past involvement with the child welfare agency or believing that young people cannot make important decisions is likely to impede one's ability to develop an effective partnership and promote meaningful engagement.
	• Look for ways to share power. Remember that what youths and families bring to the helping process is as valid and important as what agency staff bring. It is important for agency staff to remain open to criticisms youths and families may have of the system and its policies. Though it may initially be uncomfortable, working through such discussions as a team will strengthen the effectiveness of caseworkers, youths, and families.
	• Be thoughtful about how to support the long-term engagement of youths and families. Take the time to make sure that they have all the information they need to be effective but also provide the name of a person who can be contacted with additional questions. As in the other domains of engagement, it is important to establish a comfort level that encourages inquiry and participation.
Peer	• Take a comprehensive, systemic approach to planning and implementing a parent mentor or youth leadership program. Secure the endorsement of agency leadership; identify hiring criteria for parent mentors and youth leaders; develop strategies for recruiting and training them; clarify their roles and responsibilities with child welfare and court staff; develop guidelines as to how the parties will work together; develop adequate staff support and supervision.
	• Respect participants' time. Devise a way to honor the contributions of youths and families through compensation and reimbursement for expenses. Remember, if youths or families are not employed by the state or a local child welfare agency as employees or contractors, then they are not being paid to be there, and, in some cases, their participation has a cost—time away from work or school, travel expenses, and child care. Make it feasible for youths and families to participate.

Table 5-3. Implementation Supports at Casework, Peer, and Systems Levels (*Continued*)

Level of Approach	Implementation Tips
Peer (*Continued*)	• Do not expect parent mentors or youth leaders to function like trained social workers. They have their own expertise, skills, and knowledge base from which to draw as they work with youths and families. A solid program will include training for parent mentors and youth leaders on the child welfare system, how to maintain healthy boundaries with families, and time management and other professional skills, as well as on-the-job supervision. However, they should not be expected to be mini social workers. Good parent mentors and youth leaders are clear on their roles and understand and accept that they are not frontline caseworkers.
Systems	• Consider engaging families and youth to get feedback on existing services; hosting facilitated forums involving families, youths, and staff to build trust and explore what a local parent mentor or youth leader program should include; identifying training needs of families and agency staff; and reviewing or revising policies to support a parent mentor or youth leader program.
	• Laying the groundwork for new programs, infrastructure, and strategies takes time. It is not useful or realistic to expect that everything will run without a hitch or that the system will change overnight. There are necessary learning curves associated with the implementation of any new approach. Meaningful family engagement beyond the case plan will require agencies to be creative and persistent during program development and management.
	• Be open to youth and family feedback. Anticipate it by bringing youths and families to participate at this level. Some comments may make agency staff uncomfortable, but if the goal is to improve systems and outcomes, it is important to take feedback seriously and look for ways to demonstrate to youths and families that they have been heard.
	• Consider expanding the social work curriculum to include a greater focus on youth and family engagement, including teaching strategies for involving youth and family members in decision making and planning, and ways that social workers can contribute to the development of casework-, peer-, and systems-level engagement efforts throughout their careers.

Future Directions and Conclusion

As public child welfare agencies continue the difficult work of reforming systems and improving outcomes, youths and families are becoming a powerful constituency for change. Like no one else at the decision-making table, youths and families know first-hand what they need and what the system's service experience really is, not what the theoretical frameworks or policies and procedures say it should be. Youths and families often bring to the table an unparalleled level of passion for the system and its improvement. They help professionals "keep it real" by identifying when and how agency practice falls short or is inconsistent. Likewise, they are in the perfect position to determine when and how the system and its staff are doing great work.

However, if there is no institutional expectation for youths and families to participate authentically and meaningfully in decision making, agencies and their staff will undoubtedly miss the invaluable insights that youths and families can bring. In efforts to build a collaborative culture in which meaningful youth and family engagement is the status quo, it is necessary to establish organizational spaces for direct, respectful, shared engagement with all stakeholders within the system, including families and youths (FRIENDS National Resource Center for Community-Based Child Abuse Prevention, 2010; Bushe, 2006; Lasker & Weiss, 2003). Professionals and organizations cannot assume that extending an invitation for youths and family members to speak, or conducting focus groups with youths and families to solicit their feedback and ideas, will achieve meaningful collaborative engagement. Youths and families must be empowered participants rather than tokens whose voices are treated as afterthoughts.

Although there is increasing evidence for the value of family and youth engagement to the achievement of safety, permanency, and well-being for children and youths in care, child welfare agencies continue to struggle to engage youths and families in day-to-day practice (Altman, 2005, 2008a, 2008b; Collins, in press; Dawson & Berry, 2002). As youths and families move into partnerships within child welfare systems, they often encounter policies and procedures that have not caught up with the practice innovations that brought them to their new roles (Frame et al., 2010; National Technical Assistance and Evaluation Center for Systems of Care, 2010). Despite the growing consensus that child- and family-serving systems benefit from the meaningful involvement of youths and families as partners in reform efforts, systemic barriers such as lack of adequate compensation or other stakeholder supports impede long-term sustainability of agency–family–youth partnerships (Bossard, 2011; Hornberger & Smith, 2011; Horwath & Morrison, 2007).

Once established, meaningful engagement must be systemically, intentionally, and persistently nurtured in order for it to become a natural and established part of the organizational culture. Schools of social work must offer more instruction in and exploration of youth and family engagement models, both in the classroom and through field education and supervision.

A number of practice and research activities could be of great benefit as child welfare agencies continue to develop partnerships with youths and families. Among them are a comprehensive review and dissemination of practice approaches and models; the development of financial and other forms of support for youth leaders and parent mentors; continued research on the impact of parent mentor and youth empowerment programs on child safety, permanency, and well-being; writing or co-authoring by parent mentors and youth leaders of resources for distribution to families receiving child welfare services and for publication; exploration of the kinds of supports that parent mentors and youth leaders need to continue carrying out their work (including ways to help them cope with secondary trauma); and continued exploration of the impact of partnering with youths and families on caseworker job satisfaction and workload.

References

ACT for Youth. (2011). *Authentic youth engagement.* Retrieved from http://www.actfor youth.net/youth_development/engagement/authentic.cfm

Adams, J., Biss, C., Burrell-Mohammad, V., Meyers, J., & Slaton, E. (2000). *Learning from colleagues: Family–professional relationships, moving forward together.* Alexandria, VA: National Peer Technical Assistance Network's Partnership for Children's Mental Health. Retrieved from http://www.ncdhhs.gov/mhddsas/services/serviceschild-family/Toolbox/partnering/iii-learningfromcolleagues.pdf

Allen, T., Malm, K., Williams, S. C., & Ellis, R. (2011). *Piecing together the puzzle: Tips and techniques for effective discovery in family finding* (Child Trends Research Brief #2011-31). Retrieved from http://www.childtrends.org/Files/Child_Trends-2011_12_01_RB_FamilyFindingTips.pdf

Altman, J. (2005). Engagement in children, youth, and family services: Current research and promising approaches. In G. Mallon & P. Hess (Eds.), *Child welfare for the 21st century: A handbook of practices, policies, and programs* (pp. 72–86). New York: Columbia University Press.

Altman, J. (2008a). A study of engagement in neighborhood-based child welfare services. *Research on Social Work Practice, 18,* 555–564.

Altman, J. (2008b). Engaging families in child welfare services: Worker versus client perspectives. *Child Welfare, 87,* 41–61.

Ansell, D., Finck, C., Peck, R. W., Sutter, K., Screechowl, E., Zanghi, M., & Burns, P. (2007). *2007 CFSR toolkit for youth involvement: Engaging youth in the Child and Family Services Review.* Retrieved from http://muskie.usm.maine.edu/helpkids/rcpdfs/CFSRtoolkit.pdf

Anthony, E., Berrick, J., Cohen, E., & Wilder, E. (2009). *Partnering with parents: Promising approaches to improve reunification outcomes for children in foster care.* Retrieved from http://ccyp.berkeley.edu/pdfs/parenting_with_parents_final_report.doc

Antle, B. F., Barbee, A. P., Christensen, D. N., & Martin, M. H. (2008). Solution-based casework in child welfare: Preliminary evaluation research. *Journal of Public Child Welfare, 2,* 197–227.

Berg, I. K., & De Jong, P. (2004). Building solution-focused partnerships in children's protective and family services. *Protecting Children, 19,* 3–13.

Berrick, J. D., Young, E. W., Cohen, E., & Anthony, E. (2011). "I am the face of success": Peer mentors in child welfare. *Child & Family Social Work, 16,* 179–191.

Biehle, K., & Goodman, D. (2012). *Icebreaker meetings: A tool for building relationships between birth and foster parents.* Retrieved from http://www.aecf.org/~/media/Pubs/Topics/Child%20Welfare%20Permanence/Permanence/IcebreakerMeetingsToolkit/IcebreakerMeetingsToolkit.pdf

Birrell, P., & Freyd, J., (2006). Betrayal trauma. *Journal of Trauma Practice, 5,* 49–63.

Bossard, N. (2011). *Enough hope to spare: The transformative experience of birth parents as leaders in child welfare* (Doctoral dissertation, Antioch University). Retrieved from http://etd.ohiolink.edu/view.cgi?acc_num=antioch1311032360

Braxton, A. (2006). *A woman with an issue: A mother's memoir of addiction, loss, redemption and recovery.* Charleston, NC: Advantage Books.

Burford, G., Pennell, J., & Edwards, M. (2011). Family team meetings as principled advocacy. *Journal of Public Child Welfare, 5,* 318–344.

Bushe, G. (2006). Sense making and the problems of learning from experience: Barriers and requirements for creating cultures of collaboration. In S. Schuman (Ed.), *Creating a culture of collaboration: The International Association of Facilitators handbook* (pp. 151–172). San Francisco: Jossey-Bass.

California Evidence-Based Clearinghouse for Child Welfare. (2011a). *Motivational interviewing (MI).* Retrieved from http://www.cebc4cw.org/program/motivational-interviewing/

California Evidence-Based Clearinghouse for Child Welfare. (2011b). *Solution-based casework.* Retrieved from http://www.cebc4cw.org/program/solution-based-casework/

Center for the Study of Social Policy. (2002). *Bringing families to the table: A comparative guide to family meetings in child welfare.* Retrieved from http://www.cssp.org/publications/child-welfare/child-welfare-misc/bringing-families-to-the-table-a-comparative-guide-to-family-meetings-in-child-welfare.pdf

Cheng, T. C. (2010). Factors associated with reunification: A longitudinal analysis of long-term foster care. *Children and Youth Services Review, 32,* 1311–1316.

Children's Bureau. (2012). *The Children's Bureau Training and Technical Assistance Network: 2012 directory.* Retrieved from http://www.acf.hhs.gov/sites/default/files/cb/tta_network_directory_2012.pdf

Children's Bureau. (n.d.). *Child and family services reviews fact sheet.* Retrieved from http://www.acf.hhs.gov/sites/default/files/cb/cfsr_factsheet.pdf

Child Welfare Information Gateway. (2008). *Systems of care.* Bulletin for Professionals, February. Retrieved from http://www.childwelfare.gov/pubs/soc/soc.pdf

Child Welfare Information Gateway. (2010). *Family engagement.* State Manager Series, Bulletin for Professionals, June. Retrieved from http://www.childwelfare.gov/pubs/f_fam_engagement/f_fam_engagement.pdf

Child Welfare Information Gateway. (2011). *Family reunification: What the evidence shows.* Issue Brief, June. Retrieved from http://www.childwelfare.gov/pubs/issue_briefs/family_reunification/family_reunification.pdf

Child Welfare League of America. (2003). *Engaging families in child welfare: A brief review of the literature.* Retrieved from http://www.pacwcbt.pitt.edu/Organizational%20Effectiveness/Practice%20Reviews/EngagingFamilies.doc

Child Welfare League of America. (2005). *CWLA standards of excellence for transition, independent living and self-sufficiency services.* Retrieved from http://www.cwla.org/programs/standards/standardsintroindependentliving.pdf

Child Welfare Organizing Project. (2006). *A parent leadership curriculum: Developing the potential of parents as advocates, organizers, and a positive force for public child welfare reform.* New York: Author.Chrislip, D. (2002). *The collaborative leadership fieldbook: A guide for citizens and civic leaders.* San Francisco: Jossey-Bass.

Chrislip, D., & Larson, C. (1994). *Collaborative leadership.* San Francisco: Jossey-Bass.

Cohen, E., & Canan, L. (2006). Closer to home: Parent mentors in child welfare. *Child Welfare, 85,* 867–884.

Collins, M. E. (in press). Promoting youth development and transitional living services for youth moving from foster care to adulthood. In G. P. Mallon & P. McCartt Hess (Eds.), *Child welfare for the twenty first century: A handbook of policies, practices, and programs* (2nd ed.). New York: Columbia University Press.

Corbett, D., & Wilson, B. (2000). *Didn't know I could do that.* Retrieved from http://70.61.88.126/download/teleconference/aug15files/didnotknow.pdf

Corwin, T. (2012). *Strategies to increase birth parent engagement, partnership, and leadership in the child welfare system: A review.* Seattle: Casey Family Programs. Retrieved from http://www.casey.org/Resources/Publications/pdf/BirthParentEngagement.pdf.

Council on Accreditation. (2008). *COA public standards—child protective services* (8th ed.). New York: Author. Retrieved from http://www.coastandards.org/standards.php?navView=public

Crampton, D., & Jackson, W. L. (2007). Family group decision making and disproportionality in foster care: A case study. *Child Welfare, 86,* 51–69.

Crampton, D. S., Usher, C. L., Wildfire, J. B., Webster, D., & Cuccaro-Alamin, S. (2011). Does community and family engagement enhance permanency for children in foster care? Findings from an evaluation of the Family-to-Family initiative. *Child Welfare, 90,* 61–77.

Daniels, A., Grant, E., Filson, B., Powell, I., Fricks, L., & Goodale, L. (Eds.). (2010). *Pillars of peer support: Transforming mental health systems of care through peer support services.* Retrieved from http://www.pillarsofpeersupport.org/

Dawson, K., & Berry, M. (2002). Engaging families in child welfare services: An evidence-based approach to best practice. *Child Welfare, 81,* 293–317.

de Boer, C., & Coady, N. (2007). Good helping relationships in child welfare: Learning from stories of success. *Child & Family Social Work, 12,* 32–42.

DePanfilis, D., & Salus, M. (2003). *Child protective services: A guide for caseworkers.* Washington, DC: U.S. Department of Health and Human Services, Administration for Children and Families, Administration on Children, Youth and Families, Children's Bureau, Office on Child Abuse and Neglect. Retrieved from http://www.childwelfare.gov/pubs/usermanuals/cps/cps.pdf

Diorio, W. (1992). Parental perceptions of the authority of public child welfare workers. *Families in Society: The Journal of Contemporary Human Services, 73,* 222–235.

Doolan, M. (2005). *The family group conference: A mainstream approach in child welfare decision-making.* Englewood: American Humane Association. Retrieved from http://www.americanhumane.org/assets/pdfs/children/fgdm/pc-fgdm-conf-fgc2004.pdf

Drake, P. (1996). Consumer and worker perceptions of key child welfare competencies. *Children & Youth Services Review, 18,* 261–279.

Frame, L., Berrick, J., & Knittel, J. (2010). Parent mentors in child welfare: A paradigm shift from traditional services. *The Source: Helping Professionals Help Families Affected by Drugs and/or HIV, 20*(1), 2–5.

Frame, L., Conley, A., & Berrick, J. (2006). The real work is what they do together: Peer support and birth parent change. *Families in Society, 87,* 509–520.

FRIENDS National Resource Center for Community-Based Child Abuse Prevention. (2007). *Parent engagement and leadership: Factsheet #13.* Retrieved from http://www.family-treemd.org/files/414_Friends%20Parent%20Leadership%20Fact%20Sheet%2013.pdf

FRIENDS National Resource Center for Community-Based Child Abuse Prevention. (2010). *Meaningful parent leadership: A guide for success.* Retrieved from http://www.friend-snrc.org/direct-download-menuitem/doc_download/59-meaningful-parent-leadership-a-guide-for-success

Gockel, A., Russell, M., & Harris, B. (2008). Recreating family: Parents identify worker–client relationships as paramount in family preservation programs. *Child Welfare, 87,* 91–112.

Goldman, J., Salus, M., Wolcott, D., & Kennedy, K. (2003). *A coordinated response to child abuse and neglect: The foundation for practice.* Washington, DC: National Clearinghouse on Child Abuse and Neglect Information. Retrieved from http://www.childwelfare.gov/pubs/usermanuals/foundation/

Hartling, L., Sparks, E. (2008). Relational-cultural practice: Working in a non-relational world. *Women & Therapy, 31,* 165–188.

Henderson, A., Jacob, B., Kernan-Schloss, A., & Raimondo, B. (2004). *The case for parent leadership.* Lexington, KY: Center for Parent Leadership, Prichard Committee for Academic Excellence.

Hohman, M. M. (1998). Motivational interviewing: An intervention tool for child welfare case workers working with substance-abusing parents. *Child Welfare, 77*, 275–289.

Hornberger, S., Gardner, S., Young, N., Gannon, N., & Osher, T. (2005). *Improving the quality of care for the most vulnerable children, youth, and their families: Finding consensus.* Washington, DC: Child Welfare League of America Press.

Hornberger, S., & Smith, S. (2011). Family involvement in adolescent substance abuse treatment and recovery: What do we know? What lies ahead?. *Children and Youth Services Review, 33*(1), 70–76.

Horwath, J., & Morrison, T. (2007). Collaboration, integration and change in children's services. *Child Abuse & Neglect*, 31, 55–69.

Huebner, R. A., Werner, M., Hartwig, S., White, S., & Shewa, D. (2008). Engaging fathers: Needs and satisfaction in child protective services. *Administration in Social Work, 32*(2), 87–103.

James, J., Green, D., Rodgriguez, C. & Fong, R. (2008). Addressing disproportionality through undoing racism, leadership development, and community engagement. *Child Welfare, 87*(2), 279–296.

Jennings, J. (2002). *Parent leadership: Successful strategies.* Retrieved from http://www. http://friendsnrc.org/print-materials

Jeppson, E., Thomas, J., Markward, A., Kelly, J., Koser, G., & Diehl, D. (1997). *Making room at the table: Fostering family involvement in the planning and governance of formal support systems* (facilitators guide). Chicago: Family Resource Coalition of America.

Juhila, K., Pösö, T., Hall, C., & Parton, N. (2003). Introduction: Beyond a universal client. In C. Hall, K. Juhila, N. Parton, & T. Pösö (Eds.), *Constructing clienthood in social work and human services: Interaction, identities and practices* (pp. 11–26). London: Jessica Kingsley.

Kemp, S., Marcenko, M. O., Hoagwood, K., & Vesneski, W. (2009). Engaging parents in child welfare services: Bridging family needs and child welfare mandates. *Child Welfare, 88*, 101–126.

Landsman, M., & Boel-Studt, S. (2011). Fostering families' and children's rights to family connections. *Child Welfare, 9*(4), 19–40.

Larsen-Rife, D., & Brooks, S. (2009). *The importance of family engagement in child welfare services.* Retrieved from http://academy.extensiondlc.net/file.php/1/resources/LR-FamilyEngagement.pdf

Lasker, T. D., & Weiss, H. L. (2003). Broadening participation in community problem solving: A multidisciplinary model to support collaborative practice and research. *Journal of Urban Health, 80*(1), 14–47.

Lee, C. D., & Ayón, C. (2004). Is the client–worker relationship associated with better outcomes in mandated child abuse cases? *Research on Social Work Practice, 14*, 351–357.

Lemon, K., D'Andrade, A., & Austin, M. J. (2005). *Understanding and addressing racial/ethnic disproportionality in the front end of the child welfare system.* Retrieved from http://cssr.berkeley.edu/bassc/public/DISPRO_PDF.pdf

Lohrbach, S., & Sawyer, S. (2004). Creating a constructive practice: Family and professional partnership in high-risk child protection case conferences. *Protecting Children, 19*(2), 26–35.

Louisell, M. J. (2006). *Six steps to find a family: A practical guide to family search and engagement (FSE)*. Retrieved from http://www.hunter.cuny.edu/socwork/nrcfcpp/downloads/SixSteps.pdf

Malm, K., & Allen, T. (2011). *Family finding: Does implementation differ when serving different child welfare populations?* (Child Trends Research Brief #2011-27). Retrieved from http://www.childtrends.org/Files/Child_Trends-2011_10_17_RB_FamilyFinding.pdf

Malm, K., Murray, J., & Geen, R. (2006). *What about the dads? Child welfare agencies' efforts to identify, locate and involve nonresident fathers*. Retrieved from http://aspe.hhs.gov/hsp/06/cw-involve-dads/report.pdf

Marcenko, M., Brown, R., DeVoy, P., & Conway, D. (2010). Engaging parents: Innovative approaches in child welfare. *Protecting Children, 25*, 23–34.

Marts, E. J., Eun-Kyoung, O. L., McRoy, R., & McCroskey, J. (2008). Point of engagement: Reducing disproportionality and improving child and family outcomes. *Child Welfare, 87*, 335–358.

McGlade, K., & Ackerman, J. (2006). A hope for foster care: Agency executives in partnerships with parent leaders. *Journal of Emotional Abuse, 6*, 97–112.

Merkel-Holguin, L. (2003). Promising results, potential new directions: International FGDM research and evaluation in child welfare. *Protecting Children, 18*, 1.

Merkel-Holguin, L., Nixon, P., & Burford, G. (2003). Learning with families: A synopsis of FGDM research and evaluation in child welfare. *Protecting Children, 18*(1–2), 2–11. Retrieved from http://www.americanhumane.org/assets/pdfs/children/fgdm/pc-pc-article-fgdm-research.pdf

Milner, J. (2003). *Changing the culture of the workplace*. Closing plenary session, Annual Meeting of State and Tribes, January 29. Retrieved from http://www.acf.hhs.gov/programs/cb/cwmonitoring/changing_culture.htm

Milner, J., Mitchell, L., & Hornsby, W. (2005). Child and Family Services Reviews: An agenda for changing practice. In G. Mallon & P. McCartt Hess (Eds.), *Child welfare for the twenty-first century: A handbook of practices, policies, and programs* (2nd ed., pp. 707–718). New York: Columbia University Press.

Mitchell, L., Lynch-Thomas, M., & Parker, B. (in press). Child and Family Services Reviews: A catalyst for improving practice and measuring results. In G. P. Mallon & P. McCartt Hess (Eds.), *Child welfare for the twenty-first century: A handbook of practices, policies, and programs* (2nd ed.). New York: Columbia University Press.

Moore, T. (2002). *Results oriented management in child welfare*. Retrieved from http://www.rom.ku.edu

Morse, J. M., Markowitz, N., Zanghi, M., & Burns, P. (2003). *Partnering with youth: Involving youth in child welfare training and curriculum development.* Portland: Edmund S. Muskie School of Public Service, Institute for Public Sector Innovation, University of Southern Maine.

Munson, S., & Freundlich, M. (2008). *Families gaining their seat at the table: Family engagement strategies in the first round of Child and Family Services Reviews and Program Improvement Plans.* Retrieved from http://www.americanhumane.org/assets/pdfs/children/fgdm/pc-fgdm-cfsr-pip-review.pdf

National Association of Social Workers. (2005). *NASW standards for social work practice in child welfare.* Retrieved from http://www.socialworkers.org/practice/standards/NASWChildWelfareStandards0905.pdf

National Child Welfare Resource Center for Family-Centered Practice. (2000). Can we put clothes on this emperor? *Best Practice/Next Practice, 1*(1), 7–11.

National Conference of State Legislatures. (2010). *Legislative strategies to safely reduce the number of children in foster care.* Retrieved from http://www.ncsl.org/documents/cyf/strategies_reducing_the_number_of_children_in_foster_care.pdf

National Resource Center for Permanency and Family Connections. (2009). *Family engagement: A Web-based practice toolkit.* Retrieved from http://www.hunter.cuny.edu/socwork/nrcfcpp/fewpt/index.htm

National Resource Center for Permanency and Family Connections. (2011). Meaningful family partnerships. *Permanency Planning Today*, Winter. Retrieved from http://www.nrcpfc.org/newsletter/ppt-winter-2011.pdf

National Technical Assistance and Evaluation Center for Systems of Care. (2007). *A closer look: Family involvement in public child welfare driven systems of care.* Retrieved from http://www.childwelfare.gov/pubs/acloserlook/familyinvolvement/

National Technical Assistance and Evaluation Center for Systems of Care. (2010). *Family involvement in the Improving Child Welfare Outcomes through Systems of Care initiative.* Retrieved from http://www.childwelfare.gov/management/reform/soc/communicate/initiative/evalreports/reports/FamilyInvolvement_Report.pdf

Nilsen, W., Affronti, M., & Coombes, M. (2009). Veteran parents in child protective services: Theory and implementation. *Family Relations, 58,* 520–535.

Olson, K. B. (2009). Family group conferencing and child protection mediation: Essential tools for prioritizing family engagement in child welfare cases. *Family Court Review, 47*(1), 53–68.

Osher, T. (2005). Collaboration for family-driven systems and services. In S. Hornberger, S. Gardner, N. Young, N. Gannon, & T. Osher (Eds.), *Improving the quality of care for the most vulnerable children, youth, and their families: Finding consensus* (pp. 51–62). Washington, DC: CWLA Press.

Osher, T., deFur, E., Nava, C., Spencer, S., & Toth-Dennis, D. (1999). New roles for families in systems of care: Federation of families for children's mental health. Washington, DC: Center for Effective Collaboration and Practice, American Institutes for Research.

Parents Anonymous. (2005). *Pathways to meaningful shared leadership*. Retrieved from http://www.parentsanonymous.org/paTEST/publications1/Pathways_Final_sm.pdf

Pecora, P. J., Reed-Ashcraft, K., & Kirk, R. S. (2001). Family-centered services: A typology, brief history, and an overview of current program implementation and evaluation challenges. In E. Walton, P. Sandau-Beckler, & M. Mannes (Eds.), *Family-centered services* (pp. 1–33). New York: Columbia University Press.

Pennell, J., Burford, G., Connolly, M., & Morris, K. (2011). Introduction. In J. Pennell, G. Burford, M. Connolly, & K. Morris (Eds.), Taking child and family rights seriously: Family engagement and its evidence in child welfare. *Child Welfare, 90*(4), 9–18.

Pennell, J., Edwards, M., & Burford, G. (2010). Expedited family group engagement and child permanency. *Children & Youth Services Review, 32,* 1012–1019.

Pitchal, E. (2012). "Engagement is the reform": The role of youth, foster parents and biological parents in child welfare litigation. In Center for the Study of Social Policy (Ed.), *For the welfare of children: Lessons learned from class action litigation* (pp. 56–68). Retrieved from http://www.youthlaw.org/fileadmin/ncyl/youthlaw/publications/Lessons-Learned.pdf

Polinsky, M., & Pion-Berlin, L. (2001). *Research on parent leadership: Significance and findings* (Research Profile No. 2). Retrieved from http://www.parentsanonymous.org/paTEST/publications1/PA_ResearchProfilePurple05.pdf

Rauber, D. B. (2009). From the courthouse to the statehouse: Parents as partners in child welfare. *Child Law Practice, 28*(10), 149–156. Retrieved from http://www.hunter.cuny.edu/socwork/nrcfcpp/info_services/parentpartner1.pdf

Rauber, D. B. (2010). Working with parent partners to achieve better case outcomes for families. *Child Law Practice, 28*(11), 165–170. Retrieved from http://www.hunter.cuny.edu/socwork/nrcfcpp/info_services/parentpartner2.pdf

Richardson, B. (2008). Comparative analysis of two community-based efforts designed to impact disproportionality. *Child Welfare, 87,* 297–317.

Ronnau, J. (2001). Values and ethics for family-centered practice. In E. Walton, P. Sandau-Beckler, & M. Mannes (Eds.), *Balancing family-centered services and child well-being: Exploring issues in policy, practice, theory, and research* (pp. 34–54). New York: Columbia University Press.

Saint-Jacques, M., Drapeau, S., Lessard, G., & Beaudoin, A. (2006). Parent involvement practices in child protection: A matter of know-how and attitude. *Child & Adolescent Social Work Journal, 23,* 196–215.

Search Institute. (2005). *The power of youth and adult partnerships and change pathways for youth work: Executive summary*. Retrieved from http://www.search-institute.org/system/files/KelloggExecSummary_0.pdf

Sheets, J., Wittenstrom, K., Fong, R., James, J., Tecci, M., Baumann, D. J., & Rodriguez, C. (2009). Evidence-based practice in family group decision-making for Anglo, African American and Hispanic families. *Children and Youth Services Review, 31,* 1187–1191.

Shireman, J. (2003). *Critical issues in child welfare.* New York: Columbia University Press.

Smith, B. (2008). Child welfare service plan compliance: Perceptions of parents and caseworkers. *Families in Society, 89,* 521–531.

Smith, N. (2006). Empowering the unfit mother: Increasing empathy, redefining the label. *Affilia, 21,* 448–457.

Steib, S. (2004). Engaging families in child welfare practice. *Children's Voice, Sept./Oct.* Retrieved from http://www.cwla.org/programs/r2p/cvarticlesef0409.htm

Tam, T. S., & Ho, M.K.W. (1996). Factors influencing the prospect of children returning to their parents from out-of-home care. *Child Welfare, 75,* 253–268.

Taylor, R., Rivera Richart, A., Hall, L., Stolebarger, C. Held, M., Rau, D., et al. (2010). In their own voices: Why peer-to-peer mentoring works. *The Source: Helping Professionals Help Families Affected by Drugs and/or HIV, 20*(1), 20–21.

U.S. Department of Health and Human Services. (2006). *Child and Family Services Reviews: Statewide assessment instrument.* Retrieved from http://www.acf.hhs.gov/programs/cb/resource/cfsr-statewide-assessment

U.S. Department of Health and Human Services, Children's Bureau. (2004). *Findings from the initial Child and Family Service Reviews, 2001–2004.* Retrieved from http://www.acf.hhs.gov/programs/cb/resource/findings-from-the-initial-2001-2004-cfsr

U.S. Department of Health and Human Services, Children's Bureau. (2009). *Results of the 2007 and 2008 Child and Family Services Reviews.* Retrieved from www.acf.hhs.gov/programs/cb/cwmonitoring/results/agencies_courts.pdf

Virginia Department of Social Services, Child Protection Unit. (2011). Parent leadership and family engagement in CPS and foster care. *Virginia Child Protection Newsletter, 92*(Fall).

Webb, S. (2000). The politics of social work: Power and subjectivity. *Critical Social Work, 1.* Retrieved from http://www.uwindsor.ca/criticalsocialwork/the-politics-of-social-work-power-and-subjectivity

Weiss, H. & Stephen, N. (2009). *From periphery to center: A new vision for family, school, and community partnerships.* Retrieved from http://www.hfrp.org/family-involvement/publications-resources/from-periphery-to-center-a-new-vision-for-family-school-and-community-partnerships

Whipple, C., & Zalenski, J. (2006). *The other side of the desk: Honoring diverse voices and restoring effective practice in child welfare and family services* (FRIENDS Learning Tool 9). Retrieved from http://friendsnrc.org/joomdocs/diverse_voices.pdf

Williams, S. C., Malm, M., Allen, T., & Ellis, R. (2011). *Bringing family to the table: Tips & techniques for effective family engagement* (Child Trends Research Brief #2011-32). Retrieved from http://www.childtrends.org/Files/Child_Trends-2011_12_2011_RB_Family-toTable.pdf

Williamson, E., & Gray, A. (2011). New roles for families in child welfare: Strategies for expanding family involvement beyond the case level. *Children & Youth Services Review, 33,* 1212–1216.

Yatchmenoff, D. (2005). Measuring client engagement from the client's perspective in nonvoluntary child protective services. *Research on Social Work Practice, 15,* 84–96.

Zeldin, S., McDaniel, A., Topitzes, D., & Lorens, M. B. (2001). Bringing young people to the table: Effects on adults and youth organizations. *CYD Journal, 2*(2), 20–27.

The Children's Bureau

Chapter 6

ENSURING A SUCCESSFUL TRANSITION TO ADULTHOOD FOR FOSTER YOUTHS

Roxana Torrico Meruvia

In 2010, approximately 28,000 young people transitioned out of foster care (U.S. Department of Health and Human Services, 2011) and faced harsh adult realities, including a scarcity of jobs and affordable housing, high tuition rates, and lack of sufficient (or any) support, challenges to which their life skills were often not adequate. Many of these young people are of color, as African American, Native American, and Hispanic children and youths are disproportionately represented in the child welfare system (National Association of Social Workers [NASW], 2009) and are more likely than white children and youths to leave foster care without a family (Hill, 2006). Regardless of race or ethnicity, older foster youths too often must prematurely confront a daunting number of adult decisions without the support of a permanent family.

Although many of today's young adults take much longer to reach social and economic maturity (Berlin, Furstenberg, & Waters, 2010) and may rely on their families for support well into adulthood, older foster youths are forced to struggle on their own. Given the long-term effects of abuse and neglect, the trauma and loss that many have experienced, and the absence of a solid support network, it is not surprising that former foster youths experience high rates of educational failure, unemployment, poverty, single parenthood, homelessness, and health problems (Courtney & Heuring, 2005).

The Children's Bureau has been instrumental in supporting programs to help prepare youths to transition out of foster care. Though no single system can address all of the critical needs of youths leaving care, there are a number of practice and policy approaches that recognize and address them. Champions across the country, including policymakers, system administrators, state and local leaders, philanthropists, advocates, and social workers have created meaningful, innovative opportunities to help older foster youths transition into adulthood. This chapter describes the critical issues facing young people as they transition out of foster care and provides a historical perspective on the policies that support them. It also highlights some of the comprehensive approaches that address older foster youths' needs and the critical role of the social work profession in this process.

Critical Issues Facing Foster Youths

Most young people transitioning out of foster care are significantly affected by the instability that comes with long periods of foster care placement, multiple school transfers, and the challenge of preserving relationships with their biological family members (Torrico, 2010). Unlike their peers, youths leaving foster care risk experiencing a number of hardships including inadequate educational preparation, economic insecurity, and limited employment and housing opportunities. With limited life skills and a lack of resources, older youths have to struggle to secure housing, navigate education systems, obtain employment and health benefits, and learn to live independently. Unfortunately, many youths preparing to leave foster care do not have the benefit of a family or a support network to help them learn and practice the skills needed to meet life's demands.

Like other young people, youths in foster care need healthy, permanent connections with family and other caring adults as they prepare to enter adulthood. Despite the evidence that young people who are engaged in permanent relationships with supportive adults are more likely to experience positive outcomes (Bernat & Resnick, 2006), too many youths leave the child welfare system without them. In fact, 25 percent of foster youths "age out" of care lacking a permanent connection (Golonka, 2010). Without a connection to someone committed to their well-being, youths are forced to make important life decisions and overcome life's challenges when they are inexperienced and unprepared.

Access to education is critical to meeting life's basic needs. However, multiple school changes, lack of guidance and support, emotional and behavioral issues, and feelings of being unprepared academically can negatively affect the educational trajectory of foster youths. Not surprisingly, young people who transition out of foster care lag behind their peers when it comes to educational attainment (Courtney, Dworsky, Lee, & Raap, 2010). A recent study found that by age 23 or 24, approximately 25 percent of its representative sample of youths did not have a high school diploma or GED and only 6 percent had a two- or four-year degree (Courtney et al., 2010). Another study found that approximately 2 percent of foster care alumni completed a bachelor's or higher degree (Pecora et al., 2005), compared with 27.5 percent of the general population (U.S. Census Bureau, 2011). This study also found that fewer than 16 percent of foster care alumni completed a vocational degree (Pecora et al., 2005). All of these trends are particularly alarming given the critical role that higher education plays in a young adult's future earning potential.

Youths preparing to age out of foster care have to overcome several barriers to access higher education. They often lack economic security, year-round housing, transportation, access to health care, and emergency funds. Some have children of their own and cannot afford child care. Youths in foster care often have little support in filling out applications for admission and financial aid. Despite these challenges, most young people aging out of foster care have a desire to further their education. More than 80 percent of foster youths hope to experience postsecondary education (Courtney, Terao, & Bost, 2004).

Safe, stable, and affordable housing is essential for youths preparing to leave foster care. With inadequate guidance, limited income, and sparse housing options, older foster youths often face housing instability. Young people aging out of foster care are experiencing periods of homelessness or housing instability at alarming rates. Between 12 percent and 36 percent of former foster youths experience homelessness (Courtney et al., 2010; White & Rog, 2004), and 32 percent report changing living situations five or more times within two to four years of exiting the foster care system (Casey Family Programs, 2008). Youths leaving foster care face the challenge of obtaining a security deposit, furnishing a home, and making monthly rental payments. These responsibilities, coupled with a shortage of housing options and limited earning potential, make the transition to adulthood difficult. Housing stability is critical not only to young people's well-being, but also to their ability to maintain a healthy support network, obtain stable employment, and pursue higher education. The significant number of former foster youths who are parents must also care for their children (Courtney et al., 2010; Reilly, 2003; Torrico & Bhat, 2009).

Policies that Support Older Youths in Foster Care

Child welfare advocates began in the 1980s to push for dedicated funding to support older foster youths preparing to transition into adulthood. Many of these advocacy efforts stemmed from concerns that older youths were simply left on their own without any support after leaving foster care (Courtney & Heuring, 2005). Too often, youths exited foster care only to return to the attention of the state as adults through the welfare, criminal justice, or homeless systems (Child Welfare League of America, 2005). However, over the past 25 years, the federal government has recognized the vulnerability and needs of older youths in foster care and has provided funding to prepare them to transition into adulthood.

Several laws, including the Foster Care Independence Act of 1999 (P.L. 106-169) and the Fostering Connections to Success and Increasing Adoptions Act of 2008 (P.L. 110-351), which is regulated and administered by the Children's Bureau, have helped to support older youths and address their needs. In 1985, Congress authorized the Independent Living Initiative through the Consolidated Omnibus Budget Reconciliation Act of 1985 (P.L. 99-272) to support older foster youths in the transition to adulthood (Courtney & Heuring, 2005). Six years later, the Foster Care Independence Act of 1999 established the John H. Chafee Foster Care Independence Program and doubled funding from $70 million to $140 million. This law extended services (such as room and board, Medicaid, mentoring, and counseling) for current and former foster youths to age 21 (Courtney & Heuring, 2005). In 2000, Congress amended the Family Unification Program[1] under P.L. 106-337, making youths ages 18 to 21 who left foster care at age 16 or older eligible for housing vouchers (Fernandes, 2008).

The Promoting Safe and Stable Families Amendments of 2001 (P.L. 107-133) authorized the Education and Training Vouchers program as part of the John H. Chafee Foster Care Independence Program, allowing states to pay tuition, room and board, and other school attendance costs for students aging out of foster care up to age 23 (Child Welfare Information Gateway, 2011). Under Title I of the Workforce Investment Act of 1998 (P.L. 105-220), states receive funding to deliver a wide array of services (such as tutoring, summer employment, skills training, and leadership development) to low-income youths with barriers to employment (U.S. Department of Labor, Employment and Training Administration, n.d.). Reauthorized in 2008, the Higher Education Opportunity Act (P.L. 110-315) recognized that students from the foster care system have unique needs that require specialized support and expanded the definition of an independent student to include youths in foster care or youths who were wards of the court at age 13 or older. It also requires that the Federal TRIO programs, which are designed to identify and provide services to those from disadvantaged backgrounds, support foster care students (Bassett & Emerson, 2010; U.S. Department of Education, n.d.).

The Fostering Connections to Success and Increasing Adoptions Act of 2008 (P.L.110-351), the most significant child welfare reform legislation in over a decade, shifted federal policy toward a socially comprehensive approach to supporting older foster youths (Osgood, Foster, & Courtney, 2010). While some states have already taken meaningful steps to support youths transitioning out of foster care by allowing them to stay in care past the age of 18, this law gives states the option to receive entitlement funding to continue services up to age 21 if youths are engaged in school, work, or other activities that will promote their independence. It also mandates that states develop a personalized transition plan with youths in foster care no later than 90 days prior to their 18th birthday (later if the state extends care beyond age 18). Each plan is expected to address housing, health insurance, employment, supportive services, workforce supports, and education. More than 10 states have begun implementing this option by

---

[1] The Family Unification Program was authorized by Congress in 1990 under the Cranston-Gonzalez National Affordable Housing Act (P.L. 101-625). The Family Unification Program provides families involved with child welfare with Section 8 housing subsidies and the supportive services necessary to reunite with their children or avoid foster care placement altogether. Congress added youths as an eligible population for Family Unification Program in 2000.

enacting legislation to keep youths in care past age 18 (Fostering Connections Resource Center, n.d.). This act can be particularly important for youths over the age of 18 who are completing high school or attending a university, college, or vocational school, because they may be eligible for foster care services while in school.

In addition to federal policies, states have also taken meaningful steps to support older youths. For example, between 2004 and 2007, nine states enacted legislation promoting supportive services to strengthen older foster youths' academic performance (Munson & Freundlich, 2008). These policies address the development of post–high school plans, transitional service plans, outreach programs to ensure that high school students are aware of tuition waivers (Munson & Freundlich, 2008), and housing options.

To build the capacity of state, local, tribal, and other publicly administered or supported child welfare agencies and family and juvenile courts, the Children's Bureau created a Training and Technical Assistance Network (U.S. Department of Health and Human Services, n.d.) with several national resource centers covering a range of federal requirements administered by the Children's Bureau. These include the National Resource Center on Youth Development, which supports states and tribes in providing services to current and former foster youths and other at-risk youths (National Resource Center on Youth Development, n.d.) and offers support to address legislative requirements and promote youth involvement in child welfare policy, planning, and program development (U.S. Department of Health and Human Services, n.d.), and the National Resource Center for Permanency and Family Connections, which provides information services and training and technical assistance to ensure the well-being of children, youths, and families. The Children's Bureau also funds five regionally based implementation centers, which expand the reach of the Training and Technical Assistance Network (U.S. Department of Health and Human Services, n.d.).

Comprehensive Approaches to Supporting Older Youths in Foster Care

A growing number of communities are providing social and logistical supports designed to address older youths' needs. The following section reviews key programs that address the educational, financial, and housing needs of youths aging out of foster care.

Educational Support

No single agency has the comprehensive resources necessary to support all the educational expenses of older youths in foster care. Given the constellation of unique needs, it takes a number of people across systems to effectively support youths as they pursue higher education. Communities across the country have supported youths through a range of approaches including partnerships, policy changes, tuition waiver programs, scholarships or grants, and campus support programs.

A number of states use a child welfare and higher education systems approach (Bassett & Emerson, 2010). Some of these states have formed planning coalitions that include higher education and child welfare system leaders and staff as well as representatives from local agencies and advocacy organizations to develop broad strategies to address the obstacles that older foster youths face in higher education. In addition, some states hold annual conferences to bring together individuals representing postsecondary institutions, local child welfare systems, and community agencies as well as community advocates, policymakers, philanthropists, and foster youths (Bassett & Emerson, 2010). Each conference aims to

- increase awareness of opportunities in postsecondary education and the unique educational challenges of older foster youths
- create effective collaborations between educational, child welfare, and community agencies
- learn about promising practice and policy approaches that have improved educational access for students transitioning out of foster care
- introduce the Casey Family Program's (2010) *Supporting Success: Improving Higher Education Outcomes for Students from Foster Care,* a comprehensive framework to support postsecondary students from foster care
- discuss action planning and establish a point of contact for future work.

The *Supporting Success* framework is being used by a number of educational institutions and state higher education and child welfare collaborations to improve services and increase students' academic success (Bassett & Emerson, 2010). The core elements are illustrated in Table 6-1. Comprehensive approaches that incorporate strong leadership, meaningful partnerships, shared visions and goals, data-driven decision making, multiple resources, and long-term planning are essential to help youths succeed academically (Bassett & Emerson, 2010).

Financial Support

Financial constraints are a common barrier facing youths aging out of foster care and pursuing higher education (Courtney et al., 2010). Fortunately, several resources are available to address this barrier. The Education and Training Vouchers program, Chafee Foster Care Independence Program, and other scholarships and grants are among the resources that can help youths achieve their educational goals. Thirty states fund scholarships, tuition waivers, or grants for foster youths (Bassett & Emerson, 2010).

Housing Support

Too often, foster youths experience housing instability or homelessness while in school. Unlike most of their fellow students, they face housing needs not only during the school year but also during school breaks. Some four-year colleges and universities have taken

Table 6.1. Casey Family Program's *Supporting Success: Improving Higher Education Outcomes for Students from Foster Care*

A Framework for Program Enhancement: Core Elements at a Glance[1]	
Six Elements *Necessary for Program Development*	
1. Designated leadership	Youth from foster care need a caring, trusted staff person or designated lead who has primary responsibility for identifying them and consistently providing guidance in navigating higher education.
2. Internal and external champions	Support champions within and outside of the college community provide direct and indirect program support through their influence and advocacy.
3. Collaboration with community agencies	College support programs should have strong connections with local social services agencies, foundations, and the independent living programs operated by state child welfare systems.
4. Data-driven decision making	Decisions on individual support and program development should be based on data collection and analysis.
5. Staff peer support and professional development	New and established support program staff benefit from belonging to a network of peers in other colleges who support youth from foster care.
6. Sustainability planning	Explicit planning should be undertaken to sustain successful support initiatives.
Three Elements *to Provide Direct Student Support (Phase 1)*	
7. Year-round housing and other basic needs	Youth from foster care need to have priority for available campus housing and access to year-round housing. For campuses without dormitories, they need assistance in finding stable, safe, affordable housing, transportation and food services.
8. Financial aid	Youth from foster care need a financial aid package that maximizes funds to cover the cost of attendance and minimizes or eliminates the need for loans.
9. Academic advising, career counseling, and supplemental support	Youth from foster care benefit from frequent contact with knowledgeable academic and career counselors with whom they can develop a trusting relationship.
Three Additional Elements *to Provide Direct Student Support (Phase 2)*	
10. Personal guidance, counseling, and supplemental support	Personal guidance, mental health counseling, supplemental support, and health insurance are essential for youth coming from care because of their early independence, history of abuse, neglect or abandonment.

(Continued)

Table 6.1. Casey Family Program's *Supporting Success: Improving Higher Education Outcomes for Students from Foster Care* (Continued)

A Framework for Program Enhancement: Core Elements at a Glance[1]	
Six Elements *Necessary for Program Development*	
11. Opportunities for student community engagement and leadership	Youth from foster care benefit from inclusion and engagement with campus activities. Some seek out opportunities to be with other youth from foster care while others choose to avoid such association. Colleges should provide opportunities for students to engage in college life including developing a sense of community and developing leadership and advocacy skills.
12. Planned transitions: to college; between colleges; and from college to employment	Youth from foster care need assistance in planning for college, making applications and beginning their college careers. Once on track to complete an associate of arts degree, many require help transferring to a four-year college. As they near completion of college, most students need help making a successful transition to a career. Each of these three transitions involves letting go of one academic home and adjusting to a new one. This adjustment has a different meaning for youth without family support.

[1]Core Elements at a Glance, "*Supporting Success: Improving Higher Education Outcomes for Students from Foster Care,*" pg. 13. Casey Family Programs ©2010, 2013. All rights reserved. For a copy of the complete publication, contact Casey Family Programs at (206) 282-7300.

innovative approaches to address the unique needs of current and former foster youth. States also play a critical role in ensuring that foster youths' housing needs are met. For instance, California passed the Priority Housing for Foster Youth on College Campuses bill (AB 1393), which requires public postsecondary education systems to give foster youths priority for on-campus housing. This bill also requires California State University campuses keep housing open for foster youths during school breaks (California Youth Connection, n.d.).

Community colleges and vocational schools usually do not offer on-campus housing. Community college systems have taken a range of approaches to housing assistance for students, including working with local child welfare agencies. While not housing experts, child welfare and independent living workers are generally familiar with housing resources and local housing options. For example, 30 percent of Chafee Foster Care Independence Program funds can be used for housing, including housing counseling, modest rental subsidies, security deposits, and payments for furniture. Program funds can also be used for emergency assistance.

The Illinois Department of Children and Family Services (2009) uses Chafee funding to support a housing assistance program for youths under 21 who are preparing to leave the foster care system or are at risk of becoming homeless. The Youth Housing Assistance Program works with youths to identify and secure affordable housing. It also provides cash assistance (for example, for a security deposit, essential furniture, or household items). In some instances, help with urgent needs such as rent and utility arrears is also available after a case is closed. The program can also provide youths who have already aged out of foster care with a housing subsidy for up to 12 months. Subsidies are gradually reduced to help the young person become self-sufficient once the program ends (Torrico & Bhat, 2009).

Another housing option available through child welfare partnerships is the federal Family Unification Program. This vital housing resource can help youths avoid homelessness and make a successful transition into adulthood. Through a local-level partnership between child welfare agencies and public housing authorities, it provides youths with time-limited Section 8 housing subsidies and supportive services (which can be funded out of child welfare budgets). For example, a young person attending a community college or vocational school can secure housing with a Family Unification Program voucher. Colorado is one state that has put these funds to work. The Colorado Department of Human Services was awarded 100 Family Unification Program vouchers in 2001. It worked through the Division of Supportive Housing and Homeless Programs, a state housing agency, to distribute the vouchers. The Division of Supportive Housing and Homeless Programs later began to work with child welfare and community agencies to ensure that young people leaving foster care had access to case management and necessary services. In 2009, it partnered with Mile High United Way, county governments, and local providers of youth services to develop a comprehensive network of support for former foster youths with housing needs and to ensure that youths are self-reliant at the end of the 18-month program (Torrico & Bhat, 2009).

Child welfare administrators can also partner with local housing authorities to tap into other housing resources such as low-income apartments or Section 8 vouchers. Some local housing authorities, for example in New York City, have established a priority code for local child welfare agencies enabling them to access Section 8 vouchers for young people in foster care (New York City Administration for Children's Services, n.d.). Depending on the services available in the community, youths may have access to time-limited transitional housing with case management services (for example, scattered site apartments, semisupervised apartments, and host homes) or in some cases, permanent housing with or without services (with the help of a housing subsidy or in a public housing unit, for example). Permanent housing with services can be particularly important for young people with disabilities.

Cross-system partnerships are critical to addressing the housing needs of young people. Social workers within child welfare agencies can partner with local housing authorities to access housing resources for youths. They can also serve as valuable resources to staff at educational institutions by connecting them with a broad range of local youth-serving agencies. The National Center for Housing and Child Welfare (www.nchcw.org) links housing resources to local, regional, and national child welfare agencies to prevent family homelessness, reduce the need for out-of-home placement, and ensure that older youth obtain safe, stable, and affordable housing when they exit the foster care system. The Center has also worked with Congress to support the Family Unification Program.

Supporting Connections between Foster Youths

Lack of stability can increase the sense of isolation that foster youths experience. Post-secondary education can give them new opportunities to belong and build long-term relationships. Whereas some youths do not want others to know about their foster care experience, others seek opportunities to connect and network with their peers. Through partnerships with child welfare and youth-serving agencies, universities, colleges, and vocational schools can connect students to foster care alumni organizations. For example, Foster Care Alumni of America, FosterClub, and Foster Care to Success (formerly the Orphan Foundation) engage foster youths through networking, mentoring, leadership, and advocacy opportunities. FosterClub, a national network for young people in foster care, provides youths with a range of leadership development opportunities and can link them to local youth boards. A number of state and local foster youth groups and organizations exist as well, such as the California Youth Connection (www.calyouthconn.org), which teaches leadership and advocacy skills in an effort to engage directly with policymakers to improve the foster care system. These formalized networks can help young people to develop their strengths, interests, and leadership skills while expanding their support system.

Networks for Current and Former Foster Youths

FosterClub (www.fosterclub.org) is a national network for young people in foster care that produces youth-friendly publications and provides training and leadership opportunities.

Foster Care Alumni of America (www.fostercarealumni.org/), a national nonprofit association founded and led by alumni of the foster care system, carries out networking and policy advocacy. Foster Care to Success (www.fc2success.org/), formerly Orphan Foundation of America, provides college and vocational school scholarships along with internships and mentoring. It administers Educational Training Vouchers for several states.

Role of the Social Work Profession

NASW, the largest membership organization of professional social workers in the world, supports child welfare policies that are designed to provide the best care for all children in need of foster care (NASW, 2009). It recognizes the range of hardships that older foster youths face and the important role that social workers play in providing youths with knowledge and guidance during critical points in their lives. NASW is committed to improving social work practice by building bridges across policy and practice. Over the years, it has supported landmark legislation, including the Foster Care Independence Act and the Fostering Connections to Success and Increasing Adoptions Act. In an effort to help social workers implement recent child welfare policies, such as the Fostering Connections to Success Act, NASW has developed an educational series (such as webinars, publications, and tools) addressing many of the critical needs of this population (NASW, n.d.). NASW believes that with access to knowledge, training, and tools, social workers can make a significant difference in the lives of young people transitioning out of foster care.

Conclusion

Like their nonfostered peers, foster youths have high hopes and dreams for their future. They look forward to pursuing higher education, getting their first job, moving into their first apartment and furnishing it to their liking, and developing meaningful relationships that will enhance their lives. Regrettably, foster youths have many more obstacles to overcome to achieve these important milestones of adulthood.

Although there has been significant progress over the last 25 years, critical gaps remain in services for older youths in foster care. Though their number may be small, neglecting the needs of youths aging out of foster care can become very costly to states and communities. An increasing number of communities are advocating, partnering, and collaborating to address their needs, but these efforts have not reached all systems or communities. Child welfare has changed, and there is a need for innovative efforts to build more bridges between child welfare and other youth-serving systems—efforts to help systems capture accurate data, avoid duplication of services, increase resources, and improve outcomes for older foster youths. The Fostering Connections to Success and Increasing Adoptions Act of 2008 provides states with opportunities to promote the well-being of young people in foster care and prepare them to thrive as young adults. With the Children's Bureau's strong leadership and support, states can continue to build on current work in the field and significantly invest in the lives of young people.

References

Bassett, L., & Emerson, J. (2010). *Supporting success: Improving higher education outcomes for students from foster care.* Seattle: Casey Family Programs. Retrieved from http://www.casey.org/Resources/Publications/pdf/SupportingSuccess.pdf

Berlin, G., Furstenberg, F., Jr., & Waters, M. C. (2010). Introducing the issue. *Future of Children, 20*(1), 3–18.

Bernat, D. H., & Resnik, M. D. (2006). Healthy youth development: Science and strategies. *Journal of Public Health Management and Practice, 12*(6), S10–S16.

California Youth Connection. (n.d.). *Legislative accomplishments.* San Francisco: Author. Retrieved from http://calyouthconn.org/legislative-accomplishments

Casey Family Programs. (2008). *Improving outcomes for older youth in foster care*. Seattle: Author. Retrieved from http://www.casey.org/Resources/Publications/pdf/White-Paper_ImprovingOutcomesOlderYouth_FR.pdf

Casey Family Programs. (2010). *Supporting success: Improving higher education outcomes for students from foster care*. Retrieved from http://www.casey.org/resources/publications/SupportingSuccess.htm

Child Welfare Information Gateway. (2011). *Major federal legislation concerned with child protection, child welfare and adoption*. Retrieved from http://www.childwelfare.gov/pubs/otherpubs/majorfedlegis.pdf

Child Welfare League of America. (2005). *CWLA standards of excellence for transition, independent living and self-sufficiency services* (Rev. ed.). Washington, DC: Author.

Consolidated Omnibus Budget Reconciliation Act of 1985. P.L. 99-272, 42 U.S.C. § 12307 (1986).

Courtney, M. E., Dworsky, A., Lee, J. S., & Raap, M. (2010). *Midwest evaluation of the adult functioning of former foster youth: Outcomes at ages 23 and 24*. Chicago: University of Chicago, Chapin Hall Center for Children. Retrieved from http://www.chapinhall.org/sites/default/files/Midwest_Study_Age_23_24.pdf

Courtney, M. E., & Heuring, D. H. (2005). The transition to adulthood for youth "aging out" of the foster care system. In D. W. Osgood, C. A. Flanagan, & E. M. Foster (Eds.), *On your own without a net: The transition to adulthood for vulnerable populations* (pp. 27–67). Chicago: University of Chicago Press.

Courtney, M. E., Terao, S., & Bost, N. (2004). *Midwest evaluation of the adult functioning of foster youth: Conditions of youth preparing to leave state care*. Retrieved from http:/www.chapinhall.org/sites/default/files/CS_97.pdf

Fernandes, A. (2008). *Youth transitioning from foster care: Background, federal programs, and issues for Congress*. Retrieved from http://assets.opencrs.com/rpts/RL34499_20080521.pdf

Foster Care Independence Act of 1999, P.L. 106-169, 42 U.S.C.§ § 101-121 (1999).

Fostering Connections Resource Center. (n.d.). *Enacted older youth legislation*. Retrieved from http://www.fosteringconnections.org/resources/topic_legislation?id=0005

Fostering Connections to Success and Increasing Adoptions Act of 2008, P.L. 110-351, 42 U.S.C. §§ 201-202 (2008).

Golonka, S. (2010). *The transition to adulthood: How states can support older youth in foster care*. Retrieved from http://www.nga.org/files/live/sites/NGA/files/pdf/1012FOSTERCARE.PDF

Higher Education Opportunity Act, P.L. 110-315, 20 U.S.C. § § 401,403,473 (2008).

Hill, R. (2006). *A synthesis of research on disproportionality in child welfare: An update*. Retrieved from http://www.cssp.org/reform/child-welfare/other-resources/synthesis-of-research-on-disproportionality-robert-hill.pdf

Illinois Department of Children and Family Services. (2009). *Youth housing assistance*. Springfield: Author. *http://www.state.il.us/dcfs/library/com_communications_yhouse.shtml*

Munson, S., & Freundlich, M. (2008). *Educating children in foster care: State legislation 2004–2007*. Retrieved from http://www.ncsl.org/print/cyf/foster_care_education.pdf

National Association of Social Workers. (n.d.). *Children, youth and families*. Retrieved from https://www.socialworkers.org/practice/children/default.asp

National Association of Social Workers. (2009). Foster care and adoption. In *Social work speaks: National Association of Social Workers policy statements 2009–2012* (8th ed., pp. 146–153). Washington, DC: Author.

National Resource Center on Youth Development. (n.d.). *About us*. Retrieved from http://www.nrcyd.ou.edu/about-us

New York City Administration for Children's Services. (n.d.). *Housing resources for families and youth*. Retrieved from http://www.nyc.gov/html/acs/html/support_families/housing.shtml#3

Osgood, D. W., Foster, E. M., & Courtney, M. E. (2010). Vulnerable populations and the transition to adulthood. *Future of Children, 20*(1), 209–229.

Pecora, P., Kessler, R., Williams, J., O'Brien, K., Downs, A. C., English, D., et al. (2005). *Improving family foster care: Findings from the northwest foster care alumni study*. Retrieved from http://www.casey.org/resources/publications/pdf/improvingfamilyfostercare_es.pdf

Promoting Safe and Stable Families Amendments of 2001, P.L. 107-133, 42 U.S.C. § 201 (2001).

Reilly, T. (2003). Transitions from care: Status and outcomes of youth who age out of foster care. *Child Welfare, 82,* 727–746.

Torrico, R. (2010). *Youth aging out of foster care: Supporting their transition into adulthood*. Washington, DC: National Association of Social Workers.

Torrico, R., & Bhat, S. (2009). *Connected by 25: Financing housing supports for youth transitioning out of foster care*. Washington, DC: The Finance Project.

U.S. Census Bureau. (2011). *State and county quick facts*. Retrieved from http://quickfacts.census.gov/qfd/states/00000.html

U.S. Department of Education. (n.d.). *Higher Education Opportunity Act 2008*. Retrieved from http://www2.ed.gov/policy/highered/leg/hea08/index.html

U.S. Department of Health and Human Services, Administration for Children and Families. (2011). *Adoption and foster care analysis and report (AFCARS)*. Retrieved from http://www.acf.hhs.gov/sites/default/files/cb/afcarsreport18.pdf

U.S. Department of Health and Human Services, Administration for Children, Youth and Families, Children's Bureau. (n.d.). *Training and technical assistance*. Retrieved from http://www.acf.hhs.gov/programs/cb/tta/

U.S. Department of Labor, Employment and Training Administration. (n.d.). *Summary of workforce development provisions of the Workforce Investment Act of 1998 (P.L. 105-220)*. Retrieved from http://www.doleta.gov/usworkforce/wia/summarywia.cfm

White, R., & Rog, D. (2004). Introduction [Special section]. *Child Welfare, 5,* 389–392.

Workforce Investment Act of 1998. P.L. 105-220, 29 U.S.C. § § 126-129 (1998).

Chapter 7

PARADIGM SHIFTS IN CHILD PROTECTION: FROM INVESTIGATION TO FAMILY SUPPORT

Brenda G. McGowan

P roblems of child maltreatment have been documented since the Biblical accounts of Moses, Abraham, Isaac, and Jesus. Yet those concerned about child welfare are still struggling to agree on the best ways to protect and care for children who are abused or neglected. This chapter explores the changing—and sometimes reversing and contradictory—paradigms for child protective services and examines the role of the Children's Bureau in these shifts. The roles of social work and educational preparation of social workers in child protection are explored, and recommendations for the next century of child protection practice are offered.

Early Initiatives

Violence against children and child abandonment were long tolerated in this country. The first formalized effort to address the needs of maltreated children was the establishment of the New York Society for the Prevention of Cruelty to Children (NYSPCC) in 1875. Similar societies were quickly established in other parts of the country, and their number reached more than 250 by 1900. Although the founders' original objective was to remove children from abusive caretakers, their attention turned rapidly to prosecuting the abusers. Their primary function became law enforcement, not provision of direct services to children or parents, although they continued to remove children from abusive home settings.

This model of practice was followed by all of the early NYSPCCs and continued well into the twentieth century. However, this orientation was challenged, at least implicitly, by the initial leaders of the Children's Bureau. Although concern about child abuse and neglect was not part of the official work of the early Children's Bureau, this problem was brought to its attention by the many letters received at the Bureau expressing concern about parental brutality to children. But according to an official from the Library of Congress speaking about the history of the Children's Bureau, the Bureau's first chief, Julia Lathrop, took

> the position that the Hull House brain trust of women on the whole took. And that is, that the brutal working conditions that the parents faced, and the terrible economic problems in their own lives, prompted them to be abusive to their family members. . . . [Lathrop and the others believed that] the dysfunctional family that prompts abuse and neglect of children is a family that is far too hard-pressed economically. . . . Parents who are brutalized will brutalize their children. (Tichi, 2007, p. 13)

Changing Views

One can hear echoes of this sentiment today, and it was definitely restated by David Gil, author of *Violence Against Children: Physical Child Abuse in the United States* in 1970. Yet the local, state, and private agencies established to address child maltreatment in the first part of the twentieth century continued to emphasize investigation, protection, and often removal of children—not family preservation. It was not until after World War II that the umbrella organizations for child protective services began to emphasize a more family-focused approach in their service standards. To illustrate, the American Humane Association, a federation of 750 societies seeking to prevent cruelty to children and animals, issued standards for Child Protective Services agencies in 1951, which stated, "Protective service is a service to parents on behalf of their children and is directed not so much at rescuing the child from the home, as preserving, where possible, the home for the child" (quoted in Bremner, 1974, p. 853).

The Child Welfare League of America took a somewhat similar position in its standards for child protective services, issued in 1960:

> The service, on behalf of the child, has as its purpose to help parents recognize and remedy the conditions harmful to the child, and to fulfill their parental roles more adequately; or to initiate action, either with parental cooperation and consent or through petition to the court, to obtain substitute care for the child whose parents are unable, even with available help, to meet his minimum needs. (quoted in Bremner, 1974, p. 859)

This statement appears to be the first codification from a standard-setting body to incorporate both the child protection and family preservation paradigms of service.

In 1962, Dr. Henry Kempe called for physicians to recognize and diagnose the problem of physical abuse correctly and to report "willful trauma" to the police department or a local child protective service. It concluded, "Above all, the physician's duty and responsibility to the child requires a full evaluation of the problem and a guarantee that the expected repetition of trauma will not be permitted to occur" (quoted in Bremner, 1974, p. 868). This and other publications by physicians created much public concern about the problem of child abuse, increasing attention to the potential value of reporting and investigating allegations of abuse.

Vincent DeFrancis, head of the American Humane Association, conducted a survey of the status and availability of child protective services in 1967. The survey revealed that voluntary, private protective services such as the NYSPCC's were available in only 10 states, whereas public protective services existed in 47 states. This indicated a significant trend away from voluntary agency provision of protective services, due in large measure to financial pressures. Although the expansion of public services was viewed as positive, concern was expressed by Dr. DeFrancis about the limited capacity of these services and the potential overreliance on law enforcement agencies, which took a more punitive approach: "To impose a burden for protective services on law enforcement agencies negates the basic Child Protective philosophy which requires a helping, non-punitive approach" (cited in Bremner, 1974, p. 863).

The 1967 survey also reported that all 50 states, as well as the District of Columbia, the Virgin Islands, and Guam, had enacted child abuse reporting laws. Moreover, 25 of the states, the District of Columbia, and the Virgin Islands had incorporated a specific purpose clause in their reporting laws. The laws all specified the protection of children as a key purpose and usually mentioned some type of reporting mechanism, which was not federally required and therefore some states did not have a reporting mechanism. A number of the states responded that protective services should be made available to prevent further abuse and "preserve family life whenever possible" (Bremner, 1974, p. 881).

Legislative Mandates

Thus it appears that the states had moved heavily in the direction of child abuse reporting and investigation by public agencies, yet there was no federal law related to child maltreatment prior to the 1970s. Some of the major legislation passed since then is described in this section, demonstrating the significant shifts in focus between child abuse investigation and family preservation. The Children's Bureau is responsible for developing regulations and implementing the legislation described here.

The Child Abuse Prevention and Treatment Act (CAPTA) of 1974 (P.L. 93-247) was the first federal law directed solely to problems of child abuse and neglect. Its passage reflected not only mounting public concern about child battering, but also the shift toward more reporting and investigation. The law provided a small amount of funding to states for research and demonstration projects dealing with child maltreatment, but its main emphasis was reporting. It stipulated that in order to qualify for funding, states had to pass child abuse and neglect laws requiring mandated reporting of suspected and known cases of maltreatment, immunity for reporters, confidentiality, and a number of other minor provisions.

Unfortunately, the law did not specify how child abuse or neglect were to be defined or operationalized or how these problems should be treated. This lack of clarity resulted in states establishing their own definitions and created innumerable problems over time for clients as well as social service and court personnel. CAPTA focused enormous public attention on child abuse and led every state to pass a mandatory child abuse reporting law. However, it has been funded at relatively low levels, leading to many unfulfilled expectations; and despite its title, its focus has consistently been on reporting, not prevention or treatment. Thus, this law temporarily confirmed investigation as the primary paradigm for state response to child maltreatment.

Contradicting this orientation were the provisions of the Adoption Assistance and Child Welfare Act (AACWA) (P.L. 96-272), passed in 1980. Hailed as the most important piece of child welfare legislation enacted in decades, this law required states to establish programs and make procedural reforms to serve children in their own homes, prevent out-of-home placement, and facilitate family reunification following placement. It officially introduced the concept of permanency planning as a primary objective of federal child welfare policy. Specific components were aimed at redirecting funds from foster care to preventive and adoption services; providing due process for all people involved; decreasing the time children spend in foster care; ensuring placement for children in the least detrimental alternative setting; and ensuring state planning and accountability. Perhaps most important for later developments in child welfare services was the law's requirement that states make "reasonable efforts" to prevent foster care placement.

Enacted in response to increasing criticism of the child welfare system's failure to find permanent homes for children in foster care and the documented success of several demonstration projects aimed at keeping children out of care, the bill did not explicitly address child maltreatment. Moreover, no effort was made to reconcile potential conflicts between the new law and CAPTA.

Since 1980, more than 20 bills have been passed amending CAPTA and AACWA and addressing other issues related to financing foster care and adoption services through Title IV-B and Title IV-E of the Social Security Act, yet none have explicitly addressed the potential conflict between the mandates for child abuse investigation and family preservation, and a number have focused on increasing adoption opportunities for children in care, implicitly undercutting family preservation initiatives.

The Family Preservation and Support Services Program Act of 1993 (P.L. 103-66) amended Title IV-B to encourage states to create a continuum of family support services, required states to engage in comprehensive planning to develop more responsive family support and preservation programs, and defined both family preservation and family support services. The definition of family preservation services explicitly noted that these are services for families in crisis when the child is at risk of placement due to abuse or neglect.

Although these services, especially those known as intensive family preservation services, continued to expand during the 1990s, several forces converged to raise concern about their value. These included a continued increase in child abuse reports, leading to increased numbers of foster placements; in contrast with earlier reports about the success of intensive family preservation services, carefully designed studies began to document the limitations of this model of service (Nelson, 1997; Schuerman, Rzepnicki, & Littell 1994).

Moreover, a resurgence of conservative political forces began to legitimize public attacks on families in poverty (MacDonald, 1994). Also, public exposés about isolated cases in which children in families that had received family preservation services were later re-abused by their parents precipitated widespread debate about the relative value of family preservation versus child protection and the need to give priority to child safety (Farro, 2001).

The Child Abuse Prevention and Treatment Amendments of 1996 (P. L. 104-235) reauthorized CAPTA and modified it by creating the Office of Child Abuse and Neglect in the Children's Bureau; defined child abuse to include death, serious physical or emotional injury, sexual abuse, or imminent risk of harm; and authorized federal grants for the establishment of three or more citizen review panels for several purposes including "a review of the extent to which the State child protective services system is coordinated with the foster care and adoption programs established under Title IVE" (Child Welfare Information Gateway, 2009, p. 15).

The Adoption and Safe Families Act of 1997 (ASFA) (P.L. 105-89), designed to promote the adoption of children in foster care, was the first federal law to specify restrictions on permanency planning for children in foster care emphasized by AACWA and to emphasize safety for abused and neglected children at every step of the planning process, including the "reasonable efforts" to prevent placement mandated by AACWA. More specifically, this act reauthorized the Family Preservation and Support Services Program, renaming it the Safe and Stable Families Program; required states to initiate court proceedings to free children for adoption once they have been in care for at least 15 of the past 22 months; provided incentive funds to states that increased the proportion of adoptions of children in care; and required states to initiate permanency planning hearings no later than one year after children entered care. These provisions shifted the emphasis in permanency planning away from family reunification on the presumption that the best interests of the child could be secured through adoption.

The Child Abuse Prevention and Enforcement Act of 2000 (P.L. 106-177), was passed in response to increasing concern about the number of children in placement being returned to biological parents or grandparents where they were in continuing risk of maltreatment. This law emphasized child protective services as a form of law enforcement and authorized the use of federal law enforcement funds for a range of investigatory activities related to data collection and sharing of information. It also permitted use of federal funds for cooperative programs between law enforcement and media organizations to collect, retain, and disseminate information useful in identification and apprehension of criminal offenders.

The Keeping Children and Families Safe Act of 2003 (P.L. 108-36), was passed to reauthorize, amend, and improve CAPTA. It expanded a longitudinal research program and made provisions for expanded training of protective service workers regarding their legal responsibilities to protect the rights and safety of children and families. It also emphasized linkages between child protection services and public health, mental health, and developmental disability services. This could reflect increased concern about enabling children to remain with their families, but no mention was made of this objective.

The Adam Walsh Child Protection and Safety Act of 2006 (P.L.109-248) focuses on protecting children from violent crime and sexual exploitation. It emphasizes comprehensive strategies across federal, state, and local lines to prevent sex offenders from having access to children. It also requires fingerprinting of prospective foster and adoptive parents and checks of state child abuse and neglect registries regarding the prospective parents and any other adults living in the home. This law clearly reflects an emphasis on investigation as the primary mode of service for children at risk of maltreatment.

In contrast, the Child and Family Services Improvement Act of 2006, P.L. 109-288, emphasizes family preservation as the primary paradigm for service to children at risk. It amends Title IV-B to permit a broader array of services and to expand funding under the Promoting Safe and Stable Families Amendments of 2001 (P. L. 107-133). One of its components authorizes competitive grants to regional partnerships to encourage services and activities "designed to increase the well-being of, improve permanency outcomes for, and enhance the safety of children who are in out-of-home placement or are at risk of being placed . . . as a result of a parent's or caretaker's methamphetamine or other substance abuse" (Child Welfare Information Gateway, 2009, p. 6). This suggests increasing recognition of the need to take both family preservation and child protection into account.

The Fostering Connections to Success and Increasing Adoptions Act, P.L. 110-351, was enacted in 2008. This law, which amends Titles IV-B and IV-E of the Social Security Act, is geared primarily to connecting children in need of placement with caregivers who are relatives, providing kinship guardianship payments for children living with a relative who has legal guardianship, extending the age at which foster children can receive financial assistance, and improving incentives for adoption. However, it also reiterates provisions of the Adam Walsh Child Protection and Safety Act requiring fingerprinting and checks of criminal records and child abuse and neglect registries for guardians and other adults living in the home. This suggests that lawmakers were still struggling to balance investigation and family preservation concerns.

Recent Developments

Several recent developments at the federal level suggest increasing efforts to balance the family preservation and investigation paradigms for child protective services. For example, Child and Family Services Reviews were introduced in 2000 by the U.S. Department of Health and Human Services (HHS). These reviews were the first effort to focus on the outcomes rather than the processes of the various child welfare programs supported by Title IV-B and Title IV-E of the Social Security Act. Child and Family Service Reviews are administered by the Children's Bureau, which is located in the Administration for Children and Families in HHS, in collaboration with the states. In addition to ensuring accountability, they are designed to help states improve child welfare services by achieving specific outcomes related to safety, permanency, and child and family well-being. These outcomes are defined as follows:

Safety

Children are first and foremost protected from abuse and neglect.
Children are safely maintained in their homes whenever possible and appropriate.

Permanency

Children have permanency and stability in their living situations.
The continuity of family relationships and connections is preserved for families.

Family and Child Well-Being

Families have enhanced capacity to provide for their children's needs.
Children receive appropriate services to meet their educational needs.
Children receive adequate services to meet their physical and mental health needs. (Children's Bureau, n.d.).

These desired outcomes place child safety and family preservation on essentially the same level. The outcomes are measured by a two-stage process consisting of a statewide assessment using aggregate data provided by the Children's Bureau on each state's foster care and in-home services and an on-site review of service outcomes and service systems. There are a number of limitations to this review system, and efforts are underway to improve it. However, it lays out clear policy objectives for the states, placing balanced emphasis on child protection and family preservation.

The most recent legislation related to child maltreatment, the Child Abuse Prevention and Treatment Act Reauthorization Act of 2010, P.L. 111-320, offers a somewhat different perspective from earlier laws designed to reauthorize CAPTA. In addition to renewing grants for child abuse prevention and treatment, as well as those for investigation and prosecution, it requires that state plans include provisions and procedures for "differential response in triage procedures for the appropriate referral of a child not at risk of imminent harm to a community organization or voluntary preventive service" (section 106(b)(2)(B)(v)). Like emergency medical triage, these procedures are designed to encourage states to distinguish between high- and low-risk cases during screening and intake.

These triage procedures include programs such as the one in New York State called Family Assessment Response. Unlike the traditional child protective investigation, this approach focuses on family engagement. The worker is expected to make a family assessment and, based on an understanding of family needs, work with family members to identify solutions and services that can meet their immediate needs. An evaluation completed in January 2011 of the approximately 9,000 cases that had been assigned to the Family Assessment Response track in New York at that time concluded that this approach "leads to improved satisfaction, increased linkages to needed services, a reduced need for traditional public child welfare services, and fewer petitions filed in Family Court" (Schuyler Center for Analysis and Advocacy, 2011, p. 1).

Similar findings have been reported in other states. For example, Waldfogel (2008) reported that at least 26 states had some type of differential response in place, as well as the traditional investigatory approach. Based on a review of the evaluation studies in a number of these states, she concluded:

> To the extent that child safety and repeat maltreatment can be measured, children seem to be as well, or better, off on these indicators under differential response. And, families seem to be receiving more services and to be more satisfied with them, although long run outcomes for children and families have yet to be evaluated. (Waldfogel, 2008, p. 240)

What these findings suggest is that the paradigm of family preservation may now be viewed on a parallel with that of investigation and reporting for families in need of help in which children are not at imminent risk. This approach opens the door for an alternative approach to the vast majority of child protective referrals that involve neglect, not abuse. The most recent available data indicate that in 2010 there were an estimated 695,000 children who were victims of child maltreatment (9.2 victims per

1,000 children), and that 78.3 percent of these children suffered from neglect (HHS, Children's Bureau, 2011a, p. ix). Based on these numbers, it seems that many more children reported as possible victims of neglect could benefit from a differential response and receive a range of services designed to support their families. Yet of the nearly two million reports of child maltreatment that were screened and received a child protective services (CPS) response in 2010, only 9.7 percent received a differential response (HHS, Children's Bureau, 2011a, p. viii).

Research on Traditional Child Protective Services

The move toward increasing reliance on family preservation strategies in cases of child maltreatment is supported by research findings demonstrating the questionable value of investigation and out-of-home placement for children. In a longitudinal study of 595 children designed to determine whether child protective investigation is associated with later child risk factors such as social support, family functioning, poverty, and child behavior problems, Campbell, Cook, LaFleur, and Keenan (2010) discovered that investigation of suspected child maltreatment is not associated with relative improvement in common risk factors for children at age 8. The only exception was that maternal depression was higher in families that had been investigated. This finding suggests that although child abuse investigation may be essential to protect children at imminent risk of serious harm, the investigation in itself does nothing to protect children.

Unfortunately, research also indicates that child protective services are doing little to protect children while preserving family life. Reporting on the results of a number of studies of the data collected in the National Survey of Child and Adolescent Well-Being, Haskins, Wulczyn, and Webb (2007) reached several troubling conclusions:

> CPS is failing in most cases to achieve family reunification or stable placements after children have been removed from their homes. Two-thirds of children removed from their homes are still in placement after a year and a half; half are still in placement after three years. . . . Most children remain at home following the investigation of a maltreatment report. Of those who remain at home, about one-quarter will be the subject of further maltreatment reports within eighteen months. (Haskins, Wulczyn, & Webb, 2007, p. 18)

Preparing Practitioners for a New Approach

Despite the gradual policy move toward increased emphasis on family preservation rather than investigation, one need only listen to child protective workers' stories of sleepless nights, fearing they may wake up to newspaper headlines about a child abuse investigation that failed, to realize what a difficult change this is for them. Their training focuses on investigation and allegation-based fact finding. The first question they are required to pose to themselves is, "Is there imminent danger to the life or health of the child?" Even if they think the answer is no, the second question they must pose is, "Can reasonable efforts be made to prevent or eliminate the need for removal?" (cited in Cohen, Gimein, Bulin, & Kollar, 2009, p. 301). Unfortunately, as many workers know, there are severe limits on the resources and services that are available to the family. Hence, it is no wonder that a decision for removal often appears much safer to the social worker investigating a case than referral for needed services. Given this, it is somewhat surprising, but encouraging, that increasing numbers of child protective workers have become slower to recommend placement and are instead recommending alternative services for families at risk.

Such decision making requires skills in family assessment and engagement. The increase in recommendations for alternative services may reflect the fact that more child protection workers have received professional knowledge and skills through Title IV-E funding for social work education. However, it points to the need for more training and supervision in family-centered practice for all protective service workers. Schools of social work could certainly take the lead in offering such training and encouraging public child welfare workers, as well as other students, to balance efforts at child protection and family preservation.

In 2010, the NASW Center for Workforce Studies and Social Work Practice, in conjunction with the National Child Welfare Workforce Institute and Casey Family Programs, sponsored a Think Tank Symposium on Supervision: The Safety Net for Front-Line Child Welfare Practice (Center for Workforce Studies and Social Work Practice, 2010). Panelists discussed the complex issues confronting child welfare supervisors and the critical nature of preparing and supporting supervisors, who are the key workforce supporting this transition to family-centered practice and integrating the skills needed to both assess risk and safety and engage families in developing strategies to maintain children at home.

Other examples of professionalization efforts are discussed at length in the chapters in this volume on traineeship programs and partnerships between universities and child welfare agencies. Traineeship programs that fund BSW and MSW students interested in a career in child welfare provide an important resource for preparing employees and future leaders with the skills needed for the complex work of assessing safety and risk and engaging families. Efforts such as this are bringing national attention to the critical role that supervisors and a skilled workforce play in achieving the goals of safety, permanence, and well-being aspired to in the Adoption and Safe Families Act.

Future Trends

The historic shift to increased emphasis on family preservation seems clear. Perhaps most emblematic of this shift are the developments at the NYSPCC, the agency that started the whole process of child abuse investigation. This eminent organization is still very active in the child maltreatment arena, but it has turned all its investigatory responsibilities over to civic authorities and now runs a wide range of child abuse prevention, mediation, and education programs. These include Positive Parenting Plus, the trauma recovery program, the child empowerment program, crisis debriefing services (resiliency restoration training for public and voluntary child welfare staff), child permanency mediation, custody and visitation mediation, and a professional education program (training mandated reporters about identifying and reporting child abuse and neglect and legislative advocacy). These programs all speak to NYSPCC's current emphasis on prevention and early intervention as well as child abuse reporting.

In contrast, on the day I was preparing to write the conclusion to this chapter, highlighting the shift to a family preservation paradigm, an article appeared on the front page of the *New York Times* pointing out that

> hundreds of New Yorkers who have been caught with small amounts of marijuana, or who have admitted to using it, have become ensnared in civil child neglect cases in recent years, though they did not face even the least of criminal charges, according to city records and defense lawyers. A small number of parents in these cases have even lost custody of their children. (Secret, 2011, p. 17)

The article reported that localities across the country have loosened penalties for marijuana use but struggle with how to handle cases in which children are present.

> California, where the medical marijuana movement has flourished, now requires that the child welfare officials demonstrate actual harm to the child from marijuana use in order to bring neglect cases. . . . But in New York, the child welfare agency has not shied away from these cases. For those parents, the child welfare system has become an alternative system of justice, with legal standards on marijuana that appear to be tougher than those of criminal court or, to some extent, of society at large. (Secret, 2011, p. 17)

The city's rationale is that parental use of any drug can put children in danger of neglect or abuse, and many of the cases involving marijuana use also involve other allegations of neglect.

I have quoted this story in some detail because it so clearly illustrates the potential conflict between the investigation and family preservation paradigms of protective service for children. There are definitely times that allegations of child maltreatment need to be investigated and children need to be protected from serious abuse. However, as anyone who has worked in foster care knows, separation of children from their primary caretakers can be traumatic and harmful, suggesting that the relationship of children to their parents should be retained whenever practicable. (See chapter 9 on trauma-informed practice.) The tension between those most concerned about using police powers to protect children and those most concerned about sustaining family life for children seems likely to continue.

What seems most promising are the recent efforts to balance these concerns by using triage procedures to decide which cases pose risk of imminent danger and which can benefit from a differential range of support services. Increased use of this differential response approach would not only retain both the investigation and family preservation paradigms for child protective services, but also greatly reduce the number of children who are unnecessarily placed in foster care.

The only major impediment to expansion of this approach is a series of current and proposed cutbacks in discretionary funding at the local, state, and federal levels. These cuts will result in major cutbacks in many essential programs for families at risk, such as Head Start; child care support; Women, Infants, and Children; parenting education; after-school programs; and child abuse prevention programs. Child advocacy organizations across the country are asking Congress to "hold children harmless" in future debt ceiling negotiations, but programs of direct benefit to low-income families such as domestic violence programs funded under the Office on Violence Against Women, U. S. Department of Justice, Medicaid, the Supplemental Nutrition Assistance Program, and the Social Service Block Grant are also threatened. Without adequate funding, it will be very difficult for child protective workers to feel safe referring families for services rather than investigating and possibly making findings of child neglect.

The Children's Bureau could assume a lead in several ways to strengthen the move toward differential response for children who may be at risk. First, it could take the lead in monitoring and advocating against threatened cutbacks in support programs for families and children at risk. Second, it could work to ensure that the education and training programs funded under Title IV-E and the other child welfare training programs it administers emphasize family preservation as well as child protection. Third, and most easily, it could publicize and distribute widely its 2011 resource guide *Strengthening Families and Communities,* (HHS Children's Bureau, 2011b). This guide, which was developed in collaboration with a range of national organizations, federal agencies, and parents, presents an excellent overview of ways to support families and strengthen communities. For example, it identifies five protective factors linked to a lower incidence of child maltreatment. This could be of enormous benefit to all child protective workers attempting to implement a differential response to families in which there has been an allegation of child maltreatment, and to community providers of services for families and children. At relatively low cost, the Children's Bureau could give the many groups working with families and children easy access to this guide and draw public attention to the importance of differential response for children at risk.

Finally, in the administration of the Child and Family Services Review System, the Children's Bureau could assume a stronger role in ensuring that states give equal attention to the desired outcomes of permanency and child and family well-being as well as child safety. The recent Information Memorandum *Promoting Social and Emotional Well-Being for Children and Youth Receiving Child Welfare Services* (HHS, Children's Bureau, 2012) provides guidance for this refocusing. The memo defines child well-being as "those skills, capacities, and characteristics that enable young people to understand and navigate their world in healthy, positive ways" (p. 1). It lays out a framework to guide understanding of what well-being entails for children and youth, which is developmental and includes four domains: cognitive functioning, physical health and development, behavioral and emotional functioning, and social functioning. The guidance in the memo challenges CPS to move from a point-in-time assessment of safety and risk to a functional assessment of a child reported for investigation that provides a more holistic view and a baseline for assessing changes in functioning over time and across intervention domains. These data will provide important information for service planning and family engagement strategies.

The guidance offered by the Information Memorandum on social and emotional well-being also invites child welfare systems to consider whether structural changes might support more effective practice. Extending this idea to child protection, managers can ask whether CPS units are structured in the best way to carry out a family-focused, child-centered, and trauma-informed assessment during an investigation. Would a structural modification create the potential for improved investigations and assessments? For example, what if CPS teams had staff with expertise across the developmental stages so that everyone on the team could confer on a case and benefit from the deep developmentally specific knowledge that different team members possess? How would functional assessments be added into the work of the investigation? Could protective services workers team with a colleague who is specially trained in functional assessments to go out in the early part of the investigation? Could small groups of team members confer on cases daily, looking at data from the safety and risk assessment and functional assessment to help a worker prepare the case plan? Such an approach would support critical thinking, with team members posing various hypotheses about the meaning of the information at hand and identifying important questions that the worker can pursue to ensure the investigation has a clear picture of the risks, assets, and needs for each case. Such an environment would offer new opportunities for both scaling up evidence-informed practices in protective services investigation and reducing ineffective practices.

Approaches like the one described earlier also provide the opportunity to partner with schools of social work to host mini-courses and trainings that emphasize assessment practices that incorporate a functional assessment tool, team-building practices, case conferencing, and coaching in new practices.

Current supervisors may find these practice changes challenging to implement given the current emphasis on investigation and safety and risk assessments. One example of supporting supervisors to try new practices and receive support can be found in Indiana. The public child welfare agency is using the National Child Welfare Workforce Institute's Leadership Academy for Supervisors online training to support implementation of the state's practice framework. Supervisors are given protected time away from their regular job responsibilities to complete the online training, and social work faculty from Indiana University are providing coaching for the supervisors as they implement the practice model in their units. The evaluation of this initiative was still underway as this chapter was written, but it is a promising approach that both supports supervisors as leaders and sets expectations for practice strategies that can move the agency toward its goals (personal communication with M. McCarthy, co-principal investigator, National Child Welfare Workforce Institute, Albany, NY, June 12, 2012).

Since the founding of the Children's Bureau, its leaders have been advocating family-focused services that support families and children who have reduced opportunity by virtue of their community, poverty, experience of violence, education, and other contextual factors. Today's Children's Bureau leaders are providing the platform for the next century of practice. The attention to the social and emotional well-being of children and youths who have experienced maltreatment is an important call to action. The framework and guidance that have been set out offer important directions for states, tribes, and voluntary agencies to consider scaling up evidence-based approaches across all program areas.

The child and family service reviews have put a spotlight on repeat maltreatment reports, helping those charged with investigation to reconsider practices and approaches, thereby increasing the likelihood that children and families will receive needed services. Legislation supporting an alternative to a full investigation for cases in which there is no imminent risk of harm to a child offers well-documented strategies for engaging families in services that provide real assistance in areas of high priority to the family. The possibilities for fully realizing family-centered practice starting with protective services have never been better.

References

Adam Walsh Child Protection and Safety Act of 2006, P. L. 109-248. 120 Stat. 587 (2006).

Adoption and Safe Families Act of 1997, P.L.105-89, 111 Stat. 2115 (1997).

Adoption Assistance and Child Welfare Act of 1980, P.L. 96-272, 94 Stat. 500 (1980).

Bremner, R. H., Ed. (1974). *Children and youth in America: A documentary history: Vol. 3. 1935–1973*. Cambridge, MA: Harvard University Press.

Campbell, K. A., Cook, L. J., LaFleur, B. J., & Keenan, H. T. (2010). Household, family, and child risk factors after an investigation for suspected child maltreatment [Abstract]. *Archives of Pediatric and Adolescent Medicine, 164*, 943–949.

Child Abuse Prevention and Enforcement Act of 2000, P. L. 106-177, 114 Stat. 35 (2000).

Child Abuse Prevention and Treatment Act, P.L. 93-247, 88 Stat. 4 (1974).

Child Abuse Prevention and Treatment Amendments of 1996, P. L. 104-235, 110 Stat. 3063 (1996).

Child Abuse Prevention and Treatment Act Reauthorization Act, P.L. 111-320. 124 Stat. 3459 (2010).

Child and Family Services Improvement Act of 2006, P. L. 109-288, 120 Stat. 1233 (2006).

Children's Bureau. (n.d.). *Child and Family Services Reviews fact sheet.* Washington, DC: U.S. Department of Health and Human Services, Administration for Children and Families.

Child Welfare Information Gateway. (2009). *Major federal legislation concerned with child protection, child welfare, and adoption.* Washington, DC: U.S. Department of Health and Human Services.

Cohen, C. S., Gimein, T., Bulin, T., & Kollar, S. (Eds.). (2009). *Real cases: Integrating child welfare practice across the social work curriculum.* New York: Administration for Children's Services.

Family Preservation and Support Services Program Act, P.L. 103-66, 107 Stat. 312 (1993).

Farro, F. (2001). *The shifting policy impact of intensive family preservation services.* Chicago: University of Chicago, Chapin Hall Center for Children.

Fostering Connections to Success and Increasing Adoptions Act, (2008), P. L. 110-352. 122 Stat. 3949 (2008).

Gil, D. G. (1970). *Violence against children: Physical child abuse in the United States.* Cambridge, MA: Harvard University Press.

Haskins, R., Wulczyn, F., & Webb, M. B. (2007). Using high-quality research to improve child protection practice: An overview. In R. Haskins, F. Wulczyn, & M. B. Webb (Eds.), *Child protection: Using research to improve practice* (pp. 1–33). Washington, DC: Brookings Institution.

Keeping Children and Families Safe Act of 2003, P. L. 108-36. 117 Stat. 800 (2003).

MacDonald, H. (1994). The ideology of family preservation. *Public Interest, 115,* 45–60.

Nelson, K. E. (1997). Family preservation—What is it? *Children and Youth Services Review, 19,* 101–118.

Promoting Safe and Stable Families Amendments of 2001, P.L. 107-133,115 Stat. 2413 (2002).

Schuerman, J. K., Rzepnicki, T. L., & Littell, J. H. (1994). *Putting families first: An experiment in family preservation.* New York: Aldine de Gruyter.

Schuyler Center for Analysis and Advocacy. (2011). *SCAA children's policy agenda.* Albany, NY: Author.

Secret, M. (2011, August 18). No cause for marijuana case, but enough for child neglect. *New York Times.*

Tichi, C. (2007). *Justice, not pity: Julia Lathrop, first head of the U.S. Children's Bureau.* Lecture presented to the Federal Interagency Workgroup, Administration for Children and Families, U.S. Department of Health and Human Services, September.

U.S. Department of Health and Human Services, Administration for Children and Families, Administration on Children, Youth and Families, Children's Bureau. (2011a). *Child maltreatment 2010.* Washington, DC: Author.

U.S. Department of Health and Human Services, Administration for Children and Families, Administration on Children, Youth and Families, Children's Bureau. (2011b). *Strengthening families and communities, 2011 resource guide.* Washington, DC: Author.

U.S. Department of Health and Human Services, Administration for Children and Families, Administration on Children, Youth and Families, Children's Bureau. (2012, April 17). *Promoting social and emotional well-being for children and youth receiving child welfare services* (ACYF-CB-IM-12-04). Washington, DC: Author.

Waldfogel, J. (2008). The future of child protection revisited. In D. Lindsay & A. Shlonsky (Eds.), *Child welfare research* (pp. 235–241). New York: Oxford University Press.

Chapter 8

PREVENTION OF CHILD MALTREATMENT FATALITIES

Theresa M. Covington and Michael Petit

The death of children at the hands of people who are supposed to love them and care for them is the most tragic outcome of child abuse and neglect. Children are affirmations of life. When they die, we all lose expectations for a future filled with promise, memories, and innocence. When they die from abuse and neglect, it usually means people failed them in the worst way: certainly their caretakers who caused their death, perhaps neighbors who never spoke out, teachers who didn't report suspicious injuries, a child welfare system that didn't investigate or provide services, or a mental health system that didn't help the caregivers.

Fatal maltreatment is as old as human history. Children have too often been the victims of death at the hands of those responsible for their care. Applying a cultural lens to our history, one can identify religious and cultural justifications for many of these deaths. One needs only to read the story of the sacrifice of Abraham for evidence. Today the United Nations Convention on the Rights of the Child rejects the notion of cultural relativism in favor of a universal approach that transcends cultural, religious, historical, and economic differences to assert that all deliberate harm to children is unacceptable.

This chapter explores the work that has been done in the past 100 years, though mostly in the past twenty, to better understand the scope of child maltreatment deaths and efforts to learn from, and respond to these deaths. It closes with a call to action for greater efforts to ensure that America's children do not die at the hands of those who are supposed to love and protect them.

One Hundred Years of Attention to Child Fatalities

From its establishment in 1912, the Children's Bureau has always had a major focus on understanding and preventing child deaths. The 62nd Congress ruled that the Bureau shall investigate and report upon all matters pertaining to the welfare of children and child life among all classes of our people, and *shall especially investigate the questions of infant mortality*, the birth rate, orphanage, juvenile courts, desertion, dangerous occupations, accidents and diseases of children, employment, [and] legislation affecting children in the several States and Territories. [italics added] (62d Cong., 2d session. S. 252. Public, No. 116; http://archive.org/stream/babysavingcampai00unit/babysavingcampai00unit_djvu.txt).

In 1914, the U.S. Department of Labor, Children's Bureau issued a report titled *Baby Saving Campaigns*. The introduction began, "What American cities are doing and can do toward preventing infant mortality and the too common high death rate of children under five years of age is to be the subject of an annual bulletin by the Children's Bureau." As early as 1914, the Children's Bureau was encouraging a multidisciplinary approach toward preventing child deaths. The Baby Saving Campaign report described how city health departments should work to address child deaths:

> The health department should cooperate in every way possible with all the private social agencies that are at work in the city. When, as is sometimes the case, no private entities exist with which to cooperate, the health officer often resorts to agitation to bring them into existence . . . emphasizing the number of preventable deaths each week from causes so largely social in their nature that the individual parents cannot be considered wholly to blame. (U.S. Department of Labor, 1914)

One of the Children's Bureau's first major undertakings was to determine how many children in the United States died before their first birthday, and why. Eight American cities were selected, representing different conditions in different regions. Bureau staff, volunteers, and members from women's clubs visited the homes of approximately 23,000 babies in these cities. They documented conditions and discovered risk factors leading to differences in infant death rates.

The Children's Bureau then developed programs to address these causal factors and launched the first Children's Year (1918–1919) with the slogan "Save 100,000 Babies," mobilizing 11 million volunteers to help reduce infant deaths. During this year, many states were also persuaded to form their own child welfare programs. By 1921, the U.S. infant mortality rate had fallen 24 percent. Efforts continued with passage of the 1921 Sheppard-Towner Maternity and Infancy Protection Act of 1921 (P. L. 67-97), which provided states with matching funds administered by the Children's Bureau to reduce infant and maternal mortality. In effect, the Sheppard-Towner Act extended the work of the Children's Bureau to the states, and it was the first time that the federal government provided direct support for social welfare (Theerman, 2010).

Title V of the landmark 1935 Social Security Act further funded the Children's Bureau to issue maternal and child health grants to states to promote maternal and infant health, especially in depressed areas, and to establish child welfare programs for "the protection and care of homeless, dependent, and neglected children, and children in danger of becoming delinquent." In 1946 the Children's Bureau was transferred to the Social Security Administration and over the next 30 years underwent numerous reorganizations while expanding its emphasis on child welfare. In 1969, the Title V Maternal and Child Health and Crippled Children's programs were kept together and transferred, as the Maternal and Child Health Service, to the Health Services and Mental Health Administration, a major new component of the Public Health Service. Health Services and Mental Health Administration and now resides in the Health Resources and Services Administration, (Hutchins, 1994). Still, it was not until the mid-1960s that states began to mandate reporting of suspected cases of child abuse and neglect and to offer those who made the reports protection from retaliatory litigation.

In the early 1970s, as the public became more aware of and concerned about child abuse and neglect, questions arose about the scope of the problem and the adequacy of existing mechanisms for protecting children. The Senate Subcommittee on Children and Youth held hearings in 1973, which resulted in the 1974 Child Abuse Prevention and Treatment Act (CAPTA) (P. L. 93-247), which created the National Center on Child Abuse and Neglect (NCCAN), separate from the Children's Bureau but within the Department of Health, Education and Welfare. The center's charge was to support state and local efforts for the prevention and treatment of child abuse and neglect It was fully operational by 1981.

In 1986 the Children's Justice Assistance Act (P. L. 99-401) was passed with four goals: to reduce trauma to child victims, increase the rates of prosecutions for child abuse, address the needs of child victims with disabilities, and improve the handling of child fatalities resulting from abuse. Most of the act's funds stayed within the Department of Justice, but a substantial amount went to the NCCAN for grants to states.

During this time, more public attention began to be paid to fatal maltreatment, although far too many child abuse deaths still went undiagnosed or unreported. Lisa Steinberg, a six-year-old-who died after being tortured for years by her father in New York City, galvanized national attention in the late 1980s. A small but influential group from the American Professional Society on the Abuse of Children representing medicine, child welfare, law enforcement, and justice began promoting child death review (CDR) as a community-based and multidisciplinary process to better identify, respond to, and prosecute child abuse deaths.[1] This was followed by publication of *A Nation's Shame: Fatal Child*

---

[1] Child death review is a process in which a multidisciplinary team of professionals meets to share case information on individual deaths of children in order to improve investigation, provision of services, agencies' policies and prevention strategies, and, in cases of murder, criminal prosecution. It exists in all 50 states (at local levels in 38 states and at state level in 12 states).

Abuse and Neglect in the United States in 1994, issued by the U. S. Advisory Board on Child Abuse and Neglect (1995) and sponsored by the Administration for Children and Families.

This report came out at a time when there were increasing demands in the United States for national attention and policy to end fatal abuse. NCCAN followed this report with a Children's Justice Act grant to the American Bar Association to provide technical assistance, develop a training curriculum, and hold a national conference to promote CDRs. In 1996, Congress reauthorized CAPTA (P. L. 104-235) and included attention to fatal maltreatment through requirements for public disclosure of child maltreatment fatalities, restrictions on reuniting parents with children when those parents had killed another child, and the establishment of Citizens Review Panels (CRPs). These panels were authorized to review and make recommendations for improvements in the areas of child abuse fatalities, foster care and adoption, and prevention. CAPTA permitted existing review bodies, such as child fatality review teams, to serve as the states' CRPs. During these years, the Children's Bureau was not directly involved in efforts to address child abuse and neglect fatalities. Yet by the time NCCAN was dissolved and the new Office of Child Abuse and Neglect was established within the Children's Bureau in 1998, systems were in place to ensure a strong role for the Children's Bureau in addressing fatalities.

Since that time, the Children's Bureau has supported the development and continuance of fatality review teams at state and local levels. It supports the use of state Children's Justice Act and CAPTA funds for the development and maintenance of CDR. Many states would not likely have been able to establish their death review programs without these funds. As of 2011, 10 states continued to utilize portions of these funds to review and respond to child abuse fatalities. Coming full circle in a sense since 1912, the Maternal and Child Health Bureau (managing Title V block grants to states and now located within the Health Resources and Services Administration) began funding the National Center for the Review and Prevention of Child Deaths in 2002. This resource center provides training and technical support to all states to help establish and improve the review process. The center also manages a national CDR Case Reporting System. Currently, 41 states are voluntarily submitting all of their review data to this database. The Center also manages a number of other efforts in conjunction with the U. S. Centers for Disease Control and Prevention (CDC), to further study data in this system, especially related to violent deaths and sudden and unexplained infant deaths.

In 2011, the Administration on Children, Youth and Families, through the Children's Bureau, funded a new project in recognition of the expansion of other types of fatality reviews, including infant mortality and domestic violence reviews. This project was a one-year assessment of the state of the field in fatality reviews, an exploration of opportunities to improve coordination among reviews to improve child welfare, and an assessment of improvements to child welfare as a result of reviews. The project culminated in a national meeting of states in 2012 to share project findings and further advancements in the field of child fatality review.

Types of Child Maltreatment Fatality

Sadly, children die from many types of maltreatment, ranging from persistent torture and battering to neglect that results in fatal injury. One taxonomy classifies maltreatment deaths into five broad groups: infanticide and covert homicides; severe physical assaults; deliberate and overt homicides; neglect and deprivation; and deaths related to but not directly caused by maltreatment (Sidebotham, Bailey, Belderson, & Brandon, 2011). Examples from each classification are described in Table 8-1. Although deaths are classified into single categories, there can be overlap. Covert homicides are described as those in which the caregivers try to hide not only the death but the birth of a child, such as abandoning infants in trash containers. Overt homicides are those more commonly associated with physical abuse and child battering.

Table 8-1. A Taxonomy of Child Maltreatment Deaths

Classification	*Examples*
Infanticide and covert homicide[a]	Infants dying from hyperthermia when abandoned at birth; infants purposely suffocated; deaths occurring as a result of concealment of pregnancy; deaths resulting from in utero drug intoxication
Extreme neglect and deprivation	Deaths in which caregiver did not intend to kill but deliberately neglected the child, including deaths resulting from denial of food or from medical problems for which caretaker refused to seek medical attention
Severe physical assault	Deaths resulting from battering, beating, shaking, or other assault that was not intended to kill the child
Deliberate homicide[a]	Deaths in which the caretaker intended to kill the child, including shootings, strangulations, and beatings—often occur among children who are past infancy and may include the deaths of other family members
Death caused or contributed to by caretaker actions or neglect	Deaths resulting from accidental injury in which absent or poor supervision put the child in peril, such as drownings, fire deaths, suffocations in bedding, falls from windows, and accidental poisonings, and deaths in which a child should have been using a safety device (such as a car seat or bicycle helmet) but caregiver did not provide one

Source: Borrowed in part from a taxonomy suggested in Sidebotham, Bailey, Belderson, & Brandon (2011). pp. 301–302.

Classifying child maltreatment fatalities is complicated by the fact that some deaths are caused by acts of commission, such as violent assaults, while others are caused by acts of omission, such as poor supervision. There can also be overlap between these classifications, as some deaths may have multiple causes.

Classifying child deaths within a maltreatment framework is further complicated by the different standards, evidentiary requirements, and interpretations of criminal law, child welfare law, and public health frameworks. Deaths of children may or may not be classified as maltreatment depending on the entity doing the classification and reporting of the death. For example, a public health official would most likely describe a drowning death in which a child was unsupervised for a brief moment as neglect; a coroner or medical examiner would classify the death as an accident; child protective services (CPS) may take a report on the death (if, in fact, they are even alerted to it) but may not substantiate it as neglect; law enforcement may not make an arrest; and a prosecutor may not consider charges. Deaths due to neglect, whether from failure to supervise, provide appropriate medical attention, or provide other essentials such as food and shelter, are particularly challenging and often misclassified. Most states have their own laws and policies that dictate CPS and criminal decisions on the classification. The CDC published a set of public health definitions to guide the classification within a public health context for prevention (Lee, Paulozzi, Melanson, Simon, & Arias, 2008). Table 8-2 provides examples of how different agencies might classify and respond to different types of deaths.

Number of Child Maltreatment Fatalities

We do not know the true answer to the question of how many children die from maltreatment each year in the United States. Such deaths are routinely undercounted in most reporting systems, such as vital statistics data, CPS reports, and crime databases. A number of studies in the 1980s and early 1990s identified the problem of underreporting of child maltreatment fatalities on death certificates (Crume, DiGuiseppi, Byers, Sirotnak, & Garrett, 2002; Ewigman, Kivlahan, & Land, 1993; Herman-Giddens et al., 1999). One study found that maltreatment fatalities were classified on death certificates in the state of Colorado less than half of the time (Lee et al., 2008); while another found that in North Carolina child abuse homicides were under-reported by almost 60 percent (Crume et al., 2002). All of these studies found that child abuse homicides were incorrectly or ambiguously coded as natural, accidental, or undetermined deaths. The U.S. Advisory Board on Child Abuse and Neglect (1995) report *A Nation's Shame: Fatal Child Abuse and Neglect in the United States* estimated that 85 percent of childhood deaths from abuse and neglect are underreported:

> As a result of this misclassification and misdiagnosis, we do not have a reliable source to determine accurately why or exactly how many children die from

Table 8-2. Potential Differences in the Classification of Child Deaths by Different Agencies

Circumstances of Death	Probable Classification of Death, by Agency			
	Coroner	CPS	Police	Prosecutor
Fetal death; there is evidence of opiate exposure.	Accidental poisoning	Natural death—report screened out; fetal deaths are not considered live births	No report received	No report received
Toddler drowns in swimming pool during family party; adults were present but distracted.	Accidental drowning	Neglect due to poor supervision—report accepted and parent education provided	Accident—no arrest made due to the fact that family has suffered enough	No report received
Child dies from trauma to the brain; parent states child fell from couch.	Abusive head trauma, homicide	Child abuse—other children removed, case substantiated for abuse	Father arrested	Jury trial and conviction for felony child abuse
Three-year-old ingests mother's methadone, which was left on kitchen table.	Accidental poisoning	Neglect substantiated, services offered	No arrest; mother trying to beat drug addiction	No charges filed
Infant was found not breathing while wedged into pillows and sleeping in bed with intoxicated mother.	Undetermined cause	Neglect, suffocation. This is second child to die in similar circumstances. Mother had received parent education on safe sleep.	Arrest for neglect	Charges dropped due to belief that case not winnable given social norms regarding bed sharing

abuse and neglect. Each national information system is incomplete as a source of comprehensive information on child abuse and neglect deaths. Vital Statistics, the FBI's Uniform Crime Reports and the State Child Abuse Indices each track just one limited part of the picture. (p. xxvii)

The U.S. Government Accountability Office (GAO) was commissioned by Congress to study the undercounting of fatalities as reported to the National Child Abuse and Neglect Data System (NCANDS). Their report, issued in July 2011, found that

more children have likely died from maltreatment than are reflected in the national estimate of 1,770 child fatalities for fiscal year 2009. According to our survey, child welfare officials in 28 states thought that the official number of child maltreatment fatalities in their state was probably or possibly an undercount. . . . It is estimated that every year in the United States, approximately 2,500 children die at the hands of their caregivers. (GAO, 2011, p. 9)

There are many reasons for this undercount, none of which have yet been remedied on a national scale. Some of these reasons were discussed above—absence of definitions, inconsistent application of existing definitions, differing legal standards, and lack of consensus among disciplines as to how deaths should be classified. Another reason is that death investigations are inconsistent, sometimes ineffective, and may not be carried out at all. Investigations can be made especially difficult because many forms of fatal maltreatment can be easily disguised by perpetrators as accidents or misinterpreted by investigators as due to other causes. Sometimes there is insufficient medical evidence to classify a death as maltreatment. And the multiple sources of reports on child deaths, none of which captures all of the deaths, are not coordinated.

The GAO report focused on the latter problem. As discussed previously, death certificates have been shown to be a poor source for obtaining accurate death data. In a survey of state child welfare agencies, the GAO study also found great discrepancies in the manner in which fatalities are reported to NCANDS. Twenty-four states reported that they do not include deaths of children previously unknown to CPS in their NCANDS reports. A study of child maltreatment deaths in Michigan found that the state's uniform crime reporting database of police reports correctly reported 26 fatal abuse assaults in one year (as did other state reporting sources), but had no records of the three times as many neglect-related deaths that same year (Schnitzer, Covington, Wirtz, Palusci, & Verhoef-Ofetedahl, 2008).

Efforts to Better Count Child Deaths from Maltreatment

The CDC funded three states' efforts to design models to improve the counting of child maltreatment fatalities using public health surveillance approaches. The three states (California, Michigan, and Rhode Island) all compared the maltreatment deaths found in multiple sources, including death certificates, hospital records, crime reports, CPS records, and CDRs. They found that no source captured all of the deaths and that only by gathering data from all sources could a more complete count of maltreatment deaths be attained. The states also found that CDR captured the highest number of cases but still did not identify all deaths.

In 2001, the U. S. Maternal and Child Health Bureau funded the National Center for Child Death Review (NCCDR) to provide training and technical assistance in building and sustaining review programs. The Center has developed and implemented a national CDR Case Reporting System, in use by 40 states as of January 2012, that collects comprehensive information on deaths including those caused by abuse and neglect. The CDC is funding a pilot study to match data from its National Violent Death Case Reporting System in 16 states with CDR data to determine how well deaths are being captured by both systems (personal communication with T. Covington, executive director, NCCDR).

The GAO report (2011) said that officials from 23 states reported that they need additional assistance in collecting and reporting on child abuse and neglect deaths, including assistance with multidisciplinary coordination across data sources. It made four recommendations for executive action at the national level to improve the collection of data on child maltreatment:

1. Identify ways to help states strengthen the completeness and reliability of data they report to NCANDS. These efforts could include identifying and sharing states' best practices, particularly those that foster cross-agency coordination and help address differences in state definitions and interpretation of maltreatment and/or privacy and confidentiality concerns.
2. Expand, as appropriate, the type and amount of information HHS makes public on the circumstances surrounding child fatalities from maltreatment.Use stronger mechanisms to routinely share analyses and expertise with HHS partners on the circumstances of child maltreatment deaths, including insights that could be used for developing prevention strategies.
3. Estimate the costs and benefits of collecting national data on near fatalities and take appropriate follow-up actions. (GAO, 2011, p. 35).

Children Most at Risk of a Child Maltreatment Fatality

Evidence suggests that one cannot predict precisely which children are most at risk of dying from maltreatment or which caregivers are more likely to kill their children. We still do not know why some caregivers respond with extreme violence to normal child-rearing challenges while other parents can handle them without resorting to violence, or why some parents supervise their children diligently while others do not. Many child maltreatment deaths are unintended, in that the children's caregivers did not set out to kill them although they may have meant them harm. It is likely that the characteristics of these children and their caregivers are much the same as those who are abused and who abuse without a fatal outcome.

NCANDS data indicate that in 2009 a little more than half of all child homicide victims were under the age of one and that at least 80 percent were under the age of four (U.S. Department of Health and Human Services [HHS], 2007). An estimated one-half of all infant maltreatment deaths occur by four months of age (Overpeck, Brenner, & Trumble, 1998). Neglect was the cause of death in 35.8 percent of these deaths, physical abuse in 23.3 percent, and multiple forms of neglect in 36.7 percent, although these causes are not mutually exclusive. The vast majority of physical abuse deaths are due to head trauma.

Caregiver characteristics differ depending on the age of the child and type of death. Women are more likely to commit infanticide (either physical abuse or neglect) in the first six months and fatal neglect at all ages, while men are most often perpetrators of all forms of physical abuse. Studies of infanticide, and more specifically neonaticide (killing shortly after birth), have focused on women. Mental health disorders, personal experience as victims of maltreatment, and poor prenatal care are characteristics of women who commit neonaticide (Overpeck et al., 1998; Paulozzi, 2002; Spinelli, 2001, 2002).

Some characteristics of mothers who commit infanticide or fatally neglect their children have been identified: young age, low level of education, social isolation, poor prenatal care, unmarried status, and low income. Characteristics of infants who are more likely to be victims of infanticide include low birth weight, premature birth, drug exposure, male sex, and low Apgar score (Cummings, Theis, & Mueller, 1994). Caregiver risks associated with physical abuse include young age (under 20), low income, and presence of a nonbiological caregiver in the residence (Anderson et al., 1983; Overpeck et al., 1998). Recent studies have found that children living with unrelated adults (usually a parent's romantic partner) were 27 times more likely to die of maltreatment than children in homes with two biological parents (Schnitzer & Ewigman, 2005).

A high percentage of children who die from abuse or neglect have had prior contact with child welfare services. For example, NCANDS data indicate that in 2007, children whose families had received family preservation services within the child welfare system in the past five years accounted for 11.9 percent of child fatalities. Slightly more than 2 percent of the children who died had been in foster care and had been reunited with their families in the past five years (HHS, 2009). Recent evidence indicates that children reported as having experienced nonfatal maltreatment have a higher risk for intentional and unintentional injuries (accidents) during their first year of life. One study estimated that children associated with a prior allegation of maltreatment died from a later intentional injury at 5.9 times the rate of children with no reports, and from unintentional injuries at twice the rate of other children (Putnam-Hornstein, 2011). It is unclear if the association between prior contacts with CPS and fatality means that child welfare is doing a good job identifying high-risk families or if it means that the children died because the system failed to recognize the fatal risks earlier and take the correct action. Either way, these findings suggest that there may be opportunities for improved case identification, assessment, protection, and prevention.

Efforts to Better Understand Maltreatment Deaths and Improve Agency Policies and Practices

Most states began establishing CDR teams in the early 1990s. The growth of CDR teams was accelerated in the 1990s through the support of the Children's Bureau and the Department of Justice. Standardized protocols, model legislation, and trainings were made available to states and communities with federal funding support to the American Bar Association. The Children's Bureau supported states' use of their federal Children's Justice Act and CAPTA funding for the development and support of death review processes. In the early 1990s, most CDR programs were located in state social service agencies. This led to the widespread expansion of CDR teams such that today every state has a comprehensive CDR program. And as mentioned earlier, the NCCDR has developed and implemented a national CDR Case Reporting System (Covington, 2011).

Around the same time, states were establishing CAPTA CRPs at the state or local level. Some states established joint CDR–CRP teams,[2] which conduct intensive case reviews of child maltreatment deaths and issue reports with recommendations for system improvements. The majority of state child welfare agencies are also conducting their own internal reviews of child deaths due to maltreatment, and some coordinate these findings with state CDR and CRP findings to improve practice and policy. Some states utilize their office of the child advocate or children's ombudsman to conduct independent case reviews of maltreatment fatalities.

Comprehensive review of a case enables a state or community to study the complex set of circumstances leading up to and causing the child's death. The actions of the caregivers and child; the child's environment; the role of agencies in the early identification of harm, provision of services, and response to the death are discussed in detail. Quality reviews should lead to recommendations in a number of areas including

- early identification of risks and harm
- appropriate reporting, intake, and assessment of harm for children at risk

---

[2] As of 2012, the states with combined CDR-CRP panels are Florida, Georgia, Illinois, Indiana, Iowa, Kansas, Maryland, Michigan, Missouri, New Hampshire, New Jersey, North Dakota, Oklahoma, South Carolina, Texas, Virginia, and Wisconsin.

- effective services for caregivers, children, and the community
- comprehensive and multidisciplinary investigations of fatalities
- accurate determinations of cause and manner of death and accurate reporting across disciplines
- appropriate actions by the criminal justice system in responding to the deaths and protecting other children from further harm
- development of effective prevention strategies

One national study collected recommendations from reviews in 2000–2009 in 27 states. Over 300 recommendations for change from child fatality teams reviews of child maltreatment deaths were grouped into 11 categories (Douglas & Cunningham, 2008). A number of these recommendations were directed specifically at improvements to agency practices. Douglas and Cunningham (2008) concluded their study with the following observation:

> When combined, the recommendations paint a picture of problems that plague the professions that respond to child maltreatment in the US. The recommendations that were summarized in this paper deserve serious attention, as they reflect the failures of the nation's social service system, as identified by those working "in the trenches," with, fatal maltreatment. (p. 347)

A number of states are very systematic in how they document their case findings and use their reviews to implement systems change in policy and practice. For example, Illinois law requires that findings related to maltreatment deaths be reported to the state director of human services and a response be provided within 90 days. Nevada conducted intensive case reviews of over 100 suspected abuse and neglect deaths, resulting in a blue-ribbon panel that developed a multiyear state plan to address the findings and recommendations from these reviews. A major finding was that a large number of deaths were never reported to CPS, and that among those that were reported, adequate risk and safety assessments were not conducted for surviving children. A large percent of children who died were also known to the system, and the reviews of their case histories also found many lost opportunities to follow up on recommendations for services and treatments for the caregivers. Table 8-3 describes a number of key findings and the action plans developed to address them.

As these review processes are relatively new, there have only been a scattering of published studies demonstrating the power of reviews to better count maltreatment deaths, improve understanding of them, and improve services and policies. One paper described the outcomes of the Michigan Child Death Review Team's Citizen Review Panel on Child Maltreatment Fatality (Palusci, Yager, & Covington, 2010). This team uses a systematic method to identify problems with the child welfare system associated with mal-

Table 8-3. Improving the Child Welfare System Following Intensive Child Death Case Reviews: The Michigan Citizen Review Panel on Child Fatality

Finding from Death Case Review	Problem with System	Change Made following Recommendation
Failure among medical professionals to diagnose and report suspected abuse or neglect	Noncompliance	Statewide training for physicians
Unaddressed mental health needs leading to the death of a child	Inadequate policy	New protocol for family assessment by foster care agencies
Lack of accuracy or consistency by medical examiners in categorizing cause or manner of sudden, unexpected deaths in children	Poor practice	New state protocol to determine cause and manner of sudden child deaths
Inappropriate screening out of complaints and delay in acceptance of complaints and case assignment	Noncompliance	New CPS peer review program
Unacceptable time lapses between assignment and contact with families	Noncompliance	New CPS peer review program
Failure of CPS supervisor to sign off on child abuse/neglect assessments and/or to review the case materials in accordance with established procedures	Noncompliance	New mandatory CPS supervisor training
Poor communication among law enforcement and Michigan Department of Human Services (MDHS) and failure to perform joint investigation resulting in the whole picture of the child and family's condition not being properly investigated	Poor practice	New protocol for joint investigation; development of Child Advocacy Centers
Inaccurate assessment and improper coding of the five-tiered system	Poor practice	New training at CPS training institute for new hires
Failure to perform complete investigations regarding medically fragile children	Poor practice	New protocol and training sessions on medically fragile infants and Munchausen syndrome by proxy
Failure to comply with policy that positive drug screen in newborn requires automatic finding of preponderance of evidence of failure to protect	Noncompliance	New birth match system linking birth certificates with CPS records

(Continued)

Table 8-3. Improving the Child Welfare System Following Intensive Child Death Case Reviews: The Michigan Citizen Review Panel on Child Fatality (*Continued*)

Finding from Death Case Review	Problem with System	Change Made following Recommendation
Failure to properly investigate for complaints when otherwise indicated because of inability to contact parents without evidence of due diligence	Noncompliance	New protocols for joint investigation and multiple complaints
Failure of worker to properly assess well-being of child(ren) in the home or recognize imminent danger and take protective custody	Poor practice	New protocol for joint investigation
Failure to recognize and respond to parents' repeated and clear indications that they do not want the child(ren)	Poor practice	Passage of Safe Delivery Act allowing parents to safely leave infants at hospitals and other facilities
Safety assessment completed incorrectly or not at all	Noncompliance	Statewide CPS training on assessment tools and data system upgrades
Risk assessment completed incorrectly or not at all	Noncompliance	Statewide CPS training on assessment tools and data system upgrades
Totality of case inaccessible to the caseworker, including timelines, substantiations and unfounded reports	Other issues	Data system upgrades
Failure to cooperate with or coordinate investigations with day-care licensing officials	Poor practice	New mandatory CPS supervisor training
Failure to remove subsequent children after a finding of preponderance in infants with positive toxicology results	Noncompliance	New mandatory CPS supervisor training
Improperly returning a child to a home that had lost its foster care license	Noncompliance	Data system upgrades
Criminal history check incomplete or not done at all	Noncompliance	New terminals for criminal history checks placed in CPS offices

Table 8-3. Improving the Child Welfare System Following Intensive Child Death Case Reviews: The Michigan Citizen Review Panel on Child Fatality (*Continued*)

Finding from Death Case Review	Problem with System	Change Made following Recommendation
Failure of courts, investigators, or guardian ad litem to access complete CPS file, leading to poor decision making	Poor practice	Amendment of Juvenile Code requiring L-GAL to complete independent investigation
Failure of MDHS to provide important information to court or failure of court to share important information with CPS	Poor practice	Data system upgrades

Source: Adapted from Palusci, Yager, & Covington (2010).

treatment deaths. They submit their findings with recommendations to the state child welfare agency. The state agency analyzes the feasibility and appropriateness of all the recommendations; it provides a written response to the state CDR team with its justifications for not implementing some of the recommendations and its plans for implementing others. The state tracked the implementation of six years of recommendations based on specific findings of problems with the child welfare system. It tracked the number of deaths associated with each finding and found a significant decrease in deaths associated with specific systems problems when the state implemented their recommendations. There was a 35 percent decrease in findings of problems and a 9 percent decrease in the number of deaths associated with those findings (Palusci et al., 2010).

Implications for Child Protection Workers

A number of important lessons for case workers can be distilled from the findings in the case reviews described earlier. They include the following:

- Meet your community's death investigators, including your medical examiner or coroner and your homicide or child abuse detectives. Encourage them to report all child fatalities to you so that you can conduct your own background search on family histories.
- Pay attention not only to physical abuse fatalities but also to children who die in accidents and from unexpected medical complications of illnesses. Don't screen these cases out because they do not fit the standard of physical abuse. Seek information on the circumstances in these deaths and share CPS case histories with investigators.

- Be persistent in locating the histories of families of fatality victims, especially if they are new to your jurisdiction.
- Recognize that multiple noninvestigated or unsubstantiated reports can be a marker for children at risk for neglect or chronic abuse and pay special attention to these reports. Seek a supervisor's oversight when there are multiple reports on caregivers.
- Conduct a complete risk and safety assessment when warranted, and never manipulate the scoring system to avoid opening a case for a child at risk.
- When conducting an investigation on a child at risk, pay attention to the co-occurrence of domestic violence, animal abuse, physical abuse, and poor supervision and other forms of neglect.
- When you develop a service plan for caregivers, make sure referrals are followed up on, appointments are kept, and the service plan is adhered to. Follow up diligently as needed to ensure caregiver compliance, and coordinate with other agencies as necessary to ensure services are obtained.
- Don't hesitate to educate and inform other service providers on the signs of abuse and neglect. Engage them as your partners in the early identification of harm.
- Always seek supervisor input when you need help with decision making.
- Document all assessments, recommendations, interactions and outcomes completely.
- Take care of yourself and seek help when the cases overwhelm your own well-being.

The Case for Systems Change and a Focus on Primary Prevention

Many of the processes described above address problems with specific agency policies and practices and at times even with individual professional behaviors. Identifying and improving policies and practices within the child welfare system are important steps in the prevention of child deaths. It is also important, however, to focus on broader systems improvements and primary prevention.

There is evidence supporting the effectiveness of many well-known and universally accepted prevention interventions for child abuse and neglect (Palusci & Haney, 2010). Some of these include improvements in child welfare interventions to children already harmed, and primary intervention services for families at risk, including parent education, home visitation, family wellness programs, and family-based parenting interventions. Over the last 30 years, a vast amount of research has been conducted both on how to prevent maltreatment from occurring and on how to curb maltreatment once it has begun. For many of the millions of children reported as abused or neglected to public CPS agencies, lives are improved and families are strengthened because of these interventions. For many others who may not be helped, it is not because of a lack of knowledge on how to protect children from abuse and neglect.

Unfortunately, much of this knowledge has not been acted on because the costs of implementing change can be high—child protection is labor intensive. There also are great differences in the capacity of each state's social safety net to broaden support to families and protect children by fostering safe neighborhoods, good schools, well-paying jobs, and easy access to health and social services—all elements in preventing child abuse and neglect. Consequently, some states actually do have lower incidences of child maltreatment and maltreatment deaths, resulting both from stronger social systems emphasizing prevention and from stronger CPS, characterized by lower staff caseloads, well-trained workers and supervisors, easier access to treatment services, and higher degrees of cooperation with colleagues from other systems that have a role in protecting children.

What is less known and understood are interventions that can prevent maltreatment deaths. As review processes better understand the circumstances of maltreatment deaths, our understanding of the interplay between deaths and child welfare policies and services will improve, but it is fair to state that understanding of how to prevent maltreatment deaths is still in its infancy. The reviews do, however, provide a great deal of information as to the role of child welfare generally, and they suggest the need for much greater coordination across systems.

So, while taking a degree of comfort from the knowledge that much of what we already are doing does protect children, and that if there were enough money to bring every CPS agency into compliance with national standards a reduction in maltreatment would follow, we still must acknowledge that, as now constituted, the child welfare system has been unable to prevent the murders of at least 2,700 children each year, and probably many more.

Most of this chapter focuses on protecting children at imminent risk of fatal maltreatment injuries. For many of them, the time for early intervention and prevention has passed, and it is only when the entire child welfare system works in a coordinated fashion that their lives may be saved. Many reviews of child maltreatment deaths identify profound failures in interagency communication and coordination surrounding children at risk. We believe that over the next 100 years, attention to children must focus on forging close working relationships with other systems, characterized by deep and specific coordination of their respective policies, resources, and individual case practices. Only then can the protection everyone wants for highly vulnerable children be achieved. The following sections summarize important system changes that must occur among all agencies working in child welfare. They are consistent with the recommendations for policy and practice generated by the review programs described previously.

Improving Cross-System Coordination and Integration

Intense cross-system coordination of the response to children already known by CPS to be at the highest risk can significantly reduce maltreatment fatalities for these children.

Of the approximately 3 million children reported as abused or neglected each year, fewer than 1 percent are in mortal danger—but even that small percentage equals thousands of children. Even so, since many of the deaths occur in households in which neglect rather than physical abuse was reported—the vast majority of all cases—it is a challenge, though not impossible, to accurately identify many of the households at the greatest risk.

As stated previously, the families most at risk of abuse or neglect have parents who are poor, young, and without a high school diploma. Many parents that fit this description do not physically harm their children. Frequently, however, there are other risk factors present that should receive special attention, including domestic violence (actual or threatened), mental illness, substance abuse, a prison record, or prior involvement with CPS in another jurisdiction. Improving communication and record sharing across all agencies that are familiar with these families will better identify and protect children at risk. The benefits of cross-system coordination are illustrated by the establishment of formal Children's Advocacy Centers (CACs) across the United States, which bring together different local systems of protection in a structured and staffed effort to provide protection to a child in one setting. The CAC movement has grown to include more than 700 centers serving almost 300,000 children annually in over 2,000 counties, covering about two-thirds of local jurisdictions in the United States. CACs are funded by the Department of Justice and local, state, and private funds. Most are affiliated with the National Children's Alliance in Washington, DC, a nonprofit organization that accredits local CACs, develops best practice standards, conducts training and ongoing staff development, conducts research, publishes articles and other materials, and provides technical assistance to local CACs.

The CAC model has been evaluated extensively and shown to be effective when intervening in many cases of sex abuse. It is possible that with sufficient time and additional resources, CACs could adapt their well-developed child sexual abuse model to include intervening rapidly when potentially life-threatening situations of physical abuse and neglect are brought to their attention. While the problem of sex abuse is different from child fatality, the process and players needed to protect a child are remarkably similar, in large part because each involves civil and criminal legal proceedings to protect children and hold abusers criminally liable. CACs bring together a multidisciplinary team comprising of law enforcement, CPS, prosecution, medical, mental health, and victim advocacy practitioners. The challenge is whether it could incorporate child fatalities as part of its mission and whether it could be adequately funded to do so.

Coordination of Case Reports

It is well documented that the true count of maltreatment fatalities can only be obtained when case records are matched across agencies (Schnitzer, Covington, Wirtz, Palusci, & Verhoef-Oftedahl, 2008). Formal systems should be put in place to ensure the linking of case records so that fatalities as well as high-risk children are better identified. Barriers to the sharing of case information across agencies need to be eliminated rather than built higher under the banner of privacy protection. Child death reviews are an important first step in synthesizing case records on deceased children. An important next step will be the development of interagency data-sharing agreements to protect living children at high risk. A number of states and communities have begun this process. For example, in Michigan, the state departments of health and social services agreed to electronically link real-time health department birth records with a social services roster of caregivers who have had their rights terminated or who have previously killed a child. When an electronic link is made between a birth and a caregiver, an email alert is sent to the CPS office in the county in which the birth occurred. This email triggers a CPS safety assessment of the newborn infant. This system has proven to be highly effective in identifying very-high-risk infants, such that approximately 30 percent of all birth matches lead to further CPS actions to protect the infants.

Identifying Risks and Supporting High-Risk Families

Half or more of all child maltreatment fatalities occur among children who were unknown to CPS or other systems, seemingly almost at random. For these children, different approaches may help identify their risks. For example, unrelated adult males have been shown, in at least one study, to be more than 50 times more likely to be involved in a killing than a related adult male (Schnitzer & Ewigman, 2005). This points to the need to develop support and interventions targeting caretakers. For prevention to be effective, much more research is needed in identifying which families and households are at greatest risk of a fatal event and what specifically can help support them. Home visitation services can be important, especially if they are provided immediately after the birth of a child to families with risk profiles for possible maltreatment. Wide-scale home visitation programs will soon be in place in every state as a result of the 2010 Affordable Care Act. These services are effective in defusing risky circumstances at the earliest stages of parenthood.

Ensuring a Rapid Response to Fatalities

Preparing for a rapid, coordinated local response to a possible fatal child injury is a challenge given how few such cases occur in any one local jurisdiction. Sometimes years may pass between fatalities or near fatalities. And because only half or fewer of fatalities occur among children previously known to the child protection system, there are even fewer severe, high-risk cases for which to prepare a rapid response. A somewhat parallel situation faces fire departments: in many jurisdictions, fires are relatively rare, yet the consequences of fire can be so severe that the department gears up to fight the most severe fires even if they occur infrequently. This effort typically includes forming relationships with other agencies. Similarly, a child death by maltreatment is such an unacceptable event that comprehensive planning and assignment of clear roles and responsibilities is a must. One notable example is the State Technical Assistance Team in the state of Missouri, which makes highly trained experts from law enforcement, CPS, and forensics available around the clock to local communities to assist in child maltreatment and fatality investigations.

Improving the Differential Response to Abuse and Neglect

Bringing more protective interventions to bear on the most serious maltreatment cases is not a new idea. For more than a decade, a number of states have implemented a differential response model in CPS, which attempts to sort cases according to the severity of the presenting problem and then respond accordingly. This generally means a more community-based response to less urgent cases, and greater collaboration with other systems, especially law enforcement in the most serious cases. There is a growing literature showing the benefits of a differential response in preventing further abuse and enabling children to remain safely with their families.

Improving Civil and Criminal Court Interventions

It is critical to implement policies and programs that will improve the lives of families early on and prevent child maltreatment. But many of the case reviews of maltreatment deaths have found that real-time actions related to individual cases should have occurred to prevent further harm to a child, and in many cases, death. There are many cases in which it is apparent that a child is at serious risk and the question is how to bring the civil and criminal authorities to intervene in what has become a clear public safety issue. Child protective agencies have the power to activate a judicial process that can result in children being moved from their home into protective custody. This is a powerful authority, which can lead to termination of parental rights. In order to allow for the immediate removal of a child from a home where there is a known or suspected abuser, the standard of proof—usually a preponderance of the evidence—is intentionally lower than in a criminal case. There the standard of proof—beyond a reasonable doubt—is much higher, since imprisonment may result. But this lower standard of proof is also an extraordinarily powerful tool in the protection of children, because it can remove the suspected perpetrator from the child's home by a restraining order or, eventually, by arrest and incarceration.

When the System Fails and How It Can Be Improved

The following passage provides an example, drawn from a real case, of the challenges facing both children and the community that wishes to protect them, a case in which a fragmented and uncoordinated application of powerful laws and resources allowed a small girl to slip through the safety net meant to protect her. It is not an uncommon story (Maine Department of Human Services, 1984a, 1984b).

CPS had been involved with Jim Jones's various families for several years, in all three of his marriages. In each case, a child was seriously injured and physical force was used against his wife or another woman. One child was removed from the home. After the third assault, Jones was arrested and the district attorney brought criminal charges against him.

Pending his trial, CPS received a call from the hospital that two-year-old Mary Jones had been seriously abused. Upon investigation by the district attorney, state police, and CPS, it was discovered that Mary also had been seen months earlier in the hospital with severe bruising, but no one had called Social Services. It was also discovered that two years earlier another of Mr. Jones's children had been admitted to the hospital because of a skull fracture. Referrals to CPS by the hospital were slow in coming. Eventually, CPS was granted a preliminary protection petition to temporarily remove the child from her family with parent visits to be supervised.

Additional indictments were brought against Mr. Jones. Then, when CPS decided to seek more permanent custody of Mary, because of Mr. Jones's frequent visits to the home even though he was supposed to stay away, and because both parents and Mrs. Jones's mother, a frequent caretaker for Mary, denied any abuse had occurred, the presiding judge ordered that the permanent custody hearing be postponed for six months until the criminal proceedings against Mr. Jones were resolved.

Mary remained in foster care while Mr. Jones was free on bail. Six months later, even though Jones's criminal charges had not been resolved, the long delayed permanent custody hearing took place, and Social Services was ordered to retain legal custody while also returning Mary to her mother over Social Services's objection. Again, Mr. Jones was ordered to maintain a separate residence—but not to stay away from Mary's home. During this time, Jones's lawyer advised him not to participate in any counseling or meetings with CPS since it would amount to admission of guilt during his forthcoming trial for the earlier injuries to his children.

The judge in the custody hearing instructed Social Services to return in not sooner than six months, unless Mary was once again assaulted before then. The CPS worker and the CPS attorney, while unhappy with the order to return Mary to her home, were reluctant to challenge the judge. They sought neither an amendment to the judge's order nor an appeal to a higher court. The CPS worker was in and out of the home. Six months later, with no further harm to the child, all parties agreed that legal custody of Mary be restored to Mrs. Jones, who said she did not intend to reunite with Mr. Jones. He was not mentioned in the judicial order that ordered CPS to supervise the situation for six months.

A month after CPS's last visit, Mary was killed in her home and Mr. Jones was charged with her murder. Twenty months had elapsed from the time charges were brought against him to the time of Mary's death. Jones was never tried for the earlier charges. Seven trial dates were set, and seven continuances requested by the defense attorneys were granted by the judge without question and with no objections by the prosecutor. Subsequently, Jones was sentenced to life in prison.

To those who work in child protection, there is nothing extraordinary about this case. Indeed, it could have been much more complicated: There was no known substance abuse, there was only one direct abuser in the household, and while family income was modest, the family was neither impoverished nor living in squalor. Yet the community was ill prepared to protect Mary. The simultaneous need to protect Mary and to bring Jones to justice for his earlier violence created competition between two complex systems—the civil system, which could have kept Mary safe from Jones by removing her from the home as long as needed, and the criminal system, which could have kept Jones away from Mary by trying, convicting, and incarcerating him.

The private physician who suspected abuse and the emergency room physicians who confirmed it could have made more timely reports to CPS. CPS should not have relied on an inexperienced lawyer to represent its position in court, and its policies were not clear about appealing a court decision it opposed. The police could have better enforced a restraining order directing Jones to stay away from Mary. The defense attorney's repeated stalling of Jones's trial was a factor in Mary's death. In the end it did not help Jones, now in prison for life.

In short, the juncture at which all of the different systems meant to protect children are meant to converge failed. Cross-system coordination was strictly informal—there was no written memorandum of understanding among the different parties, no full sharing of information, no single case plan, and no mutual accountability among professionals.

In many jurisdictions there are multidisciplinary teams that do possess the coordinating vehicle needed to protect children. Written cross-system protocols exist, and the entire protective capacity of a community is drawn together to serve the child. Nothing less is required to reduce the endless killing of children. But in many communities there is no such coordinated rapid response to a child in dire danger.

This chapter does not propose an expansion of the criminal justice system's involvement in the vast majority of maltreatment cases that are best left to the family, the community, CPS, and the civil legal system. With adequate funding for manageable caseloads, prevention and treatment services, and staff training, and a heavier emphasis on a public health model of support for families, there would be little need for law enforcement to become involved in most cases. But, in the most high-risk cases an aggressive response by police, prosecutors, and the criminal courts to violent abusers is essential for reducing fatalities and near fatalities.

Need for Coordinated National Action

Excellent work is already being done along similar lines to those proposed here. But child fatalities demand a coordinated cross-system response in every jurisdiction as well as development of and experimentation with different models as needed. As potentially useful as the CAC model might be, there may be other approaches that could succeed, and indeed may already be in place and functioning as intended.

The authors of this chapter are both members of the national Coalition to End Child Abuse Deaths, whose members include the National Children's Alliance, the National District Attorneys Association, and the National Association of Social Workers. Since its formation in 2010, the coalition helped prompt the GAO study of data collection on child abuse deaths and has met with the Children's Bureau and the federal Administration on Children, Youth and Families, briefed White House staff, conducted congressional staff briefings, testified at a Congressional hearing on maltreatment fatalities, and worked with congressional sponsors to introduce legislation creating a national commission to end child abuse deaths.

We are encouraging the Children's Bureau to fund new research on maltreatment fatalities. An inventory and review of existing written cross-system protocols would be useful, as would studies to better profile the characteristics of those who have killed a child. Many risk-profile and risk-assessment instruments have been developed, but we are unaware of any that specifically address factors common in fatalities. It will also be important for the Children's Bureau to continue its collaborative efforts with other federal agencies working on child maltreatment prevention, including with the Health Resources Services Administration and the Centers for Disease Control and Prevention.

Conclusion

No doubt the existing constellation of agencies working to protect children prevents many child abuse deaths each year. But with more than 2,500 such deaths occurring annually, much more needs to be done. While the incompleteness of current knowledge will limit the number of deaths that can be prevented, we are certain that even within limited budgets a renewed focus on stopping maltreatment fatalities can be successful.

Ensuring that primary prevention programs are implemented and that efforts to protect children at risk are better coordinated is the best way to honor the memories of the 2,500 and more children who will die every year in the United States in ways not imaginable to most Americans.

References

Anderson, A., Ambrosino, R., Valentine, D., & Lauderdale, M. (1983). Child deaths attributed to abuse and neglect: An empirical study. *Children and Youth Services Review, 5,* 75–79.

Child Abuse Prevention and Treatment Act of 1974, P.L. 93-247, 88 Stat. 4 (1974).

Child Abuse Prevention and Treatment Act Amendments of 1996, P.L. 104-235, 110 Stat. 3063 (1996).

Children's Justice and Assistance Act of 1986, P. L. 99-401, 100 Stat. 903 (1986).

Covington, T. (2011). The US national child death review case reporting system. *Injury Prevention, 17*(Supplement 1), 34–37.

Crume, T. L., DiGuiseppi, C., Byers, T., Sirotnak, A., & Garrett, C. (2002). Under ascertainment of child maltreatment fatalities by death certificates, 1990–1998. *Pediatrics, 110,* e18.

Cummings, P., Theis, M., & Mueller, B. (1994). Infant injury death in Washington state, 1981 through 1990. *Archives of Pediatrics & Adolescent Medicine, 148,* 1021–1026.

Douglas, E., & Cunningham, J. (2008). Recommendation from child fatality review teams: Results of a nationwide exploratory study concerning maltreatment fatalities and social service delivery. *Child Abuse Review, 12,* 331–351.

Ewigman, B., Kivlahan, C., & Land G. (1993). The Missouri Child Fatality Study: Underreporting of maltreatment fatalities among children younger than five years of age, 1983 through 1986. *Pediatrics, 91,* 330–337.

Herman-Giddens, M. E., et al. (1999). Under ascertainment of child abuse mortality in the United States. *JAMA, 281,* 463–467.

Hutchins, V. (1994). Maternal and Child Health Bureau: Roots. *Pediatrics, 94,* 695–702

Lee, R., Paulozzi, L., Melanson, C., Simon, T., & Arias, I. (2008). *Child maltreatment surveillance: Uniform definitions for public health and recommended data elements, version 1.0.* Atlanta: Centers for Disease Control and Prevention, National Center for Injury Control and Prevention.

Maine Department of Human Services. (1984a). *Child protective report on the death of Garrianna Quinn, April 9.* Augusta, ME: Author.

Maine Department of Human Services. (1984b). *Protecting our children: Not without changes in the legal system, The Report of the Governor's Working Group on Child Abuse and Neglect Proceedings.* Augusta, ME: Author.

Maternal and Infancy (Sheppard-Towner) Act of 1921, P.L. 67-97, ch. 135, 42 Stat. 224 (1921).

Overpeck, M., Brenner, R., & Trumble, A. (1998). Risk factors for infant homicide in the United States. *New England Journal of Medicine, 339,* 1211–1216.

Palusci, V., & Haney, M. (2010, Winter). Strategies to prevent child maltreatment and integration into practice. *APSAC Advisor,* pp. 8–17.

Palusci, V. J., Yager, S., & Covington, T. M. (2010). Effects of a citizens review panel in preventing child maltreatment fatalities. *Child Abuse & Neglect, 34,* 324–331.

Paulozzi, L. 2002. Variation in homicide risk during infancy—United States, 1989–1998. *Morbidity and Mortality Weekly Report, 51,* 187–189.

Putnam-Hornstein, E. (2011). Report of maltreatment as a riskfactor for injury death: A prospective birth cohort study. *Child Maltreatment, 16*(3), 163–174.

Schnitzer, P., Covington, T., Wirtz, S., Palusci, V., & Verhoef-Ofetedahl, W. (2008). Public health surveillance of fatal child maltreatment: Analysis of three state programs. *American Journal of Public Health, 98,* 296–303.

Schnitzer, P., & Ewigman, B. (2005). Child deaths resulting in inflicted injuries: Household risk factors and perpetrator characteristics. *Pediatrics, 116,* 687–693.

Sidebotham, P., Bailey, S., Belderson, P., & Bradnon, M.(2011). Fatal child maltreatment in England, 2005–2009. *Child Abuse & Neglect, 35,* 299–306.

Spinelli, M. G. (2001). A systematic investigation of 16 cases of neonaticide. *American Journal of Psychiatry, 158,* 811–813.

Spinelli, M. G. (2002). *Infanticide: Psychosocial and legal perspectives on mothers who kill.* Washington, DC: American Psychiatric Association.

Social Security Act of 1935, ch. 531, 49 Stat. 620 (1935).

Theerman, P. (2010). Julia Lathrop and the Children's Bureau. *American Journal of Public Health, 100,* 1589–1590. doi: 10.2105/AJPH.2009.188185

U.S. Advisory Board on Child Abuse and Neglect. (1995). *A nation's shame: Fatal child abuse and neglect in the United States* [Executive summary]. Washington, DC: Author.

U.S. Department of Health and Human Services, Administration for Children and Families, Children's Bureau. (2007). *Child maltreatment.* Washington, DC: Author.

U.S. Department of Health and Human Services, Administration for Children and Families, Children's Bureau. (2009). *Child maltreatment.* Washington, DC: Author.

U.S. Department of Labor, Children's Bureau. (1914). *Baby saving campaigns: A preliminary report on what American cities are doing to prevent infant mortality* (4th ed.) (Infant Mortality Series No. 1, Bureau Publication No. 3). Washington, DC: Authors Retrieved from http://archive.org/stream/babysavingcampai00unit/babysaving-campai00unit_djvu.txt (Section 12).

U.S. Government Accountability Office. (2011, July). *Child maltreatment: Strengthening national data on child fatalities could aid in prevention* (Publication No. GAO-11-599). Retrieved from GAO Reports Main Page via GPO Access database: http://www.gpoaccess.gov/gaoreports/index.html

Chapter 9

TRAUMA-INFORMED CHILD WELFARE PRACTICE

Virginia C. Strand

Making child welfare systems trauma informed is a major challenge at the beginning of the 21st century. Bryan Samuels, commissioner of the Administration on Children, Youth and Families, recently stated:

> The research is clear that the experience of abuse or neglect leaves a particular traumatic fingerprint on the development of children that cannot be ignored if the child welfare system is to meaningfully improve the life trajectories of maltreated children, not merely keep them safe from harm. . . . These mental health, behavioral health and social and emotional needs are the core challenge before us. If we are to put children who have been maltreated and exposed to trauma on a positive life trajectory, we must build a child welfare system that responds effectively to these compelling and complex needs. (*Reauthorization of Title IV-B*, 2011)

The imperative to incorporate new knowledge about trauma and its impact is reflected in the NASW *Code of Ethics*, which states: "Social workers should strive to become and remain proficient in professional practice and the performance of professional functions. Social workers should critically examine and keep current with emerging knowledge relevant to social work" (National Association of Social Workers, 2008, p. 22, section 4.01). Since social workers continue to have a clear and active presence in the child welfare field, the obligation to further trauma-informed practice is clear.

An important pathway to better outcomes for child welfare agencies is the creation of trauma-informed child welfare practice. Trauma theory is used to advocate more effective infusion of knowledge about trauma, its impact, and empirically supported interventions in child welfare agencies in order to inform practice with children and families. Development of such knowledge can also help improve the organizational culture in many public child welfare agencies.

This chapter provides a reflection on the role that the Children's Bureau has played in raising public awareness about traumatic social conditions, reviews the recent literature on prevalence of trauma exposure in child welfare populations, identifies important contributions to the understanding of trauma, and outlines a widely accepted conceptual framework for trauma interventions. Finally, it offers a blueprint for developing practice strategies for frontline and supervisory staff.

Historical Antecedents and the Role of the Children's Bureau

Awareness of the ways in which human behavior can be profoundly traumatizing, from intra-family violence to war, has been with us since ancient times. However, society has oscillated between mobilizing to address the impact of traumatic events, both individually and systemically, and ignoring it. Social injustices are a violation of the social contract—the expectations of the child, family, and community that society will provide a safe and supportive social environment—and often result in traumatizing conditions and situations. In the early years of the Children's Bureau, particularly under its first director, Julia Lathrop, Bureau staff and volunteers provided leadership in social advocacy, education, and legislative reform to address many of the traumatizing social conditions of the time.

The causes endorsed by the Children's Bureau can be understood as advocacy for social policies that addressed traumatizing social conditions such as infant mortality. A decrease in infant mortality was advanced through strategies of birth registration and mortality prevention. Emerging data suggest that, in particular, the emphasis on improving parenting behavior through education and knowledge sharing advanced by the Children's Bureau was a major contribution to the decline of infant mortality during the second decade of the twentieth century (Almgren, Kemp, & Eisinger, 2000). The social condition of women was addressed through education about children's health, child care, and other issues viewed as helpful to parents. Another important contribution was the bureau's legal advocacy for the provision of public pensions to mothers, which established a template for what would later become the Aid to Families with Dependent Children program under the Social Security Act of 1935 (P.L. 74-271) (Machtinger, 1999). The bureau's legislative impact was evident in the contribution of its staff to the sections of the Social Security Act dealing with children.

Like society's attention to trauma issues, the prominence of the Children's Bureau, and society's support for child welfare interventions, have waxed and waned. During the 1970s, the identification of battered child syndrome and subsequent advocacy to identify and intervene with abused and neglected children resulted in the infusion of resources over the next three decades into an expanded child welfare system. Today this system responds to about 2 million reports a year and cares for approximately 425,000 children in substitute care.

Child welfare systems have historically served a range of victimized, exploited, and traumatized children and parents, but only recently have we come to understand the long-term impact of trauma exposure on children entering the child welfare system. Child welfare's constant interaction with families who have experienced trauma in one form or another underscores the need for trauma-informed practice knowledge and organizational cultures sensitive to the impact of trauma on clients and staff. By definition, children who are reported for child maltreatment are likely to have experienced child abuse and neglect or sexual abuse or witnessed domestic violence. These children and their families are also often exposed to community violence, war-related refugee experiences, combat violence in the case of returning veterans, medical trauma, natural disaster, or traumatic loss. There is increasing evidence that, when these experiences are not addressed, children and their parents are at greater risk for a range of behavioral, emotional, educational, and social problems in childhood and later in life.

The majority of traumatized children are not found in mental health clinics but in child welfare, juvenile justice, and other child-serving systems (Harris, Lieberman, & Marans, 2007). In reference to child welfare in particular, Griffin, Martinovich, Gowron, and Lyons (2009) found in a study in Illinois that 85 percent of children entering state custody had at least one type of traumatic experience, and the majority had multiple exposures. Children in foster care have higher-than-average rates of mental health problems (Pecora, 2010). Recently, Kolko et al. (2010) documented a 19 percent prevalence of post-traumatic stress symptoms in children placed in care. In a sample from a child protective service database, Sprang, Staton-Tindlall, and Clark (2008) found a high prevalence of traumatic exposure among drug-endangered children.

A major role of the Children's Bureau has been to fund research examining conditions affecting children and the child welfare interventions that address them. Funding for training and demonstration projects, national resource centers, and more recently Quality Improvement Centers has demonstrated the Bureau's commitment to knowledge development and knowledge management (Brodowski, Flanzer, Nolan, Shafer, & Kaye, 2007). Efforts to address workforce issues specifically have been emphasized since 2003, with the funding of eight five-year grants focused on recruitment and retention, and the current five-year funding of the National Child Welfare Workforce Institute, which seeks to implement many of the lessons learned from the original recruitment and retention grants through leadership training. Encouragement for institutions to incorporate an understanding of trauma more directly into child welfare practice is reflected in the five-year awards made in 2011 to five states to develop trauma-informed child welfare systems (Administration for Children, Youth and Families, 2011).

Evidence-Informed Trauma Principles

Impact of Trauma on Children

The impact of trauma on children, youths, and families has been widely studied and has led to the development of principles that can guide practice. The complex impact of trauma on children and families has been well articulated (Cook et al., 2005; Courtois, 2004). When children have been exposed to chronic or severe trauma, their functioning is often compromised across a number of domains. A prominent concern is the effect on the development of secure attachment, but affective, cognitive, behavioral, and somatic functioning are also typically affected. The child's perception of self and others may become distorted, and the world in general may come to seem unsafe. As children and adolescents seek to cope with these adverse experiences and changed worldviews, they may use avoidance strategies, demonstrate hyperarousal to trauma reminders, and have difficulty modulating feelings or regulating behavior. Interpersonal relationships may be perceived as a source of danger, leading to isolation or hostile interactions with others.

A history of abuse and neglect brings children to the attention of the child welfare system. However, intervention placing children in out-of-home care in order to keep them safe may inadvertently place children at risk for secondary adversities as they confront new challenges, losses, and stressors. The cumulative impact of these stressors, if unaddressed, often leads to additional emotional difficulties and behavioral disruptions. The challenge for child welfare is thus threefold: (1) to offer children and their families trauma-sensitive services from a skilled workforce; (2) to identify, train, and support resource parents or foster parents in what they need to know to parent children with histories of severe neglect, exploitation, and victimization; and (3) to prepare and sustain frontline staff and supervisors who are affected daily by direct or vicarious exposure to traumatic events.

Critical to working with traumatized children and adolescents is the need to understand the role of trauma triggers—which cause involuntary, automatic responses leading over time to emotional, cognitive, and behavioral dysregulation—in the child and family's social environment. According to the U.S. Substance Abuse and Mental Health Services Administration (2010), "trauma informed organizations, programs, and services are based on an understanding of the vulnerabilities or triggers of trauma survivors that traditional service delivery approaches may exacerbate, so that these services and programs can be more supportive and avoid re-traumatization."

The experience of overwhelming danger that occurs at the time of a traumatic event affects the body's neurobiology, which mobilizes to ward off danger, often through flight-or-fight responses. With severe and persistent trauma, even when the child is safe and emotionally regulated, the body responds to an association with past dangers—an event, person, smell, sound, or activity—as if the danger was occurring in the present. For such children and those around them—parents, caregivers, teachers, and peers—these inadvertent, automatic responses can appear irrational and unprovoked. Caregivers and other staff who work with children need to be attuned to such reactions to trauma triggers. Thus, there is a critical need for trauma-informed services in child welfare agencies.

Common reactions and responses of traumatized children and adolescents include the following:

- hypervigilance
- guardedness
- withdrawal and isolating behavior
- depression and suicide ideation or attempts
- fighting with peers
- irritability
- impulsivity
- inability to concentrate
- disrespect to authority figures
- physical complaints

Caseworkers, foster parents, other foster family members, supervisors, counselors, teachers, physicians, and other service providers must be attuned to these behaviors and their link to previous trauma, or helping runs the risk of becoming another form of hurting.

Approaches to Trauma Intervention

A great deal is known about what works effectively with traumatized children, adolescents, and adults; this knowledge can be used to inform the development of a trauma-informed workforce. Phase-oriented trauma treatment is widely accepted as a defining characteristic of trauma-informed interventions (Brown, Scheflin, & Hammond, 1998; Courtois, 2004). Phase-orietnted trauma treatment refers to a progression in treatment from helping a client establish physical and psychological safety to reducing symptom distress and building coping capacities *prior* to helping a client process trauma memories. Interventions to process trauma are undertaken to develop a coherent, integrated understanding of the trauma (connecting physiological, emotional, and cognitive aspects), and include activities to identify trauma or loss reminders, identify worse moments, and unpair thoughts, reminders, or discussions of the traumatic event from overwhelming negative emotions, with the goal of mastering or reintegrating traumatic or painful memories. A number of evidence-based trauma treatments have been found to be effective with violence-exposed children (Cohen, Mannarino, Murray, & Igelman,

2006). Most interventions acknowledge either explicitly or implicitly thisthree-stage approach for effective intervention:

- *stabilization*—establishing physical safety and emotional stability, characterized by an emphasis on the present; developing adaptive coping strategies to better modulate affect dysregulation, stress responses, behavioral dysregulation, and cognitive distortions
- *integration* of traumatic experience into ongoing life, characterized by a focus on acknowledging the reality of traumatic events and harmful relationships and making meaning of past events
- *consolidation*—returning to a normal developmental trajectory, characterized by the consolidation of personal and interpersonal growth and mobilization of energy to focus on the future

Applying Trauma Theory to Agency Practice

Trauma-informed practice is possible in child protective, preventive, foster care, and adoption services. Using the framework for intervention identified with successful treatment of traumatized children and adults, the first emphasis in work with children coming to the attention of the child welfare system should be on stabilization. This fits well with the organizational emphasis on safety reflected in the mandate for child protective services.

First and foremost, preservice training for all child welfare staff should include information about the impact of trauma on children and birth and foster parents as well as the impact of working with traumatized populations on child welfare workers. An excellent resource for staff training is the *Child Welfare Trauma Training Toolkit* (National Child Traumatic Stress Network, 2008). This training provides a foundation in nine essential elements of child welfare practice: (1) maximizing the child's sense of safety; (2) helping the child to reduce overwhelming emotion; (3) helping the child make new meaning of his or her trauma history and current experiences; (4) addressing the impact of trauma and subsequent changes in the child's behavior, development, and relationships; (5) coordinating services with other agencies; (6) making a comprehensive assessment of the child's trauma experiences and their impact on his or her development and behavior, and using it to guide services; (7) supporting and promoting positive and stable relationships in the life of the child; (8) providing support and guidance to the child's family and caregivers; and (9) managing professional and personal stress.

The phase-oriented approach to trauma treatment can be aligned with the goals of the child welfare system for children's safety, permanency, and well-being. The concept of safety, long understood in child welfare as physical safety, is expanded here to include an emphasis on emotional safety and security. The integration of trauma memories in aligned with interventions undertaken by the child welfare system—usually through preventive or foster care services—to establish permanency. It is argued that it will be difficult for a child to be maintained in a permanent home without disruption unless there is attention to treatment geared specifically to integration of the traumatic experiences. Consolidation of trauma memories and posttrauma growth is equated with foundation concepts of child well-being.

Child Protective Services. The concept of safety can be expanded to include the child's sense of internal or psychological safety and the actions that need to be taken in the external environment with parents or other caregivers so the adults act in ways that help a child establish that sense of safety. Three concepts are used to differentiate strategies designed to stabilize children's external environment from those to stabilize a child's internal, emotional environment: safety actions, safety promoting interventions, and safety planning interventions (Strand, Hansen, Young, & Courtney, 2011).

Safety actions in the external environment include those designed to assure physical safety and reduce concerns about immediate physical risk to the child. This may mean removal, or in extreme cases, arrest of a perpetrator. More commonly it requires referral of a nonoffending parent to a domestic violence shelter, advocacy services, or preventive services for support related to reduction of inadequate care.

Less well understood is the need for psychological safety, which is addressed through safety promoting and safety planning interventions. *Safety promoting interventions* include strategies to achieve internal emotional, behavioral, or cognitive stability when a child is at risk of immediate harm or self-injurious behavior. These include actions to reduce dangerously escalating behavior on the part of a parent or child or to intervene with a parent to protect the child. Interventions are directed at helping the child and family achieve internal emotional security and behavioral stability.

Safety planning interventions can be used when the child is safe and there are no concerns about immediate physical risk. They focus on plans for achieving internal control, with an emphasis on activities that help maintain the child, caregiver, and family's physical and emotional safety. They include identification of triggers and predictable stressors that have led to crises in the past and strategies to prepare in advance to stay in control. They may also include education about paying attention to one's sense of danger, body ownership (for example, "good touch–bad touch" explanations), risks involved with keeping secrets, and identification of key people the child can go to with safety concerns and ways to ask for help when feeling unsafe, along with the identification of other high-risk situations for abuse.

Child protective services are best positioned to help with safety actions and often with safety planning; foster care workers and foster parents can assist with safety planning; and preventive workers are ideally situated to implement safety promoting strategies.

Engaging parents is often key to successful intervention by child protective services. Because the overwhelming majority of substantiated cases seen by child protective services workers are not referred to family court, the ability to engage parents in understanding and accepting the need for help increases the likelihood that they will follow through with referrals. Evidence suggests that child protective workers could be more effective by using a partnering rather than an authoritative approach with families (Dumbrill, 2006). Family engagement better positions child protective workers to provide psychoeducation about the impact of trauma on children. The fact that traumatic events often result in impulsive behaviors and emotional states that are, to a large degree, involuntary is an important message to communicate and if understood, may make parents more willing to accept referrals. Using reflective listening, which can be taught in preservice training, demonstrating empathy, and being knowledgeable about trauma-specific resources are also key components for effective practice.

Preventive Services. The preventive services worker is typically involved with a family once the child has been determined to be physically safe. The risk of placement may still be present, and there are often ongoing concerns about the child becoming unsafe in the current living situation. This is a key point for safety promoting and safety planning interventions targeting both parents and children. An important skill for preventive services workers to build is the capacity to intervene with a family or parent–child dyad, because efficiency often requires that the child is not seen alone.

The possibility of traumatic exposure in the history of the birth parent is important to explore, as the child is typically living with the birth parent while receiving preventive services. If the parents have a history of abuse and neglect themselves, this will increase the likelihood of their responding impulsively and at times inappropriately in the care of their children. As with the child who has experienced trauma, the adult, too, may be dealing with emotional and behavioral dysregulation that is affecting their parenting. It may be important to identify this as an issue for the parents and work to help them accept a referral to a trauma-specific service to augment the help from preventive services.

Intervention with a child or adolescent often requires attention to behavioral, emotional, cognitive, and physical dysregulation. If the preventive services worker has the appropriate training, he or she can help the child identify, regulate, and express feelings. Help with behavioral regulation often requires that children or adolescents be helped to identify trauma reminders in their environment that may trigger actions that get them into trouble with peers, parents, and teachers.

If the preventive services worker is not trained to undertake this work and makes a referral to a trauma-specific service, he or she may still need to coordinate services so that the important people in the child's school and family network are involved. This may involve psychoeducation with school personnel about trauma and the potential of trauma triggers at school to interfere with attendance, learning, and appropriate behavior. Trauma work with the parent to support the child's growth is also important, whether it is carried out by the preventive worker or another provider. Placement prevention can be improved by the extent to which the preventive services worker can undertake and reinforce safety promoting interventions with the child and family.

Another key component for parents whose children are at risk for placement is parent training. Preventive services workers need to be aware of the range of evidence-based parent training that is currently available. Evidence suggests that didactic parenting classes are only minimally effective, if at all, in changing parenting practice (Casanueva, Martin, Runyan, Barth, & Bradley, 2008). On the other hand, research has identified a range of parent education programs with promising outcomes in changing abusive and neglectful parenting. Four of these have consistently been demonstrated to be effective in a variety of studies: the Incredible Year (Webster-Stratton & Hammond, 1997), Multisystemic Therapy (Henggeler et al., 1998), Parent Training (Forgatch & Martinez, 1999), and Parent–Child Interaction Training (Eyberg & Robinson, 1982). Although not specifically trauma-focused, they have demonstrated effectiveness with parents coming to the attention of the child welfare system (Barth, 2009).

Foster Care Services. As with the preventive services worker, the role of the foster care worker is to provide safety promoting and safety planning services, but with the foster parents. An excellent resource for foster care workers is the workshop Caring for Children Who Have Experienced Trauma (National Child Traumatic Stress Network, 2010). Ideally, it should become part of the mandatory training for foster parents, but when that is not the case, the curriculum provides excellent content and language that the foster care worker can use in educating foster parents about the impact of trauma and working with them to identify strategies they can use in their home.

While from the system's point of view, placing children in foster care removes them from a physically unsafe environment, the child may not experience it this way. Given the heightened concern with danger and safety experienced by traumatized children, there are specific steps that foster parents can take to familiarize children in their care with their new environment, which will help them feel secure. This includes making them familiar not only with the physical environment but also with the structure and rules of the family. Foster parents also need to be prepared for common disruptions in eating and sleeping. Not only do children have trouble falling asleep, but sleep may also be disturbed by nightmares or night terrors (it's important for foster parents to know the difference), and children may have trouble waking up in the morning.

In terms of safety promoting interventions, it is as important for foster parents as for children to be aware of and able to use basic coping techniques to decrease arousal and dysregulation. These include strategies to calm down—listening to music, deep breathing, taking a time out, playing sports, talking, writing, or doing art—whatever works for a particular child. Foster parents will have an easier time and there is less likelihood of disruption if they can help the child regulate emotions and behavior.

Trauma-specific services are often crucial to a child's recovery. A number of evidence-based trauma treatments have been found to be effective with children in foster care. Weiner, Schneider, and Lyons (2009) found that three such treatments—Child–Parent Psychotherapy, Trauma-Focused Cognitive-Behavioral Therapy, and Structured Psychotherapy for Adolescents Responding to Chronic Stress—were equally effective in reducing symptoms and improving functioning in children in foster care. These treatments were implemented with a racially diverse sample of youths, and results were found to be equally effective when making culturally sensitive adaptations to the model. Between them, the three models are able to reach a wide age range; they are designed, respectively, for children under five, school-age children and their families, and adolescents who may not have a primary caregiver actively involved in treatment.

Adoption Services. Services for adoption preparation as well as supportive services to families after adoption appear to be an important factor in maintaining permanency (Coakley & Berrick, 2008). Relatively little attention has been paid to making these services trauma-informed.

The risk of adoption disruption for children with a preadoptive history of child sexual abuse is high, due to a number of factors. These include the behavioral and emotional problems resulting from sexual abuse, the tendency to have had more moves in care, and the difficulty these children have in attaching to the adoptive mother (Nalavany, Ryan, Howard, & Smith, 2008). This underscores the need for trauma-informed preadoption services. Research supports the need for workers to have the time to complete child and family assessments In addition, the assessment should be expanded to include readiness to adopt a traumatized child; whether it is a kinship or stranger adoption, prospective adoptive parents should be trained in parenting traumatized children and adolescents (Coakley & Berrick, 2008).

One of the keys to successful adoption or kinship guardianship for traumatized children and adolescents is to help the child successfully resolve the impact of trauma—specifically, to decrease emotional and behavioral dysregulation and strengthen cognitive coping, particularly in the areas of attention and concentration, two areas in which the child will need to function well in order to complete school. The availability of a permanent home implies the opportunity for the development of a positive, secure attachment figure. As part of the preparation for the move to permanent status, it is important that the preadoptive parents are familiar with the impact of trauma, have the necessary skills to reinforce coping behaviors, and have worked on the development of their relationship with the child as a safe, secure emotional base. These developments will reduce the possibility of permanency disruption.

Impact on Staff of Working with Trauma

Working with traumatized children and adolescents, as well as family perpetrators who may also be trauma survivors, can often negatively affect staff, sometimes in ways that they may not recognize. This is referred to in the literature as vicarious trauma, secondary traumatic stress, or compassion fatigue. Vicarious trauma is generally defined as a change in cognitive *schemas*—beliefs, assumptions, and expectations related to psychological needs—that organize the experience of self and the world (McCann & Pearlman, 1990). It is thought to result from hearing about traumatic events. Secondary traumatic stress is often thought to result from exposure to actual traumatic events, as is the case for police and firefighters and child protective workers (Figley, 1995; Stamm, 1995). Workers' exposure to vicarious trauma and secondary traumatic stress can result in behavioral change, specifically the emergence of symptoms similar to those seen in post-traumatic stress disorder, which can include intrusive thoughts related to clients' traumatic disclosures, avoidance, physiological arousal, distressing emotions, and functional impairment (Bride, Hatcher, & Humble, 2009). Compassion fatigue, arising from both direct and indirect exposure, is associated with sadness and depression, sleeplessness, and general anxiety (Cerney, 1995).

Conrad and Keller-Guenther (2006) found that over 50 percent of child protective workers in one state system reported a high risk of compassion fatigue, even though an equally high percent reported high compassion satisfaction. Littlechild (2005) reported on research documenting that violence and threats of violence were widespread sources of stress for child welfare workers. Horwitz (2006) found a positive association between traumatic events experienced directly and indirectly by workers and the presence of negative workplace effects. Caringi (2007), in an exploration of individual and organizational factors that contribute to secondary traumatic stress, found that two factors were relevant: the unintentional choice of child protective services work ("happening" into the job), and consequently, lack of education or training for the work.

Behaviors reflective of secondary traumatic stress can include the following:

- avoidance of work responsibility or specific tasks
- impulsive behaviors reflected in decision making that is not well thought out or modulated
- verbal aggression or verbal retaliation with coworkers and sometimes clients
- absence from work due to fatigue and other somatic complaints
- preoccupation with psychological danger and physical safety in the work environment
- secondary adversities (increased tension with supervisors or coworkers resulting from increased use of sick days, erratic behavior on the job, distractibility, and irritability)

- development of risk-avoidant supervisory and management approaches
- sense of breakdown in the social contract (recognition that the agency may not only fail the client but also fail to protect staff from negative societal responses)

From Crisis-Driven Reactions to Trauma-Informed Systems

Efforts to create more trauma-informed, supportive organizational environments are often challenged by agency cultures that are more deficit-oriented in their appraisal of parents, privilege safety over well-being, are held hostage to computerized information systems driven by the need for accountability, and have to curtail professional discretion in decision-making. These characteristics, interacting with the nature of the client population served and the impact on staff of serving that population, have resulted in a risk-averse and reactive organizational culture in many child welfare agencies.

Changing such an organizational culture in order to establish a climate that promotes both physical and psychological safety for staff can be a major challenge. Supervision must become more client-centered and worker-supportive to counter the emphasis on accountability that has come to characterize child welfare. Trauma content needs to be introduced into already full preservice training curricula, and agencies need to establish ongoing training to build staff knowledge about the range of evidence-informed trauma treatments available in their community. Staff will also need ongoing support to cope with home visits in violent neighborhoods, hostile clients, and reoccurring exposure to traumatic experiences such as child fatalities. What exists to guide an agency as it attempts to meet these challenges? The following section incorporates knowledge about important areas of development for child welfare in the coming decades.

Future Directions and Practice Implications

Diversity and Disproportionality

Trauma-informed practice will need to address the role of historical trauma in achieving culturally responsive practice, because understanding historical trauma is central to understanding disproportionality and disparity in child welfare. *Disproportionality* refers to the overrepresentation of children from particular groups (such as African American and Native American) in the child welfare system. *Disparity* refers to unequal treatment received by children of color in the child welfare system. *Historical trauma* has been defined as the "cumulative and collective emotional and psychological injury over the life span and across generations, resulting from a cataclysmic history of genocide" (Struthers & Lowe, 2003, p. 258). A common manifestation of historical trauma is distrust of the mainstream culture, of which the child welfare system is part. This distrust is inherent in guardedness in approaching child welfare, resistance to services, and poor communication between the population and staff in child welfare, particularly where staff members represent the dominant culture.

In a study of factors contributing to disproportionate treatment of African American children by the child welfare system, Dettlaff and Rycraft (2010) identified five barriers to reducing disproportionality. Two of these are directly related to the impact of trauma—cultural bias and the climate of fear characteristic of child welfare agencies. Cultural bias is reflected in misconceptions and stereotypes attributed to a population, which may in turn be directly related to lack of awareness of how the historical relationship to the dominant culture has been transmitted in an attitude of fear and mistrust. An example of this bias would be when caseworkers apply their own values and knowledge about appropriate parenting rather than carefully assessing risk and protective factors for an individual child based on their interactions with the family and child.

A fearful agency climate is characterized by heightened awareness of the risk of individual liability for caseworkers and their supervisor if a child is not removed from a dangerous situation. The lack of familiarity with parenting and family norms can lead to precipitous removal of children due to the influence of an agency climate in which removal is perceived as protecting staff from potential liability. Adding to this fear is the tendency for media attention to focus on child welfare agencies when a child dies or is seriously injured, and to produce stories that result in negative public perceptions of the agencies and their staff.

Implications for the Social Work Profession

These insights have implications both for social work practice and the training of social workers.

Social Work Practice. The profession needs to continue its dedication to creating and sustaining trauma-informed agencies, organizations, and services. Child welfare organizations need to assume responsibility for addressing the barriers in their organizational culture to becoming trauma sensitive, with an emphasis on developing physical and psychological safety for staff. Staff training is essential on the impact of trauma on individuals and families, the range of evidence-based trauma treatments, and their fit for populations at different points in the service trajectory of child welfare, including child protective services, prevention, foster care, and adoption services. Training and ongoing institutional support to counter the effects on staff of working with traumatized populations remains a critical challenge. More needs to be done to study the effectiveness and impact of trauma-informed systems.

Social Work Education. Schools of social work need to be creative in incorporating the concept of historical trauma into analyses of oppression, social injustice, and human rights. Students need to be introduced to trauma-specific coursework, and schools of social work could partner with agencies to design field placements in which students would be exposed to evidence-informed intervention and treatment. Coursework could emphasize preparing for practice with traumatized populations, relevant for many social work settings. The military has developed a curriculum that reduces the impact of exposure by helping soldiers to use coping strategies when faced with traumatic events (Frappell-Cooke, Gulina, Green, Hacker-Hughes, & Greenberg, 2010), and this concept could be transferred into social work curricula. Finally, students could be exposed in their education program at both the BSW and MSW levels to strategies for coping with vicarious trauma or secondary traumatic stress.

Trauma training for child welfare practitioners is long overdue. Now that we have the knowledge and strategies to prepare practitioners to interact in a trauma-sensitive manner with clients, it is time to take action.

References

Administration for Children, Youth and Families. (2011). *Integrating trauma-informed and trauma-focused practice in Child Protective Service (CPS) delivery* (HHS-2011-ACF-ACYF-CO-0169). Retrieved from http://www.acf.hhs.gov/programs/cb/resource/discretionary-grant-awards-2011

Almgren, G., Kemp, S. P., & Eisinger, A. (2000). The legacy of Hull House and the Children's Bureau in the American Mortality Transition. *Social Service Review, 74*(1), 1–27.

Barth, R. P. (2009). Preventing child abuse and neglect with parent training: Evidence and opportunities. *Future of Children, 19*(2), 95–118.

Brodowski, M. L., Flanzer, S., Nolan, C., Shafer, J., & Kaye, E. (2007). Children's Bureau discretionary grants: Knowledge development through our research and demonstration projects. *Journal of Evidence-Based Social Work, 4*(3/4), 3–20.

Bride, B. E., Hatcher, S. S., & Humble, M. N. (2009). Trauma training, trauma practices, and secondary traumatic stress among substance abuse counselors. *Child Maltreatment, 5*(2), 95–105.

Brown, D., Scheflin, A. W., & Hammond, D. C. (1998). *Memory, trauma treatment and the law.* New York: W. W. Norton.

Caringi, J. (2007). Secondary traumatic stress in New York state child welfare workers. *Dissertation Abstracts International: Section A, 68*(10), 4476.

Casanueva, C., Martin, S. L., Runyan, D. K., Barth, R. P., & Bradley, R. H. (2008). Quality of maternal parenting among intimate-partner violence victims involved with the child welfare system. *Journal of Family Violence, 23*, 413–427.

Cerney, M. S. (1995). Treating the "heroic treaters." In C. R. Figley (Ed.), *Compassion fatigue: Coping with secondary traumatic stress disorder in those who treat the traumatized* (pp. 131–149). Philadelphia: Brunner/Mazel.

Coakley, J. F., & Berrick, J. D. (2008). Research review: In a rush to permanency: Preventing adoption disruption. *Child and Family Social Work, 13*(1), 101–112.

Cohen, J. A., Mannarino, A. P., Murray, L. K., & Igelman, R. (2006). Psychosocial interventions for maltreated and violence-exposed children. *Journal of Social Issues, 62,* 737–766.

Conrad, D., & Keller-Guenther, Y. (2006). Compassion fatigue, burnout, and compassion satisfaction among Colorado child protective workers. *Child Abuse & Neglect, 30,* 1071–1080.

Cook, A., Spinazzola, J., Ford, J., Lanktree, C., Blaustein, M., Cloitre, M., et al. (2005). Complex trauma in children and adolescents. *Psychiatric Annals, 35,* 390–398.

Courtois, C. A. (2004). Complex trauma reactions: Assessment and treatment. *Psychotherapy: Theory, Research, Practice, Training, 41,* 412–425.

Dettlaff, A. J., Rycraft, J. R. (2010). Factors contributing to disproportionality in the child welfare system: Views from the legal community. *Social Work, 55,* 213–224.

Dumbrill, G. C. (2006). Parental experiences of child protection intervention: A qualitative study. *Child Abuse & Neglect, 30,* 27–37.

Eyberg, S. M., & Robinson, E. A. (1982). Parent–child interaction therapy: Effects on family functioning. *Journal of Clinical Child Psychology, 11,* 130–137.

Figley, C. R. (1995). *Compassion fatigue: Coping with secondary traumatic stress disorder in those who treat the traumatized.* New York: Brunner/Mazel.

Forgatch, M. S., & Martinez, C. R. Jr. (1999). Parent management training: A program linking basic research and practical application. *Journal of Consulting and Clinical Psychology, 67,* 711–724.

Frappell-Cooke, W., Gulina, M., Green, K., Hacker-Hughes, J., & Greenberg, N. (2010). Does trauma risk management reduce psychological distress in deployed troops? *Occupational Medicine, 60,* 645–650.

Griffin, G., Martinovich, Z., Gowron, T., & Lyons, J. S. (2009). Strengths moderate the impact of trauma on risk behaviors in child welfare. *Residential Treatment for Children and Youth, 26,* 105–118.

Harris, W. W., Lieberman, F. A., & Marans, S. (2007). In the best interests of society. *Journal of Child Psychology and Psychiatry, 48,* 392–411.

Henggeler, S. W., Schoenwald, S. K., Borduin, C. M., Rowland, M. D., & Cunningham, P. B. (1998). *Multisystemic treatment of antisocial behavior in children and adolescents.* New York: Guilford Press.

Horwitz, M. J. (2006). Work-related trauma effects in child protection social workers. *Journal of Social Service Research, 32*(3), 1–18.

Kolko, D., Hurlburt, M. J., Zhang, J., Barth, R. P., Leslie, L. K., & Burns, B. J. (2010). Posttraumatic stress symptoms in children and adolescents referred for child welfare investigation. *Child Maltreatment, 15*(1), 48–63.

Littlechild, B. (2005). The stresses arising from violence, threats and aggression against child protection social workers. *Journal of Social Work, 5,* 61–82.

Machtinger, B. (1999). The Children's Bureau and Mother's Pensions Administration, 1912–1930. *Social Service Review, 73*(1), 105–118.

McCann, I. L., & Pearlman, L. A. (1990). Vicarious traumatization: A contextual model for understanding the effects of trauma on helpers. *Journal of Traumatic Stress, 3*(1), 131–149.

Nalavany, B. A., Ryan, S. D., Howard, J. A., & Smith, S. L. (2008). Preadoptive child sexual abuse as a predictor of moves in care, adoption disruption and inconsistent adoptive parent commitment. *Child Abuse & Neglect, 32,* 1084–1088.

National Association of Social Workers. (2008). *Code of ethics of the National Association of Social Workers.* Retrieved from http://www.socialworkers.org/pubs/code/default.asp

National Child Traumatic Stress Network. (2008). *Child welfare trauma training toolkit.* Retrieved from http://www.nctsn.org/products/child-welfare-trauma-training-toolkit-2008#q6

National Child Traumatic Stress Network. (2010). *Caring for children who have experienced trauma: A workshop for resource parents.* Retrieved from http://www.nctsn.org/products/caring-for-children-who-have-experienced-trauma

Pecora, P. J. (2010). Why current and former recipients of foster care need high quality mental health services. *Administration and Policy in Mental Health and Mental Health Services Research, 37*(102), 185–190.

Reauthorization of Title IV-B–subpart 1: The Child Welfare Services Program and subpart 2: The Promoting Safe and Stable Families Program (PSSF): Hearing before the Subcommittee on Human Resources, Committee on Ways and Means of the U.S. House of Representatives, 112 Cong. (2011) (testimony of B. Samuels, Washington, DC). Retrieved from http://waysandmeans.house.gov/UploadedFiles/Bryan_Samuels_Testimony.pdf

Social Security Act of 1935, P.L. 74-271, 49 Stat. 620, Title IV. Retrieved from http://www.enotes.com/social-security-act-1935-reference/social-security-act-1935

Sprang, G., Staton-Tindlall, S., & Clark, J. (2008). Trauma exposure and the drug endangered child. *Journal of Traumatic Stress, 21,* 333–339.

Stamm, B. H. (Ed). (1995). *Secondary traumatic stress: Self-care issues for clinicians, researchers, and educators.* Baltimore: Sidran Press.

Strand, V., Hansen, S., Young, S., & Courtney, D. (2011). *Core curriculum on child trauma (CCCT) coding manual.* Unpublished manuscript, Fordham University Graduate School of Social Service, New York.

Struthers, R., & Lowe, J. (2003). Nursing in the Native American culture and historical trauma. *Issues in Mental Health Nursing, 24,* 257–272.

Webster-Stratton, C., & Hammond, M. (1997). Treating children with early-onset conduct problems: A comparison of child and parent training interventions. *Journal of Consulting and Clinical Psychology, 65,* 93–99.

Weiner, D. A., Schneider, A., & Lyons, J. S. (2009). Evidence-based treatments for trauma among culturally diverse foster care youth: Treatment retention and outcomes. *Children and Youth Services Review, 31,* 1199–1205.

Chapter 10

SERVING FAMILIES WITH CO-OCCURRING CHALLENGES

Brenda D. Smith

The multiple challenges facing many poor families have been evident to observers for years. Although the stated policy of one of the early U.S. child welfare organizations, the Massachusetts Society for the Prevention of Cruelty to Children, was that it never removed children from their homes for reasons of poverty alone, historian Linda Gordon aptly observed, "but poverty was never alone" (Gordon, 1988, p. 95).

Today, just as poverty rarely occurs alone, neither does involvement with child welfare services. In addition to poverty, families involved with child welfare services often face co-occurring challenges with substance abuse, mental health, domestic violence, trauma and traumatic stress, housing, or other concrete needs. The multiple potential challenges families face when also involved with child welfare services contribute to systemic challenges and tensions in planning appropriate policy and practice responses. High quality, helpful practice may be promoted if child welfare caseworkers properly identify the various challenges families face. Focused attention on assessing any family's multiple problems, however, can lead to unintended labels, stigma, and a deficit-based approach in which strengths and informal resources are overlooked (Sousa, Ribeiro, & Rodrigues, 2006).

This chapter addresses some of the service delivery challenges that are exacerbated when families face multiple co-occurring challenges. It begins with a look at twentieth century practice and policy approaches to serving families with co-occurring challenges, including various efforts to coordinate services, with a focus on the response of the Children's Bureau. It summarizes research on coordinated service models, including a comprehensive, family-centered service delivery model known as "systems of care." It addresses the social work profession's potential and partially realized role in theorizing co-occurring challenges in relation to social, economic, and political environments, including communities and larger systems. Finally, it addresses future challenges by highlighting practice and policy approaches that may best serve families with co-occurring challenges as the Children's Bureau moves forward with its agenda for the next 100 years.

Historical Antecedents

Since their origins, the social work profession and the Children's Bureau have worked to identify and respond to families with multiple co-occurring challenges. The early practice responses to such challenges reflect priorities, tensions, and contradictions that endure today. One priority established by the Children's Bureau is a commitment to the use of evidence in the development of social welfare policies and practices. From the beginning, Children's Bureau staff worked with leaders in the developing social work profession to promote the idea that social problems could be solved scientifically (Gordon, 1994). Children's Bureau leaders and some early social work leaders believed, however, that a scientific approach to social problems, including families with multiple challenges, went hand-in-hand with a compassionate and political approach to social problems.

Edith Abbott, an early social work leader who worked with Children's Bureau colleagues, emphasized the importance of economic and political change as a strategy to meet the needs of multiply disadvantaged families. When friendly visiting was a typical response to families facing multiple challenges, Abbott reportedly argued that "if social workers were truly committed to alleviating suffering, then they must work to adjust economic and political relationships so no one need[s] a friendly visitor's patronage" (Muncy, 1991, p. 82). While Abbott's position may have been a minority view among social workers in the 1920s, her comment illustrates the ongoing tension between direct individual or family-centered helping and efforts to promote larger systems change through political action. Abbott and Sophinisba Breckenridge, early leaders of the University of Chicago School of Social Service Administration, one of the first schools of social work, emphasized social and political reform in the social work curriculum. They particularly emphasized the need for economic reform as a means to address social problems, and they directly linked economic challenges to the range of challenges families faced. If families' economic needs were addressed, they argued, "then such problems as juvenile delinquency, substandard housing, hunger, and poor health could be eliminated" (Muncy, 1991, p. 83).

Another enduring tension, illustrated in the early years of the Children's Bureau and related to the needs of families with multiple challenges, involves the relative merit of services specifically targeted to particular needs versus widely available, comprehensive, and preventive services. Among social workers arguing for a scientific approach to social problems were those who advocated diagnosis and the provision of particular services targeting particular needs. Although a "scientific casework" approach had good intentions to match specific needs to specific services, the approach led to categorization and to separate treatment of different family needs. Hence, categorization of services often derided today, grew out of sensible arguments for specific targeting of resources to needs and a sensible observation that specific and particular needs could not be met well through a general, standardized approach. Then as now, however, seemingly efficient targeting of resources and specialized services risked the unintended consequence of stigma and service gaps. In addition, a focus on specialized categories of services competed with a universal, preventive service orientation in which services would be widely available rather than matched to need.

In the early years of the Children's Bureau, at the same time that casework, service targeting, and categorization were gaining acceptance, a competing, preventive, universal approach was also gaining popularity through networks of women's organizations. The latter approach culminated in the Sheppard-Towner Act, formally titled the Materity and Infancy Act of 1921 (P.L. 67-97), which called for a preventive, universal, public health approach to serving young families. Children's Bureau history suggests that if categorization eventually became the predominant mode of service provision for families with multiple challenges, that result may have less to do with service philosophy than with pragmatic and political choices. Regarding social work and Children's Bureau activity surrounding the development of the 1935 Social Security Act and referring to plans for the new Aid to Dependent Children Program, Gordon wrote, "lacking the power to create universal welfare provisions without stigma, these ever-practical activists sought to remove a particular program from the pejorative ... welfare" (Gordon, 1994, p. 105). Gordon quoted Edith Abbott's sister and Children's Bureau leader, Grace Abbott, as noting that the families and children who would be eligible for the initial Aid to Dependent Children program would be "really nice," implying that those children and families who were not nice, or those with many problems, could be excluded (Gordon, 1994).

The Children's Bureau history suggests that a tendency toward service fragmentation grew, in part, from a desire to appropriately and specifically target services when responding to the needs of families with co-occurring challenges and, in part, from a desire to separate certain types of challenges from others so families might at least receive some services without stigma. It seems to be an unintended consequence of these well-intentioned motives that services for many multiply challenged families have become stigmatizing as well as fragmented and difficult or even impossible to obtain. Moreover, despite a historical and enduring emphasis on the importance of data and research in service development, even today many services available to poor families have unproven effectiveness and lack funding for research to study their effectiveness.

Practice and Policy Approaches for Families with Co-occurring Challenges

Prevalence of Co-occurring Challenges

Co-occurring challenges in family life have been reported for years, primarily on an anecdotal basis. Only recently have researchers made substantial progress in estimating prevalence rates or other specific measures of co-occurring challenges, and these estimates are based on samples and methods of varying quality and validity. One reputable source, the U.S. Public Health Service (2000), estimated that 92 percent of children using services from one system, such as child welfare, also use services from at least one additional system, and 19 percent use services from four or more service systems.

A recent Illinois study sought to assess multisector service use among families undergoing a child welfare investigation or using food stamps. Of those families, 34 percent used services from one additional service sector and 23 percent used services from two or more additional sectors. Families using services from multiple sectors accounted for 86 percent of the resources used for all families included in the study. The same study estimated that of all families with children in Illinois, about 7 percent used services from multiple service sectors (Goerge, Smithgall, Seshadri, & Ballard, 2010). Another Illinois study addressed families involved with child welfare services who also had substance abuse problems. The researchers found that, in addition to substance abuse, the families faced challenges with domestic violence, housing, and mental health. Only 8 percent of the families in the study had no other problems besides child welfare and substance abuse; 30 percent had at least one other problem; 35 percent had two other problems; and 27 percent had three (Marsh, Ryan, Choi, & Testa, 2006).

Studies based on the Children's Bureau–funded National Survey of Child and Adolescent Well-Being (NSCAW), a nationally representative sample of children and families having contact with child welfare services, have documented a range of co-occurring challenges. For example, half of children in the study sample had experienced a special health care need, such as asthma or a learning disability, in the past three years (Ringeisen, Casanueva, Urato, & Cross, 2008); 31 percent of female caregivers had reported an incident of domestic violence in the past year (Kohl, Barth, Hazen, & Landsverk, 2005); and about 25 percent of female caregivers had experienced major depression (Administration for Children and Families, 2008). Mental health problems in children are also among the co-occurring challenges families having contact with child welfare face. One study estimated that about half of the children in the NSCAW sample have an emotional or behavioral problem (Burns et al., 2004); another estimated that 42 percent have a mental health problem (Hurlburt et al., 2004). About 33 percent of children in the NSCAW sample receive services from more than one service sector (Farmer et al., 2010).

Among the challenges families involved with child welfare services face, several relate to poverty and concrete needs. Estimates based on the NSCAW study suggest that more than half of children having contact with child welfare services live in a household with an income below the federal poverty line. For an estimated 21 percent, the household income is less than 50 percent of the federal poverty line. Of those families undergoing a maltreatment investigation, NSCAW data suggest that 65 percent have a household income below $25,000 (NSCAW, 2005). Courtney, McMurtry, and Zinn (2004), in one of the few studies to specifically investigate housing problems among families involved with child welfare services, found that among families receiving in-home protective services, 14 percent had been evicted, 22 percent had resorted to moving in with family or friends, and 10 percent had been homeless. The prevalence of housing problems was even higher among families with children in foster care. Among those families, 26 percent had been evicted, 42 percent had moved in with family or friends, and 29 percent had been homeless. The same study identified other co-occurring challenges among the sample of families involved with the child welfare system: About half of the parents had less than a high school education, and 26 percent had a disability or mental health challenge that hindered daily activities. Finally, studies have suggested that families facing multiple challenges often live in communities with relatively high rates of poverty, residential instability, unemployment, and inadequate child care resources (Coulton, Korbin, Su, & Chow, 1995; Freisthler, Merritt, & LaScala, 2006; Lery, 2009).

Services for Families with Multiple Challenges

Although it is widely accepted that families involved with child welfare services face co-occurring challenges, evidence suggests that many families do not receive services to address those challenges. With co-occurring substance abuse, for example, NSCAW data indicate that among parents with past-year alcohol abuse or illicit drug use, only 18 percent were identified by child welfare caseworkers to have a substance abuse problem (Gibbons, Barth, & Martin, 2006). A similar discrepancy between caregiver and caseworker reports has been found for domestic violence. Whereas about one-third of caregivers in the NSCAW sample reported past-year domestic violence, 12 percent of caregivers were identified by caseworkers as domestic violence victims. Also, of the caregivers who experienced domestic violence, only 20 percent received domestic violence services (Kohl et al., 2005). Another study focusing on parents with substance abuse problems involved with child welfare services found that about half of the parents received substance abuse treatment; 23 percent were offered treatment but did not receive it; and 23 percent were not offered treatment (SAMHSA, 1999). A more recent study found that of parents with substance abuse problems, only 22 percent completed substance abuse treatment (Choi & Ryan, 2006).

Similar service gaps have been found related to other co-occurring challenges. Of children involved with child welfare services who face mental health challenges, one study found that only about 28 percent receive mental health services (Hurlburt et al., 2004). Service gaps may be greatest when challenges pertain to concrete service needs, such as housing or cash assistance. Whereas about half of families in a Milwaukee child welfare study reported that they needed help finding a place to live or help with repairs or maintenance of their homes, only 21 percent were provided or referred to housing services (Courtney et al., 2004).

Coordination to Address Service Gaps

In attempting to explain the substantial service gaps for families facing multiple challenges, observers have noted that a partial explanation may relate to how services are structured (Marsh, Smith, & Bruni, 2011). In particular, observers have questioned the merit of services that are fragmented or delivered by separate service systems (Lawson & Barkdull, 2001). To better serve families with multiple challenges, policymakers and service providers have worked to develop and implement various models of service integration and coordination.

Several distinctions among forms of service delivery, although not universally used, can be helpful—including use of the term *service coordination* for arrangements between service providers and *service integration* for the offering of two or more service types in the same location. A distinction can also be made between service coordination at the systems level (agreements among agencies) and at the family or practice level (case management to ensure that clients receive services from different sectors) (Bunger, 2010; Chung, Domino, & Morrissey, 2009; King & Meyer, 2006).

The systems-of-care approach to services coordination involves both a service philosophy and logistical components. It was developed in response to the observation that families of children with mental health challenges faced fragmented services, stigma, and barriers to services including difficulty in finding culturally appropriate services. The goal was to create a service system that is driven by families, centered on children's needs, community based, culturally competent, and that involves naturally occurring informal supports (Stroul & Friedman, 1986). Services should involve collaboration and cooperation among providers who uphold systems of care principles. Ideally, families facing multiple challenges would have access to a comprehensive range of formal services and informal supports in their communities. Each family would then work with service coordinators to design its own individualized service plan.

While this approach is rarely fully implemented (Kutash, Greenbaum, Wang, Boothroyd, & Friedman, 2011), the principles create a model for communities to aspire to and develop. As discussed later, however, any service coordination model, regardless of its thoughtful and sensible design, is unlikely to help families if the services it coordinates have not been demonstrated to help when implemented in routine settings.

Evidence on Service Coordination and Integration

Assessment of the effectiveness of a coordinated services program have generally involved questions such as whether the program has been implemented as intended, whether it has increased service use, including services matched to needs, and whether integrated services lead to better outcomes. Studies of systems- and case-level service coordination have found that such efforts do increase the number of services used and/or the length of service participation.

The Starting Early Starting Smart integrated services model, for example, involves integrated preventive parenting, mental health, and substance abuse services in settings that families can easily access, such as pediatric health clinics and early childhood education centers. An evaluation found that services integration promoted overall service use and the use of services matched to needs (Morrow et al., 2010). A study using NSCAW data found more precise matching of mental health need to service receipt when services were better coordinated (Hurlburt et al., 2004). Specifically, when child welfare agencies had more ties with mental health service providers, children with greater mental health service needs were more likely to receive mental health services, and children with lesser mental health service needs were less likely to receive services. These studies did not assess whether greater service use led to improved child outcomes.

Whereas conventional wisdom suggests that systems-level services coordination and interagency collaboration are central components of effective treatment, a number of studies focused specifically on coordinated service systems have failed to find positive effects (Bickman, 1996; Glisson & Hemmelgarn, 1998). Perhaps the best known of these studies involved a services coordination demonstration project known as the Fort Bragg Project, which evaluated the effects of a coordinated system of care for children in military families who were referred for mental health treatment. Among the coordinated services were outpatient counseling, in-home services, 24-hour crisis management, and residential services. The services were community-based and provided and coordinated by multidisciplinary teams that worked to match individualized services to each child's needs. The project was evaluated using a quasi-experimental design in which families receiving coordinated services were compared to families receiving services available through the usual referrals to distinct providers.

The study found that families receiving coordinated services did indeed receive more services and were more satisfied with services than those families receiving standard care. However, mental health outcomes were found to be no different for families in the two groups (Bickman, 1996), a finding that evoked much surprise and controversy. No better outcomes were found in subsequent longitudinal studies or with a subsequent replication of the study among poor civilian families in Stark County, Ohio (Bickman, Lambert, Andrade, & Penaloza, 2000). The authors concluded that, rather than service delivery systems, attention should focus on service quality. Others interpreting the study findings have noted that while there was no difference in outcomes between the two groups, outcomes for children in both groups improved (Hoagwood, 1997). Such findings raise the possibility that even routine services involve some forms of service coordination. The findings also raise questions about service coordination that should be further explored along with efforts to improve service quality.

Other studies of services coordination and service delivery mechanisms have also failed to find service system effects on outcomes. Littell (1997), for example, found that coordinated family preservation services did not lead to expected outcomes even when services were provided as intended. A study of the effects of service coordination through interagency collaboration in children's mental health found that interorganizational relationships were unrelated to service outcomes and had a negative effect on service quality (Glisson & Hemmelgarn, 1998). These authors concluded that system-level efforts to coordinate or integrate services could detract attention from families and service quality.

Some studies of service-level coordination have found positive effects. Bai, Wells, and Hillemier (2009), for example, used NSCAW data to assess whether service intensity, or the number of ties between child welfare agencies and mental service providers, was associated with the number of services used and mental health outcomes. The researchers found that a greater number of ties increased service receipt and the likelihood of improved child mental health.

In Illinois, multiply challenged parents with children in foster care were linked with a substance abuse *recovery coach* who not only helped the parents stay in substance abuse treatment but also helped them access services addressing their other challenges. An evaluation using a randomized control design found that parents with a recovery coach were somewhat more likely than parents receiving typical services to achieve reunification from foster care and to avoid a new substance-exposed birth (Ryan, Choi, Hong, Hernandez, & Larrison, 2008; Ryan, Marsh, Testa, & Louderman, 2006). The recovery coach research also showed that the likelihood of reunification was much improved when families made progress in the problem areas for which they received services (Marsh et al., 2006). The findings underscore the importance of ensuring that families with co-occurring problems have access to effective services that are demonstrated to help.

Other promising system-level service integration strategies include family treatment drug courts and service co-location. Modeled on criminal drug courts, family treatment drug courts integrate child welfare, substance abuse, and other services via court mandates. Evaluations suggest that they lead to greater treatment enrollment, faster treatment enrollment, and increased chances of reunification from foster care (Boles, Young, Moore, & DiPirro-Beard, 2007; Green, Furrer, Worcel, Burrus, & Finigan, 2007; Worcel, Furrer, Green, Burrus, & Finigan, 2008). The co-location of substance abuse treatment counselors in child welfare offices is still under evaluation, but initial findings suggest that it can lead to increased understanding among child welfare and substance abuse staff, improved relationships among service providers, and better coordination of services for clients (Lee, Esaki, & Green, 2009; McAlpine, Courts-Marshall, & Harper-Doran, 2001). Systems of care and other service coordination models remain popular, but we have much to learn about how or whether particular service system mechanisms or service delivery components lead to positive outcomes.

In summary, while it is clear that coordinated service systems are generally associated with increases in service utilization and some improved outcomes (Bruder et al., 2005; SAMHSA, 2005), it is not yet clear what role, if any, the service delivery systems play in influencing family and youth outcomes. Paradoxically, even as service providers face increased pressure to report service outcomes, rarely are providers in routine settings asked to link outcomes to particular services, and services are rarely subjected to impact evaluations with research designs suited to assess their effects.

On balance, certain generalizations can be drawn from studies of service coordination for families with multiple challenges. One is that coordinated service systems seem successful at promoting service utilization, but using more services does not inevitably lead to improved outcomes. Another is that service quality must be sustained to achieve positive outcomes. A well-coordinated system of care will be unable to help families if the services being coordinated are not effective or implemented as intended. Finally, many families involved with child welfare services and facing other co-occurring challenges are not receiving services with demonstrated effectiveness.

Disappointing findings from a range of service coordination and integration studies has shifted the attention of some researchers and policymakers from service delivery systems to the quality of particular services and the importance of determining whether services addressing co-occurring challenges lead to their intended outcomes. Coordination of services in systems of care is a popular and enduring idea, perhaps for good reason. The idea that additional benefit can come through structures and service delivery systems can be better tested, however, when the services in question are of sufficient quality to help families.

Fortunately, a number of services in mental health, substance abuse, parenting, and other areas have been demonstrated to help families. While it remains challenging to implement evidence-supported interventions in routine community settings, efforts to develop evidence-based mechanisms for disseminating and implementing evidence-based interventions are growing (Fixsen, Naoom, Blase, Friedman, & Wallace, 2005; Proctor, Landsverk, Aarons, Chambers, Glisson, & Mittman, 2009). In addition to increasing the availability of evidence-based, high-quality services in routine settings, however, we also need further investigation of informal supports and the impact of community contexts on service need, service receipt, and service outcomes. Multiply challenged families often live in troubled communities, and knowledge is growing on the connections between community contexts and family members' physical and mental health.

Social Work and Families with Co-occurring Challenges

The social work profession is thoroughly familiar with families facing multiple challenges. Moreover, coordinated service systems and, particularly, the systems-of-care philosophy and practice are consistent with social work values, theory, and practice. Through the profession's history, social workers have struggled with the tensions and conundrums associated with services for families with multiple challenges, such as the potential conflicts between targeted and comprehensive services, and between a services approach and political efforts at social reform. Responding to families with co-occurring challenges is clearly among the profession's priorities, and social work has the potential to play an even stronger leadership role in advancing responses to families with multiple challenges. The 100th anniversary of the Children's Bureau can be a reminder of the potential for social workers to be leaders at the federal level. Perhaps the profession can be inspired not only to emphasize the importance of integrated, strengths-based, family-focused systems of care, but also to be national leaders in the implementation and evaluation of such efforts.

Social workers not only have firsthand experiences working with families, but also have a strengths-based, holistic view that sees the merits of integrated, comprehensive systems of care. With such a view, they can be prepared to identify informal sources of support in family networks and to see family strengths. Social workers are also trained to have a macro perspective and the capacity to see how any family's multiple problems likely reflect systemic and structural deficits that need to be changed. Social workers understand that families are more likely to have informal sources of support when they live in a strong, healthy community.

Future Directions

With support from the Children's Bureau, practitioners and policymakers have made progress in meeting the needs of families with multiple challenges. As the Children's Bureau continues its efforts to address practice challenges that can be exacerbated for families with multiple co-occurring challenges, some contemporary practice challenges seem similar to those facing the very first social workers and the Children's Bureau's founders. We still struggle, for example, with the relative merits of targeted and matched services versus comprehensive, widely available, preventive services. Other contemporary practice challenges, however, are new. Not only is it important to develop evidence-supported practices, for example, but we now see more clearly the challenge of implementing such practices in routine settings. Following are some of the practice priorities for serving families with co-occurring challenges as the Children's Bureau begins its second 100 years.

First, efforts continue to promote thorough, comprehensive, and family-centered assessments of service needs. The best assessment teams are not only aware of the full range of challenges families may face but also have the skills to adequately identify a family's challenges (Smithgall, Jarpe-Ratner, Yang, DeCoursey, Brooks, & Goerge, 2009). The best assessments focus on the needs and challenges that families identify, rather than only on those that are apparent to professionals from the outside, and they identify family strengths and informal resources in the family and community (Friesen, Koroloff, Walker, & Briggs, 2011; Sousa, Ribeiro, & Rodrigues, 2006). The best assessment practices are also ongoing to ensure that early perceptions can be modified when appropriate and to provide the fullest opportunity for families to have continuous input as partners in service delivery. Family group conferencing models are an example of a means toward comprehensive, culturally appropriate, and family-centered assessments (Burford & Hudson, 2000).

Second, efforts continue to develop evidence-based interventions that are demonstrated to promote positive outcomes. Social workers not only are involved in research to develop evidence-based interventions, but also have an important role to play in the challenge of implementing evidence-based interventions in routine, publicly funded community settings (Proctor, 2007; Proctor et al., 2009). Some particularly innovative approaches to the development and implementation of effective services enable practitioners to receive ongoing quantitative feedback on various elements of the treatment process and thereby build evidence in practice settings. For example, practitioner researchers at Vanderbilt University have developed contextualized feedback systems, a means through which service providers can use advanced technology to track services and client outcomes and use data to inform practice (Bickman, Riemer, Breda, & Kelley, 2006; Kelley & Bickman, 2009).

Third, interdisciplinary collaborations and interprofessional working teams continue, as do collaborations across specializations in which practitioners work hand-in-hand with administrators, policymakers, and researchers. To promote such efforts, some states and localities are developing flexible or braided funding mechanisms to overcome the funding "silos" that often characterize human service systems (Marsh et al., 2011). Also, as the need for evidence-supported cross-sector service coordination becomes more apparent, so does the need for integrated data systems. California and Illinois have been leaders in integrating state-level services data. Integrated databases enable policymakers and practitioners to more easily identify co-occurring service needs, identify areas of practice strength and weakness, and more clearly plan coordinated interventions. To strengthen interprofessional practice, researchers are developing mechanisms to measure it (Bronstein, 2002; Mellin, Bronstein, Amorose, Ball, & Green, 2010) and establishing goals for more rigorous and effective cross-sector training (Hoge et al., 2009).

Finally, the development of strong, evidence-based interventions and well-functioning systems of care is ongoing and important but even at its best will still only offer remedies to the problems families face after those problems emerge. Social work practitioners, policymakers, and researchers must remain aware of the need to work toward programs and social reforms that prevent family problems as well as respond to them.

The founders and early leaders of the Children's Bureau were committed to both research and advocacy. They resisted pressures to create an agency committed to dispassionate use of research findings. They saw the potential in using data and research findings as tools in advocacy for social reform. Later generations of social workers inspired by the Children's Bureau continue its commitment to research and have expanded efforts to improve social work practice. At the 100th anniversary, however, as we reflect on latter-day efforts to maintain and strengthen the founders' vision, we might use their inspiration to fortify efforts at social reform. Especially as budgets for public services are reduced and political environments place additional burdens on poor families, social workers must remember the profession's roots in social reform and advocacy as well as service provision. Families with multiple challenges may benefit in the short term from effective services, but longer term gains and prevention of co-occurring challenges will require social reforms that lead to stronger, safer, healthier communities and more equitable and just distribution of resources.

References

Administration for Children and Families. (2008). *Depression among caregivers of young children reported for child maltreatment* [National Survey of Child and Adolescent Well-Being Research Brief]. Washington, DC: Author.

Bai, Y., Wells, R., & Hillemeier, M. M. (2009). Coordination between child welfare agencies and mental health service providers, children's service use, and outcomes. *Child Abuse & Neglect, 33,* 372–381.

Bickman, L. (1996). A continuum of care: More is not always better. *American Psychologist, 51,* 689–701.

Bickman, L., Lambert, E. W., Andrade, A. R., & Penaloza, R. E. (2000). The Fort Bragg continuum of care for children and adolescents: Mental health outcomes over five years. *Journal of Consulting and Clinical Psychology, 68,* 710–716.

Bickman, L., Riemer, M., Breda, C., & Kelley, S. D. (2006). CFIT: A system to provide a continuous quality improvement infrastructure through organizational responsiveness, measurement, training, and feedback. *Report on Emotional and Behavioral Disorders in Youth, 6,* 86–87.

Boles, S. M., Young, N. K., Moore, T., & DiPirro-Beard, S. (2007). The Sacramento drug dependency court: Development and outcomes. *Child Maltreatment, 12,* 161–171.

Bronstein, L. R. (2002). Index of interdisciplinary collaboration [Instrument development]. *Social Work Research, 26,* 113–126.

Bruder, M. B., Harbin, G. L., Whitbread, K., Conn-Powers, M., Roberts, R., Dunst, C. J., Van Buren, M., Mazzarella, C., & Gabbard, G. (2005). Establishing outcomes for service coordination: A step toward evidence-based practice. *Topics in Early Childhood Special Education, 25,* 177–188.

Bunger, A. C. (2010). Defining service coordination: A social work perspective. *Journal of Social Service Research*, 36, 385–401.

Burford, G. & Hudson, J. (Eds.). (2000). *Family group conferences: New directions in community-centered child and family practice.* Hawthorne, NY: Aldine de Gruyter.

Burns, B. J., Phillips, S. D., Wagner, H. R., Barth, R. P., Kolko, D. J., Campbell, Y., et al. (2004). Mental health need and access to mental health services by youths involved with child welfare: A national survey. *Journal of the American Academy of Child and Adolescent Psychiatry, 43,* 960–970.

Choi, S., & Ryan, J. P. (2006). Completing substance abuse treatment in child welfare: The role of co-occurring conditions and drug of choice. *Child Maltreatment, 11,* 313–325.

Chung, S., Domino, M. E., & Morrissey, J. P. (2009). Changes in treatment content of services during trauma-informed integrated services for women with co-occurring disorders. *Community Mental Health Journal, 45,* 375–384.

Coulton, C. J., Korbin, J. E., Su, M., & Chow, J. (1995). Community-level factors and child maltreatment rates. *Child Development, 66,* 1262–1276.

Courtney, M. E., McMurtry, S. L., & Zinn, A. (2004). Housing problems experienced by recipients of child welfare services. *Child Welfare, 83,* 393–422.

Farmer, E.M.Z., Mustillo, S. A., Wagner, H. R., Burns, B. J., Kolko, D. J., Barth, R. P., & Leslie, L. K. (2010). Service use and multi-sector use for mental health problems by youth in contact with child welfare. *Children and Youth Services Review, 32,* 815–821.

Fixsen, D. L., Naoom, S. F., Blase, K. A., Friedman, R. M., & Wallace, F. (2005). *Implementation research: A synthesis of the literature* (Florida Mental Health Institute Publication No. 231). Tampa: University of South Florida, Louis de la Parte Florida Mental Health Institute, National Implementation Research Network.

Freisthler, B., Merritt, D. H., & LaScala, E. A. (2006). Understanding the ecology of child maltreatment: Review of the literature and directions for future research. *Child Maltreatment, 11,* 263–280.

Friesen, B. J., Koroloff, N. M., Walker, J. S., & Briggs, H. E. (2011). Family and youth voice in systems of care: The evolution of influence. *Best Practices in Mental Health, 7*(1), 1–25.

Gibbons, C. B., Barth, R. P., & Martin, S. L. (2006). *Substance abuse among caregivers of maltreated children.* Unpublished manuscript, University of North Carolina at Chapel Hill.

Glisson, C., & Hemmelgarn, A. (1998). The effects of organizational climate and interorganizational coordination on the quality and outcomes of children's service systems. *Child Abuse & Neglect, 22,* 401–421.

Goerge, R. M., Smithgall, C., Seshadri, R., & Ballard, P. (2010). *Illinois families and their use of multiple service systems.* Chicago: Chapin Hall at the University of Chicago.

Gordon, L. (1988). *Heroes of their own lives: The politics and history of family violence: Boston 1880–1960.* Urbana: University of Illinois Press.

Gordon, L. (1994). *Pitied but not entitled: Single mothers and the history of welfare 1890–1935.* New York: Free Press.

Green, B. L., Furrer, C. J., Worcel, S. D., Burrus, S.W.M., & Finigan, M. W. (2007). How effective are family drug treatment courts? Results from a four-site national study. *Child Maltreatment, 12,* 43–59.

Hoagwood, K. (1997). Interpreting nullity: The Fort Bragg Experiment—a comparative success or failure? *American Psychologist, 52,* 546–550.

Hoge, M. A., Morris, J. A., Stuart, G. W., Huey, L. Y., Bergeson, S., Flaherty, M. T., et al. (2009). A national plan for workforce development in behavioral health. *Psychiatric Services, 60,* 883–887.

Hurlburt, M. S., Leslie, L. K., Landsverk, J., Barth, R. P., Burns, B. J., Gibbons, R. D., et al. (2004). Contextual predictors of mental health service use among children open to child welfare. *Archives of General Psychiatry, 61,* 1217–1224.

Kelley, S. D., & Bickman, L. (2009). Beyond outcomes monitoring: Measurement feedback systems in child and adolescent clinical practice. *Current Opinion in Psychiatry, 22*(4), 363–368.

King, G., & Meyer, K. (2006). Service integration and co-ordination: A framework of approaches for the delivery of co-ordinated care to children with disabilities and their families. *Child Care, Health & Development, 32,* 477–492.

Kohl, P. L., Barth, R. P., Hazen, A. L., & Landsverk, J. A. (2005). Child welfare as a gateway to domestic violence services. *Children and Youth Services Review, 27,* 1203–1221.

Kutash, K., Greenbaum, P. E., Wang, W., Boothroyd, R. A., & Friedman, R. M. (2011). Levels of system of care implementation: A national study. *Journal of Behavioral Health Sciences & Research, 38,* 342–357.

Lawson, H. A., & Barkdull, C. (2001). Gaining the collaborative advantage and promoting systems and cross-systems change. In A. L. Sallee, H. A. Lawson, & K. Briar-Lawson (Eds.), *Innovative practices with vulnerable children and families* (pp. 245–270). Dubuque, IA: Eddie Bowers.

Lee, E., Esaki, N., & Green, R. (2009). Collocation: Integrating child welfare and substance abuse services. *Journal of Social Work Practice in the Addictions, 9,* 55–70.

Lery, B. (2009). Neighborhood structure and foster care entry risk: The role of spatial scale in defining neighborhoods. *Children and Youth Services Review, 31,* 331–337.

Littell, J. (1997). Effects of the duration, intensity and breadth of family preservation services: A new analysis of data from the Illinois Families First experiment. *Children and Youth Services Review, 19,* 17–39.

Marsh, J., Ryan, J., Choi, S., & Testa, M. (2006). Integrated services for families with multiple problems: Obstacles to family reunification. *Children and Youth Services Review, 28,* 1074–1087.

Marsh, J. C., Smith, B. D., & Bruni, M. (2011). Integrated substance abuse and child welfare services for women: A progress review. *Children and Youth Services Review. 33*(3), 466–472.

Maternity and Infancy (Sheppard-Towner) Act of 1921, P.L. 67-97, 42 Stat. 224 (1921).

McAlpine, C., Courts-Marshall, C., & Harper-Doran, N. (2001). Combining child welfare and substance abuse services: A blended model of intervention. *Child Welfare, 80*(2), 129–149.

Mellin, E. A., Bronstein, L. R., Amorose, A. J., Ball, A., & Green, J. (2010). Measuring interprofessional team collaboration in expanded school mental health: Model refinement and scale development. *Journal of Interprofessional Care, 24,* 514–523.

Morrow, C. E., Mansoor, E., Hanson, K. L., Vogel, A. L., Rose-Jacobs, R., Genatossio, C. S., Windham, A., & Bandstra, E. S. (2010). The Starting Early Starting Smart integrated services model: Improving access to behavioral health services in the pediatric health care setting for at-risk families with young children. *Journal of Child and Family Studies, 19,* 42–56.

Muncy, R. (1991). *Creating a female dominion in American reform 1890–1935.* New York: Oxford University Press.

National Survey of Child and Adolescent Well-Being. (2005). *CPS sample component Wave 1 data analysis report.* Washington, DC: U.S. Department of Health and Human Services, Administration for Children and Families.

Proctor, E. K. (2007). Implementing evidence-based practice in social work education: Principles, strategies, and partnerships. *Research on Social Work Practice, 17,* 583–591.

Proctor, E. K., Landsverk, J., Aarons, G., Chambers, D., Glisson, C., & Mittman, B. (2009). Implementation research in mental health services: An emerging science with conceptual, methodological, and training challenges. *Administration and Policy in Mental Health, 36,* 24–34.

Ringeisen, H., Casanueva, C. E., Urato, M. P., & Cross, T. P. (2008). Special health care needs among children in child welfare. *Pediatrics, 122,* 232–241.

Ryan, J. P., Choi, S., Hong, S. J., Hernandez, P., & Larrison, C. R. (2008). Recovery coaches and substance exposed births: An experiment in child welfare. *Child Abuse & Neglect, 32,* 1072–1079.

Ryan, J. P., Marsh, J. C., Testa, M. F., & Louderman, R. (2006). Integrating substance abuse treatment and child welfare services: Findings from the Illinois Alcohol and Other Drug Abuse Waiver Demonstration. *Social Work Research, 30,* 95–107.

Smithgall, C., Jarpe-Ratner, E., Yang, D. H., DeCoursey, J., Brooks, L., & Goerge, R. (2009). *Family assessment in child welfare: The Illinois DCFS integrated assessment program in policy and practice.* Chicago: Chapin Hall at the University of Chicago.

Sousa, L., Ribeiro, C., & Rodrigues, S. (2006). Intervention with multi-problem poor clients: Towards a strengths-focused perspective. *Journal of Social Work Practice, 20*, 189–204.

Stroul, B., & Friedman, R. (1986). *A system of care for children and youth with severe emotional disturbances.* Washington, DC: Georgetown University Child Development Center, CASSP National Technical Assistance Center for Children's Mental Health.

Substance Abuse and Mental Health Services Administration (SAMHSA). (1999). *Blending perspectives and building common ground: A report to Congress on substance abuse and child protection.* Washington, DC: U.S. Government Printing Office.

Substance Abuse and Mental Health Services Administration (SAMHSA). (2005). *Comprehensive Community Mental Health Services for Children and Their Families Program— evaluation findings: Annual report to Congress.* Washington, DC: Author.

U.S. Public Health Service. (2000). *Report of the Surgeon General's Conference on Children's Mental Health: A national action agenda.* Washington, DC: U.S. Department of Health and Human Services.

Worcel, S. D., Furrer, C. J., Green, B. L., Burrus, S.W.M., & Finigan, M. W. (2008). Effects of family treatment drug courts on substance abuse and child welfare outcomes. *Child Abuse Review, 17*, 427–443.

Chapter 11

SOCIAL WORK TRAINEESHIP PROGRAMS

Gary R. Anderson, Kathleen Coulborn Faller, and Robin Leake

Assuring the safety of children, promoting lifelong connections for children with loving adults who are committed to each child's development and future, and supporting the well-being of children through attentiveness to health care, mental health, and education are daunting professional challenges. Achieving these goals involves decisions that require weighing competing principles and practicing in uncertain and risky circumstances. The goals of safety, permanency, and well-being are advanced by complex organizations, often in stressed and under-resourced communities. The professionals who operate within these service agencies, navigate and network in these communities, and address the needs and risks facing vulnerable children and family members must possess a special combination of competencies and traits. Identifying, recruiting, orienting, training, supporting, and retaining this special professional workforce is essential to promote child welfare's high goals and principles. Without a well-prepared workforce, the best programs and the most successful interventions will flounder.

Dedicated to the development of this workforce, the Children's Bureau has been pivotal in supporting its professional education through child welfare traineeship programs provided by social work education programs across the country. This chapter briefly describes the historical development of traineeship programs and discusses the most recent traineeship programs that have been supported through the National Child Welfare Workforce Institute, funded by the Children's Bureau. A range of themes relevant for an effective child welfare workforce (such as leadership, systems of care, and cultural competency) drive the curricular, field, and student support innovations associated with these traineeships. The challenges and opportunities for building a diverse workforce through traineeships are discussed, as well as the role evaluation plays in shaping the implementation of traineeship programs. Finally, the implications of traineeship programs for social work education and social work practice in the future are discussed.

Historical Development of Traineeship Programs

The preparation of the child welfare workforce has been a federal interest for a number of decades. The most extensive educational programs, funded by Title IV-B (Social Security Act, 42, U.S.C. § 426) and IV-E of the Social Security Act (42, U.S.C. § 471-479B), support the child welfare–relevant education of both prospective and current child welfare workers through enrollment in social work programs in which students are engaged in child welfare courses and field placements and are expected to work in a child welfare setting upon graduation.

Federally supported traineeship programs designated a social work degree as the academic qualification most relevant for child welfare employment. This preference recognized that many social work programs had evidenced a substantial commitment to the field of child welfare through coursework, specializations, field placements, and university–agency partnerships. A number of state agencies either required or prioritized social work education.

As the evaluation of the child welfare workforce and its preparation has increased in recent years, often aided by Title IV-E–funded social work programs, promising findings have supported the role of social work education as appropriate and relevant preparation for child welfare work. These studies have noted a correlation between a social work education and higher worker retention rates and intent to stay in one's position (Ellett, Ellett, & Rugutt, 2003) and a "goodness of fit" between child welfare and social work education (Bernotovicz, n.d.; Landsman, 2001; Rycraft, 1994). Professionals with social work degrees were found to be more likely to achieve permanency for children, and the reduction of worker turnover associated with a social work education also had a positive effect on permanency efforts (Albers, Reilly, & Rittner, 1993; Hess, Folaron, & Jefferson, 1992). One study noted that social workers with an MSW were inclined to have more positive views of clients (McGowan & Auerbach, 2004; Social Work Policy Institute, 2010).

Traineeship Program Design

Over the decades, traineeship programs primarily provided stipends for students pursuing a social work education with a child welfare focus. The creation of the National Child Welfare Workforce Institute (NCWWI) in 2008 introduced a number of programmatic innovations. The NCWWI traineeship programs share the features, opportunities, and challenges of traditional programs but enhanced the educational experience and innovations associated with social work programs dedicated to preparing the child welfare workforce. The traineeships encourage curricular attention to central child welfare themes such as leadership, systems of care, diversity, and organizational culture. Supported by peer networks and incorporating a range of innovations, NCWWI traineeships help prepare students for the child welfare workforce and future programmatic leadership. With enhanced attention to curriculum, field education, and academic innovations, the traineeships have built on traditional traineeship program features.

Program Features

Over the years, a common core of objectives, processes, and program elements has been evident throughout traineeship programs. These Children's Bureau–supported programs encourage the development of a well-prepared child welfare workforce through the following steps:

- Recruiting students to specialize in an enriched or enhanced curricular experience. Each school also identified a specific number of students who would be recruited for this program and offered financial assistance. This number of students supported varies from program to program and may depend, in part, on the cost of tuition as social work programs with lower tuition costs may be able to provide support for more students.
- Developing or enhancing an academic specialization in child welfare. This ensures that trainees have a coherent, integrated core of academic courses and field education experiences.
- Employing special features of a program to enrich the educational experience of the trainees. This can include recruitment of minority students, development of interdisciplinary experiences, specific content such as legal training or cultural competency, or specific challenges such as supporting mental or physical health.

Requirements for traineeship programs include successful completion of coursework and field education and confirmation by the social work program that the trainee is in good academic standing. Trainees are required to enter public child welfare employment upon graduation. This employment time that a trainee must work in a child welfare agency after graduation is called a payback, or repayment period, as a condition of receiving the traineeship's financial support. The length of the payback period is generally equivalent to the number of years that the student trainee received federal funds while in the social work program.

Each traineeship program pays careful attention to field education, as an internship in a child welfare agency plays a central role in a social work curriculum and in the student's preparation for child welfare work. Traineeship requirements for colleges and universities usually include an on-site field instructor with an MSW and a field liaison with knowledge of child welfare and the agency in which the student is placed.

Academic advising, practice classes, specialized child welfare courses, and a range of seminars and student support groups complement the field educational experience.

Social work traineeship programs often lead to curriculum development—courses (which may require additional faculty or staff), specialized field placements, dedicated support services, and other program features. This is a fiscal challenge, as traineeship budgets are predominantly earmarked for student financial support.

Overall, the benefit of a traineeship program is the training of a cohort of child welfare workers who can deliver high quality services to children and families. Benefits for the field of child welfare include (1) recruiting students to study child welfare; (2) preparing students through a specialized child welfare education; (3) providing financial support for students that encourages a career in child welfare; and (4) providing talented trainees to public child welfare agencies during the field experience component of the training and as potential future employees. Ultimately, children and families benefit from having a well-educated, well-trained social work professional in the front lines of child welfare service provision, assuring greater child safety, attentiveness to permanency, and prioritization of child and family well-being.

Outcomes for these traineeship programs are generally stated in terms of number of students in good standing, followed by the number of students who graduate and the number who enter the public child welfare workforce in a timely manner. These outcomes are typically measured simply by tracking student progress before and after graduation. Some programs propose enhanced measurement activities, such as pre- and posttests associated with courses and the overall traineeship experience; but with almost no funding for evaluation, it is challenging for programs to expand their assessment beyond simple counts.

These features have characterized traineeship programs for decades. Building on them, the NCWWI introduced a number of innovations in the design and delivery of traineeship programs, many in response to challenges experienced by earlier programs.

Program Challenges

Traineeship programs face a range of challenges:

- recruiting a strong and culturally diverse cohort of students
- managing the distinction between education and training
- preparing students for the complexity of the child welfare environment, including the breadth of knowledge needed for effective practice and the depth of skill needed to address difficult cases and support effective family engagement
- preparing students for a range of employment options across the continuum of child welfare services—family support, family preservation, child protective services, foster care, kinship care, therapeutic foster homes, group homes, residen-

tial care with a range of confinement and programming options, and adoption and postadoption services

- preparing students to understand and work with federal and state laws and court procedures
- responding to a range of stressors in the external environment

Traineeships have implemented a range of recruitment strategies. The opportunity may be announced to the entire BSW and MSW student population, or there may be targeted recruitment of trainees from a subpopulation of students—usually those who have already selected a child and family focus or indicated an interest in a child welfare field placement. An advantage of recruiting from the broader population is the possibility of attracting students to child welfare who might not otherwise consider this field of practice. A potential disadvantage is that a student's interest in the traineeship program may be unduly influenced by the funding support rather than a genuine and enduring interest in child welfare. Students who have already selected a child welfare field placement or curriculum specialization have demonstrated some interest in the field prior to learning about the availability of financial support.

Trainees can also be recruited from potential applicants to the social work program, either through partnerships with child welfare agencies (aimed at recruiting existing child welfare workers) or by providing information to the general applicant population.

Even with the financial support of the stipends and relatively modest expectations and responsibilities, some traineeship programs have experienced recruitment challenges, including competition from potentially more popular fields of practice and negative perceptions of child welfare work. Recruitment might be further complicated if traineeship programs are designed to attract a special subset of students such as students of color or students from rural regions. A number of programs, due to their urban locations, agency support, or history of strong child welfare partnerships and employment, experience high student interest and consequently develop a more demanding and extensive selection process.

Selection of trainees is accomplished through a number of approaches, beginning with an application to ascertain student interest and commitment and ensure successful student achievement. Many programs use an advisory committee to review applications and make recommendations for selection. Some committees are diverse and elaborate (with faculty members, alumni, agency representatives, and others); others are made up of the program's lead faculty members.

The application process also provides an opportunity to communicate expectations and responsibilities. As a requirement for receiving the significant financial support that the traineeship offers, students are expected to sign an agreement that they will work in a public child welfare agency upon graduation. This expectation is clearly stated in applications and early communications; students are expected to provide continuing contact and employment information to the social work program after graduation. Some programs treat this continuing contact as an opportunity to engage graduates in future traineeship program efforts, such as assisting in selection and mentoring of participants, communicating about work in child welfare, or providing other advice to the social work program.

Student agreement to work in child welfare after graduation (or repay the traineeship stipend) is typically secured at the time of the application or soon after selection. The process of honoring this obligation can be complicated if the student relocates to another state, if no appropriate positions are available, or if the student seeks employment in a related field rather than a traditional child welfare position.

There are sometimes debates about how relevant and how closely related an academic social work curriculum should be to public agency needs and practice. For example, social work programs often view themselves as providing a well-rounded educational experience that includes a critique of child welfare systems and attentiveness to multiple systems. An agency may prefer that training focus on the agency's specific practice model or position descriptions, or on practical day-to-day case management. Social work programs expose students to a range of theories and models and encourage critical thinking; agencies may have a preferred set of principles and models consistent with their approach and procedures.

In addition to resolving the differences between an educational approach and an agency-specific training perspective, social work education must provide both a generalist educational foundation and the specialized knowledge needed for child welfare work. Understanding the policy-making process and relevant local, state, and national policies is generally a key component of social policy classes, but this content could be broad, extensive, and dynamic in nature. In addition, a student could have a field placement in foster care or a course that focuses on adoption but then find that the employment opportunity upon graduation is in child protective services. Traineeship programs affirm that a social work education that is aligned with the standards of the Council on Social Work Education addresses the foundational knowledge and specialized preparation needed to work in child welfare. The relevance to child welfare practice is reinforced through child welfare electives and related courses that might address such topics as substance abuse or mental health. Consequently, traineeship programs typically craft a preferred or required course of study that includes specialized coursework with a foundation of social work knowledge and skills.

With regard to external environmental stressors, in addition to academic challenges, a range of challenges can arise in field placements—securing effective supervision, managing a caseload that is too small or too large, juggling autonomy and oversight in cases with high risk, agency staff turnover, and budget cutbacks and their ramifications for services and staffing. Many traineeship programs use the limited funds available beyond stipends to dedicate advisors and field liaisons to support student learning in the field and to reinforce the connection between classroom learning and agency-based learning.

National Child Welfare Workforce Institute Traineeship Program

Features and Structure

Traditional traineeships maintained the same structure for a number of decades, with some variation in the targeted student population (BSW or MSW) or number of years supported (typically three). During this time, hundreds of social workers were prepared for child welfare service and entered the workforce. Four issues emerged: (1) Was it possible to provide additional support for curriculum and programming to enrich the student experience? (2) Was it possible to foster innovations in social work programs that could advance knowledge about preparation for child welfare? (3) To what extent could traineeship programs help address the need for a diverse workforce and the challenge of racial disproportionality in child welfare? (4) Could evaluation of the traineeship programs be expanded so that the experience of students, schools, and agencies could be better documented and lessons learned could be more clearly identified?

The development of a new approach to traineeships—as demonstrated by the funding and scope of work associated with the federally funded NCWWI—has provided opportunities to design a range of activities and strategies to address the recruitment, selection, and support of students, the development of curriculum, and other innovations to support student preparation and advance social work education, address the development of a diverse workforce, and advance the evaluation of these activities and identify the process and outcomes associated with this new approach to traineeships.

The NCWWI, funded in 2008 by the Children's Bureau, included a traineeship program, which selected and now administers 12 social work traineeship programs that are set to continue through 2013. The NCWWI traineeships differ from earlier programs in the following ways:

- They include BSW, MSW, and combined BSW/MSW programs, while most short-term traineeship programs have focused primarily on MSW programs.
- They address a number of themes in curriculum and training, including leadership, systems of care, diversity, worker recruitment and retention strategies, and the goals measured by federally administered child and family service reviews.
- Unlike previous traineeships funded under Title IV-B, but similar to Title IV-E programs, they have received modest funds beyond those earmarked for student stipends so that social work programs could develop new initiatives and strengthen child welfare content in the programs.

- There is the expectation that the initiatives and innovations developed by the 12 traineeship schools will be shared with the broader social work education community.
- They were funded for multiple years (nine for five years and three for four years) so that innovations could be planned, implemented, refined, evaluated, and disseminated.
- They use an enhanced communication strategy to provide support through student trainee peer networks and a team of faculty and field education leaders who are also connected to each other and in communication through their own peer networks. Regular communication with deans, directors, and chairs of social work programs assures and recognizes institutional support.
- They participate in a process and outcome evaluation led by NCWWI to inform their work and to better understand their challenges, successes, and impact on workforce development.

In addition to the 12 NCWWI traineeship programs, five Comprehensive Workforce Projects funded at the same time have also developed traineeship programs. Predating these traineeships and operating concurrently, social work programs supported by federal Title IV-E funds have also been engaged in advancing the child welfare competency of the workforce through social work education. Combined, the NCWWI traineeships and Comprehensive Workforce and Title IV-E programs constitute a significant commitment to preparing the child welfare workforce. The communication and exchange of knowledge between these groups is an additional innovative aspect of the NCWWI.

Innovations

For the NCWWI traineeships, modest increases in funding, additional support through peer networks, and expectations with regard to curricular and program development that could strengthen child welfare content in social work programs led to implementation of a number of innovations. These innovations begin with the student recruitment and selection process, as social work programs rely on diverse advisory groups (including agency leaders, faculty, and consumer families), traineeship alumni, and a detailed application process to select trainees. One program met with prospective students and their families in recognition that students will need a support system to succeed in the social work program. Other program innovations include the following:

- Enhancement of curriculum. This includes revising existing courses to introduce child welfare or traineeship-relevant content, developing new courses—for example, on leadership, systems of care, and child welfare work with specific populations (such as communities of color or rural populations), and aligning coursework with public agency preservice training requirements.

- Enrichment of the student experience. This includes offering student-led seminars, encouraging creation of student portfolios, development of capstone projects, and encouraging student participation in professional conferences.
- Exploration of varied field education models and practices. This includes the use of a rotation model (with students placed in public, private, and federal agencies), support for linguistic competency, and mentoring by traineeship alumni and agency leaders.
- Strengthening of agency partnerships. Activities include agency-based design teams to address workplace climate and processes, representative advisory groups, and aligning curriculum and training with agency-identified evidence-based practices.

In addition to curriculum improvements, student enrichment activities, field education models, and agency partnerships, the NCWWI traineeship programs have identified several special issues arising from student experiences, and programs are responding to student needs and learning opportunities. These issues are student retention in social work programs, challenges associated with the transition to professional agency-based experience after graduation, distinctions between BSW and MSW programs, the value of clinical work in child welfare, and the role of geography, particularly preparing for rural and tribal child welfare practice.

Programs have addressed themes such as leadership development, systems of care and child well-being, evidence-based practices (for example, motivational interviewing), and workforce issues such as factors that promote retention. This enhanced traineeship model supports a special attentiveness to building a diverse workforce and is important to the evaluation of the traineeship programs in general.

Building a Diverse Workforce through Traineeships

The NCWWI traineeship initiative provides an opportunity to focus on special challenges for the child welfare workforce. Historically there have been marked racial imbalances in child welfare. Children and families of color are overrepresented as child welfare clientele, while the child welfare workforce is predominately white and female. Valued in the initial development of the NCWWI traineeships and identified as an important program consideration in the program application process, many of the social work programs used the traineeships to recruit, select, and nurture professionals and students underrepresented in the child welfare workforce. Between the NCWWI and Comprehensive Workforce traineeships, there are 17 programs. Five programs have specifically targeted Native American students, two have targeted students at historically black colleges and universities, and three are focused on Spanish-speaking trainees. Even those that have not specifically targeted students of color have assertively reached out to them. Two of the traineeships have reported that all of their students, past and present, come from underrepresented populations.

There has been an ongoing examination of these programs with regard to their successes, challenges, and lessons learned. One issue that has been a theme in program success is the importance of *establishing and maintaining strong relationships with constituencies of color*. These may be institutional—for example, nurturing relationships with tribal and urban community colleges and undergraduate programs with substantial constituencies of color, or reaching out to agencies with substantial numbers of employees and clientele of color. They may also be individual—for example, cultivating promising employees of color and urging them to apply to traineeship programs, or reaching out to supervisors and administrators of color who may channel potential applicants of color to the traineeship. Going into the community and participating in social activities sponsored by underrepresented populations is another strategy employed by some programs. Fostering these relationships requires persistence. Agencies and people of color may not readily trust or respond with enthusiasm to these overtures. The NCWWI experience to date is that even programs that have had initially disappointing response rates have not given up but have redoubled their efforts.

Having *high-visibility faculty and staff of color* lends credibility to traineeships and makes it easier to recruit. So too does having *current students and graduates of color* whom traineeship programs can showcase. Programs have featured these students on their websites and in their brochures. They have fostered presentations by their students that serve both to socialize them into the social work profession and to demonstrate the accomplishments of their trainees.

Conversely, programs whose staff and faculty are primarily white have struggled more. One of the greatest challenges is recruiting BSW students from an undergraduate program that is mostly white. Similarly, recruiting from diverse undergraduate and community college programs into a mostly white university is difficult.

Programs that recruit trainees from the current child welfare workforce rather than from incoming or current students have had fewer challenges. Although this workforce is not as diverse as we hope it to be, it is more diverse, particularly in urban areas, than many undergraduate programs and even than incoming MSW students. However, one of the ironies is that sometimes child welfare agencies do not appear to share the same level of commitment to diversity as the traineeships. When these agencies are given the responsibility of recruiting or recommending staff for traineeships, they may choose white employees.

To date, the NCWWI traineeship experience has demonstrated that diversity begets diversity. Over 50 percent of traineeship recruits in the first three years of the traineeships have been students of color, with a high percentage in the first year (73 percent of students recruited) and continuing strong percentages in following years (for example, 43 percent of students in the second year). Altogether the 17 traineeship programs are increasing the diversity of the child welfare workforce. The development of creative and persistent strategies for improving the diversity of the child welfare workforce remains a traineeship and educational priority. It is important that child welfare agencies share the traineeships' commitment to diversity.

In summary, factors that increase success in recruiting diverse trainees are as follows: developing strong bonds and abiding relationships with diverse populations, placing faculty and staff of color in key positions, establishing a history of educating students of color, having a diverse student body at both the BSW and MSW levels to recruit from, and being located in an ethnically diverse community.

Building Evaluative Evidence for the Traineeship Experience and Outcomes

With limited funds for anything other than student stipends, social work programs are generally unable to conduct evaluation activities beyond tracking student grades and asking limited follow-up questions about employment and reflections on academic experiences. One of the benefits of the NCWWI traineeships is the evaluation of a large cohort of students across more than 20 social work programs (primary traineeship social work programs and their partner schools). This discussion is based on the analysis and experience of the program evaluation team with access to traineeship reports. The NCWWI cross-site evaluation is able to conduct a standardized longitudinal assessment of students throughout their traineeships and after graduation, focusing on gathering information to answer these key questions:

- How successfully are traineeships using recruitment strategies to increase the number of qualified and diverse applicants?
- How are traineeship programs implementing innovative educational strategies that effectively prepare child welfare workers?
- To what extent are local child welfare issues affected by and affecting education, training, and university–agency partnerships?
- To what extent do traineeships prepare students with the knowledge and skills to work effectively in child welfare?

A collaborative and participatory evaluation approach was used that relied on active engagement of all of the traineeship partners to develop a mixed-methods evaluation design and assessment tools. This cross-site evaluation team also played a critical role in addressing logistical challenges associated with the project, including obtaining students' informed consent to share contact information and participate in the evaluation, and ensuring compliance with internal review boards from each school for the protection of human subjects.

The evaluation design includes annual interviews with traineeship principal investigators and students and graduates, reviews of semiannual progress reports from each traineeship program, collection of student demographic and educational performance data, competency ratings from faculty and field instructors, and a standardized Web-based self-report survey for students. The survey, titled the Stipend Student Inventory (SSI), comprises a standardized child welfare competency assessment, as well as demographic information and measures of satisfaction with the program (coursework, fieldwork, and instructors), stress and coping, and workforce issues. The SSI is administered to all students at the beginning of the academic year in which they first receive a stipend and then annually through the life of the program. This design enables researchers to follow students beyond graduation and throughout their time of employment that is part of the graduates' formal repayment period in return for accepting the traineeship stipend. During these initial years of employment, the researchers can learn how traineeship graduates are transferring their knowledge and skills to the workplace and explore factors that influence job retention, satisfaction, and commitment.

In the hope that the cross-site data can be used by individual schools to evaluate the effectiveness of their traineeships, the SSI was designed with maximum flexibility. Schools were encouraged to customize the survey beyond the standardized measures to capture unique elements of their program. NCWWI evaluators collect all of the data and share program-level results with each school upon request. In this way, the capacity of traineeship programs for enhanced evaluation is strengthened through participation in the cross-site evaluation, and schools have greater buy-in for the process.

Evidence of the collaborative work of the cross-site evaluation group is the development of a standardized set of competencies across eight domains of child welfare: relevant federal policy, organization of child welfare services, organization of other programs related to child welfare practice, human behavior in the social environment, current approaches to child welfare service delivery, skills, ethics, and cultural issues. Using a common set of standardized child welfare competencies for multiple schools of social work can be a challenging and complicated endeavor, as many programs have their own unique competencies or are invested in developing their own competencies that align with their mission, values, and instructional objectives. However, for the purposes of standardized cross-site evaluation, this collaborative work group agreed to use the same basic competencies. Preliminary analyses indicate that these competencies have demonstrated reliability and show differential gains among BSW and MSW students. Further, exploratory factor analysis also confirms that competencies are grouped into discreet constructs or topic areas.

The SSI has an average response rate of approximately 80 percent of the traineeship students. Findings show high levels of satisfaction among both BSW and MSW students with their overall education experience, including course offerings, quality of instruction, support from faculty, and field placements. About half (52 percent) of the students reported increased commitment to the field of child welfare as a result of their field placement, while only 11 percent said they were less likely to consider a career in child welfare as a result of their field experience.

Both BSW and MSW students showed significant competency gains during their educational preparation. Competency self-ratings were significantly higher for MSW compared to BSW students, and for students currently working in a child welfare agency. Significant differences in competency ratings persisted between BSW and MSW students one year after graduation, suggesting that it takes more than one year of experience for BSW students to "catch up."

Inter-rater reliability between students' self-ratings of competencies and rating by faculty and field instructors has been low. Faculty and field instructors tend to rate students much higher than the students rate themselves, using the high end of the rating scale with frequency. These cross-site results confirm anecdotal reports of grade inflation and suggest it to be a common occurrence. They also suggest that field instructors may have a different frame of reference than students in regard to the competencies. For example, instructors may be rating students based on their valuation of where a beginning student should be at this stage of development, while students might be rating their own competencies against a different metric, such as their perceptions of a proficient professional worker in the field. These early findings suggest the need for more exploratory work in self-competency ratings, if this is to be a useful measure of student skills development. Field instructors have also identified a number of areas for student development through open-ended responses, including the need for students to be exposed to a broader array of child welfare practice areas in their field experiences, and for students to learn how to engage with families, particularly those with different cultural and ethnic backgrounds.

The cross-site evaluation includes longitudinal assessment of students after they graduate to learn about workforce factors that have been shown to influence retention, such as agency culture and climate, job satisfaction, salary and benefits, and supervision (Calahane & Sites, 2008; Dickinson & Perry, 2002; Glisson & Hemmelgarn, 1998). Early data from traineeship participants one year after graduation show that over 70 percent believe their traineeships prepared them for their job and that they have the skills they need to do their job effectively. Almost 60 percent reported high job satisfaction, and most reported strong support from supervisors and peers. However, about one-third of graduates reported that they plan to leave child welfare after their repayment period. Interviews have suggested that many graduates have a strong commitment to working with underserved children and families, but not necessarily through public or private child welfare. Some of the graduates expressed frustration that child welfare leadership and innovation skills are not valued and encouraged on the job, and said they would like more opportunities to use the advanced skills obtained in their social work education programs.

Thus far, the NCWWI evaluation has yielded valuable information about student competencies, program innovation, partnership initiatives, and student outcomes that inform the programs and provide lessons learned for the broader field of social work education. With a significant financial investment and a desire for future support, the ability to address the outcomes and success of the program has heightened importance. The feedback from multiple standpoints combined with large sample sizes and longitudinal features promote the acquisition of meaningful information to support ongoing program improvement.

Traineeships and the Future of Social Work Education and Practice

The enhanced evaluation of traineeship programs and the attentiveness to recruiting and preparing a diverse workforce should enrich the lessons learned from this significant investment of federal funding to strengthen the preparation and leadership of child welfare professionals. With increased attention to the systematic identification and development of promising practices and evidence-based practices, and the recognition of the crucial clinical role of child welfare workers in supporting the education and physical and mental health of children as well as their safety and permanency, the important role of social work education is highlighted. Schools of social work can identify evidence-based and promising practices that have application in child welfare settings, advance the use of these practices in field education by supporting field instructors and agency partners, and ultimately encourage improved practice through partnerships that extend beyond graduation and benefit from the placement of graduates in the workplace. These training partnerships will also facilitate knowledge from the agency being introduced and infused in the curriculum.

In the future, traineeship programs could continue to benefit from the initiation of innovative educational supports for students, such as the development of leadership through seminars and peer networks, the identification of knowledge and skills through portfolios, and the experience of networking and presenting at professional conferences. Other opportunities abound:

- There is the opportunity to gain specialized information—for example, about effective recruitment practices through community and family engagement and strong student support through mentoring and peer networking.
- Understanding of child welfare competencies can be expanded and enriched by comparing and contrasting the experiences of BSW and MSW students, social work students who are concurrently in school and employed in child welfare and newly recruited social work students without a work history in child welfare, rural and urban students, and other diverse student categories.

- University–agency partnerships can be strengthened to improve student preparation and help trainees to make the transition from student status to employee and professional. Models of networking and mentoring can be crafted that move from school-based programs to agency based, and other avenues of connectivity and support can be created.

Traineeship programs present a special opportunity to develop student, agency, and academic leaders and to develop innovations and support systems with wide applicability to social work education and the field of child welfare. By adding and strengthening coursework, focusing field education, enriching the educational experience with opportunities for peer networks, coaching, and mentorships, and then extending relationships into the agency following graduation, traineeships have provided a testing ground for program development. What lies ahead are new opportunities to continue learning with the agencies how best to prepare and support a professional workforce.

Ensuring that social work education has the curricular content, field education competencies and experiences, and programmatic supports that students need is essential for this contribution to workforce preparation. In addition, partnerships with child welfare agencies help ensure that social work programs are engaged with the content and challenges faced by agencies and that agencies are informed and benefit from an ongoing relationship with a child welfare–focused social work program. A number of these lessons have been learned from traineeship programs and evidenced by the enhancement of social work educational programs. Strengthening connections to agencies and extending relationships after trainees graduate can build on the curriculum and programmatic features of traineeship programs. These investments and the lessons learned from these partnerships and programs will result in a steady influx of competent child welfare professionals into the workforce who are able to provide ethical, skillful leadership supporting the delivery of effective services to children and families.

References

Albers, E., Reilly, T., & Rittner, B. (1993). Children in foster care: Possible factors affecting permanency planning. *Child and Adolescent Social Work Journal, 10,* 329–341.

Bernatovicz, F. (n.d.). *Retention of child welfare caseworkers: A report.* Retrieved from www.muskie.usm.maine.edu/helpkids/pubstext/retention.html

Calahane, H., & Sites, E. (2008). The climate of child welfare employee retention. *Child Welfare, 87,* 91–111.

Dickinson, N., & Perry, R. (2002). Factors influencing the retention of specially educated public child welfare workers. *Journal of Health and Social Policy, 15*(3–4), 89–103.

Ellett, A., Ellett, C., & Rugutt, J. K. (2003). Executive summary. In *A study of personal and organizational factors contributing to employee retention and turnover in child welfare in Georgia: A report prepared for the Georgia Department of Human Resources/Division of Family and Children Services*. Retrieved from http://www.louisville.edu/kent/projects/iv-e

Glisson, C., & Hemmelgarn, A. (1998). The effects of organizational climate and interorganizational coordination on the quality and outcomes of children's service systems. *Child Abuse & Neglect, 22,* 401–421.

Hess, P. M., Folaron, G., & Jefferson, A. B. (1992). Effectiveness of family reunification services: An innovative evaluative model. *Social Work, 37,* 304–311.

Landsman, M. (2001). Commitment in public child welfare. *Social Service Review, 75,* 386–419.

McGowan, B., & Auerbach, C. (2004, January). *A survey of MSW graduates at New York City Administration for Children's Services.* Presentation at 2004 Society for Social Work and Research Conference, New Orleans.

Rycraft, J. R. (1994). The party isn't over: The agency role in the retention of public child welfare caseworkers. *Social Work, 39,* 75–80.

Social Work Policy Institute. (2010). *Professional social workers in child welfare work: Research addressing the recruitment and retention dilemma.* Retrieved from http://www.socialworkpolicy.org/research/child-welfare-2.html

Chapter 12

SOCIAL WORK EDUCATION IN TRIBAL AND URBAN INDIAN CHILD WELFARE SETTINGS

Virginia Whitekiller, Katharine Cahn, Heather Craig-Oldsen, and James Caringi

The Indian Child Welfare Act (ICWA) (P.L. 95-608), enacted in 1978, made numerous changes in how states are required to interact with tribal nations regarding Native children. Passed before the landmark Adoption Assistance and Child Welfare Act of 1980 (P.L. 96-272), ICWA put in place a strong framework for child welfare practice with American Indian and Alaska Native children. For example, it called for "active" (not just "reasonable") efforts to prevent out-of-home placement, maintain tribal ties, and return children to family, tribe, or tribal culture in a timely way. ICWA called for tribal notification and the involvement of tribal expertise in making child placement decisions.

Despite this early policy framework, as the U.S. child welfare system completes its first century, American Indian and Alaska Native children continue to be placed in foster care away from their own families, tribes, and tribal cultures at rates higher than children from other racial or ethnic groups. Similarly, workforce development efforts for tribal child welfare have lagged behind those for state and county workers. While there are close to 80 partnerships between schools of social work and state or county child welfare agencies, only a handful of partnerships exist between social work education programs and tribal or urban Indian child welfare providers.

Children's Bureau traineeships funded by Title IV-B of the 1962 amendments to the Social Security Act, involving 426 grants to schools and departments of social work, have been an important means of investment in child welfare workforce development, both in general and for tribal agencies. In 2008 the Children's Bureau funded the National Child Welfare Workforce Institute (NCWWI), which included a mandate to administer 12 traineeship programs. Of the twelve traineeships selected, five focused entirely or in part on social work students committed to working in tribal or urban Indian child welfare. This may be the largest concentration of direct grant funding to date for the preparation of American Indian and Alaska Native social work students for child welfare careers with Indian families.

This chapter is written by lead faculty from four of these traineeships. It is the hope of the authors that specific lessons learned from these four programs might offer a window into the larger history of social work education and workforce development for Indian child welfare.

Though operating in distinct regional and cultural settings, each university and tribal partnership held in common the desire to recruit and retain social workers committed to effective, legal, and respectful work with Native families. Though program histories differ, each program's historical context is based on the local community and school's experience with and unique local response to tribal jurisdiction. Beginning with a discussion of each university's unique historical, cultural, and regional context, the chapter reviews lessons learned and draw on these lessons to discuss future workforce development efforts for full implementation of ICWA. The chapter concludes with a summary of the innovations and lessons learned that emerge from the collective experiences of the four universities and the tribes with which they partner.

Briar Cliff University's Siouxland Indian Child Welfare Traineeship Project

Over the years as a result of federal incentives, job opportunities, proximity to tribal lands, and other reasons, the three-state area around Sioux City, Iowa, became home to many Native American families. Known as Siouxland, the area is the home of a culturally and ethnically diverse population including members of the Santee Sioux, Omaha, Ponca, Winnebago, and Yankton Sioux tribes. All but the Ponca tribe have reservation land near Sioux City. In 2009, the community became the home of the Siouxland Indian Child Welfare Traineeship Project, one of the 12 NCWWI child welfare traineeships.

Because of the legacy of the boarding school experience, wholesale removals of Native children from their homes, and other negative experiences with the child welfare system, the Native community of Siouxland had a strong mistrust of non-Native public and private child welfare agencies. In part because of the lack of Native and culturally competent child welfare workers, the number of Native children in Siouxland's child welfare system became and has remained disproportionately high into the second decade of the 21st century.

As early as 1991, Native community members in Siouxland began to share stories of losing their children and grandchildren to the child welfare system. The community organized and began meeting monthly with local Iowa Department of Human Services staff and a variety of other stakeholders, including the Sioux City Human Rights Commission, the courts, private providers, area colleges and universities, health providers, police, and other service providers. They called themselves the Community Initiative for Native Children and Families (CINCF) and became the forum for understanding how and why Native children were disproportionately present in the child welfare system. One repeatedly identified cause was the lack of Native and culturally responsive social workers.

In 2003 CINCF organized the first annual Memorial March to Honor Our Lost Children to draw attention to the issue, sparked by the recent deaths of two children and the adoption of others by non-Native families. Native members of CINCF formed the Recover our Children group and met with the governor of Iowa to express their concerns. In the same year, an Iowa Indian Child Welfare Act was passed, largely as a result of CINCF's efforts. The Iowa Indian Child Welfare Act was intended to increase ICWA compliance through better definitions of active effort, eligibility, and review requirements. In 2004, the Iowa Department of Human Services awarded new Minority Youth and Family Initiative funding to Sioux City and Woodbury County to advance practices aimed at reducing the number of Native children in the child welfare system. This stemmed partly from the federal Child and Family Service Review[1] (CFSR). for which Woodbury County was one of four counties in Iowa with on-site reviewers. The CFSR findings on disparate treatment of Native American families supported the need for culturally sensitive services.

The Specialized Native American Project, known simply as the Native Unit to those in Siouxland, was launched by the Department of Human Services in January 2005. Among other workers, the unit employed Native American family and tribal liaisons who primarily worked with local tribes, as well as with many other federally recognized tribes throughout the United States. This specialized team exclusively worked with children and families that self-identified as Native. The team used active efforts as required by ICWA. Relative placements increased, and collaboration with the tribes strengthened services to reunify children with their families in all cases including relative placement and collaboration with the tribes.

These practice changes, along with increased systems coordination and a growing trust between the Native community and public and private child welfare agencies, began to reduce the number of Native children in out-of-home placement. Families involved with the Native Unit showed reduced risk of re-abuse and increased family functioning. Tribes became more involved. In 2006 the CINCF collaboration caught the attention and support of national organizations including the Annie E. Casey Foundation (now the Alliance for Children and Families), Georgetown University, the National Indian Child Welfare Association, and the Child Welfare League of America. Despite

---

[1] According to the Children's Bureau Web site, the Child and Family Services Reviews (CFSRs) enable the Children's Bureau to ensure conformity with Federal child welfare requirements, to gauge the experiences of children, youths, and families receiving state child welfare services, and to assist states as they enhance their capacity to help families achieve positive outcomes.

other practice advances, all partners from local to national levels agreed that a primary barrier to better serving Native children and families and reducing their number in the child welfare system was the lack of Native social workers.

According to tribal leaders, Siouxland had many excellent Native American workers who provided volunteer services or were paid for general service provision but who were lacking social work credentials to enable them to be hired as child welfare workers. Many had college credits but had been unable to complete a degree. Consequently, in 2009 Siouxland had both a limited number of and a great need for Native American child welfare workers.

Building upon community partnerships, Briar Cliff University proposed the development of the Siouxland Indian Child Welfare Traineeship Project. The project's primary goal was to provide financial support for Native American students who were committed to careers in child welfare, preferably in Siouxland, to complete their BSW degrees. A community advisory board representing the public child welfare agency and the Omaha, Ponca, Santee Sioux, Winnebago, and Yankton Sioux tribes produced deeper knowledge of effective community and tribal recruitment and retention of Native American social work students.

Essential to the success of the program is the active leadership of the tribes in recruiting, selecting, and providing ongoing support to the trainees. Tribal members chair the family and tribal team meetings during which each applicant to the program learns from Native American graduates of the social work program, faculty, and advisors what they might expect during their academic work. This leads to informed decisions by the applicants, their family members who will provide support during the educational process, the social work program faculty, and the advisors who are instrumental in the final selection decisions.

University of Montana

As is true in much of the nation, tribal children are over-represented in the child welfare system in Montana, which is home to seven federally recognized tribes and seven reservations. Whereas American Indians represent 10 percent of the state population, they represent over one-third of children in care statewide. It is also likely this estimate is low due to data tracking and reporting difficulties (Horne, Travis, Miller, & Simmons, 2009). The state has a history of attempts to increase ICWA compliance and is currently invested in efforts to better understand the over-representation of Native children in care. Regardless of these difficulties, Native tribes in Montana are able to build on the strengths of their communities in cultural and traditional ways. The diverse tribal systems of Montana demonstrate tremendous resilience, internal capacity, and potential for positive transformation. It is imperative that future tribal, state–tribal, and university partnerships support tribes in using their own capacity to positively affect child and family welfare in their communities.

Collaboration between the University of Montana and tribes has been a priority for the university since its establishment in 1970. The initial partnership showed promise but was not without difficulties. A small faculty, vast distances to travel to collaborate, and a lack of knowledge of the cultures of local tribes created barriers to be addressed by what was then the Department of Social Work. However, in 2002 with the addition of an MSW program and formation of a School of Social Work, as well as movement of the school from the College of Liberal Arts to the College of Health Professions and Biomedical Sciences, there was a renewed impetus to increase Title IV-E state and tribal collaboration.

Collaboration with tribes continues to grow at the University of Montana. The School of Social Work has a strong commitment to social justice, which informs its vision and curriculum. The state of Montana is also unique in that each of its seven reservations has a tribal college. Much of the school's effort has consisted of building relationships with tribal colleges by developing "2 plus 2" programs in which students can stay in their home communities and receive a bachelors degree in social work from the University of Montana. Although the school has had a Title IV-E–funded BSW and MSW program for some time, the NCWWI traineeship grant has greatly increased its ability to engage with Native students who have an interest in working in tribal child welfare. The flexibility of this funding, allowing students to pay back their stipend by working in a state, private, or tribal child welfare agency, has increased the number of Native students obtaining degrees through traineeships.

Native students are engaged in both tribal and state-run practicum sites. Curricular developments include a course on ICWA specific to Montana tribes and two courses that address traumatic stress as related to child abuse and neglect. Current efforts to recruit more Native students to the traineeship program include hiring two cultural consultants who are both tribally enrolled MSW graduates.

Another success is the school's relationship with the National Native Children's Trauma Center, which is housed in the interdisciplinary Institute for Educational Research and Service. The Institute and the School of Social Work recently received a grant from the Children's Bureau to create trauma-informed child welfare systems in Indian Country. This joint effort in concert with Title IV-E and NCWWI funding forms the basis for future collaboration with tribes in Montana and nationally.

Northeastern State University

Northeastern State University (NSU) has a long history of providing higher education to Native Americans. In 1851, after the Cherokees' forced removal from the eastern United States, the Cherokee Nation established the Cherokee Male and Female Seminaries in Tahlequah, Oklahoma, now the capitol of the Cherokee Nation. The purpose of these educational institutions was to provide private higher education to Cherokee men and women; curricula were designed to formally train Cherokee teachers to practice their profession in Indian Territory. Following statehood on March 6, 1909, the Cherokee Nation Female Seminary was purchased by Oklahoma to provide public education to state residents as a normal school; it later became a state college. In 1974, what began as a progressive system of formal tribal education to fulfill a stipulation in the Treaty of 1835 between some representative Cherokees and the U.S. government became Northeastern State University.

In keeping with its history of culturally diverse student representation, NSU continues to lead the nation in Native American student enrollment and bachelor's degree conferrals. In 2011, undergraduate Native students made up 28.9 percent (2,751) of the total university enrollment, of 9,519, with 348 (24.3 percent) undergraduate degree conferrals for Native Americans out of 1,434 for the total university. This percentage also correlates with the Native student enrollment in the BSW program, which has about 180 students total with 52 Native American students and 60 total graduates a year, with 15 (25 percent) being Native American.

NSU also maintains a national reputation for the implementation of programs and curricula that address Native American populations and issues. An element of this legacy is the Annual Symposium of the American Indian, ongoing since 1972. Each year this free three-day program hosts a wide array of national and international indigenous presenters in the areas of education, arts, social sciences, health, and community mobilization. Furthermore, the university offers a bachelor's degree through the Cherokee Education Degree Program, which prepares students to be teachers and speakers of the Cherokee language and to promote the Cherokee culture and life ways.

The social work program further serves as a scholarly resource and institutional support for Native populations. For example, the department partnered with the Cherokee Nation to promote the annual Preserving Family, Culture, and Caregivers Child Welfare Conference on the NSU Tahlequah Campus from 1994 to 2009. In spring 2010, former Cherokee Nation Chief Wilma Mankiller, an NSU Sequoyah Fellow, and Virginia Whitekiller, an NSU social work faculty member, taught the first Native American leadership seminar. This annual course offering has become institutionalized by the Cherokee Nation as a requirement for its academic scholarship recipients.

NSU's social work program has always incorporated Native issues and practice into its curriculum. Under the new Council on Social Work Education standards, the program has added a core competency of "cultural awareness in the provision of services to Native Americans" (Whitekiller-Drywater, 2012, p. 31). Outcome indicators for this competency are to

(1) acquire and apply knowledge of the historical oppression and tribal diversity of Native American populations; (2) identify the social issues that colonization has had upon Native American tribal populations; and (3) analyze social

work practice models to determine their compatibility in working with Native Americans. (Whitekiller-Drywater, 2012, p. 31)

The BSW program offers extensive preparation in the field of child welfare. Accredited in 1992, the program served as a Title IV-E subcontractor from 1994 to 2010; NSU led in the number of Native and non-Native social work graduates placed in child welfare service in Oklahoma counties. In 2005, NSU placed the first tribal Title IV-E student in an Indian child welfare practicum, and in 2010, it was selected for NCCWI traineeship with a primary purpose of preparing Native American BSW students to work in Indian child welfare systems. Through this award, the social work program was able to create the state's first child welfare specialization with an emphasis on working with Native American populations. This innovative specialization exchanges the standard 11-semester-hour social work minor for a structured curriculum that addresses various facets of child welfare. The traineeship program has eight students at different stages of completing work toward graduation; they receive a stipend covering educational expenses and some travel costs for attending professional conferences and commuting to practicums.

This specialized funding also supports the development of partnerships with tribal agencies and governments to promote collaboration directed at enhancing the child welfare systems that serve Native American populations through workforce development and program innovations. For example, NSU's traineeship program continues to work with the Cherokee Nation and the United Keetoowah Band of Cherokee Indians in Oklahoma to refine partnerships that best meet the child welfare workforce needs of their populations. The partnerships begin with practicum placements for both Native and non-Native students in their tribal child welfare programs. Trainees are guaranteed to receive in-depth training and experience on tribal child welfare practices and policies that align with the Indian Child Welfare Act. They also receive direct experience in working with Native families, the state child welfare system, tribal and state courts, and other affiliated tribal child welfare systems.

Due to Indian preference in hiring, trainees who opt to be placed at tribal practicum sites do not automatically expect employment with the tribes upon graduation. As at many employment sites, hiring is dependent upon such factors as job availability, experience, and the students' fit with the agency. However, there is an increased likelihood, especially for the Native students, of hire upon graduation due to their excellent preparation of having a child welfare specialty and 440 practicum hours in a tribal child welfare agency.

Portland State University

Portland State University (PSU)'s School of Social Work is the only public school of social work in Oregon, a state where nine federally recognized tribes are located. In addition, Portland is home to a large urban Native population and social service agencies serving primarily American Indians and Alaska Natives. While located in an urban area, the School of Social Work at PSU has a history of workforce development to strengthen social work practice in both urban and tribal child welfare settings, and has drawn on community, state, and federal support for this work.

For example, in the 1990s, PSU hosted a Children's Bureau traineeship grant focusing on child welfare workforce development in communities of color. PSU later played a leadership role in designing and delivering the Building on Strengths tribal traineeships, a Children's Bureau–funded program based at the University of Washington School of Social Work but serving social work schools and departments across the Pacific Northwest. Building on Strengths provided support to tribally enrolled or affiliated students with a career commitment to improving tribal child welfare outcomes (Bending, DeMello, Crofoot, & Cahn, 2000). Tribally enrolled social work faculty and elders developed the curriculum competencies and teaching approaches. Cultural and peer learning experiences were offered to traineeship students to supplement their classroom education.

The traineeship program provided rich culturally based learning experiences to social work students with the cultural capital and commitment to serve tribal children and families. Lessons learned remain in the curriculum and culture of several participating schools, and graduates of this traineeship have gone on to form tribal child welfare programs or serve as Indian child welfare unit supervisors and staff. The program also left a legacy of learning at the participating schools. A strong sense of community for tribal social work students, specific classes, customized field experiences, and a network of faculty–tribal relationships is still in place in some participating schools. PSU faculty who participated in this program infused learning into the PSU curriculum and the Child Welfare Partnership (Title IV-E funded) stipend program.

Tribal partnership and workforce development are also part of the Child Welfare Partnership, a training and research program founded in 1993 by the state child welfare agency and the university, supported by federal (Title IV-E) and state (university and agency) dollars. The Child Welfare Partnership in-service and caregiver (foster, adoptive, and kinship) trainings are open to both tribal and state child welfare workers. The child welfare education program offers stipends to an average of 50 social work students per year who are committed to a career in child welfare, including students of American Indian descent. A MSW distance education program, now fully incorporated into the social work program, was incubated by the Child Welfare Partnership to serve the workforce development needs of Oregon's rural and tribal settings.

Specialized grant funding from the Children's Bureau has helped the Child Welfare Partnership strengthen the curriculum content and training approach for rural and tribal child welfare staff. Between 2003 and 2008, a five-year rural training grant supported the development of a range of training and classroom materials on social work practice in rural and tribal child welfare for Oregon and rural Alaska. Tribal child welfare directors and Alaska village chiefs, as well as the Oregon Indian child welfare liaison and manager, contributed to and advised on curriculum development using face-to-face and distance education approaches. Through this grant, the Child Welfare Partnership has strengthened relationships with the tribes, and Partnership staff regularly attend the quarterly meetings of all tribes with the Indian child welfare liaison to identify and promote workforce development for those serving tribal children. Partnership staff have served the tribes in hosting a yearly Indian child welfare conference, and in action planning for improved Indian child welfare compliance in the state.

PSU also has a long-standing relationship with the National Indian Child Welfare Association, based in Portland, which has historically offered field placements and research opportunities for social work students. Participants in the rural and tribal training program took the association's online training on the Indian Child Welfare Act. This partnership continues to provide avenues for advancing tribal child welfare practice and policy and for the development of tribally affiliated social workers with much-needed social work skills in policy advocacy, research, and administration to conduct social work at the systems level.

Based on this history of strength, and a shared knowledge of what was needed in tribal child welfare workforce development, the PSU Child Welfare Partnership successfully applied for one of the NCWWI traineeships. The purpose of this program has been to invest in leadership development and to increase the number of culturally responsive leaders in tribal, state, and private child welfare agencies. Social work students selected for this program are experienced in communities of color and demonstrate strong leadership potential and career commitments to child welfare. American Indian and Alaska Native participants have been identified by their tribe or urban agency as currently serving or having the potential to serve in a leadership role for tribal or urban Indian child welfare client families.

The Culturally Responsive Leadership program provides students with enriched financial and educational supports, connecting Native students with Native faculty and with field placements that support their educational goals. The program offers a monthly student-led seminar designed to offer an "empowerment zone" within the larger curriculum as well as to provide leadership education. Tribally enrolled social work students may also take advantage of the programming and sense of community offered by the Native American Cultural Center on campus, and support from American Indian faculty in social work and other departments on campus. Graduation for these students includes an honor ceremony hosted by the Native American Cultural Center, bringing together extended family and tribal connections to acknowledge the communal accomplishment of their graduation. Student leaders from this program have gone on to work with urban, tribal, and national Indian child welfare programs.

Lessons Learned across Programs: Bridging the Gap between University and Tribal Communities

The traineeships described in this chapter have produced many lessons that can shape Children's Bureau policy going forward into the next century. We have found that bridging the gap between universities and tribal communities is an essential first step in developing child welfare traineeships with Native Americans. This has not been an easy task; the lessons learned have been laborious, with change occurring gradually at best. In the past 200-plus years, federal education and social service policies have been inconsistent and disruptive to Native people and have rarely honored the practices, values, and beliefs of the populations they were designed to serve. As a result, Native Americans continue to struggle with a variety of alien institutions and policies.

Academic institutions have not been exempt from these subjugating practices. The provision of education for Native Americans by the federal government was a direct result of historical obligations based on treaties under which Native Americans exchanged land and the accompanying natural resources for education and health care (Pevar, 1992). Education was used as a means to assimilate Native Americans into mainstream society. Even in modern academic programs, including social work programs that are built upon a foundation of social justice that embraces cultural diversity, educational practices can fail to incorporate theories, practices, and skills that address different ways of knowing.

For example, contemporary practice models are based on the belief that families are experts in their own lives. In this vein, our traineeship programs have come to acknowledge that the tribal communities with which we partner are experts in their own relevant practices and challenges, and it is imperative that we learn from them and value what they have to offer as integral participants in the search for solutions. One educator said, "It is through the multiple and rich interpretation of their [Native American] stories that we can better understand the relationship between the individual, the community and institutions of higher education" (Oritz & HeavyRunner, 2003, p. 218). In keeping with this revelation, while developing child welfare traineeships for Native populations, we have had to ask: How can we place ourselves in positions to hear the stories of child welfare challenges and remedies in Native communities and open our hearts to receive this knowledge?

The Challenge of Time: Program Relationship Building

One important lesson from our programs is that effective bridging between universities and tribal communities requires an investment of time for all involved. Appropriate, ethical, and respectful relationships do not come about overnight but are the products of the hard work of all participants. This poses a challenge, as both current and past traineeships have been time-limited rather than ongoing. Though the current traineeship cycle is funded for periods of four to five years, this is a minimal amount of time in which to develop ongoing and meaningful relationships, especially when building a foundation of trust that has either never been established or has been broken by mainstream institutions.

Considering that social work education for tribal child welfare is best designed within a sense of community, our program representatives have found it essential to take the time to establish a physical presence by going out to the Native communities to meet individually with key leaders or in group gatherings, rather than asking tribal representatives to come to the universities. These efforts have not been limited to one visit but have involved multiple excursions to nourish the relational seeds that have been planted. The financial costs to the program in time and travel expenses have been extensive, but our persistence has led to reciprocity when Native communities have been invited to attend cultural activities.

In one instance, a traineeship program representative offered to share knowledge by providing an overview on family group conferencing for a small tribe with limited training funds. This was enthusiastically received by the Indian child welfare staff, and in return, a traditional Native meal was prepared for the program visitor; it was enjoyed with the entire social services department. Visits are not just for the purpose of program planning but encompass a range of cultural and relational activities. Faculty in traineeship schools attend powwows and traditional honor ceremonies, participate in gift-giving and baby showers, and prepare and serve food for tribal community events. These are all activities well beyond the traditional role of a typical faculty member and are not recognized in promotion and tenure requirements, but they are central to authentic relationship building in tribal and urban Indian settings.

The Challenge of Shared Power: Building True Partnerships

Experiences from the child welfare traineeships described in this chapter indicate strongly that a successful traineeship program must also include conscious and deliberate efforts to reach out and initiate true partnerships with Native communities—partnerships that involve shared ownership between the traineeship programs and the tribal communities, not just agreements in paper documents such as grant proposals and program evaluations. The tribal "participation" indicated in some grant proposals is too often reduced to acting as token committee advisors or dependent consumers of a service, echoing the era when Native Americans were labeled as wards of the government. Educational institutions too often perpetuate colonized practice in weak attempts to "provide" empowerment, something that is not theirs to give: "It is the Native American families and communities, not the educational institutions, who set the precedence for their own empowerment" (Whitekiller-Drywater, 2010, p. 17). Building true partnerships means building meaningful ongoing political participation by tribal representatives, and privileging cultural ways of knowing and teaching over time.

Although we have not fully achieved true partnerships with Native communities, tribes and schools across the programs described in this chapter have made considerable progress toward this goal. Ways that schools of social work have worked toward establishing true partnerships include inviting Native community members to assist in the recruitment, interviewing, and selection of trainees. We have also engaged Native community members as program consultants to aid in the development of best practices, not only from an academic perspective but from a community perspective as well. Tribal elders and tribally enrolled faculty have established both competencies and approaches to teaching that fit tribal needs and cultural healing practices. Field placements in tribal and urban Indian settings and policy-making bodies have also given power to the tribal setting as an educational niche. Tribally enrolled field instructors and placements have placed the role of educator within cultural communities.

The Challenge of Belonging: Making a Cultural Home on College Campuses

Core to American Indian and Alaska Native identity is the experience of being part of a whole, being located in and attentive to a network of reciprocal connections, support, and community. This experience is well supported on campuses that are close to or on reservation land or that are tribally owned or have a majority Native student population. Research has noted that tribal members are much more likely to attend school when it is close to home, reducing the cost of travel and the distance that might otherwise make it difficult to fulfill family and tribal obligations (HeavyRunner & DeCelles, 2002; Lee, Donlan, & Brown, 2010). Proposing a family education model for tribal colleges, researchers HeavyRunner and DeCelles (2002) said that "replicating the extended family structure within the college culture enhances the student's sense of belonging and leads to higher retention rates" (p. 29).

When students attend social work programs far from home, or on campuses where curriculum policy and practices are based on Euro-American culture, it can be very lonely and stressful. The typical academic culture in such settings is designed around being an individual, separate from (and sometimes competitive with) others, figuring out rules and policies by reading or looking them up online, writing papers by oneself, and putting school before family and community obligations. While people raised in an individualistic culture might feel quite at home and even flourish in this sort of academic setting, people raised in the more collaborative, relational worldview that is more typical of Native culture can feel quite isolated. Successful social work education will focus on building a sense of community.

For example, a tribal elder consulting on curriculum development told faculty, "It's not what you teach; it's how you teach." This prompted the traineeship program to pay more attention to building cultural community and supports for tribal trainees and to educating faculty in more responsive teaching approaches. Faculty (several of whom were tribally enrolled) held monthly gatherings for movies and popcorn, hosted a drum circle, and supported a student-led association of American Indian social workers. On at least two of our campuses, a graduation honor ceremony is held to include family and friends, acknowledging the communal accomplishment of the graduating student's success. One campus has a Native Cultural Center where students can socialize, attend cultural events, and find a sense of home.

Traineeship faculty also worked to help existing programs become more culturally responsive, coaching other faculty to understand the needs and learning styles of tribal and urban Native students. For example, sometimes tribally affiliated students must miss class to meet compelling, non-negotiable cultural needs such as attending a funeral (which can take a week or more, including travel) or other ceremony. It is imperative to work with faculty in educating them about the diverse value system of Native populations; further exploration should be encouraged to uncover whether or not absenteeism has a cultural basis. For instance, when Native students arrive late for class or do not attend at all, it should not automatically be assumed that they do not care about their education. To acknowledge both cultural and academic priorities, faculty may wish to offer alternate ways for students to demonstrate mastery of course material. Faculty are encouraged not to base a portion of a grade on classroom attendance but instead to base grades on demonstrations of competence with the material. Educating faculty in this way can be an effective strategy for building a stronger sense of cultural welcome at schools of social work.

At the same time, advisors who are tribally enrolled or affiliated can work with students on how to walk in both cultural worlds and how to negotiate time for study and coursework with extended family and community members. One student said, "Living successfully in both worlds is a constant balancing act." Tribally enrolled faculty can provide a sense of safety and connection for students as well.

The Challenge of Geography: Expending Time and Resources for Trainees

Another lesson from the traineeship experience is that it is imperative to devote enough time and resources, not only for program relationship building but also for Native social work trainees. As stated in the previous section, students need time to participate in both tribal life and educational life, and ability to find that time is affected by geography. For example, it is common for Native students to attend college close to their home communities, as is substantiated by the high enrollment and retention figures found in states with large Native populations such as Oklahoma, Arizona, California, New Mexico, and Washington. The preference for attending school close to home may be culturally attributed, as Native students are reported to go home more frequently than their non-Native counterparts (Cibik & Chambers, 1991).

Native students interviewed for one study saw going home from a different cultural perspective than did their non-Native counterparts. Although they were aware that the personnel at their institutions viewed frequent visits home as negative or immature, students believed that going home to help their families outweighed the likely negative consequences of missing class (Benjamin, Chambers, & Reiterman, 1993). Another study found that family obligations (sometimes compounded by financial difficulties) were the most significant reasons for attrition of American Indian and Alaska Native students at a predominantly white undergraduate program at a major university (Lee et al., 2010).

Though prioritizing tribal and family obligations sometimes leads to describing students as "place bound," an alternate view might be that these students are demonstrating tribal and cultural loyalty and building the cultural capital that will make them highly effective social workers in an Indian child welfare program. Social work programs in urban areas that have a commitment to child welfare workforce development for tribes will do well to invest in or partner with programs closer to tribal homelands.

Flexibility with time matters as much as flexibility with place. Studies have indicated it is not uncommon for Native students to leave college for the reasons stated above and others, only to return to complete their degrees at a later time (Tierney, 1992). For Native trainees who advance to their field placement, the obstacles of time, distance, poverty, and lack of reliable transportation can become more pronounced and provide multiple retention challenges. Other researchers (Lee et al., 2010) have identified the importance of advising to meet these challenges. Field faculty will need to work closely with advisors, students, and the field placement to ensure a good fit.

In spite of these extraordinary circumstances, we have learned to approach each student situation on a case-by-case basis, building knowledge and respect across faculty and within field placements to increase the success of Native American students over time. All in all, we have found that it is vital to improvise our programs as necessary based upon the effects of cultural discontinuity and a variety of economic and family-related circumstances, while encouraging students to take responsibility for their academic progress.

The Challenge of Different Ways of Knowing: Building an Inclusive Curriculum

Wetsit (1997) found that compared to majority society, cultural diversity exists across the different Native populations in the areas of time management, goal orientation, sharing versus materialism, being versus doing, humility versus arrogance, harmony with nature, the importance of tradition, and reverence for elders. It is not surprising, then, that the child welfare curriculum and standards of practice that are taught in classrooms and used as a skills base in practicums do not always correlate with indigenous culture. Because of this, it is not uncommon for Native trainees to struggle to make boxed western approaches "fit" into the circular, holistic indigenous belief that all things are related. This can cause students to reach a stalemate when writing papers or taking tests; no matter how many different ways that they look at the theories and concepts, they cannot see how these would apply to Native populations.

However, there is a growing body of scholarship that is congruent with Native worldviews and practices—for example, faculty guiding students to learn about such culturally developed theories as the relational worldview (Cross, 1998), or about work on "practice-based evidence" (such as culturally validated healing practices), and to study institutional practice theories of colonization, trauma-informed organizational practice, and truth and reconciliation.

In addition to expanding course content, it can be valuable to offer a range of teaching approaches, including experiential learning. In this vein, to make a strong, successful program we have learned to encourage creativity and implement classroom innovations that are particular to Indian child welfare; many of these ideas come from students and Native community members. The incorporation of experiential learning methods encourages students to develop practical projects that will produce lasting results while maintaining academic rigor.

For example, in keeping with the purpose of ICWA to address the culture of Indian children and families, one Native student received independent study credit for the development of an annual two-day cultural camp that brought foster families, children, and Indian child welfare staff together. On another campus, a senior Native BSW student in a macro practice course identified a significant problem related to the lack of Native foster parents in an urban community located near four tribal reservations. Mobilizing members of all the local tribes, the student successfully engaged the national training organization that developed the parent training curriculum offered in the two states where those tribes were located. Drawing on advocacy skills learned in her social work practice courses, as well as the expertise and mobilized voice of her tribal communities, the student advocated successfully for culturally responsive adaptations to the curriculum. These changes have the potential to make a difference for families across the nation, wherever the curriculum is offered. In a third program, a social work student facilitated a talking circle to collect student input to the social work curriculum, demonstrating to her classmates the validity and effectiveness of traditional macro practice approaches.

Another way our programs have built a more inclusive curriculum is to allow academic credit for, or devote practicum time to, attendance at tribal symposia, statewide Indian child welfare conferences, or national conferences such as the yearly National Indian Child Welfare Association conference to gain exposure to and make connections with regional and national child welfare professionals and to develop deep knowledge of emerging best practices specific to the tribal context. Traineeship funding that supports these activities has allowed students to gain social work skills developed in and for tribal practice settings and to build cultural networks across the child welfare field to support future learning and service.

Some students are reconnecting with and deepening their own cultural knowledge and identity, which may have been lost through relocation to urban areas or out-of-tribe adoption, assimilation, or boarding school placement in prior generations. Such cultural discovery experiences can amplify the cultural ties and sense of a cultural self central to practice with American Indian and Alaska Native families. Schools can support students in developing a strong cultural sense of self by offering academic or field credit for cultural immersion experiences as part of the required or elective curriculum. For example, one program added a summer independent study guided by a tribally enrolled faculty member, which included summer travel to a traditional ceremony, listening to elders teach about traditional approaches to child protection and family support, and other cultural experiences. A faculty sponsor can support the academic credit for activities whose cultural merit is validated by elders or traditional wisdom keepers. In these and other ways, trainees can develop and implement meaningful projects with the potential to produce, not just learning, but long-lasting results that can benefit Native communities for years to come.

Curriculum development can be amplified and strengthened by respecting the validity of tribal and traditional ways of knowing. One traineeship program has added core competencies that specifically address working with Native populations by critically analyzing existing practice models prior to their use with these diverse groups. Another approach, useful in policy classes, is to examine the effect that colonization has had upon Native populations, an important subject when considering the disproportionality in contemporary Native child welfare caseloads. Other curriculum developments have involved developing courses and seminars on ICWA, social work with American Indians, and indigenous leadership. Finally, when possible, our programs are complementing existing faculty strengths by incorporating additional Native practitioners as guest speakers, program consultants, field supervisors, and adjunct faculty.

The Challenge of Leadership: A Different Way of Knowing

Developing leaders in child welfare is a pivotal part of workforce development; however, consideration needs to be given to how leadership is perceived in Native culture. It is typical in western society to find that those selected for leadership positions are extroverted and ready to express opinions and delegate assignments to others. Often these leaders acquire their positions by stepping forward, expressing ambition, or drawing attention to themselves. It is the *position* that holds meaning, not necessarily the *person* in the leadership position (American Indian Policy Center, 1997). However in

Native cultures, leaders are often those who have the ability to persuade others to do something, and they are called to leadership positions not by themselves but by others (Warner & Grint, 2006). They are usually trained for leadership positions beginning early in their lives and are reserved in their speaking, often leading by their actions (Bryant, 1998). These indigenous leaders work toward community empowerment as a measure of success (Kawulich, 2008); deflecting praise from oneself and onto others is not uncommon, resulting in an image of humility and self-deprecation (Bryant, 1998). Put simply, a leader in many traditional tribal cultures acts as a servant to others and is willing to take on any task to benefit the community. There is a major difference between the leadership model of rugged individualism that permeates majority society, and the leadership model of collectivism that usually characterizes Native cultures. Given the mission of the traineeships to develop leaders, both our programs and our Native students can find themselves in the awkward position of negotiating between these two starkly differing definitions of leadership.

One way of addressing this conundrum is to balance the traineeship program's leadership objectives with indigenous concepts of leadership. Achieving this type of balance is necessary as many Native traineeship students are bicultural, meaning they walk both in the world of their Indian culture and that of majority society. To assist in accomplishing this, we inform the students from the onset that the program has the expectation that the trainees will become leaders in child welfare in a way that is right for them and their community and identify some of the ways that we will help them in exploring this potential. For instance, some of our programs require that the students attend annual professional conferences or incorporate classroom assignments into practicum behavioral indicators, supporting the implication that these assignments and experiences make them leaders. To provide more balance, we encourage students to take the initiative to include their own objectives and tasks that reflect their values of leadership. We invite them to conduct classroom and group activities that emphasize participation and shared power, showing all students how a modest leader can bring out all voices. It can be an eye-opening experience for students from non-Native cultures to experience the power of traditional tribal approaches and processes such as the talking circle.

Call to Action

Based on the experience of these four traineeship programs as well as past experience with American Indian education, the authors of this chapter recommend the following actions for social work educators and for the Children's Bureau's workforce development efforts.

Expand the time allowed for students to complete the program. Stipend or traineeship programs should take into account the familial and tribal obligations as well as the financial challenges faced by some American Indian and Alaska Native students and allow students to leave and return to the program.

Increase funding for student and program support, and allow tribal service in return for student support. Stipend or traineeship programs should establish higher levels of funding to support American Indian and Alaska Native students, who are more likely to come from backgrounds of poverty and who may be the main source of support for many family members. Expand program funds to underwrite the advising and community-building roles played by academic advisors and the travel costs associated with the formation of university–tribe partnerships, student recruitment, culturally appropriate field learning experiences, and cultural learning experiences, such as conferences and tribal meetings, necessary to support the standard curriculum. These specialized traineeships currently allow post-traineeship child welfare service requirements to be fulfilled in tribal child welfare agencies. Similar policy changes are recommended for traineeships funded with federal support under Title IV-E.

Partner with tribal colleges and other two-year institutions to permit social work degree completion via interactive television, online classes, and courses that can be taken during consecutive blocks of time instead of taking multiple semester-long courses at once. Students with the best potential to serve tribal child welfare clients may live on the reservation, often in very rural areas. Distance education, concentrated residency, or courses offered on-site at tribal colleges are social work education models better suited to the learning needs of these students. When students must come to an urban campus, find ways to include family and tribal members in that choice.

Develop and employ indigenous leadership concepts that encompass a different way of knowing in academic programs and leadership academies. Offer an expanded curriculum for social work students with career commitments to serve in tribal and state child welfare agencies. Allow funding for course content related to tribal culture. When teaching leadership development, programs should build on indigenous models of leadership that emphasize service to the community, honoring of elders, and community-based selection of leaders rather than individual models.

Focus on how learning experiences are offered, not just what is taught. Build relationships within the academic program and between the academic program, tribal leaders, and child welfare programs. An extensive literature on indigenous ways of knowing and learning, as well as conclusive findings on supporting success for American Indian and Alaska Native learners, is now available (Aikenhead & Ogawa, 2007; Barnhardt & Kawagley, 2005; Parker, 2007; Stevens, 2008; Walker & Bigelow, 2011). Based on this literature and the experience of our traineeship programs, we believe that curricular approaches that develop strong tribal engagement in the program, foster a culturally congruent community for students on campus, offer cultural advisors, and emphasize collaborative and team-based learning approaches will be the most effective. Time for deep dialogue and the unfolding of learning at multiple levels should be incorporated into classes, rather than exclusively emphasizing strict linear models of learning.

Continue to conduct research on effective social work education to meet the needs of the tribal child welfare workforce. There is a need for more research on preparation of American Indian and Alaska Native social workers to work in Indian child welfare. While the current and past programs described in this chapter have common practices that appear to advance the success of American Indian students, there is a need to move from time-limited grants to the study of tribally supportive educational programs over the long term and extending into the impact of such programs on the delivery of child welfare services. Only with ongoing investment in educational approaches and tribal practices will social work students with strong tribal ties be able to complete their education and return to the field to serve American Indian and Alaska Native children and families.

Successful workforce development for Indian child welfare requires offering concrete supports for students and maintaining institutional flexibility toward indigenous ways of knowing while keeping academic rigor high. Even more than that, workforce development for tribes requires that social work programs invest in relationships, respect the wisdom of tribal leadership, and adopt an attitude of humbleness on the part of the educational institution. Tribes have a critical need for a child welfare workforce that has both the tribal affiliation and expertise and the social work skills to protect children, preserve family and tribal continuity, and respect tribal sovereignty.

References

Adoption Assistance and Child Welfare Act of 1980, P.L. 96-272, 94 Stat. 500 (1980).

Aikenhead, G. S., & Ogawa, M. (2007). Indigenous knowledge and science revisited. *Cultural Studies of Science Education, 2,* 539–620.

American Indian Policy Center. (1997). *Traditional American Indian leadership: A comparison with U.S. governance.* Retrieved from http://www.americanindianpolicycenter.org/research/tradlead.html

Barnhardt, R. & Kawagley, A. O. (2005). Indigenous knowledge systems and Alaskan Native Ways of knowing. *Anthropology and Education Quarterly, 36*(1), 8–23.

Bending, R., DeMello, S., Crofoot, T., & Cahn, K. (2000). *Building on strengths traineeship grant proposal.* Unpublished manuscript, University of Washington, Seattle.

Benjamin, D. P., Chambers, S., & Reiterman, G. (1993). A focus on American Indian college persistence. *Journal of American Indian Education, 32*(2), 24–40.

Bryant, M.T. (1998). Cross-cultural understandings of leadership: Themes from Native American interviews. *Educational Management Administration and Leadership, 26*(1), 7–20.

Cibik, M. A., & Chambers, S. L. (1991). Similarities and differences among Native Americans, Hispanics, blacks, and Anglos. *NASPA Journal, 28*(2), 129–139.

Cross, T. L. (1998). Understanding family resiliency from a relational world view. In H. I. McCubbin, E. A. Thompson, A. I. Thompson, & J. E. Fromer (Eds.), *Resiliency in Native American and immigrant families—Resiliency in Families Series* (pp. 143–158). Thousand Oaks, CA: Sage Publications.

HeavyRunner, I., & DeCelles, R. (2002). Family education model: Meeting the student retention challenge. *Journal of American Indian Education, 41*(2), 29–37.

Horne, A., Travis, T., Miller, B., & Simmons, D. (2009). *Court reform and American Indian and Alaskan Native children: Increasing protections and improving outcome.* Reno, NV and Portland, OR: National Council of Juvenile and Family Court Judges, and National Indian Child Welfare Association.

Indian Child Welfare Act of 1978, P.L. 95-608, 92, Stat. 3069 (1978).

Kawulich, B. B. (2008). Giving back to the community through leadership. *Advancing Women in Leadership Journal, 28.* Retrieved from http://advancingwomen.com/awl/awl_ wordpress/giving-back-to-the-community-through-leadership/

Lee, J., Donlan, W., & Brown, E. F. (2010). American Indian/Alaskan Native undergraduate retention at predominantly white institutions: An elaboration of Tinto's theory of college student departure. *Journal of College Student Retention: Research, Theory and Practice, 12,* 257–276.

Ortiz, A. M., & HeavyRunner, I. (2003). Student access, retention and success: Models of inclusion and support. In M. K. Benham & W. J. Stein (Eds.), *The renaissance of American Indian higher education* (pp. 215–239). Mahwah, NJ: Lawrence Erlbaum Associates.

Parker, J. (2007). Diversity and the academy. *Teaching in Higher Education, 12*(5/6), 787–792.

Pevar, S. L. (1992). *The rights of Indians and tribes: The basic ACLU guide to Indian and tribal rights* (2nd ed.). Carbondale: Southern Illinois University Press.

Stevens, A. (2008). A different way of knowing: Tools and strategies for managing indigenous knowledge. *Libri: International Journal of Library & Information Services, 58*(1), 25–33.

Tierney, W. G. (1992). *Official encouragement, institutional discouragement: Minorities in academe—The Native American experience.* Norwood, NJ: Ablex.

Walker, R. D., & Bigelow, D. A. (2011). A constructive Indian country response to the evidence-based program mandate. *Journal of Psychoactive Drugs, 43,* 276–281.

Warner, L. S., & Grint, K. (2006). *American Indian ways of leading and knowing.* Thousand Oaks, CA: Sage Publications.

Wetsit, D. (1997). *The Native American experience in higher education: Turning around the cycle of failure II.* Washington, DC: National Institute of Education. (ERIC Document Reproduction Services No. ED414108)

Whitekiller-Drywater, V. S. (2010). Cultural resilience: Voices of Native American students in college retention. *Canadian Journal of Native Studies, 30*(1), 1–19.

Whitekiller-Drywater, V. S. (2012). *Northeastern State University Department of Social Work: CSWE Self Study.* Unpublished manuscript, Tahlequah, OK.

Chapter 13

WORKFORCE AND LEADERSHIP DEVELOPMENT

Katharine Cahn, Freda Bernotavicz, and Cathryn Potter

Every day, vulnerable children and families come to the attention of child welfare staff in state, county, and tribal programs across the country. It is critical that these staff have the right skills, resources, and organizational supports to help these families succeed. Positive outcomes are the result of a whole system working well together, not just the skill sets of individual workers. Workforce development produces better outcomes, and leadership (by managers and supervisors) is the key to workforce development. This chapter traces the evolution of Children's Bureau goals and interventions from a focus on particular practice issues to a comprehensive approach to improving outcomes through workforce and leadership development.

Historical Antecedents: The First Century

Over the years, the Children's Bureau has engaged in partnerships with states, tribes, nonprofit organizations, and citizens to support the welfare of children. In its early years, the focus was often on policy change, as it took the lead in advancing important policy agendas for children and families. Over time, administration of programmatic change and systems improvement through child welfare funding opportunities became a significant part of the Children's Bureau's work. Currently it oversees funding to states, tribes, and communities related to child welfare services, foster care and adoption assistance, independent living, promotion of safe and stable families, state and community-based child abuse prevention and treatment, and court improvement projects (Administration for Children and Families, 2011).

Since the enactment of the Child Abuse Prevention and Treatment Act (1974), workforce development through training and traineeships has been an important focus of the work of the Children's Bureau. This has been carried out through two mechanisms: (1) direct training grants and traineeship support to schools of social work, tribes, private agencies, and states and (2) regulations that allow the use of federal funds to support training partnerships between schools of social work and states as part of state plans. Training and traineeship grants have focused on improving practice or systems responses to particular child welfare populations or issues. The latter approach is grounded in the Adoption Assistance and Child Welfare Act (1980) which amended the Social Security Act (1936) to create a new section, Title IV-E, one provision of which allows schools of social work and state agencies to match state funds with federal funds to support the education of social work students committed to careers in child welfare and to support training for child welfare workers. Currently over one hundred schools of social work are engaged in Title IV-E educational or training partnerships. Through both direct grants to schools and state–school partnerships supported by Title IV-E funds, thousands of child welfare workers have received a professional education or in-service training in child welfare services. Included in that number are many supervisors and managers.

The Children's Bureau has worked on the development of skilled child welfare staff through a variety of structural and technical assistance mechanisms as well as through discretionary grants. In 1979, regional child welfare training centers were established, creating a partnership between schools of social work, public agencies, tribes, and other regional stakeholders to strengthen child welfare training programs, focusing on the specific practice issues of each region. In the early 1980s the Bureau closed these centers and replaced them with national resource centers that provide training and technical assistance on specific topics, issues, or areas of practice.

The national resource centers have had a strong focus on workforce development. Most requests from states have included a workforce development component, and much assistance from the national resource centers has involved at least short-term training for workers and sometimes supervisors. Some national resource centers have taken on specific dimensions of workforce development for supervisors and managers. For example, the National Resource Center for Organizational Improvement has worked on strengthening child welfare supervision, and the National Resource Center on Adoption has focused on development of minority leaders in adoption practice through its Minority Adoption Leadership Development Institute.

An examination of the Children's Bureau's discretionary grant programs from 1995 through 2001 (Potter, 2012) indicates that most grants were targeted to development and evaluation of practice approaches in adoption, abandoned infants, family-based services, out-of-home care, independent living, and implementation of specific legislation. Children's Bureau requests for research proposals focused on practice development, longitudinal research on children and families, and development of stronger data capabilities in states. In the year 2000, a focus on supervisors and managers began to emerge, with requests for proposals specifically targeting these populations for implementation of the Adoption and Safe Families Act (1997) and an announcement for development of supervisor training.

Funded training projects for which final reports are available, including Virginia, Texas, Illinois, Oregon, and Kansas, show a strong focus on data-driven decision-making (Potter, 2012). Virginia trained managers in outcome-based management skills and the associated use of data. Illinois used project funds to develop an internal system of outcome indicators and data analysis and train supervisors and managers to use it. Texas trained management staff to use an online system that enables timely use of data in decision making. The Kansas project developed an Internet-based training for supervisors organized around results-oriented management and grounded in policy, and the Oregon team emphasized the development of leadership skills and decision-making frameworks (Potter, 2012).

Final reports for the supervisor training projects are available for Illinois, Michigan, Wisconsin, Kentucky, and Illinois. These projects developed supervisor trainings with attention to ongoing support for trainees. Michigan developed a three-day training on child welfare policies and best practices followed by monthly sessions emphasizing practical supervision skills. Wisconsin emphasized the supervisor's role in workers' transfer of learning to practice, developing classroom training on competency-based worker development, performance improvement approaches, and peer mentoring programs. Kentucky developed solution-focused supervision training for all supervisors using a combination of classroom training and Web-based discussion groups. Illinois targeted its supervisor training to developing supervisor knowledge and skill in assisting workers to intervene in cases involving parental substance abuse (Potter, 2012).

The year 2003 was pivotal as the Children's Bureau moved from a focus on specific practice skills or client issues to a more systemic approach, connecting workforce issues with issues of leadership, organizational culture, and systems change. Chronic and long-standing issues in the child welfare workforce, once seen as a staffing challenge (Helfgott, 1991), were increasingly viewed as a workforce crisis (Alwon & Reitz, 2000; Reitz, 2001).

Building on workforce studies in the early 2000s that drew on Child and Family Services Review (the federal program that periodically reviews state child welfare systems) data, a report by the General Accounting Office (name changed to Government Accountability Office in 2004) (GAO, 2003) found that workforce problems—high caseloads, training deficiencies, and staffing shortages—were having an impact on safety and permanency outcomes, including placement disruptions, foster care re-entry, and continued abuse and neglect. Several reports (Annie E. Casey Foundation, 2003; Child Welfare League of America, 2001; Light, 2003; Urban Institute, 2001) reinforced these findings and predicted that the situation would worsen due to several trends: a shrinking qualified labor pool as the social work workforce ages disproportionately to the overall workforce, increases in caseloads, the changing focus of the work, diminished opportunities for flexibility and autonomy, and greater demand for accountability.

The GAO called on the Children's Bureau to help child welfare agencies address workforce recruitment and retention problems by using the discretionary grant program to promote research on promising practices and by issuing guidance for states to use their performance improvement plans to address the issue. In response, the Children's Bureau put out a request for proposals on ways to improve recruitment and retention. Eight university–agency partnerships across the country were awarded five-year grants to develop organizational change models and training related to effective recruitment and retention: the University of Albany, New York, University of North Carolina at Chapel Hill, Michigan State University, University of Iowa, University of Michigan, University of Southern Maine, Fordham University, and University of Denver (Child Welfare Information Gateway & National Child Welfare Workforce Institute, 2010).

The recruitment and retention projects were data driven (using organizational assessments; human resources data; surveys and focus groups with workers, supervisors, and managers; exit interviews; and job satisfaction surveys), conducted by strong university–agency partnerships, and focused on building organizational capacity, including leadership and supervision, as well as training models.

During this period, other organizations and researchers also focused on workforce issues, including the Annie E. Casey Foundation, the American Public Human Services Association, and the National Association of Social Workers. The National Institute for Mental Health funded several studies on organizational climate that demonstrated that caseworkers who provide services in child welfare systems that have more engaged climates are more likely to have good work attitudes, are less likely to quit their job, deliver higher quality services, and are more effective (Glisson, 2010; Glisson, Dukes & Green, 2006). Other studies supported the conclusions that leadership is a key factor in organizations and can affect employees' job satisfaction (Elpers & Westhuis, 2008) and that support from supervisors is pivotal in employee retention (Jacquet, Clark, Morazes, & Withers, 2007). These findings reinforced the need for a systemic perspective on workforce development; that became the theme of two national conferences funded by the Children's Bureau in 2005 and 2006.

In addition, researchers changed their focus from inputs such as staff development to outcomes (Harvard Family Research Project, 2008) and from turnover (why workers leave) to retention (why they stay) (Ellett & Ellett, 1997; Graef, Potter, & Rohde, 2002). Perhaps the most important trend was the recognition that there are no silver bullets or easy answers for the complex, systemic issue of recruitment and retention (Cyphers, 2001) and that multiple activities and pathways link the capacity of the professional workforce and improved child outcomes (Zlotnik, DePanfilis, Daining, & Lane, 2005). These links include education and professional staff development, organizational supports, and policy supports (Harvard Family Research Project, 2008). Organizational supports—an organizational mindset that values program improvement, administrators who support training and advocate for better compensation and conditions, adequate and supportive supervision, shared decision-making, and a strong performance management structure—all require leadership at multiple levels and a systemic approach to workforce development. Consistent with this broadened, systemic perspective, the recruitment and retention projects implemented a variety of strategies, which are discussed below.

Realistic Recruitment

Workforce capacity building begins with attracting the right people to the job. To ensure long-term retention, recruitment and selection should be a streamlined process of matching the best job applicant to the job and achieving the affective commitment that helps promote long-term retention.

To attract potential applicants with the characteristics associated with retention (Ellett, 2000; Light, 2003), some of the projects developed professionally designed posters, fliers, public service announcements, and advertisements, as well as diverse recruitment strategies for agencies to use. To increase retention and reduce early turnover, the strategies used realistic recruitment approaches (CPS Human Resource Services, 2006; Graef & Potter, 2002) and found that a more realistic and user-friendly recruitment process showed a 50 percent reduction in early turnover and an improvement in new hires' perceptions of the application and hiring process (Bernotavicz, 2008).

Many projects developed realistic job preview videos to give prospective candidates a chance to understand whether the challenges and rewards of child welfare work would be right for them. Findings from one project showed that the video was effective in helping prospective recruits make a more informed decision about applying for the job and in reducing early turnover (Faller et al., 2009).

Competency-Based Screening and Selection

Competency-based selection focuses on identifying and screening for the characteristics needed at entry and those that are most likely to predict long-term success on the job. The selection process can also be enhanced by using job analysis as a basis, focusing on specific competencies, using multiple job-related assessments, standardizing the process, and providing training to interviewers (Bernotavicz & Locke, 2000; Graef & Potter, 2002).

Several recruitment and retention projects developed screening materials and training for supervisors in their use. Findings from the University of Southern Maine project showed that the competency-based screening process was a valid predictor of job performance. Candidates rated highly in the selection process were rated highly by supervisors after 12 months on the job (Bernotavicz, 2008).

Strengthening Supervision

Supervisors are the lynchpin of the child welfare agency, connecting the organizational vision to worker outcomes. A meta-analysis of research on the impact of supervision on worker outcomes found that workers who receive effective supervision reciprocate with positive feelings and behaviors toward their jobs and organizations (Mor Barak, Travis, Pyun, & Xie, 2009). Several studies have cited supportive and informed supervision as a reason child welfare workers remain on the job (Dickinson & Perry, 2002; Jacquet et al., 2007; Landsman, 2001) and lack of supportive supervision as a reason for leaving a child welfare job (Nissly, Mor Barak, & Levin, 2005). Investment in supervision has the potential to promote an organizational culture that supports learning, a sound foundation for practice improvement, and a committed and stable workforce (Collins-Camargo, 2005). Findings from a controlled research study in 33 North Carolina counties (Dickinson & Painter, 2009; Dickinson, Painter, & Lee, 2007) showed that a comprehensive package of training and technical assistance to improve the recruitment, selection, and retention skills of supervisors had a positive impact on worker retention.

All the recruitment and retention projects focused to some degree on the central role supervisors play throughout the process of recruitment, selection, and retention. They produced a variety of training materials and other resources to enhance and support supervisory skills in these areas.

Organizational Development

Several of the projects also focused on organizational development, based on findings that the climate of an organization positively affects staff turnover and retention. In New York, local agency "design teams" of workers, supervisors, and managers worked together with a trained external facilitator to identify and solve organizational problems linked to turnover and poor outcomes in order to improve the agency climate and retention rates. Agencies with such a team experienced a greater improvement in the intent-to-leave and turnover rates than comparison agencies (Strolin-Goltzman et al., 2009). The University of Denver's recruitment and retention project implemented a comprehensive intervention in five sites across three western states and concluded that sustained retention efforts require a comprehensive, organizational approach and that it is important to embed the effort within the organizational culture (Potter, Comstock, Brittain, & Hanna, 2009).

Leadership

Given the previous findings on organizational development and workforce strategies, it is clear that leadership at the management and supervisory level is of central importance to workforce development and achieving outcomes. Managers and supervisors are in the best position to motivate staff, create a positive organizational culture and vision, understand the leader–follower relationship, and foster participatory management (Elpers & Westhuis, 2008).

Managers and supervisors have been shown to influence retention by almost every study on the topic (Mor Barak et al., 2009), and most of the recruitment and retention grantees focused at least part of their intervention and research on engaging, strengthening, and partnering with leaders at the supervisory or management level. Across the New York intervention sites, relationships between agency leaders and the design teams played a central role, with agency leaders having the power to inspire, facilitate, constrain, or impede the teams (Strolin-Goltzman et al., 2009). The University of Denver project concluded that leadership support is critical and that frequent turnover in executive leadership is a reality (Potter et al., 2009). Michigan State University developed leadership training for managers and administrators with an intensive focus on recruitment and retention (Michigan State University School of Social Work & Mackenzie Associates, 2009). Fordham University evaluated a formal mentoring program in Connecticut that connects new workers with experienced workers, supervisors, and managers (Strand & Bosco-Ruggiero, 2009).

Findings from other researchers during this period reinforced the links between supervision, organizational climate, staff retention, and outcomes (Ellett, Collins-Camargo, & Ellett, 2006). Two studies in Missouri found that a comprehensive approach, including an employee selection protocol, 360-degree evaluation (using input from a variety of sources in the performance appraisal process), employee development planning, peer consultation, and support groups for supervisors, had a positive impact on worker retention, supervisory and team effectiveness, and job satisfaction (Collins-Camargo, Sullivan, Washeck, Adams, & Sundet, 2009; Renner, Porter, & Preister, 2009).

Recognizing the importance of developing a cadre of leaders to implement changes in the child welfare system, the Children's Bureau funded the University of Utah to develop the National Child Welfare Leadership Institute (2007–2009). The goal of the Institute was to provide a structured learning environment for mid-level children's services managers to develop their skills in leading change and to address current issues in child welfare. The Institute included four components: a five-day residential training, a transfer-of-learning period with coaching and technical assistance, a three-day training event, and implementation of a change initiative with follow-up coaching. The curriculum included developing skills in adaptive leadership (Heifetz & Linsky, 2002), implementation science (Fixsen, Naoom, Blase, Friedman, & Wallace, 2005), assessment, and addressing racial disproportionality and disparities and applied these skills to the development and implementation of a change initiative.

An Integrated Model for Leadership and Workforce Development

Based on findings from the recruitment and retention grantees and the Leadership Institute, the Children's Bureau released a request for proposals to develop an integrated approach to child welfare workforce development through strengthened leadership at the supervisory and management level and the use of traineeships. A partnership among nine universities under the leadership of the School of Social Welfare at the University at Albany was successful in being awarded the cooperative agreement to establish the National Child Welfare Workforce Institute (NCWWI).

In addition, the Children's Bureau awarded five workforce cooperative agreements to take a holistic approach to systems reform and workforce development. These were located in Kansas, Louisiana, New York, North Carolina, and Colorado; the fifth, based at University of Denver, had pilot sites in Colorado, Wyoming, and tribal nations in North Dakota. Examples of interventions include a workforce assessment and intervention model to improve organizational health (University of Denver), strengthening the workforce of private and tribal agencies (Kansas), exploring the relationship between organization climate and worker job satisfaction (New York) strengthening supervision and implementing best practice approaches to recruitment and retention (North Carolina and Louisiana). Professional educational opportunities through BSW and MSW traineeships and stipend programs are common strategies to attract and retain committed and competent staff.

As part of the Children's Bureau's national systems reform effort, the goal of the NCWWI is to build leadership capacity at all levels throughout the child welfare system, derive promising practices in workforce development, deliver child welfare leadership training for middle managers and supervisors, facilitate BSW and MSW traineeships, engage national peer networks, support strategic dissemination of effective and promising leadership and workforce practices, and advance knowledge through collaboration and evaluation.

A leadership model provides a conceptual framework for all NCWWI activities. This model, based on an extensive literature review, provides a holistic view that includes four leadership domains (leading change, leading in context, leading people, leading for results) supported by five leadership attributes (adaptive, collaborative, distributive, inclusive, and outcome focused); central to the model is the concept of self-knowledge (Figure 13-1).

The NCWWI also developed a model that defines competencies for each of the leadership domains, along with proficiency indicators, to create a leadership ladder from caseworker to supervisor, middle manager, and executive (National Child Welfare Workforce Institute, 2010). The competency model guides the innovative curriculum of the Leadership Academy for Middle Managers (a written curriculum delivered in five-day regional workshops by a team of three trainers with follow-up Web-based sessions and coaching) and the Leadership Academy for Supervisors (which includes both on-line asynchronous learning and follow-up synchronous sessions that are delivered either remotely or face to face).

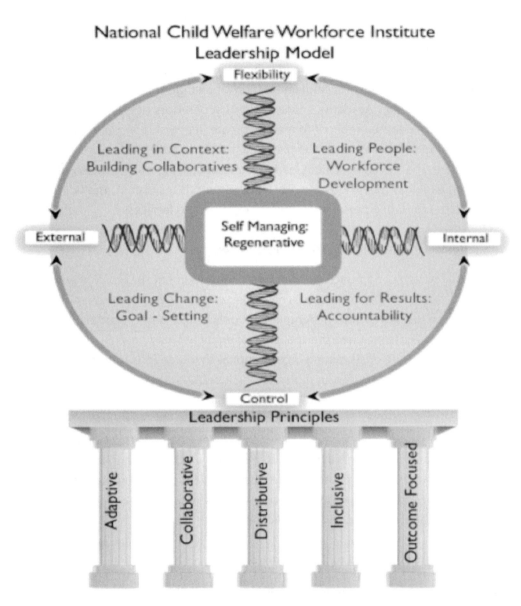

Figure 13-1. National Child Welfare Workforce Institute Leadership Model

The NCWWI's work in general, and its leadership model in particular, reflect and put into practice the Children's Bureau's evolving perspective. Moving from a single problem-solution model, they link supervision, leadership, and workforce development to outcomes for children, youths, and families in a systemic manner. Through knowledge assessment, management, and dissemination and peer networking programs, NCWWI identifies and provides best practice information in a systemic approach, addressing simultaneously the areas of leadership, systems change, and workforce development.

Its traineeships bring competent new staff into the field and provide professional development to existing workers and supervisors. Like the University of Utah curriculum, the NCWWI curriculum introduces leadership competencies and strengthens learning by training and coaching for implementation of change initiatives. By participating in NCWWI Leadership Academy, managers and supervisors develop their leadership competencies, become prepared to assume greater leadership responsibilities in their agencies through succession planning, and contribute to sustainable systems change in child welfare. The NCWWI also links leaders, supervisors, and trainees across the nation through a variety of peer networks. This intervention is a systemic, multidimensional approach to promoting better outcomes for children and families.

Challenges in Promoting a Systems Perspective

Though a systemic approach to workforce development is more effective than approaches based on a single issue, challenges to this approach remain. Recruitment and retention researchers often identified not only similar best practices but also similar challenges. These included the challenge of engaging leaders in change efforts and the related challenge of sustaining organizational change efforts in spite of leadership turnover. Infrastructure issues, in particular the lack of data systems, posed a barrier in some settings. Child welfare work, whether in state, county, or tribal settings, is busy, demanding, and acutely sensitive to external pressures. Reflecting the "permanent whitewater" of agency leadership (Vaill, 1996), it was noted that competing priorities and lack of time were barriers in most systems. Finally, workforce and leadership development and systems change are not one-shot interventions. Many sites identified the need for follow-up coaching and support, which is why peer learning and coaching were incorporated into the Leadership Academies.

Leadership Issues Related to Disproportionality

As the Children's Bureau enters its second century, workforce and leadership issues intersect with another major issue: racial disproportionality in child welfare. African American and American Indian and Alaska Native children and families (and in some jurisdictions, Hispanic children and families) are found in child welfare care in numbers disproportional to their percentage in the general population (GAO, 2007). Moving to a more systemic perspective on workforce development and leadership is key to development of a workforce capable of realizing safety, permanence, and well-being for all children, including children of color.

Workforce development started as a "colorblind" intervention. Early training and education focused on improving the worker's skill set and goodness-of-fit with the agency as it is and preparing all workers to learn current practices. Later training focused on the development of cultural understanding to better apply existing practices in the context of each family's cultural niche. This view could be seen in Children's Bureau grants that funded training and workforce development on specific practice issues related to culture, such as teaching about the Indian Child Welfare Act, recruitment of African American adoptive families, or teaching culturally sensitive or culturally responsive practice. Traineeships funded by Title IV-E and state dollars supported recruitment of staff and caregivers from all backgrounds and sometimes resulted in greater diversity among social work students and in the child welfare workforce. Traineeships funded by Title IV-B discretionary grants, which allow more flexibility than IV-E funding, sometimes focused on specific groups such as tribal members or students of color.

Through these grants, social work scholars and workforce development providers found that, while recruitment and training of staff of color may be part of the solution, one must look more broadly and consider the nature of organizational and community cultures to create more holistic solutions. Organizational culture and climate matter in the recruitment and retention of staff of color, and they make a difference in the ability to implement culturally responsive practices and form new alliances to mobilize community supports. Leadership by managers and supervisors is key to the development of an empowering and welcoming agency culture, culturally responsive practice implementation, and engaged community partnerships.

Effective workforce development strategies and practice approaches that improve outcomes for children and youths from communities of color reflect an emphasis on partnership, community engagement, leadership, and outcomes. For example, in a series of Children's Bureau training grants awarded to one of the authors of this chapter and colleagues, key principles and promising practices began to take shape for workforce development, leadership development, and improving practice outcomes for children of color (for example, Supervising for Excellence, the Northwest Child Welfare Leadership Institute, Building on Strengths Traineeship, and the Frontline Connections Quality Improvement Center, all grant-funded training programs based at the University of Washington School of Social Work).

In training programs conducted by Cahn through the Northwest Child Welfare Leadership Institute at the University of Washington in 1990 and 1991, child welfare managers of color identified the impact of organizational cultures at both child welfare agencies and schools of social work on recruitment and retention and conducted change projects to promote more empowering organizational cultures. Throughout, these programs identified the importance of leadership that embraced and modeled diversity and promoted fairness and equity in practice. Supervisors exercise leadership by building diversity within the unit, providing coaching for staff in providing responsive services, and establishing strong ties to diverse local communities. Managers exercise leadership by sending a strong and consistent message of racial equity and fairness, allocating funding to diverse community providers, and building an organizational culture that welcomes diverse approaches and voices.

Recruitment and retention of diverse staff must be supported by ongoing evolution toward more culturally effective practices. American Indian and urban African American grantees from the Frontline Connections Quality Improvement Center (a cooperative agreement with the Children's Bureau for a Quality Improvement Center on Child Protective Services at the University of Washington) demonstrated culturally responsive child protection practice models that included family engagement using community and tribal cultural healing practices to support child safety and family preservation. These programs demonstrated that tribal and cultural child welfare agencies can work on prevention and the healing of historical as well as current trauma through the use of cultural traditions and practices. Frontline Connections grantees demonstrated promising practices of family engagement by using tribal and cultural agencies as safe places for challenged or vulnerable parents to gather and learn. Supervisory and managerial leadership can build partnerships between tribal and state child welfare agencies to promote community-based solutions.

At the same time that the Children's Bureau funded the recruitment and retention projects in 2003, it also awarded training grants for rural practice. Two schools of social work demonstrated child welfare skill building with tribal youths and families (Tribal Stars at the University of California at San Diego and the Rural and Tribal Training Grant at Portland State University). Echoing earlier findings, relationship building and working in partnership with tribal or cultural elders and healers emerged as a key practice principle. Supervisors are key in coaching and supporting workers to move in these directions. Managers must provide leadership in forming such partnerships.

The findings of these programs point to the need for workforce and skill development at the level of the individual worker, supervisor, and manager, and suggest the central role leadership plays in practice development and the development of organizational climates that promote diversity and address disproportionality and disparities in staff and client outcomes. In the four domains of the NCWWI leadership model, the skill of "leading people" includes attention to building and empowering inclusive organizational cultures and welcoming diverse staff. The skill of "leading in context" emphasizes the ability to build strong partnerships between schools of social work and child welfare agencies and with traditional or cultural resource providers who are key to building child and family resilience. The skill of "leading change" involves identifying clear evidence-based and promising practices to meet the needs of families of color as well as keeping the vision alive. Finally, the skill of "leading for results" calls for uncompromising data-driven accountability for producing equitable outcomes for all children.

Looking Forward: Policy and Practice

As the history described above demonstrates, the last century of partnership between schools of social work and the Children's Bureau was marked by movement from providing training and professional development with a focus on specific practice issues to workforce development strategies carried out within a more holistic and systemic framework. The Children's Bureau enters its second century with a deeper understanding of the intersecting role of organizational, workforce, and leadership factors in producing positive outcomes for children, youths, and families. Effective practices will become part of child welfare not just as a result of practice training for individuals in the workforce, but also as a result of efforts to improve organizational culture and leadership for building community alliances to support practice change. New practice and organizational change initiatives will be led by supervisors and managers grounded in principles of leadership, workforce development, and the use of data-informed decision-making. New workers with social work degrees who have been educated in leadership and emerging practice models will enter child welfare work as leaders for change. The Children's Bureau and schools of social work should invest in research, support promising practices, and pursue other opportunities—including improvements to data systems and an array of funding options—to promote this multidimensional, systemic approach.

Investment in Research

The multilayered work on systems change proposed here needs an evidence base. Practice approaches in workforce development, leadership, and supervision must be developed and evaluated with an eye to "connecting the dots" of training and workforce development, organizational-level practices, and client outcomes. While early literature and training grants suggest there is a strong connection, much more research is needed. A national study is needed of the complex relationships between workforce development, leadership and supervision, and client outcomes. Research on practice implementation should be tailored to the unique organizational niche of child welfare.

Support for Promising Practices

Several promising practices already in effect deserve ongoing support from the Children's Bureau and child welfare administrators in tribal and state systems, particularly in the areas of staff recruitment and selection and leadership training.

Staff Recruitment. Proactive strategies to attract and educate the best employees will reduce early turnover and promote retention. Supervision and management strategies to improve recruitment include collaborating with the agency human resources office to develop a recruitment plan; encouraging the involvement of current staff in recruiting and promoting an agency-wide approach to realistic recruitment; expanding recruitment strategies to include internships; and increasing outreach to increase diversity, including strategies for attracting both older workers and workers from subsequent generations, workers of color, workers with needed linguistic and cultural skills, and students.

Support for partnerships between schools of social work and tribal and public child welfare agencies should continue and expand. These school–agency partnerships have emerged as a promising pathway into employment and a useful staff development and retention strategy. In particular, the ability of schools to attract, educate, and graduate social workers with experience in communities of color and American Indian and Alaska Native settings should be strengthened. This may include stronger partnerships with tribal colleges, community colleges, and high schools, establishing a pathway to higher education for many communities.

Staff Selection. Improved selection processes have been shown to be a fiscally prudent approach to reducing worker turnover and improving child outcomes. Supervision and management strategies to achieve this include collaborating with the human resources office to develop and use a list of entry-level worker competencies consistent with the agency's job requirements and practice model; encouraging the use of a variety of job-related screening methods in the selection process; and sharing ideas about effective strategies for rating and selecting candidates. Proven methods of screening, recruiting, and assessing goodness of fit for the job include realistic job previews and competency-based screening. Further research is needed to develop a deeper understanding of how these approaches affect recruitment across diverse cultural, ethnic, and linguistic groups. This work will also require stronger connections between child welfare leadership, employee unions, and human resources departments, which calls for adaptive and inclusive leadership skills.

Leadership Training and Education. Expanded curricula should be developed for training academies and social work school programs that emphasize the leadership and supervisory principles and practices necessary to implement practice change and to ensure the quality and effectiveness of services delivered to children and families. Supervisory training should include content on coaching for practice effectiveness and building supportive workplace cultures that promote retention. The NCWWI leadership model, in particular the "leading people" component, provides a conceptual framework for leadership training and education for supervisors. This domain involves the ability to lead people in fulfilling the organization's vision, mission, and goals. Inherent in it is the ability to provide an inclusive workplace that fosters staff members' development, facilitates cooperation and teamwork, and supports constructive resolution of conflicts. The competencies relevant to leading people are managing conflict, staff development, cultural competence, and leveraging diversity. These can be integrated in one training or offered in stand-alone modules on recruitment, screening, diversity, leadership, and coaching. Both options are available from the Leadership Academy for Supervisors offered by NCWWI.

Experience also suggests that the development of peer learning approaches and coaching to supplement traditional classroom work will have greater impact on staff skills than training alone. Child welfare is a field in which local practices and local change initiatives provide learning laboratories all over the country. Much good learning could be captured and made available through Children's Bureau–supported approaches to peer learning. Bureau leadership in connecting change initiatives and partnerships across the country would be helpful in capturing and disseminating lessons learned for implementation in other jurisdictions or classrooms.

Other Opportunities

Lessons learned from recent grantees suggest that workforce development could also be improved by making other specific changes, particularly in data systems and funding streams. A section on workforce issues could be added to the Child and Family Services Reviews. Structures for sharing data between state child welfare systems and the state and county human resources departments that serve them should be improved so as to set benchmarks for recruitment and retention, track desirable staff characteristics such as diversity, professional education, and retention, and support research on workforce issues. Data on the outcomes of workforce development efforts should be collected and reported regularly. It is important that states, tribes, and counties continue to evaluate the progress and impact of workforce development efforts to test, verify, and expand the holistic or systemic approach to workforce development. Finally, there is a need for a national study of the relationships between workforce capacity, leadership and supervision, and child outcomes.

A number of promising funding options exist. As discussed above, funding for research on workforce issues as they relate to child and family outcomes would be useful. There is also a need for continued investment in leadership development and peer learning opportunities. Finally, many child welfare systems lack financial incentives for staff to take part in continuing education or earn a professional degree. Increased funding could incentivize workers to pursue professional education and improve the competence of the child welfare workforce. Attention should be paid to the impact financial support has on workforce diversity; equal access to professional education is an important component of this fiscal driver for workforce quality and competence.

All of the proposed interventions require a strong leadership commitment to workforce development. This would result in formalized training partnerships (covered in other chapters) that promote the leadership skills needed to work in complex, collaborative, diverse settings.

Summary

In terms of connecting supervision, leadership, and workforce development, the Children's Bureau has demonstrated a change in focus from professional development around particular practice issues to long-term workforce capacity building embedded in systemic change. This broader perspective reinforces the critical role of leadership at all levels. By preparing leaders to build a competent and committed workforce and to implement sustainable change in the child welfare system, the Children's Bureau will improve outcomes for children, youths, and families. Strong supervision is the key to workforce development; it is the link between worker competence, satisfaction and retention, and positive outcomes for children, youths, and families. The leadership role of the unit supervisor links agency policy and field-level implementation. The leadership role of the manager supports supervisors, determines organizational culture, removes barriers to change, engages community partners, and initiates and sustains change strategies.

Schools of social work must continue to evolve side by side with the Children's Bureau, moving from a problem or issue focus to a systemic focus, addressing child welfare outcomes through investment in workforce capacity, and developing leadership at the supervisory and managerial levels.

References

Administration for Children and Families, (2011). The story of the Children's Bureau. Washington, DC: Author

Adoption Assistance and Child Welfare Act of 1980, 42 U.S.C., §622 (2012).

Adoption and Safe Families Act of 1997, 42 U.S.C.§670 (2012).

Alwon, F., & Reitz, A., (2000). *The workforce crisis in child welfare.* Washington, DC: Child Welfare League of America.

Annie E. Casey Foundation. (2003). *The unsolved challenge of system reform: The condition of the frontline human services workforce.* Baltimore: Author.

Bernotavicz, F. (2008). *Recruitment and retention of child welfare staff final report.* Portland: University of Southern Maine, Edmund S. Muskie School of Public Service, Institute for Public Sector Innovation.

Bernotavicz, F., & Locke. A. (2000). Hiring child welfare caseworkers using a competency-based approach. *Public Personnel Management, 29,* 33–42.

Child Welfare Information Gateway & National Child Welfare Workforce Institute. (2010). Synthesis: Developing models of effective child welfare staff recruitment and retention *training.* Retrieved from https://www.childwelfare.gov/management/funding/funding_sources/synthesis/randrt.pdf

Child Abuse Prevention and Treatment Act of 1974, 42 U.S.C. §10404 (2012)

Child Welfare League of America. (2001). *The child welfare workforce challenge: Results from a preliminary study.* Washington, DC: Author.

Collins-Camargo, C. (2005). *A study of the relationship among effective supervision, organization culture promoting evidence-based practice, worker self-efficacy, and outcomes in public child welfare* (Doctoral dissertation, University of Kentucky, Lexington).

Collins-Camargo, C., Sullivan, D., Washeck, B., Adams, J., & Sundet, P. (2009). One state's effort to improve recruitment, retention, and practice through multifaceted clinical supervision interventions. *Child Welfare, 88*(5), 87–107.

CPS Human Resource Services. (2006). *Realistic job preview: A review of the literature and recommendations.* Houston: Cornerstones for Kids.

Cyphers, G. (2001). *Report from the child welfare survey: State and county data and findings.* Washington, DC: American Public Human Services Association.

Dickinson, N., & Painter, J. (2009). Predictors of undesired turnover for child welfare workers. *Child Welfare, 88,* 187–208.

Dickinson, N. S., Painter, J. S., & Lee, J. S. (2007, January). *Child welfare worker turnover: Understanding and predicting who actually leaves.* Paper presented at the Annual Conference of the Society for Social Work and Research, San Francisco.

Dickinson, N. S., & Perry, R. E. (2002). Factors influencing the retention of specially educated public child welfare workers. *Evaluation Research in Child Welfare, 15*(3/4), 89–103.

Ellett, A. J. (2000). *Human caring, self-efficacy beliefs and professional organizational culture correlates of employee retention in child welfare* (Doctoral dissertation, Louisiana State University, Baton Rouge).

Ellett, A. J., Collins-Camargo, C., & Ellett, C. (2006). Personal and professional correlates of outcomes in child welfare: Implications for supervision and continuing professional development. *Professional Development: Journal of Continuing Social Work Education, 9*(2/3), 45–54.

Ellett, C. D., & Ellett, A. J. (1997). Statewide study of child welfare personnel factors: Who stays, who leaves, who cares? In T. Martin & M. Miah (Eds.), *A national child welfare challenge: Creating partnerships to strengthen families and children. Proceedings of the National Conference on Child Welfare* (pp. 61–71). Carbondale: Southern Illinois University.

Elpers, K., & Westhuis, D. J. (2008). Organizational leadership and its impact on social workers' job satisfaction: A national study. *Administration in Social Work, 32*(3), 26–43.

Faller, K. C., Masternak, M., Grinnell-Davis, C., Grabarek, M., Sieffert, J., & Bernotavicz, F. (2009). Realistic job previews in child welfare: State of innovation and practice. *Child Welfare, 88*(5), 23–48.

Fixsen, D. L., Naoom, S. F., Blase, K. A., Friedman, R. M., & Wallace, F. (2005). *Implementation research: A synthesis of the literature.* Tampa, FL: National Implementation Research Network. Retrieved from http://ctndisseminationlibrary.org/PDF/nirnmonograph.pdf

General Accounting Office. (2003). *Child welfare: HHS could play a greater role in helping child welfare agencies recruit and retain staff* (GAO-03-357). Washington, DC: Author.

Glisson, C. (2010). Organizational climate and service outcomes in child welfare agencies. In M. B. Webb, K. Dowd, B. J. Harden, J. Landsverk, & M. F. Testa (Eds.), *Child welfare and child well-being: New perspectives from the National Survey of Child and Adolescent Well-being* (pp. 378–406). New York: Oxford University Press.

Glisson, C., Dukes, D., & Green, P. (2006). The effects of the ARC organizational intervention on casework turnover, climate, and culture in children's services systems. *Child Abuse & Neglect, 30,* 855–882.

Government Accountability Office. (2007). *African American children in foster care: Additional HHS assistance needed to help states reduce the proportion in care* (GAO-07-816). Washington, DC: Author.

Graef, M. I., & Potter, M. E. (2002). Alternative solutions to the child protective services staffing crisis: Innovations from industrial/organizational psychology. *Protecting Children, 17*(3), 18–31.

Graef, M. I., Potter, M. E., & Rohde, T. L. (2002). *Why do they stay? Research-based implications for practice.* Washington, DC: Child Welfare League of America.

Harvard Family Research Project. (2008). Changing the conversation about workforce development: Getting from inputs to outcomes. Houston: Cornerstones for Kids.

Heifetz, R., & Linsky, M. (2002). *Leadership on the line: Staying alive through the dangers of leading.* Boston: Harvard Business School Press.

Helfgott, K. (1991). *Staffing the child welfare agency: Recruitment and retention.* Washington, DC: Child Welfare League of America.

Jacquet, S., Clark, S., Morazes, J., & Withers, R. (2007). The role of supervision in the retention of public child welfare workers. *Journal of Public Child Welfare, 1*(3), 27–54.

Landsman, M. J. (2001). Commitment in public child welfare. *Social Service Review, 75,* 386–419.

Light, P. (2003). *The health of the human services workforce.* Washington, DC: Brookings Institution.

Michigan State University School of Social Work & Mackenzie Associates. (2009). *Developing models of effective child welfare recruitment and retention training.* Ann Arbor: Michigan State University.

Mor Barak, M. E., Travis, D. J., Pyun, H., & Xie, B. (2009). The impact of supervision on worker outcomes: A meta-analysis. *Social Service Review,* 83, 2–32.

National Child Welfare Workforce Institute. (2010). *Leadership competency framework.* Albany, NY: Author.

Nissly, J., Mor Barak, M., & Levin, A. (2005). Stress, social support and workers' intentions to leave their jobs in public child welfare. *Administration in Social Work, 29*(1), 79–100.

Potter, C., Comstock, A., Brittain, C., & Hanna, M. (2009). Intervening in multiple states: Findings from the Western Regional Recruitment Project. *Child Welfare, 88*(5), 169–185.

Potter, C. (2012). *A historical review of Children's Bureau funding priorities.* Unpublished manuscript. University of Denver.

Reitz, A. L. (2001). *Responding to the workforce crisis: Strategies for recruiting agency staff.* Washington, DC: Child Welfare League of America.

Renner, L., Porter, R., & Preister, S. (2009). Improving the retention of child welfare workers by strengthening skills and increasing support for supervisors. *Child Welfare, 88*(5), 109–127.

Social Security Act of 1936, Title IV-E, 42 U.S.C., §§601–687 (2012).

Strand, V., & Bosco-Ruggiero, S. (2009). Initiating and sustaining a mentoring program for child welfare staff. *Administration in Social Work, 34*(1), 49–67.

Strolin-Goltzman, J., Lawrence, C., Auerback, C., Caringi, J., Claiborne, N., Lawson, H., et al. (2009). Design teams: A promising organizational intervention for improving turnover rates in child welfare workforce. *Child Welfare, 88,* 149–168.

Urban Institute. (2001). *Running to keep in place: The continuing evolution of our nation's child welfare system, assessing the new federalism* (Occasional Paper No. 54). Retrieved from http://www.urban.org/UploadedPDF/310358_occa54.pdf

Vaill, J. (1996). *Learning as a way of being: Strategies for survival in a world of permanent whitewater.* San Francisco: Jossey-Bass.

Zlotnik, J., DePanfilis, D., Daining, C., & Lane, M. (2005). *Factors influencing the retention of child welfare staff: A systematic review of the research.* Washington, DC: Institute for the Advancement of Social Work Research.

Chapter 14

KNOWLEDGE MANAGEMENT AND LEADERSHIP DEVELOPMENT IN CHILD WELFARE

Nancy C. McDaniel and Charmaine Brittain

The legacy of the Children's Bureau in shaping child welfare practices, programs, and polices reflects continual efforts to expand knowledge about what works and transfer that knowledge to others. This chapter explores the Bureau's evolving role in effecting change by transferring knowledge to the field and describes the impact made by the Bureau through an emerging body of knowledge about the role of leaders, the characteristics of leadership, the tools of change management, and their implications for practice. The Children's Bureau's first chief, Julia Lathrop, recognized that knowledge is not a static commodity but a dynamic process and, when captured and used effectively, is a powerful force that can sway leaders to act in the best interest of children, youths, and families.

Social, cultural, economic, and political factors have shaped the role and scope of influence exerted by the Children's Bureau over the past century. What has remained remarkably unchanged is the extent to which the Children's Bureau continues to stimulate and shape national policies and promote systemic change in services for vulnerable children and youths. Today's Children's Bureau plays a pivotal role in building the leadership capacity of the nation's child welfare workforce, as well as creating the knowledge base that guides child welfare leaders.

That history and legacy are inextricably linked with the values embedded in the social work profession. In fact, the seeds of professionalism as a basis for the work of caring of others, reflected in the field of social work and discussed later in this chapter, were sown early in the Children's Bureau's history. Lathrop recognized the importance of professionalism and insisted on hiring staff with subject matter expertise. At a time when most organized social and family services were carried out through volunteerism and by private charities, and most government agencies were primarily staffed with political appointees, Lathrop insisted that the Children's Bureau would be staffed by paid, trained professionals (Tichi, 2007, p. 5).

Founding of the Children's Bureau

As a new federal agency, established in 1912 in the Department of Commerce and Labor, the Children's Bureau found its direction through the influence of individual leaders as well as the influence of elected officials and child advocates. With an initial appropriation of $25,640 and 15 employees, the Bureau was directed to

> investigate and report . . . upon all matters pertaining to the welfare of children and child life among all classes of our people, and shall especially investigate the questions of infant mortality, the birth rate, orphanage, juvenile courts, desertion, dangerous occupations, accidents and diseases of children, employ-ment, legislation affecting children in the several States [46 in 1912] and Ter-ritories. But no official, or agent, or representative of said bureau shall, over the objection of the head of the family, enter any house used exclusively as a family residence. The chief of said bureau may from time to time publish the results of these investigations in such manner and to such extent as may be prescribed by the Secretary of Commerce and Labor. (Children's Bureau, 1912, p. 1)

The role of the Children's Bureau, as described in the report prepared by the Sen-ate Committee on Education and Labor, was purposefully limited to that of furnishing information to the States to

> enable them to deal more intelligently and more systematically and uniformly with the subject. The bill is not designed to encroach upon the rights nor relieve the States from the duty of dealing with this subject, but to furnish the information to enable them to more successfully deal with it. (Children's Bureau, 1912, p. 3)

In the years that followed, Lathrop extended the role of the Bureau beyond this limit, expanding its scope and influence.

Early Years of the Children's Bureau: Knowledge Leading to Change

From its founding, the Children's Bureau leveraged knowledge to influence policies and lead change in ways that would not be out of step with its role today. A key strategy was to gather information and use it to make a case for changes in public policy. This was accomplished by emphasizing data rather than anecdotes to sway public opinion and influence public policy. One of Lathrop's first actions, even before the federal funding for the Children's Bureau had been released, was to meet with "the Census Bureau 'with statisticians' because she knew she needed numbers" (Tichi, 2007, p. 6).

Understanding the role of the Children's Bureau as a purveyor of knowledge is not complete without exploring the differences between data, information, and knowledge. Laudon and Laudon (2002), along with others writing about public and private sector organizations, make distinctions, most often represented as a hierarchy, between *data* (a "stream of raw fact"), *information* ("data shaped into a form that is meaningful and useful"), and *knowledge*, which is described by Leung as the process in which we "make sense of the present situation and interpret it with related insights acquired from our past experiences, so that some new sensible judgment can be arrived at and action can be taken" (Leung, 2007, pp. 186, 193).

Austin, Claassen, Vu, and Mizrahi (2008) have written extensively on knowledge management in human service organizations. As stated in Davenport and Prusack (2000), "Data is defined as a set of 'unorganized facts,' discrete findings that carry no judgment or interpretation" (pp. 2–3). Austin et al. said information adds context to those findings and is data that have been "organized, patterned, grouped, or catego-rized" (Austin et al., 2008, p. 362). Knowledge adds the dimension and richness of experience and is "recreated in the present moment" (McDermott, 1999). The distinction between the three terms—data, information, and knowledge—provides a context to discuss how the early leaders of the Children's Bureau interpreted their role of aggregating and disseminating information and data about issues under their purview.

Almost a century ago, the implicit position of the Children's Bureau was that information was a prerequisite for effective public policy. The role of the Bureau was focused on obtaining and disseminating information; the next step of creating knowledge and acting on it was the responsibility of the states. This position was made explicit in the following statement:

> [The Children's Bureau's] duty is solely to study and report upon conditions affecting the welfare of children. It may publish facts it secures, in any form approved by the Secretary of the Department of Commerce and Labor. It will endeavor to secure pertinent facts and to present them promptly and clearly for use and popular distribution. Its effectiveness must depend *upon the use made of these facts by the people of the United States* [italics added]. (Children's Bureau, 1912, p. 5)

However, Lathrop recognized that the Children's Bureau needed to extend that duty and promote the creation of knowledge by presenting data and information in a way that would "be heard by the whole public which it was created to serve" (Bradbury & Eliot, 1956, p. 10), with the ultimate goal of prompting public action. In fact, the earliest legacy of the Children's Bureau was grounded in gathering information and disseminating that information to inform the public—to build knowledge leading to change. U.S. infant and maternal death rates were recognized as far higher than those of other industrial nations, but it was also recognized that without "secured reliable knowledge as to children born, there can be no reliable knowledge as to the birth rate, or as to the proportion of children who die" (Children's Bureau, 1912, p. 4).

The bureau assumed an active role in gathering information in order to inform and educate the public, and its first study was of "why babies died" (Bradbury & Eliot, 1956, p. 6). Next, the Children's Bureau began studying maternal mortality. Once the conditions contributing to infant and maternal mortality emerged from the reports, the bureau began issuing annual reports "on the incidence and trends in these deaths in various sections of the country and in various population groups" (Bradbury & Eliot, 1956, p. 8). The bureau acted as a change agent by disseminating facts, coupled with knowledge so that "some new judgment can be arrived at and action taken" (Leung, 2007, p. 193). Consequently, the role of the bureau expanded to one of advocacy for mandatory birth registration and state reporting to the Census Bureau.

The Children's Bureau produced two pamphlets that were widely distributed. In 1913, *Prenatal Care* was published, and *Infant Care*, was published the following year. It was considered somewhat daring for the government to insert itself into the private lives of citizens and was also viewed as encroaching on the medical profession by offering detailed and prescriptive advice on child rearing.

Lathrop countered criticism by saying, "There is no purpose to invade the field of the medical or nurturing profession, but rather to furnish such statement regarding hygiene and normal living every mother has a right to possess in the interest of herself and her children" (quoted in Bradbury & Eliot, 1956, p. 8). Ultimately, Congress supported the creation and dissemination of educational pamphlets as demand rose from constituents seeking more information on childhood. By 1955, more than 10 editions of *Infant Care* had been published, with a distribution of more than 34 million copies (Bradbury & Eliot, 1956, p. 9).

During her tenure of nine years, Lathrop advocated policies that were considered controversial and viewed by numerous political and professional groups as overstepping the role of the Children's Bureau. For example, she advocated setting limits on child labor at a time when children were routinely employed in industry (Tichi, 2007). The Bureau's advocacy and use of information led to improved sanitary conditions and the pasteurization of milk and was used as an argument for widows' pensions and the establishment of a minimum wage (Bradbury & Eliot, 1956, p. 8).

Evolving Role of the Children's Bureau

Today, the Children's Bureau is nested within a bureaucracy that has increased to a size and scope unimagined a century ago. The Children's Bureau is one of two bureaus within the Administration on Children, Youth and Families (ACYF), which in turn is one of 10 offices within the Administration for Children and Families (ACF), one of 12 operating divisions within the U.S. Department of Health and Human Services (HHS) (HHS, ACF, 2013; HHS, ACF, Children's Bureau, 2013a). With an annual budget of more than $7 billion, the Children's Bureau today "seeks to provide for the safety, permanency and well-being of children through leadership, support for necessary services, and productive partnerships with States, Tribes and communities" (HHS, ACF, Children's Bureau, 2013b).

Over the past century, not only has the Children's Bureau grown in size, but the scope of knowledge that falls within its purview has grown dramatically. The Children's Bureau today plays multiple roles as a convener, purveyor, and capacity builder through the dissemination of knowledge and development of leaders and has carried out its role as change agent using multiple and evolving strategies.

Knowledge Management and the Training and Technical Assistance Network

Knowledge management—capturing, organizing, managing, and disseminating knowledge—is a daunting challenge. However, the benefits have been well documented; for example, organizations that manage knowledge claim higher rates of productivity (New York State Department of Civil Service & New York State Governor's Office of Employee Relations, 2002, p. 2). Knowledge management can be a strategy to synthesize and highlight best and emerging practices while managing information overload. The *Knowledge Management/Transfer Workgroup Report* summarized three components of knowledge management: people (those "who collectively comprise the organizational culture that nurtures and stimulates knowledge sharing"), processes (methods to "acquire, create, organize, share, and transfer knowledge"), and technology, which includes the mechanisms for storage and access (New York State Department of Civil Service & New York State Governor's Office of Employee Relations, 2002, p. 6). All three components are essential for fully functional knowledge management.

Within the Children's Bureau today, the responsibility for knowledge management and its components—people, processes, and technology—cuts across every division and team, as each plays a role in capturing data, managing that data to create useable information, and building knowledge capacity. One particular strategy, the Training and Technical Assistance Network, illustrates the importance of harnessing the components of "people, processes, and technology" employed by the Bureau to effectively reach the field. Composed of 30 distinct entities, many of which consist of partnerships between multiple national organizations and universities, the Training and Technical Assistance Network includes national resource centers, quality improvement centers, regional implementation centers, other cosponsored national centers, and members providing technical assistance, consultation, and information services (HHS, ACF, ACYF, Children's Bureau, 2010). Each Training and Technical Assistance Network member relies on interrelated strategies employing people, processes, and technology to carry out the activities associated with knowledge management and, ultimately, to enhance leadership capacity and support improved practices. The Children's Bureau's historical role in dissemination of information and innovative program ideas is long-standing, encompassing strategies beyond that of this network.

Knowledge Management and Information Clearinghouses

The Child Abuse Prevention and Treatment Act (CAPTA) of 1974 (P.L. 93-247), and its subsequent amendments and reauthorizations (HHS, ACF, Children's Bureau, 2013c; California Center for Research on Women and Families, 2009, p. 1), shaped the current approach to knowledge transfer and dissemination of information. The act mandated that states define child abuse and neglect and establish reporting laws, and it established the National Center on Child Abuse and Neglect and, through the Center, initiated activities consistent with the work of the Children's Bureau today, including the following:

- compiling, summarizing, and publishing current research on child abuse and neglect
- compiling and publishing training materials
- providing technical assistance
- conducting research
- making a "full study and investigation of the national incidence of child abuse and neglect" (Child Abuse Prevention and Treatment Act of 1974, P.L. 93-247, Sec. 2. (b)(1-6))

Another critical element of CAPTA, which firmly established the present role of the Children's Bureau in dissemination of knowledge, was the establishment of an "information clearinghouse on all programs" for the "prevention, identification, and treatment of child abuse and neglect" (Child Abuse Prevention and Treatment Act of 1974, P.L. 93-247, Sec. 2. (b)(2)). The role of the first information clearinghouse was to act as a repository to collect, organize, and disseminate information about child maltreatment. In 1987, Congress established the National Adoption Information Clearinghouse. Operating separately, but with areas of overlap, each clearinghouse was responsible for collecting, organizing, and disseminating information and representing different aspects of child welfare.

Organizing and disseminating information was greatly assisted by the advent of computer technology; the Children's Bureau's approach to dissemination has been shaped by technological advances and the needs of the field. The years between 2002 and 2007 were characterized by change and growth, as the Bureau incorporated technological advances and created a more integrated approach to knowledge transfer. In 2007, the two clearinghouses were consolidated (K. Helfgott, personal communication, July 5, 2011), producing the Child Welfare Information Gateway, designed as a single point of access for information and offering a full continuum of resources promoting safety, permanency, and well-being of families. This highlighted the change in the Bureau's vision for information dissemination, from the more static process of creating and disseminating documents to creating communities of practice to promote the integration and active use of the information (Child Welfare Information Gateway, 2011a, 2011b).

In another significant change, the Children's Bureau now offers training, technical assistance, research, and consultation services to states, tribes, and territories. In January 1986, six new national child welfare resource centers were approved for funding, with an additional three approved the following summer, replacing the regional child welfare resource centers, whose funding ended in 1984. Each of the new resource centers focused on a specific area of expertise, and they would function as "national centers of excellence whose services will be sought by the field" (California Department of Social Services [CDSS], 1986, p. 2). Funding was limited to three years, with the expectation that each resource center would acquire additional income on a fee-for-service basis and focus on the "marketing of exemplary resource material, training, and consultation services" (CDSS, p. 3).

The first librarian for the national resource center on child abuse, operated by the American Humane Association (funded 1986–1991 and 1991–1996), described the challenging and time-consuming process of collecting hard copies of states' policy and procedures manuals by sending a letter of request to each state's child welfare director, and, upon receipt, storing all of the manuals on shelves and in boxes. One of her first duties was to create a card catalog listing each of the books, journals, and other documents. The library holdings were primarily used by resource center staff and by appointment upon request by local college and university faculty. The library holdings and policy manuals were not accessible to the public. The resource center maintained a toll-free number, and most requests came from the media, asking for general information, or from state government staff, asking what other states were doing in a variety of areas (R. Alsop, personal communication, June 28, 2011).

Today dissemination of information, directed toward building the capacity of state, tribal, and territorial child welfare agencies, is coordinated by the Training and Technical Assistance Network, accessed directly by states and through the Administration for Children and Families regional offices. An additional goal is to build leadership capacity to sustain systemic change. The next section discusses the effort in recent years to build not only knowledge but also capacity through leadership development.

Historical Themes in Leadership Development

Over the last 200 years, leadership principles and theories increasingly garnered attention in the search for explanations of the success of organizations, movements, governments, and even wars. Why were some efforts successful and not others? Could the explanation lie in the leadership practices of the men and women behind the efforts? What aspect of their leadership style facilitated their success?

Theories abounded, starting with a focus on the "great man" concept, posited by Thomas Carlyle, that leaders were born great and possessed certain traits that led to their success (Carlyle, 1904). Research in the early part of the 20th century sought to identify specific personality traits and physical characteristics, but this approach was ultimately disproved, as the qualities and personalities of leaders were so disparate that no common threads could be readily discerned. In the mid-twentieth century, leadership theories focused more on rational behavior in response to situations, giving rise to theories such as Theory X and Y (McGregor, 1960) and situational leadership (Hersey & Blanchard, 1972), moving from "what" makes a leader successful to "how" to effectively lead. Contingency theory of the 1960s stated that leaders fell into two camps, those who focused primarily on the task at hand and those who focused on relationships, and that the situation then determined which type of leadership was most successful (Fiedler, 1967). "Correct" analysis of the situation then leads to the "correct" response. The transformational leadership model (Bass, 1985; Burns, 1978) arose in the 1980s and called upon leaders to put aside their personal interests for the good of the group in order to transform everyone through empowerment and motivation. The relationship model of leadership and the servant leadership theory became well known in the 1990s and echoed the transformational model, with the emphasis on relationships and the goal of service to others. These more contemporary leadership theories harken back to an earlier time, with an emphasis on normative traits and a focus on inspirational leaders (Grint, 2011).

Current leadership theories incorporate past learning but have evolved to focus on the situation and the importance of a leader's ability to adapt to the current situation while inspiring followers. Adaptive leadership is the practice of mobilizing people to address difficult challenges and thrive (Heifetz, Grashow, & Linsky, 2009). Change and the capacity to embrace and orchestrate it are at the heart of adaptive leadership. According to Heifetz and Linsky's (2002) principles of adaptive leadership, some leadership challenges are adaptive, while others are technical in nature. A technical challenge is something the group already has the knowledge to fix; solving the challenge is more a management task than a leadership process. A challenge is adaptive when it requires something new—a new behavior, knowledge, action, or way of thinking that is not in the group's current repertoire. When change is adaptive in nature, people do not know how to solve the problem and, in fact, people are the problem. Adaptive challenges require people to learn new ways, change behaviors, reach new understandings, see the world through new filters, and work through problems in a collective process (Heifetz & Linsky, 2002). Leadership implications include the importance of systems thinking, relationship building, and nimbleness for addressing the adaptive challenges so prevalent in today's society.

Adaptive leadership, along with the tenets of implementation science, guide the Children's Bureau's current efforts to facilitate change within the child welfare field. Lessons learned from the past tell us that it is no longer sufficient to "build it and they will come"; rather, leadership must mobilize resources and people to bring about meaningful improvements within the child welfare field.

Capacity Building through Leadership Development and Change Management

Over the Children's Bureau's 100-year history, emphasis shifted from merely quantifying and understanding the plight of children to improving outcomes for children. At the 50th anniversary of the Children's Bureau, Chief Katherine Oettinger said, " a hardy band of practical dreamers . . . studied the past and present circumstances of children in order to chart a course for the future" (U.S. Social Security Administration, 1962). Today, it is no longer sufficient to count the number of maltreated children or units of service (for example, counseling sessions) provided; rather, the child welfare field focuses on outcomes to ensure that children are safe, permanency is achieved, and the well-being of children is improved.

Today, all Children's Bureau's sponsorships require that grantees prove that their activity makes a difference. All proposals to the Children's Bureau are required to contain a logic model. Logic models "connect the dots" to show how the inputs of a project move through program objectives to outputs and eventually to outcomes. Using a logic model brings heightened awareness of the process and its outcomes and formalizes the knowledge transfer process.

During the better part of its history, the Children's Bureau's focus was on collecting information and promoting practices to support the change process through legislation. A growing recognition of the pivotal role leadership plays in promoting and sustaining change led to an effort by the Bureau to promote effective leadership practices at multiple levels to strengthen the child welfare system and sustain change that yields improved outcomes for children, youths, and families. Today's Children's Bureau seeks to build capacity and develop leaders with the knowledge and skills to act as change agents to manifest continual improvements in the child welfare field.

More and more, organizations recognize the need for leadership at all levels—also called distributive leadership—and are encouraging the development of staff leadership skills across the organization. Not only top-level leadership but also leadership by mid-level managers and supervisors is needed to promote change. No one leader, approach, or strategy can facilitate a change; rather, multiple leaders and a multi-pronged approach that reflects implementation science are necessary for meaningful and successful change.

Change, leadership, and the transfer of knowledge are inextricably linked. Leadership provides the guidance for change to happen and, in doing so, transfers new knowledge and skills to the organization and the people within it in order to realize the desired change. Within an organization, the change process is just as important as the actual change itself. Effective change models the parallel process of casework with clients, agency leadership with staff, and agency staff with community providers (Lonne, Parton, Thomson, & Harries, 2008). Thus, authoritarian, directive approaches will be as ineffective with staff as they are with clients when it comes to realizing substantive change, either in family interactions or in agency culture. Instead, approaches that are respectful and inclusive (such as adaptive leadership) will lend themselves to more successful outcomes.

Another realization for child welfare has been the growing recognition that change occurs only with thoughtful and purposeful activities directed toward implementation. Too often, the promise of innovative practices has dissipated over the course of the project and remained unfulfilled. Implementation science connects knowledge to action so that the good ideas and cumulative knowledge do not languish but are realistically put into place to achieve the intended results. Distinct stages and specific strategies to yield incremental results guide efforts to implement any kind of change. In order for implementation to succeed, it requires leadership support and multilevel organizational structures for installation and maintenance of effort (Fixsen, Naoom, Blase, Friedman, & Wallace, 2005). The Children's Bureau has led the focus on implementation science so that new program initiatives, especially those that translate evidence-based practices into institutionalized program components, have the opportunity to succeed.

Social Work, NASW, and Child Welfare

Although issues such as substance abuse, mental illness, domestic violence, and generational poverty existed in previous generations, they did not seem to have such a profound effect on practice as they do now, making it so much more complicated and challenging to help children and families. Over the last 100 years, citizens, policymakers, and elected officials have recognized that the country's complex societal issues could not be solved solely by families and charitable organizations. Increasingly, the government is viewed as having a responsibility to address and ameliorate these issues and to ensure the safety and well-being of all citizens. The social work profession and the Children's Bureau work in tandem to do research, develop interventions, educate practitioners, and provide services to address these social problems for the betterment of all society, while increasing the social work knowledge base.

As the Children's Bureau evolved, so did the social work profession, and the National Association of Social Workers (NASW) led efforts to develop a common body of knowledge and values to guide the profession. NASW's *Code of Ethics,* approved in 1996 and revised in 2008 by the NASW Delegate Assembly, expresses the core values that drive the social work profession: service, social justice, dignity and worth of the person, importance of human relationships, integrity, and competence. Social work values manifest in Children's Bureau–sponsored activities and programs. For example, since early 2000s, there has been growing attention to the need for a strong and competent workforce, leadership development, and capacity building, which specifically reflect NASW values such as dignity and worth of the person, integrity, and competence.

There has also been a growing recognition that these values, in and of themselves, are not sufficient. Working toward social justice is an admirable goal, which is to "do the right thing," but how it is done matters just as much as whether it is achieved—that is, to do it the right way. That approach requires a specific set of skills and competencies related to managerial effectiveness and leadership.

The link between the Children's Bureau and the social work profession continues to be strong as they work to expand the knowledge base and build evidence for practices that are effective. For example, family engagement has always been important within the child welfare field, but there has been a new emphasis on improving the ways that child welfare workers engage families to achieve outcomes. Within social work education, effective family engagement practices are studied by social work educators and researchers, who then strive to bring these practices into the classroom and then to child welfare agencies. The partnership between universities and states and tribes is vital to the successful implementation of an evolving practice framework that strives to realize social work values.

Social Work Education and Child Welfare

To professionalize child welfare, many agencies partnered with schools of social work starting in 1990, using funding from Title IV-E of the Adoption Assistance and Child Welfare Act of 1980 (P.L. 96-272) and Title IV-B, Section 426(c) of the Social Security Act [42 U.S.C. Section 626] to support BSW and MSW education (Zlotnik, 2003). In social work education, the field experience or practicum has been an integral component of preparing students for professional practice (Wayne, Bogo, & Raskin, 2006, 2010), and the child welfare field has benefited from this complementary relationship (Risely-Curtiss, 2003). The academic experience integrates with the practical learning that occurs in the agency, providing a full academically and professionally grounded experience (Folaron & Hostetter, 2007; Wayne, Bogo, & Raskin, 2006). Many child welfare workers, supervisors, and administrators began their professional careers in child welfare as interns fulfilling their field education requirement. Graduates who possess a social work education are far more prepared to practice in child welfare than those from other disciplines, in large part because of the field education component (Folaron & Hostetter, 2007; Franke, Bagdasaryan, & Furman, 2009; Scannapieco & Connell-Corrick, 2003).

Strong partnerships between child welfare and schools of social work strengthen the capacity of agencies to employ evidenced-based practices (Collins-Camargo & Hoffman, 2006). Evidence-based practices are the result of a process in which potential interventions are investigated through scientific inquiry to select the most appropriate for a specific problem. Using evidence-based practices is a social work moral and professional responsibility (Collins-Camargo & Hoffman, 2006).

Partnerships with the Children's Bureau to promote evidence-based practices help to realize this vision. For example, the proliferation of kinship care as a placement option for children who cannot safely remain at home offers an opportunity to examine the effectiveness of this option (Gleeson, 1995). Use of kinship care serves many purposes, including the manifestation of social work values of the dignity and worth of the person and the importance of human relationships. Schools of social work can offer intellectual leadership by supporting research on kinship care and bringing the findings from this research into the classroom and training programs for kin care families, while also fulfilling their mandate to promote social work values and ethics, including addressing issues such as diversity, promotion of social and economic justice, and serving populations at risk (Gleeson, 1995). This is just one example of the many research and education partnerships within social work education programs that work with child welfare providers to support and improve effective practices.

Future Directions and Practice Implications

The futures of child welfare practice, social work, and NASW are inextricably linked. Ongoing partnerships between schools of social work and child welfare agencies provide the most effective way to prepare students to work in the complex field of child welfare, while promoting knowledge development and transfer (Auerbach, McGowan, & Heft LaPorte, 2007; Collins-Camargo & Hoffman, 2006; Franke et al., 2009). A continuum of support for social work study (BSW, MSW, and post-graduate), as well as ongoing professional development and competency-based training, will elevate the knowledge and practice skills of the child welfare workforce. Requiring an MSW for promotion to a supervisory position could also be encouraged (Auerbach et al., 2007) as a way to professionalize the field and reward employees who further their education.

Implementation of child welfare practice certificates demonstrates an explicit link between social work education, the goals of the NASW, and the field of child welfare and is another vehicle for recognizing the professional requirements unique to the field of child welfare. The recommended curriculum for the child welfare practice certificate includes theories of crisis intervention, human behavior, child development, family systems, grief, separation and loss, attachment and bonding, child welfare practice, and interviewing, all with a trauma-informed perspective, along with a field practicum in a child and family agency (Folaron & Hostetter, 2007).

Creating an environment in which collaboration flourishes is important. Schools of social work must engage in active partnerships with child welfare agencies to provide educational opportunities for students and employees, as well as to increase the knowledge base related to evidence-based practices. It has been said that social work is both an art and a science, and this tension is a healthy one—facilitating the rigorous testing of new interventions, while recognizing the adaptive challenges in transferring interventions to complex social environments. This partnership promotes the integration of science into a real-world setting, testing the efficacy, feasibility, and sustainability of evidence-based practices.

Child welfare agencies benefit from these partnerships through the education and preparation of a well-trained workforce, including serving as a field site to test innovative, promising, and evidence-informed practices. Social work schools will be preparing future BSW and MSW students with both the technical knowledge and skills to do their jobs and the leadership knowledge and skills to address adaptive changes that will continue moving the child welfare field forward. Doctoral programs in schools of social work are also key to knowledge development, training students to employ the rigorous skills needed to develop and test new evidence-based practices (J. H. Williams, personal communication, January 10, 2012). Child welfare staff and social work programs working together will align the knowledge and skill needs of child welfare agencies with the social work curriculum, ensuring that interventions are not only scientifically grounded but also socially and culturally relevant.

An active partnership between schools of social work and child welfare agencies offers flexibility in funding and resources to test and implement new practices. The resultant knowledge can then be infused in curricula and reflected in laws, policies, and the practices of child welfare agencies. By continuing to support and encourage such activities, the Children's Bureau raises expectations for a more professionalized and evidence-based environment. Consequently, more research, sufficient funding, improved working relationships, and use of evidence-based and evidence-informed practices will benefit all (Collins-Camargo & Hoffman, 2006).

Over the past century, the Children's Bureau has shaped child welfare law, policy, and practice. Using data and information as the basis for its authority, the Children's Bureau has exerted its influence by building the capacity of leaders as change agents through gathering, creating, and disseminating knowledge to the field of child welfare professionals. Over the next century, the challenges facing social work educators and professionals will reflect an increasingly complex society. Values of the social work profession—social justice, human dignity, and integrity—will remain a constant; however, these values will manifest differently in guiding the response of future child welfare leaders to social issues such as the long-term well-being of children, community health, global equity, and environmental and ecological respect.

Drucker (2003) said, "[Knowledge] makes itself constantly obsolete, so that today's advanced knowledge is tomorrow's ignorance. And the knowledge that matters is subject to rapid and abrupt shifts." Knowledge is not a static commodity but a dynamic interaction and transaction among individuals. The Children's Bureau has created an infrastructure to accomplish these transactions not only directly with child welfare professionals, but also through the network of training and technical assistance providers. If the present course of the Children's Bureau remains constant, the future direction is likely to be one in which technology is used to manage and increase access to the overwhelming amount of information available to the field. The use and impact of that knowledge will ultimately be reflected in outcomes for children, youths, families, and communities, and this is the true indication of its value.

Processes and technology are two components of knowledge management. The third and most important component is people. The workforce of child welfare professionals is both the subject of change management and the object by which change occurs. Changing demographics and an aging workforce have heightened the importance of leadership development. Today's young workforce will be tomorrow's agents of change. As a young woman, Julia Lathrop sat in an audience and was inspired by Jane Addams to become an agent of change, eventually becoming the first chief of the Children's Bureau. Today's actions will shape and inspire tomorrow's leaders.

References

Adoption Assistance and Child Welfare Act of 1980, P.L. 96-272, 94 Stat. 500 (June 17, 1980).

Auerbach, C., McGowan, B., & Heft LaPorte, H. (2007). How does professional education impact the job outlook of public child welfare workers? *Journal of Public Child Welfare, 1*, 55–75.

Austin, J., Claassen, J., Vu, C., & Mizrahi, P. (2008). Knowledge management: Implications for human service organizations. *Journal of Evidence-Based Social Work, 5*(1/2), 361–389. doi:10.1300/J394v05n01_13

Bass, B. M. (1985). *Leadership and performance beyond expectations.* New York: Free Press.

Bradbury, D., & Eliot, M. (1956). *Four decades of action for children—A short history of the Children's Bureau.* Retrieved from http://www.archive.org/details/fourdecadesofact00brad

Burns, J. M. (1978). *Leadership.* New York: Harper & Row.

California Center for Research on Women and Families. (2009, June). *Key Federal child welfare laws.* Retrieved from http://www.ccrwf.org/wp-content/uploads/2009/07/ccrwf-federalstatecwslawssummary-june2009.pdf

California Department of Social Services. (1986, February 19). *Subject: National child welfare resource centers* (All County Information Notice No. 1-16-86). Retrieved from http://www.dss.cahwnet.gov/lettersnotices/entres/getinfo/acin86/I-16-86.pdf

Carlyle, T. (1904). *On heroes and hero-worship and the heroic in history.* London: Oxford University Press.

Child Abuse Prevention and Treatment Act, P.L. 93-247, 88 Stat. 4 (1974).

Child Welfare Information Gateway. (2011a). *General FAQs.* Retrieved from http://www.childwelfare.gov/general_faq.cfm

Child Welfare Information Gateway. (2011b). *More on the clearinghouses.* Retrieved from http://www.childwelfare.gov/more.cfm.

Children's Bureau. (1912). *The Children's Bureau, Department of Commerce and Labor: Establishment of the bureau.* Retrieved from http://lccn.loc.gov/12029019

Collins-Camargo, C., & Hoffman, K. (2006). University/child welfare agency partnerships: Building a bridge between the ivory tower and the state office building. *Professional Development: The International Journal of Continuing Social Work Education, 9*(2), 24–37.

Davenport, T.H., & Prusack, L. (2000). *Working knowledge: How organizations manage what they know.* Cambridge, MA: Harvard Business School Press.

Drucker, P. F. (2003). *On the profession of management.* Boston: Harvard Business Review Press.

Fiedler, F. E. (1967). *A theory of leadership effectiveness.* New York: McGraw-Hill.

Fixsen, D. L., Naoom, S. F., Blase, K. A., Friedman, R. M., & Wallace, F. (2005). *Implementation research: A synthesis of the literature* (FMHI Publication #231). Tampa: University of South Florida, Louis de la Parte Florida Mental Health Institute, National Implementation Research Network.

Folaron, G., & Hostetter, C. (2007). Is social work the best educational degree for child welfare practitioners? *Journal of Public Child Welfare, 1,* 65–83.

Franke, T., Bagdasaryan, S., & Furman, W. (2009). A multivariate analysis of training, education, and readiness for public child welfare practice. *Children and Youth Services Review, 31,* 1330–1336.

Gleeson, J. (1995). Kinship care and public child welfare: Challenges and opportunities for social work education. *Journal of Social Work Education, 31*(2), 182–193.

Grint, K. (2011). A history of leadership. In A. Bryman, D. Collinson, K. Grint, B. Jackson, & M. Uhl-Bien (Eds.), *The Sage handbook of leadership* (pp. 3–28). Los Angeles: Sage Publications.

Heifetz, R., Grashow, A., & Linsky, M. (2009). *The practice of adaptive leadership.* Boston: Harvard Business Press.

Heifetz, R., & Linsky, M. (2002). *Leadership on the line: Staying alive through the dangers of leading.* Boston: Harvard Business School Press.

Hersey, P., & Blanchard, K. H. (1972). *Management of organizational behavior: Utilizing human resources.* (2nd ed.). Upper Saddle River, NJ: Prentice-Hall.

Laudon, K. C., & Laudon, J. P. (2002). *Management information systems: Managing the digital firm.* Upper Saddle River, NJ: Prentice-Hall.

Leung, Z. (2007). Knowledge management in social work—Towards a conceptual framework. *Journal of Technology in Human Services, 25*(1/2), 181–198. doi:10.1300/J017v25n01_13

Lonne, B., Parton, N., Thomson, J., & Harries, M. (2008). *Reforming child protection.* New York: Routledge.

McGregor, D. (1960). *The human side of enterprise*, New York: McGrawHill.

McDermott, R. (1999). Why information technology inspired but cannot deliver knowledge management. *California Management Review, 41*(4), 103–117.

National Association of Social Workers. (2008). *Code of ethics of the National Association of Social Workers.* Retrieved from http://www.socialworkers.org/pubs/code/code.asp

New York State Department of Civil Service & New York State Governor's Office of Employee Relations. (2002). *Knowledge management/transfer—Report of the Knowledge Management/Transfer Workgroup.* New York: Author.

Scannapieco, M., & Connell-Corrick, K. (2003). Do collaborations with schools of social work make a difference for the field of child welfare? Practice, retention, and curriculum. *Journal of Human Behavior in the Social Environment, 7*(1/2), 35–51.

Tichi, C. (2007). *Justice, not pity: Julia Lathrop, first chief of the U.S. Children's Bureau* [Audio teleconference transcript]. Retrieved from http://www.acf.hhs.gov/sites/default/files/cb/history_cb_transcript.pdf

U.S. Department of Health and Human Services, Administration for Children and Families. (2013). *Administration on Children, Youth and Families: Organizational chart.* Retrieved from http://www.acf.hhs.gov/about/offices

U.S. Department of Health and Human Services, Administration for Children and Families, Administration on Children, Youth and Families, Children's Bureau. (2010). *The Children's Bureau training and technical assistance network 2010 directory.* Washington, DC: Author.

U.S. Department of Health and Human Services, Administration for Children and Families, Children's Bureau. (2013a). *About the Children's Bureau: Organization structure.* Retrieved from http://www/acf.hhs.gov/programs/cb/about/organization_structure

U.S. Department of Health and Human Services, Administration for Children and Families. Children's Bureau. (2013b). *About the Children's Bureau: Mission.* Retrieved from http://www.acf.hhs.gov/programs/cb/aboutcb/fact_sheet_cb.

U.S. Department of Health and Human Services, Administration for Children and Families, Children's Bureau. (2013c). *The Child Abuse Prevention and Treatment Act as amended* by the *Keeping Children and Families Safe Act of 2003*. Retrieved from http://www.acf. hhs.gov/programs/cb/laws_policies/cblaws/capta03/capta_manual.pdf

U.S. Social Security Administration. (1962). *It's your Children's Bureau.* Retrieved from http:// www.ssa.gov/history/childb2.html

Wayne, J., Bogo, M., & Raskin, M. (2006). Field notes: The need for radical change in field education. *Journal of Social Work Education, 42,* 161–169.

Wayne, J., Bogo, M., & Raskin, M. (2010). Field education as the signature pedagogy of social work education. *Journal of Social Work Education, 46,* 327–339.

Zlotnik, J. (2003). Preparing social workers for child welfare practice. *Journal of Health & Social Policy, 15*(3), 5–21.

Chapter 15

UNIVERSITY–AGENCY PARTNERSHIPS TO ADVANCE CHILD WELFARE

Joan Levy Zlotnik

"**A** Battle Joined: How the School of Social Work Partners with Child Welfare Agencies to Better Young Lives in the Balance" was the feature article of the spring 2011 issue of the University of Pittsburgh School of Social Work's magazine *Bridges*. It described the partnership between the school and county child welfare agencies across the state, highlighting the partnership with Allegheny County. This is just one contemporary example of how universities are important resources for child welfare agencies and the services that they provide. This includes supporting the developmental and educational needs of the children and families served, as well as being a resource for education, research, training, strategic planning, and data analysis for agency administrators and staff. Such university–agency partnerships help the university fulfill its community service and research missions and help to ensure that the education it offers is relevant to contemporary practice.

This chapter focuses on university–agency child welfare partnerships, offering a historical perspective in the context of the Children's Bureau and providing examples of how universities contribute to the well-being of children, the improvement of organizational climate and culture, knowledge development and knowledge transfer, and the recruitment and retention of staff. The significant role of schools and departments of social work is described, and issues for the future are identified.

Federal Support for University–Agency Partnerships

University–agency partnerships in child welfare have a long history. Since the beginning of federally funded child welfare services in 1935 with the passage of the Social Security Act (P.L. 74-271), states have been encouraged to use some of their funds to support educational leave for child welfare workers to acquire a social work degree (U.S.

Department of Health, Education and Welfare, 1965). As the Children's Bureau's appropriations related to child health and child welfare programs grew in the 1950s and 1960s, so did the focus on workforce development. Especially after 1961, the Bureau expanded its involvement with schools of medicine, social work, and public health and became more directly involved in education and training in these disciplines ("*The Records of the Children's Bureau*," 1989).

Until 1969, the Children's Bureau programs focused on both child health and child welfare. In 1969, however, this changed due to reorganization in the Department of Health, Education and Welfare. The Bureau's focus narrowed, as the Maternal and Child Health Bureau and the Crippled Children's Services moved to the Public Health Service (these programs are now within the Health Resources and Services Administration). With this move, the training of physicians and public health workers was separated from child welfare training. Both the Children's Bureau and the Maternal and Child Health Bureau continued to offer some grants to social work education programs. But the reorganization undercut what should be a strong link between the health and welfare and well-being of children (Social Work Policy Institute, 2012).

Ties between the Maternal and Child Health Bureau and the Children's Bureau were recently strengthened with the creation of the Maternal Infant and Early Childhood Home Visiting Program (http://www.hrsa.gov/grants/manage/homevisiting) under the Patient Protection and Affordable Care Act of 2010 (P.L. 111-148). Implementation is occurring collaboratively as the two bureaus work together on identifying the evidence-based parameters that states will be required to use in implementing their home visiting programs.

Title IV-B, Section 426, of the Social Security Act

The 1962 Social Security amendments included provisions under Title IV-B, Section 426 as a direct response to workforce shortages. It also included a provision for a research and demonstration program that would test innovations. Section 426 (1) (C) provides for grants to public and nonprofit institutions of higher learning to train individuals to work in the child welfare field. This funding supports traineeships for undergraduate and graduate students, in-service training, and curriculum development. The applicants for the traineeship grants are most frequently social work education programs. Social work advocacy by the National Association of Social Workers (NASW) and the Action Network for Social Work Education and Research has focused on increasing annual appropriations for this funding and targeting it toward schools of social work.

A 1993 study by the General Accounting Office (now the Government Accountability Office) documented the ups and downs of this funding stream, noting that (in 1992 constant dollars) the level of appropriation had decreased 75 percent from the 1978 funding high of $8,150,000. (General Accounting Office, 1993). Section 426 funding for training was at $3.8 million from 1982 until 1995, when it increased to $4.6 million; and then in fiscal year (FY) 1996 it decreased to $2 million. Advocacy by NASW and the Action Network for Social Work Education and Research resulted in an increase in the appropriation to $7.2 million in FY 2000 (Zlotnik, 2002), where it remained until 2010, when Congress included an additional $20 million for the reduction of the need for long-term foster care (Child Welfare League of America [CWLA], 2010).

Title IV-E Training

The second major stream of funding that supports training and education partnerships between social work education programs and child welfare agencies is the Title IV-E training entitlement. Title IV-E was created in 1980, when the Social Security Act was amended through the passage of the Child Welfare and Adoption Assistance Act of 1980 (P.L. 96-272). Although provisions that can support degree education for students were included at the time of passage, schools and agencies did not begin to take full advantage of this opportunity until the early 1990s (Zlotnik, 2003; Zlotnik & Cornelius, 2000). Based on several sources, it is estimated that fewer than 40 states use this funding mechanism to support BSW and MSW students preparing for child welfare careers and to offer degree education to current child welfare workers (Council on Social Work Education [CSWE], 2012; Social Work Policy Institute, 2012). Although this funding stream has provided support for many agencies to professionalize their frontline and supervisory workforce, these efforts have been vulnerable to unclear regulations, inconsistent interpretations of the regulations, and the lack of clear administrative guidance, as well as changes in education and training priorities as state child welfare leadership changes. Actions were taken in the late 1990s to address these issues (Administration on Children, Youth and Families, 1996); however, no changes actually occurred, and lack of clarity and inconsistent interpretations continue to be a problem.

As more and more states and social work education programs engaged in Title IV-E–supported educational partnerships, an annual meeting for university and agency partners was organized in conjunction with CSWE's annual program meeting to exchange information, ideas, and resources. In addition, an electronic mailing list that provides an opportunity for subscribers to seek advice and exchange information was initiated, and a Title IV-E Web site was developed (http://www.sw.uh.edu/community/cwep/title-iv-e/index.php).

The existence of Title IV-E partnerships has also enlarged the body of research on the child welfare workforce, as efforts funded under Title IV-E are required to carry out evaluations (Zlotnik, DePanfilis, Daining, & Lane, 2005). Among the outcomes of the annual program meeting were a call for papers on the role of social work educators as advocates to enhance partnerships as well as outcomes for children and families, resulting in the publication of a special issue of the journal *Public Child Welfare* (Pasztor

& Tomlinson, 2011). The Title IV-E Web site includes information on partnerships at different universities and in different states, as well as names of the key contact people.

Technical Assistance and Other Funding

Beyond these specific funding streams that can be used to directly support the education of social workers for child welfare careers, universities also receive funding to support training and technical assistance efforts. Such funding comes from Titles IV-B and IV-E as well as from a number of other laws, including the Child Abuse Prevention and Treatment Act, the Adoption and Safe Families Act, the Fostering Connections to Success and Increasing Adoptions Act, the Promoting Safe and Stable Families Program (Title IV-B, Part II), other Children's Bureau–administered programs, Medicaid, and the Social Services Block Grant. Some programs of the Substance Abuse and Mental Health Services Administration, for example the Child Traumatic Stress Initiative, have targeted child welfare populations and may also be implemented and evaluated through university partnerships. For example, Fordham University and Hunter College are collaborating on a grant to enhance child welfare social workers' competence in trauma-informed cognitive-behavioral treatment (National Center for Social Work Trauma Education and Workforce Development, 2013).

Convening Workforce Partners

In 2000 and 2005, recognizing that addressing workforce issues is linked to child welfare service delivery reform, the Children's Bureau hosted large invitational meetings on workforce issues (http://www.childwelfare.gov/pubs/wf_institute/wf_institute .pdf), inviting child welfare agencies and representatives from universities to participate. National organizations—NASW, CSWE, CWLA, the National Association of Public Child Welfare Administrators (NAPCWA), and the Institute for the Advancement of Social Work Research (IASWR) worked closely with the Children's Bureau to plan these meetings and to ensure that both agencies and universities were actively involved. The meetings further highlighted the importance of universities as a major driver of workforce and child welfare improvements and served as an advocacy tool to encourage the Children's Bureau to more systematically support and facilitate such partnerships. The meetings also served as a mechanism to disseminate information on models of effective collaboration between agencies and universities, identify the attributes of effective partnerships (discussed in more detail below) and address sustainability efforts.

In addition, the National Association of Deans and Directors of Schools of Social Work (NADD) and NAPCWA hosted several joint conferences to help support the child welfare education and training partnerships and to identify lessons learned. Recommendations from the inaugural conference in 2002 included identification of a research agenda to investigate competencies and their linkage to outcomes and to investigate the relative effectiveness of workers with various backgrounds, including comparison of workers trained with Title IV-E funding with workers trained with other funding at both the BSW and MSW level. A joint NADD/NAPCWA committee met for several years, and advocacy efforts were encouraged, including a 2002 letter that NASW and CWLA leaders sent to governors to advise them to attend more closely to the risks inherent in their child welfare systems (Ferguson, 2002). The recommendation to create a clearing-house of information on agency–university partnerships, especially those supported by Title IV-E, was implemented through the establishment of the previously mentioned Title IV-E Web site, now housed at the University of Houston, containing Title IV-E and other child welfare partnership resource information.

Two subsequent joint symposia were convened, and child welfare administrators made presentations during the CSWE annual program meeting for several years. As leadership changes occurred in both organizations, the joint committee and the special symposium were not continued. NADD has, however, established a child welfare task force that meets twice a year, and ongoing state-level collaborations are encouraged.

In April 2011, to further strengthen the university–agency connections, Bryan Samuels, commissioner of the Administration on Children, Youth and Families, was invited to meet with NADD to discuss workforce issues and ways that universities, especially schools of social work, can contribute to child welfare system improvements and enhanced outcomes for the children and families served. Samuels stressed the need for mental health and other systems to work together, and the importance of schools of social work engaging with these systems to address client needs. He called for child welfare practitioners to develop excellent clinical skills in order to provide evidence-based interventions to meet the needs of both the children and families served. He noted that MSWs are uniquely positioned to deliver proven effective interventions that address the behavioral health and social-emotional needs of children in child welfare, suggesting that they have the motivation to help children and families and the advanced education to move beyond case management to provide such services. Samuels also stressed the importance of cultural competence and the ability to use data to drive outcome-based decision making (Samuels, 2011).

Research and Evaluation

The engagement of universities, especially schools of social work, with child welfare agencies to carry out needs assessments, collect and analyze data, and engage in research and program evaluation, also has a long history. Title IV-B includes a provision for research and demonstration grants, for which funds were appropriated only until 1996. This funding supported the testing of many model child welfare programs as well as the development of child welfare research centers in several schools of social work. The Child Welfare Research Center at the University of California, Berkeley is still in operation and plays a critical role in California, gathering, analyzing, and using child welfare data to inform child welfare practice and policy improvements.

With the loss of Title IV-B funding, child welfare researchers have had to scramble to find funding sources, and universities and agencies working together have also looked for alternate sources. Other funding sources administered by the Children's Bureau that can support university-based research and evaluation efforts include use of Title IV-E administrative funds at a 50 percent match to support research. There are provisions to support research and evaluation in the Child Abuse Prevention and Treatment Act, Adoption and Safe Families Act, Fostering Connections for Success and Increasing Adoptions Act. Sources of support outside the Children's Bureau have included foundations like the Annie E. Casey Foundation, W. T. Grant Foundation, and Casey Family Programs, as well as other federal programs including the Substance Abuse and Mental Health Services Administration, the Centers for Disease Control and Prevention, the Department of Education, the National Institutes of Health, and the Department of Justice (Institute for the Advancement of Social Work Research, 2008).

To further strengthen the connections between research and practice, the Children's Bureau created five regional implementation centers that use research to guide practice and policy improvements in states. Four of these centers are led by universities; of those, two are led by schools of social work. The National Child Welfare Workforce Institute and several of the national resource centers that are also part of the Children's Bureau Training and Technical Assistance (T/TA) Network are led by social work programs. These broad-ranging training and technical assistance programs include multi-layered partnerships, engaging with national organizations, consulting firms, the federal government, state agencies, and universities.

As can be seen from the attendees at Children's Bureau grantee meetings and presentations at the first and second National Child Welfare Evaluation Summits (http://ncwes2011.jbsinternational.com/ContentTwoColumn.aspx), university representatives, especially from social work education programs, are fully engaged in partnering with child welfare service providers to implement and test interventions, evaluate outcomes, and collect and analyze critical outcome and administrative data.

These research and evaluation efforts have resulted in policy improvements. For example, studies on youths aging out of foster care by the University of Illinois Child and Family Research Center and by Chapin Hall at the University of Chicago are considered important catalysts in the creation of the Fostering Connections legislation in 2008 and the recent Child and Family Services Improvement and Innovation Act (P.L. 112-34) that reauthorized parts I and II of Title IV-B, which includes provisions related to data collection on the use of psychotropic drugs and on child abuse deaths (Chapin Hall/National Governors Association, 2009).

Evidence-Based Practice

The Children's Bureau has, over the past decade, focused increasingly on implementation of evidence-based practices and expanded evaluation expectations in discretionary grants (Deakins, Morgan, Nolan, & Shafer, 2011). Evidence-based service delivery improvements are promoted through initiatives like the implementation centers discussed earlier and quality improvements centers funded by the Children's Bureau (http://www.acf.hhs.gov/programs/cb/tta/cbttan.pdf). In addition, it has supported a network of evidence-based home visiting programs (http://www.acf.hhs.gov/programs/cb/programs_fund/discretionary/2008.htm) and maintains a useful Web site on evidence-based practice through the National Resource Center for Community-Based Child Abuse Prevention (http://www.supportingebhv.org).

The linkages between the promotion of evidence-based practices and the use of research and evaluation findings are critical. For example, based on analysis of the findings of the Child and Family Services Reviews and the National Study on Child and Adolescent Well-being as well as other outcomes data, the Children's Bureau is focusing on better meeting the social and emotional needs of the children served by the child welfare system (Anderson, 2011; Samuels, 2011). This will require a greater focus on developing, implementing, testing, and replicating effective interventions. These interventions need to focus on well-being, as well as on safety and permanence, and need to target not only children who are in foster care, but also children who remain in their own homes or in kinship care.

As one step in implementing this agenda, in FY 2010, the Children's Bureau used the $20 million targeted at reducing long-term foster care under Title IV-B, Section 426 to fund five high-profile grants focusing on building the evidence base to achieve this goal. These grants, whether awarded to agencies or universities, require the engagement of agency staff and universities along with other community stakeholders. The grants went to the University of Kansas School of Social Welfare, the California Department of Social Services, the Los Angeles Gay and Lesbian Community Services Center, the Arizona Department of Economic Security, the Washoe County Department of Social Services in Nevada, and the Illinois Department of Children and Family Services (http://www.acf.hhs.gov/programs/cb/programs_fund/discretionary/2010.htm).

At the 2011 Rosalyn Carter Symposium on Mental Health Services, speakers highlighted the importance of using evidence-based practices, including trauma-informed treatments, to better meet the needs of the children and families served by the child welfare system (http://www.cartercenter.org/health/mental_health/symposium/2011/archives1.html). The University of Maryland School of Social Work is training child welfare Title IV-E students to use motivational interviewing, an evidence-based intervention, to work with families in the child welfare system (personal communication with F. Streeter, June 2011). The California Evidence-Based Clearinghouse for Child Welfare (http://www.cebc4cw.org)—supported by the California Department of Social Services, administered through Rady Children's Hospital in San Diego, and engaging numerous university researchers and child welfare administrators—is an increasingly valuable resource that provides child welfare professionals with easy access to vital information about selected child welfare–related programs.

Proctor (2007) highlights the critical leverage points and reciprocal roles for agencies and universities to identify evidence-based treatments, adopt and implement them, and evaluate their effectiveness. These are all critical steps in which universities and agencies can help each other to achieve practice improvements and enhanced outcomes for children and families (Institute for the Advancement of Social Work Research, 2007).

Making sure that agencies and universities understand each other and can communicate with each other to meet common goals is critical for partnerships to be successful. With a long history of university–agency connections at the local, state, and national levels related to education, training, technical assistance, research, evaluation, and identification and implementation of evidence-based practices, it is important to discuss the attributes that are needed to best develop and maintain effective partnerships. It is also important to understand the challenges that university–agency partnerships face and to identify strategies and tools to overcome the challenges. The next section addresses these issues.

Attributes of Effective University–Agency Partnerships

The signature pedagogy of social work education is field instruction (CSWE, 2008). Therefore, there should be a natural alliance between universities and agencies in social work, and child welfare is a major field of social work practice. Universities involved with training collaborations are also more likely to explore research collaborations and vice versa. Such training and research efforts also can be used to inform the BSW, MSW, and PhD curricula, create opportunities for field placements in child welfare to implement new and innovative practices, and inform professional development efforts (Collins, Amodeo & Clay, 2008; McRoy, Flanzer, & Zlotnik, 2012).

University–agency collaborations provide agencies the opportunity to draw on the resources of the university, providing access to libraries, research infrastructure, and the technological and analytical expertise that may not exist within the agency. University faculty may also bring an outside perspective to the agency and a neutral and academic perspective that is valued by policymakers and other stakeholders and critics, especially when reporting findings and outcomes. Students and staff can also be hired to assist the agency with short-term projects and initiatives. From the agency perspective, partnering with universities provides important person power and can provide a research and training capacity that may be more flexible than that developed in house. Agencies seek out university partnerships to work on practice improvements and to collect and analyze data. Several states, including California, Illinois, Minnesota, and North Carolina, have created sophisticated administrative data collection and analysis efforts based at universities. The resulting data are used to inform and improve frontline practices (Institute for the Advancement of Social Work Research, 2008).

Some attributes of effective university–agency partnerships apply to all types of partnerships, such as understanding each other's culture and context, agreeing on a process by which information can be exchanged and communicated, and developing trust. The American Public Human Services Association (2010), of which NAPCWA is a key affiliate, highlighted the importance of strategic partnerships in *Positioning Public Child Welfare Guidance*, identifying the critical dimensions of partnerships in regard to collaboration, networking, cooperation, and integration.

Lawson et al. (2006) described three categories of literature that inform university–agency partnerships—engaged university literature, social work partnership literature, and research-focused university literature—and identified the following as key partnership success factors:

- unity of purpose
- development of interdependent relationships
- negotiation of specialized roles and responsibilities
- shared power and authority
- conflict resolution mechanisms
- norms of reciprocity cemented by social trust
- strategies to break down barriers
- evaluations and continuous improvement

These attributes are exemplified in the research partnership between the University of Buffalo School of Social Work's Buffalo Center for Social Research and the Hillside Family of Agencies in New York. Two visions aligned as the two entities signed a contract to implement a research partnership, recognizing that the university and the agency had complementary competencies, with the agency staff providing practice expertise and the university providing research expertise (Bisco, 2011). Using this complementary knowledge and expertise, they were able to enter into a long-term effort that is expected, as described by Dean Nancy Smyth, to "test evidence-based practices in real time, in the real world, to help agencies make the shifts in practice that matter" (Bisco, 2011, p. 5). In this partnership and elsewhere, developing a formal research center structure has been beneficial to both partners (Institute for the Advancement of Social Work Research, 2008; Lewis, 2012; Zlotnik, 2010).

In a tool kit for university–agency child welfare research partnerships, the Institute for the Advancement of Social Work Research (2008) suggested that effective research partnerships

- develop and sustain ongoing working relationships
- learn from and understand each other's cultures and contexts
- plan for leadership transitions by garnering support and involvement of leaders while establishing peer-to-peer relationships
- establish clear parameters for project time frames
- understand the processes for data access, sharing, retention, and confidentiality
- develop procedures for review of publications and presentations from the research
- achieve institutional review board approvals in a timely manner.

Lawson et al. (2006) noted that people and organizations can serve as intermediaries to encourage entities that may not have a previous history of working together to form a partnership. This is a role that the university can play in a translational research or change process or in the adoption of evidence-based practices (Denniston, Palinkas, Tseng, & Wallin-Miller, 2011). This role can be fulfilled by professional organizations as well, as is exemplified in the NASW SHIFT project, which brought together agencies and universities and other key stakeholders to address implementation of evidence-based efforts to prevent suicide by adolescent girls (National Association of Social Workers, 2009). Professional associations can also be part of the university–agency partnership. For example, the NASW California Chapter is an active part of the California Social Work Education Center advisory group.

Challenges to Sustaining Partnerships

Like any other collaborations, partnerships between universities and agencies face challenges that need to be overcome so that the partnerships can be successful and sustained over the long term. With the high turnover in leadership in child welfare agencies, these barriers can best be addressed when, in addition to relationships between leaders, there are also peer-to-peer relationships between faculty and agency staff that can transcend leadership changes.

Support from diverse funding sources can help ensure that when one funding stream decreases or disappears, there are other sources to sustain the partnership. For example, at Washington University in St. Louis, a research center on violence and injury prevention funded by the Centers for Disease Control and Prevention includes projects and builds on studies and outreach efforts that were funded by the National Institutes of Health, Department of Justice, Department of Education, Children's Bureau, and the state over the past 15 years (Center for Violence and Injury Prevention, 2011; Rogers, 2008).

Barriers to universities and agencies' ability to work together to enhance child welfare outcomes include the following (Zlotnik, 2010):

- differing organizational values and philosophies
- differing reward systems
- differing priorities
- lack of institutional commitment for the long term
- agencies' need to work in shorter time frames than universities
- complexity of child welfare practice
- lack of emphasis on professional social work credentials in child welfare agencies (which limits incentive for social work graduates to seek employment there)
- agency bidding and contracting processes that are inconsistent with long-range partnerships
- funding streams that are not stable enough for long-range planning
- cost (in time and resources) of maintaining working relationships

Models and Examples of Partnerships

Effective partnerships require that people with different goals, talents, roles, and expertise come together and develop a mutually beneficial agenda. Many university–agency partnerships in child welfare are facilitated by the creation of centers within universities that develop the infrastructure to support and maintain the projects and initiatives. These centers are frequently multipurposed and multidisciplinary and allow some flexibility in responding to the changing needs of the agencies with which they work. A training partnership may also develop research initiatives over time and vice versa (Zlotnik, 2008; Zlotnik & Cornelius, 2000).

Many partnerships are funded by soft money. Although the lead might be a tenured faculty member, many other faculty participants might not be on a tenure track, and initiatives are often carried out by professors, research assistants, training coordinators, or organizational consultants who work only on specific projects (Zlotnik, 2008). Such partnerships may be long-standing, yet individuals without tenure often experience a level of uncertainty as projects come and go (Institute for the Advancement of Social Work Research, 2008). This flexibility of expertise on the university side, however, can be very beneficial to the agency. Especially in tight economic times, being able to engage an expert in a specific area for a limited time through a university partnership is far less cumbersome than engaging someone through the agency's standard hiring process.

While many child welfare centers target efforts in their own state or even just a region of the state, other centers, like Chapin Hall Center for Children at the University of Chicago and the Ruth H. Young Center for Children and Families in Baltimore, undertake multiple projects, with multiple funders, meeting needs at the local, state, and national levels.

To further understand the value, diversity, and breadth of university–agency child welfare partnerships from both agency and university perspectives, there have been recent efforts to document them. For more information on exemplars of child welfare university–agency partnerships, see *Strengthening University/Agency Research Partnerships to Enhance Child Welfare Outcomes: A Toolkit for Building Research Partnerships* (IASWR, 2008) (http://www.socialworkpolicy.org/wp-content/uploads/2007/06/9-IASWR-CW-Research-Partners.pdf); the Title IV-E Partnership Web site (http://louisville.edu/kent/projects/iv-e); and several special journal issues—*Child Welfare* volume 88, issue 5, which focuses on recruitment and retention partnerships; the *Journal of Health & Social Policy*'s 2002 special issue (volume 15, issues 3/4), and the 2003 special issue of the *Journal of Human Behavior and the Social Environment* (volume 7, issues 1/2). In addition, numerous articles of the journal *Public Child Welfare* describe the outcomes of partnership efforts, and examples can be found on the Child Welfare Information Gateway Web site (http://www.childwelfare.gov).

Examples of multidisciplinary partnerships are described below.

Center on Children, Families, and the Law

The Center on Children, Families, and the Law (http://ccfl.unl.edu/) was established in 1987 at the University of Nebraska-Lincoln as a home for interdisciplinary research, teaching, and public service on issues related to child and family policy and services. The knowledge generated and synthesized by the Center faculty is widely disseminated to policymakers, scholars, service providers, and the general public. Work done by the Center has served as the basis for new local, state, and national legislation and has been cited in court rulings, including by the U.S. Supreme Court.

Research by faculty in the colleges of Arts and Sciences, Law, and Education and Human Sciences is integrated with expertise from the School of Social Work at the University of Nebraska at Omaha and the University of Nebraska Medical Center. The Center's own faculty, reflecting its interdisciplinary goals, includes professionals with degrees in law, psychology, pediatrics, special education, social work, sociology, and education. The Center is located administratively within the University of Nebraska-Lincoln's College of Arts and Sciences and is a member of the College's Family Research and Policy Initiative. Among the Center's current initiatives are the Midwest Child Welfare Implementation Center (http://www.mcwic.org/) and programs targeted to children with special needs and their families as well as child care. Since the 1980s, the Center has trained new child welfare workers, and since 2005 it has been the home of the Supreme Court Commission on Children and the Courts (http://ccfl.unl.edu/projects_outreach/outreach/judicial_commission/).

Child Welfare Education and Research Programs at the University of Pittsburgh School of Social Work

The Pittsburgh partnership, Child Welfare Education and Research Programs at the University of Pittsburgh School of Social Work (http://www.socialwork.pitt.edu/research/child-welfare/index.php), incorporates a comprehensive continuum dedicated to child welfare training, education, and research across the state of Pennsylvania, working with the Pennsylvania Department of Public Welfare's Office of Children, Youth and Families and the Pennsylvania County Children and Youth Administrators. It includes the Child Welfare Training Program, the Child Welfare Education for Leadership Program, and the Child Welfare Education for Baccalaureates Program. The partnership addresses recruitment, retention, vacancies, and turnovers of staff; provides curricular support; conducts research and evaluation; and provides technical assistance and transfer of knowledge to achieve practice improvements (University of Pittsburgh School of Social Work, 2011).

California Social Work Education Center

Created in 1990, the California Social Work Education Center (http://calswec.berkeley.edu) is a consortium of 20 accredited graduate schools of social work, the 58 county Departments of Social Services and Mental Health, the state Departments of Social Services and Mental Health, the California chapter of the National Association of Social Workers, and several foundations, housed at the University of California, Berkeley. The center's efforts initially focused on child welfare, but they have been expanded to include the education and training of the mental health and aging services workforce as well. The center's goals include preparing a diverse group of social workers for careers in human services, with special emphasis on child welfare, mental health, and aging; defining and operationalizing a continuum of social work education and training; and engaging in evaluation, research, and dissemination of best practices in social work (California Social Work Education Center, 2013). It has developed and continuously analyzes the relevance of a set of core competencies and has carried out workforce research for more than 20 years. It has longitudinal information on the students who have been involved with its Title IV-E partnership and for many years hosted an annual conference on evaluation of training. It also provides research grants to faculty to help build relevant content for social work curriculums.

Barton Child Law and Policy Center

Located at the Emory University School of Law, the Barton Child Law and Policy Center (http://childwelfare.net/) has a mission to promote and protect the well-being of neglected, abused, and court-involved children in the state of Georgia, to inspire excellence among the adults responsible for protecting and nurturing these children, and to prepare child advocacy professionals. Law students and students preparing for child advocacy careers from other disciplines further their clinical education in a required partner course, Advocacy for Children in the 21st Century: An Interdisciplinary Approach to Policy Development and by operating a clinic. The center also hosts an annual symposium that is broadcast on the Internet and to distance learning sites across Georgia. During the summer, the Barton Center joins forces with the Department of Family and Children Services to sponsor internships in the field of child advocacy, which serves to assist those practicing in the field as well as to train future professionals.

Looking to the Future

As the Children's Bureau moves into its second century, the role of universities as supports to child welfare agencies at the state and local levels, and to the child welfare enterprise nationally, is probably as robust as it has ever been. With over 40 projects funded by the Children's Bureau's T/TA network, the roles of university centers and university faculty, especially in schools of social work, are multifaceted and include training, education, curriculum development, research and evaluation, consultation, knowledge transfer, and organizational development. Events like the first and second National Child Welfare Evaluation Summits provided an opportunity to highlight these roles and to identify how universities and agencies partner together as well as some of the challenges they experience (Children's Bureau, 2011). See http://ncwes2011.jbsinternational.com for the summit program and to view sessions and review presentations.

While many partnerships are currently active, both university and agency leaders are cognizant of the fact that these important relationships and activities may not be permanent. They are vulnerable to changes in leadership, potential loss of funding or a funding challenge due to a post hoc federal audit, changing funding priorities, changes in policy and procedures, and national economic conditions.

Thus, it is critically important that there be a focus on relationship development and trust as well as flexibility so that partnerships can withstand the changes that are inherent in publically funded efforts. Title IV-E educational partnerships continue to be particularly vulnerable to vague policies, the tie to the 1996 AFDC eligibility rate in the state, and inconsistent policy interpretations.

As identified in a NASW national study of licensed social workers (Whitaker, Weismiller, & Clark, 2006), the impending retirement of a large cohort of "baby boomers" will put even greater demands on child welfare services to examine the supply and demand of child welfare workers and the pathway to child welfare practice. This will require continual engagement with universities as well as outreach to high schools, in order to encourage those who are interested in serving children to consider the child welfare field. The current multipurpose National Child Welfare Workforce Institute, a consortium of nine universities, serves as a new model for addressing child welfare workforce challenges. It is critical that the Children's Bureau not only evaluate this model, but also look at how it can be sustained over the next decade. Advocates have long encouraged the Children's

Bureau to embark on a more comprehensive and integrated workforce strategy, and the current effort of the National Child Welfare Workforce Institute, supporting also Title IV-E partnerships and the Comprehensive Workforce Centers, comes closest to this vision.

National organizations including NASW, NAPCWA, CWLA, CSWE, and others can play important roles in supporting university–agency partnerships in child welfare. Deans and directors of schools of social work, national social work and child welfare organizations, and the Children's Bureau must work together to better integrate the goals of qualified, competent child welfare and social work staff with available funding for training and education. Several projects funded by the Annie E. Casey Foundation, Ford Foundation, and Casey Family Programs, and led by this author, have fostered and documented university–agency partnerships. In addition, convenings through national conferences help to disseminate information about what works and what the challenges are. National leadership, as noted in the section Convening Workforce Partners, provides concrete examples of what the outcomes of such efforts can be.

The Children's Defense Fund and Children's Rights convened national organizations together with representatives from child welfare agencies and universities to develop a national policy agenda to strengthen the child welfare workforce (http://www. childrensdefense.org/child-research-data-publications/data/promoting-child-welfare-workforce-improvements.html). Some of the recommendations have been included in the recent reauthorization of the Child Abuse Prevention and Treatment Act and in the Child and Family Services Improvement and Innovation Act that passed in 2011, and several recommendations can be implemented directly by the Children's Bureau. The implementation centers as well as the work of the National Child Welfare Workforce Institute also address some of the recommendations.

NASW can continue to play an important role in promoting partnerships. It has hosted three recent symposia to link practice, research, education, and policy through its Social Work Policy Institute (http://www.socialworkpolicy.org)—Supervision: The Safety Net for Front-Line Child Welfare Practice (November 2010); Investing in the Social Work Workforce (May 2011); and Children at Risk: Optimizing Health in an Era of Reform (November 2011). Each symposium highlighted the importance of interprofessional collaboration and the critical value of partnerships between agencies and universities that can result in improvements in practices that enhance outcomes for the children and families who are the focus of the Children's Bureau's programs.

It is increasingly obvious that there must be ongoing collaboration between child welfare, behavioral health, education, legal, and medical professionals, perhaps returning in part to the Children's Bureau's early vision of integration of child health and child welfare. Improved outcomes for children and families will not be achieved by one discipline or one agency alone. Strategies for interprofessional education and training among physicians, social workers, lawyers, nurses, and psychologists in the university should be developed, in addition to the ongoing support from the Children's Bureau for social work education for child welfare workers. Social work is the key pipeline for preparation for child welfare practice. In the past there have sometimes been attempts to focus on interprofessional education at the expense of a social work focus. Whether in education, training, research, or knowledge development, we need to do both.

Developing and sustaining partnerships will continue to be made more difficult as long as the national economy struggles and cutbacks continue in universities and in federal, state, and local governments. If we are to fulfill our obligation to our most vulnerable children, the vision of the Children's Bureau must continue to be fulfilled, and cross-disciplinary partnerships are an essential aspect of society's investment, not only in the safety of children, but also in their well-being.

References

Administration on Children, Youth and Families. (1996, August 21). Comments concerning the implementation and management of child welfare training for which federal financial participation (FFP) is available. *Federal Register, 61*(163), 43250.

American Public Human Services Association. (2010). *Strategic partnerships guidance: Positioning public child welfare guidance.* Retrieved from http://www.ppcwg.org/images/files/Strategic%20Partnerships%20Guidance.pdf

Anderson, C. (2011, May). *Preparing the child welfare workforce: What will it take to reach the next 25%.* Presentation to the Investing in the Social Work Workforce Symposium, Washington, DC.

Bisco, J. (2011). Vital connections: Vision of community-based research leads to HUB model. *Mosaics, 5*(2), 5–7.

California Social Work Education Center. (2013). *The California Social Work Education Center.* Retrieved from http://calswec.berkeley.edu/description-history

Center for Violence and Injury Prevention. (2011). *Center for Violence and Injury Prevention.* Retrieved from http://cvip.wustl.edu/Pages/Home.aspx

Chapin Hall/National Governor's Association. (2009). *Extending foster care to age 21: Benefits, costs, and opportunities for states.* Retrieved from http://www.chapinhall.org/sites/default/files/documents/GCF%20Jul09%20PowerpointPresentations.pdf

Child Welfare League of America. (2010). *Funding for selected children's programs chart, 2010 final budget.* Retrieved from http://www.cwla.org/advocacy/FY2011_Budget.pdf

Children's Bureau. (2011). National Child Welfare Evaluation Summit, Summit Programs and Materials. Retrieved from http://ncwes2013.jbsinternational.com/PastSummits.aspx.

Collins, M., Amodeo, M. A., & Clay, C. (2008). *National evaluation of child welfare training grants: Final report.* Retrieved from http://library.childwelfare.gov/cwig/ws/library/docs/gateway/Record?rpp=10&upp=0&m=1&w=+NATIVE%28%27recno%3D64247%27%29&r=1

Council on Social Work Education. (2008). *Educational policy and accreditation standards.* Retrieved from http://www.cswe.org/File.aspx?id=13780

Council on Social Work Education. (2012). 2011 Statistics on Social Work Education in the United States. Retrieved from http://www.cswe.org/File.aspx?id=62011

Deakins, B., Morgan, O. J., Nolan, C., & Shafer, J. (2011, August). *Revisiting research to practice: Children's Bureau perspectives on implementation and evaluation in child welfare initiatives.* Plenary presentation at the 2nd National Child Welfare Evaluation Summit, August 31, 2011, Washington, DC. Retrieved from http://ncwes2011.jbsinternational.com

Denniston, J. L., Palinkas, L., Tseng, V. & Wallin-Miller, H. (2011, August). *Evaluating the effectiveness of child welfare dissemination activities.* Presentation at the 2nd National Child Welfare Evaluation Summit, August 30, 2011, Washington, DC. Retrieved from http://ncwes2013.jbsinternational.com/Pdfs/2011%20National%20Child%20Welfare%20Evaluation%20Summit%20Agenda.pdf

Ferguson, S. (Ed.). (2002). *Proceedings from the Professional Education to Advance Child Welfare Practice: An Invitational Working Conference.* Retrieved from http://louisville.edu/kent/projects/iv-e/PEACWproceedings.pdf

General Accounting Office. (1993). *Federal policy on Title IV-E share of training costs.* Washington, DC: Author.

Institute for the Advancement of Social Work Research. (2007). *Partnerships to integrate evidence-based practices into social work education and research.* Retrieved from http://www.socialworkpolicy.org/documents/EvidenceBasedPracticeFinal.pdf

Institute for the Advancement of Social Work Research. (2008). *Strengthening university–agency/research partnerships to enhance child welfare outcomes: A toolkit for building research partnerships.* Retrieved from http://www.socialworkpolicy.org/publications/iaswr-publications/universityagency-child-welfare-research-partnerships-toolkit-available.html

Lawson, H., McCarthy, M., Briar-Lawson, K., Miraglia, P., Strolin, J., & Caringi, J. (2006). A complex partnership to optimize and stabilize the public child welfare workforce. *Professional Development: The International Journal of Continuing Social Work Education, 9*(2), 122–139.

Lewis, C. (2012). Research administration: Essential infrastructure for enhancing research capacity. In R. McRoy, J. Flanzer, & J. Zlotnik (Eds.), *Building research culture and infrastructure: Tools for social work educators* (pp. 83–102). New York: Oxford University Press.

McRoy, R., Flanzer, J., & Zlotnik, J. (2012). *Building research culture and infrastructure: Tools for social work educators.* New York: Oxford University Press.

National Association of Social Workers. (2009). *The NASW SHIFT Project: Suicide prevention for adolescent girls.* Retrieved from http://www.socialworkers.org/practice/adolescent_health/shift/

National Center for Social Work Trauma Education and Workforce Development (2013). About us. Retrieved from http://www.ncswtraumaed.org/about-us.

Pasztor, E., & Tomlinson, B. (Eds.). (2011). Advocacy and public relations [Special issue]. *Journal of Public Child Welfare, 5*(2/3).

Proctor, E. K. (2007). Implementing evidence-based practice in social work education: Principles, strategies, and partnerships. *Research on Social Work Practice, 17*, 583–591.

The Records of the Children's Bureau, 1912–1969. (1989). Alexandria, VA: Chadwyck-Healey.

Rogers, B. (2008, Fall). Perspectives with Melissa Jonson-Reid and Brett Drake: Changing the role of child welfare. *Social Impact,* pp. 6–9.

Samuels, B. (2011, April). Presentation by Bryan Samuels at the National Association of Deans and Directors of Schools of Social Work Meeting, , Laguna Beach, CA.

Social Security Act of 1935, P.L. 74-271, 49 Stat. 620 (1935).

Social Work Policy Institute. (2012a). *Children at risk: Optimizing health in an era of reform.* Washington, DC: National Association of Social Workers.

Social Work Policy Institute. (2012b). *Educating social workers for child welfare careers: The status of using Title IV-E to support BSW and MSW education.* Retrieved from http://www. socialworkpolicy.org/wp-content/uploads/2013/01/SWPI-IVE-Policy-Brief.pdf

University of Pittsburgh School of Social Work. (2010). *Child welfare education and research programs annual report, 2009–2010.* Retrieved from http://www.socialwork.pitt.edu/ research/child-welfare/documents/CWERP%20Annual%20Report%202009-2010.pdf

University of Pittsburgh School of Social Work. (2011, Spring). A battle joined: How the School of Social Work partners with child welfare agencies to better young lives in the balance. *Bridges,* pp. 6–8.

U.S. Department of Health, Education and Welfare. (1965). *Closing the gap in social work manpower.* Washington, DC: Author.

Whitaker, T., Weismiller, T., & Clark, E. (2006). *Assuring the sufficiency of a frontline workforce: A national study of licensed social workers. Special report: Social work services for children and families.* Washington, DC: National Association of Social Workers.

Zlotnik, J. L. (2002). Preparing social workers for child welfare practice: Lessons from an historical review of the literature. *Journal of Health & Social Policy, 15*(3/4), 5–22.

Zlotnik, J. L. (2003). The use of Title IV-E training funds for social work education: An historical perspective. *Journal of Human Behavior and the Social Environment, 7*(1/2), 5–20.

Zlotnik, J. L. (2010). Fostering and sustaining university–agency partnerships. In M. Testa & J. Poertner (Eds.), *Fostering accountability: Using evidence to guide and improve child welfare policy* (pp. 328–356). New York: Oxford University Press.

Zlotnik, J. L., & Cornelius, L. (2000). Preparing social work students for child welfare careers: The use of Title IV-E training funds in social work education. *Journal of Baccalaureate Social Work, 5*(2), 1–14.

Zlotnik, J. L., DePanfilis, D., Daining, C., & Lane, M. M. (2005). *Factors influencing retention of child welfare staff: A systematic review of research.* Retrieved from http://www. socialworkpolicy.org/wp-content/uploads/2007/06/4-CW-SRRFinalFullReport.pdf

Chapter 16

ENVISIONING THE FUTURE: TRENDS, CHALLENGES, AND OPPORTUNITIES

Anita Light, Christine James-Brown, Cecilia Fiermonte, Elizabeth Clark, and Julia M. Watkins

In this chapter, several national organizations allied with the work of the Children's Bureau—the National Association of Public Child Welfare Administrators (NAPCWA), the Child Welfare League of America (CWLA), the Alliance for Children and Families (ACF), the National Association of Social Workers (NASW), and the Council on Social Work Education (CSWE)—lay out some of their 21st-century goals for practice and policy innovation. Themes include prevention, early intervention, capacity building, empowerment of families and communities, and sustainability with ongoing supports for children and families. A major concern is effective service provision to diverse families and addressing the disproportionalities in the child welfare system. There is a need for more evidence-based, data-driven, outcome-oriented approaches to serving children and families. In addition, building the capacity for continuous quality improvement (CQI) and development of knowledge about what works are essential cornerstones for 21st-century child welfare work. Another major theme is the need for increased competencies in the child welfare workforce, and the need to treat workforce development as a research area in its own right.

Many of these themes complement key elements of the Children's Bureau agenda, including workforce development, practice competencies, trauma-informed services (including insights from neuroscience), evidence-based practices, disproportionality, family empowerment, and organizational capacity building with data-driven feedback on practice outcomes and effectiveness.

Promoting Strong Practice, Solid Research, and Healthy Organizations (NAPCWA)

The nation's child welfare leaders are taking progressive steps to transform the human services delivery system to better serve children, youths, and families. With a unified voice, members of NAPCWA have articulated a vision for the future in which outcomes for children are positive, their needs are seen and addressed holistically, they can readily access services and supports, and they are safe, healthy, living in permanent families, and preparing to be productive citizens.

In this envisioned future, abuse and neglect are first and foremost prevented from occurring; prevention strategies strengthen the community, avoid temporary and inadequate fixes, reduce costs to the system, and address problems before children are harmed. Early intervention programs short-circuit dysfunctional family dynamics before they overwhelm a family's ability to cope, reinforce and promote healthy development of children with special needs early in life, and move at-risk families onto a more positive behavioral path. These leaders recognize that capacity building strategies like fatherhood programs or transition services for youths are also needed to sustain the gains a family makes after accessing the right mix of services and supports. Prevention, early intervention, capacity building, and sustainability are all at the core of an effective 21st-century child welfare service delivery system.

To realize this vision, NAPCWA advocates eliminating policy barriers to the effective and efficient administration of child welfare programs, strengthening practice to focus on outcomes instead of outputs and to include the child and family in choosing interventions appropriate to their needs, and strengthening service delivery organizations.

As a first step, NAPCWA has called for Congress to enact legislation that would both reform child welfare financing and support an integrated child welfare system that is in alignment with the national goals set by the Children's Bureau of safety, permanency, and well-being. Resources should be invested in the front end of the system to prevent child abuse and neglect and support all children in need, helping to stabilize families before they are endangered. Additionally, improved data collection systems and policies are needed to allow interoperability among all human service programs and enable a holistic approach to service delivery.

Second, NAPCWA recognizes that for child welfare systems to know how best to serve children and families, they must continue building an evidence base that captures the most advanced research, uses the best clinical experience, and recognizes the values that are important to the children and families served. By continuously informing research, child welfare leaders keep the body of knowledge enriched and relevant as effective practices advance. This body of knowledge is critical to the development of effective public policy for the field.

Consideration must also be given to the ever-changing environment in which children and families live and its impact on the type of workforce needed to provide services and supports. As the environment changes, and practice evolves, the academic programs that prepare the workforce must align with this evolution. Orienting and training the workforce to be strength-based and inclusive of the family in finding solutions that work for them is an essential principle.

Third, policies and practices are only as effective as the organizations in which they are implemented. NAPCWA strongly supports efforts to improve business practices, ensure efficiency, eliminate redundancies, and in particular, strengthen the CQI process. A robust agency tracking and monitoring system, capable of linking performance to outcomes, ensures that children are being well served and that resources are well spent. In addition, many child welfare systems are hampered by outdated technology that cannot keep up with a workforce that has better resources at home than at the office. Investments are critical in this arena if public agencies are to have a chance at becoming an employer of choice.

Public child welfare leaders have long recognized that the problems of abused and neglected children are multifaceted and occur when families and communities are ill-equipped to deal with the challenges of mental illness, substance abuse, unemployment, poor housing, lack of adequate health care, economic instability, and other problems. We know the solutions that will secure the right outcomes for the children and families we serve. Taking the right steps now to see that policies are appropriate, practice is well researched and implemented by a committed workforce, and organizations are functioning at maximum capacity will ensure a safe, healthy future for our children.

Raising the Bar so All Children Can Succeed and Flourish (CWLA)

The Children's Bureau's 100-year anniversary is a good time to celebrate the agency's tremendous leadership and significant accomplishments. From its founding, the bureau charted new ground for children as it sought to understand the extent and causes of infant mortality and address the critical health concerns of babies and their mothers. Throughout its history, the agency has fostered the development of new and more effective responses to family problems through its work with states and tribes. The bureau's success offers an opportunity to take stock of the nation's progress and look to future considerations as we continue to raise the bar for children who have been abused or neglected.

Since its beginning at the first White House Conference on the Care of Dependent Children in 1909, CWLA has worked with the bureau to improve the lives of the most vulnerable children and families. Through this partnership, the United States was able to respond to the child care needs of women entering the workforce during World War II, promote adoption and reunification for children in foster care in the 1970s and 1980s, and focus on family support and early permanency in the 1990s and 2000s.

Despite these successes, the work is not done; challenges old and new continue to confront child welfare. In this age of technology and media bombardment, problems like poverty, isolation, discrimination, and disenfranchisement are more complex than ever. Still, at critical points over the past 100 years, both CWLA and the Children's Bureau have established a fresh awareness of the problems facing children and families and found the means to reinvent our work and better accomplish our goals. As we enter a new century of service, it seems that we are again at a watershed moment where we must answer two critical questions. First, what does it mean to push toward a brighter future for all of America's children and families? Second, how do we achieve it?

Perhaps history provides some answers. Although they described it in the language of a different era, the child welfare field's founders saw a critical need to address the welfare of children, provide for their safety, and ensure them the opportunity to live in a permanent family. Comprehensive and community-based approaches were viewed as an organizing vehicle by which the nation could achieve better outcomes for children. These child welfare leaders also expressed the need to make certain that reforms used standardized best practices that were derived from data and information. Finally, a committed and well-trained workforce was viewed as essential to ensure fidelity to these methods and excellence of service.

In 1915, in a presentation to the National Conference of Charities and Corrections titled *Report of the Committee: A Community Plan in Children's Work*, C. C. Carsten, the first head of CWLA, called for the collection of "successful experiences" that could be "woven in to a harmonious whole" and put in place "for communities to provide for the proper safeguarding of the children's interests" (The Social Welfare History Project, 2013, p. 1). Perhaps his words reverberate today in new calls for the development of evidence-based practices and a comprehensive capacity in each community to improve outcomes for children and families.

These fundamental goals are still relevant even if they are more difficult to realize. Today, complex funding structures support a wide assortment of service models. In many jurisdictions, public- and private-sector organizations are experiencing enormous shifts in roles and responsibilities. States are also bearing greater responsibility for the delivery of child welfare services. As a result, state policies and resource decisions can have a significant effect on the nature and effectiveness of child and family services. At the same time, there is remarkable diversity in the children and families that we serve, and communities face significant challenges to their capacity to respond to the needs of their most vulnerable residents. These and related concerns persist against a daily onslaught of increasingly negative public perceptions of child welfare services.

There have been enormous strides in evaluating and improving the child welfare system. However, the responsibility for improving outcomes for children goes beyond creating a more functional system. To get it right for children and families, it is necessary to reexamine and extend the meaning of child welfare, returning to a broader focus that, rather than simply reacting to families in trouble and attempting to balance the demands of safety, permanency, and well-being, increases attention to the needs and interests of each child. It does not matter if the system is more efficient or even if it is smaller if (1) every child who enters the system is not better off spiritually, emotionally, physically, and developmentally; and (2) children at risk of entering the system and their families are not provided the supports they need for the children to grow up safely in their own homes and communities and reach their full potential.

America's families and communities are more ethnically and linguistically diverse than ever. Within this context, new policies must be created that embed the well-being of children within communities and support the ability of communities to meet the needs of all children and families. This transition will not happen quickly, so it is also necessary to consider how to function during the transition. It is important to begin by clarifying roles and accountablities so that families, communities, and allied child-serving organizations can work with the child welfare system more effectively to understand and achieve agreed-on outcomes.

It is also important for child welfare to eliminate an overreliance on unevenly applied approaches that merely seem right and sometimes work. Instead, there must be a deeper commitment to excellence and consistency or standardization. The simple principles of making certain that children and families receive the right intervention, at the right time, and in the right measure continue to apply. However, selecting and applying the right intervention must be guided by the evidence with just the right amount of practice-based wisdom.

Child welfare has become increasingly sophisticated in its understanding of how well systems are doing in achieving broad goals. Still, a stronger focus on practice-level research, evaluation, and data analysis will help us better understand what works to help children and families succeed. This focus will also help us understand the relationship between case-level interventions, case outcomes, and systemic improvements.

To support improved case practice, it is important to consider the evolving needs of today's workforce. First, it must be uniformly well equipped with the knowledge and skills needed for child welfare practice. To ensure better outcomes, boilerplate service plans must be replaced with a nuanced approach to determining which interventions will effectively build on family and community strengths and meet individual child and family needs. Second, we must understand that the workforce is diverse and includes social workers, case managers, resource families, allied professionals, informal and community-based supports, parents, youths, and others who must also be well-informed and well-integrated into the work of child welfare.

In this light, it is important that information and research be more readily available to those who need it. Too often new ideas exist in pockets within geographic areas and even within organizations. When innovations show success or even promise, they must be lifted up so that the knowledge base can be further explored and the resulting evidence can be embedded in day-to-day practice. No child or family should be untouched by this high-quality process. Where a child happens to live cannot determine whether he or she will have the opportunity to reach their full potential.

To achieve this CWLA has developed the CWLA National Blueprint for Excellence in Child Welfare, which is based on the premise that everyone has responsibility for the well-being of children. It begins with their families and extends to the broader community far beyond traditional child welfare organizations. To achieve true success in child welfare, the blueprint articulates a vision where all children will grow up safely in loving families and supportive communities, with everything they need to flourish, and will connect to their culture, ethnicity race, and language. It lays out the road map to achieve this, including an increased focus on the development of evidence-based practices and a comprehensive capacity in each community to improve outcomes for children and families. A key goal of the National Blueprint is to be a catalyst for change: to broaden the thinking of individuals and groups and to help them see how their specific pieces fit into and enhance the whole.

The National Blueprint is designed to move us towards a brighter future for all of America's children. CWLA will work with its member agencies and partners at the Children's Bureau and across the country to advance the CWLA National Blueprint. CWLA firmly believes that a common vision and new direction that is crafted and shared by families, communities, the child welfare system, and all those who serve and interact with children is not only achievable but necessary and requires that we redouble our collective efforts to push for a brighter future for every child and family.

Uncharted Territory: Leading through Innovation and Excellence (ACF)

ACF represents some of the strongest and most innovative leaders in child welfare in the private sector. Together, our member organizations deliver more than $3.6 billion in services annually to more than three million people in over 8,000 communities across the United States. Our mission is to lead our members in providing services that deliver sustained, high-quality results for children and families. We do this by providing our members with intellectual capital that strengthens their capacity to serve and advocate for children, families, and communities.

The tide is turning toward increasingly privatized child welfare systems, with much uncharted territory and many potential opportunities. We will be leading our members in finding the best ways to work with government in reaching the outcomes that we want for our children. As we strive for those outcomes, we have analyzed the trends that are likely to shape the 21st century. Many factors will come into play, shifting the landscape and creating disruptive forces, such as purposeful experimentation and integrating science creating the dynamic human services agencies of the future: flexible, purposeful, high impact, and highly knowledgeable (ACF, 2011). One of the strongest disruptive forces facing our members is the need to experiment and yet at the same time be more purposeful. Shrinking budgets and greater demand for impact call for solutions that deliver results. Alliance members have been at the forefront of experimentation on improving practices. The following insights from Alliance members were obtained during interviews carried out in June 2012.

When Jeremy Kohomban, president and chief executive officer of Children's Village in Dobb's Ferry, New York, which provides services to youths aging out of foster care and some residential services, sought to redefine that agency's residential system, he looked at longitudinal data to examine how youths fared after leaving the program. The numbers led him to believe that a quick drop-off in services was destructive. The agency found a way to intensify after-care service, which sometimes now lasts up to five years. They also identified a quick fix: working with the school system to ensure that children enroll in and attend school immediately after discharge. The results are promising, with 85 percent of youths showing positive outcomes after discharge. Kohomban says this represents a unique opportunity. "We have reduced reliance on residential care, but every night a child needs a bed." He said that this is a chance to redefine services in a positive way that meets the needs of youths in care.

Kohomban's success illustrates the way private providers can react quickly and creatively to need in a way that government often cannot. Yet Alliance members believe that it is not a private-versus-public issue but a matter of true collaboration between government and service providers. Government can provide the big-picture support that allows providers to craft creative solutions.

Rather than test ideas blindly, providers often rely on hard data that support their theories. They believe in both evaluation and rigorous research. Program evaluations show what approaches are promising and where further research is needed to make it possible to advance good practice. Dennis Richardson, president and chief executive officer of the Hillside Family of Agencies in Rochester, New York, said that child welfare research often falls short because of small sample size. He noted that the federal government could facilitate more countrywide research, thus providing the large numbers necessary for a meaningful evidence base. He argued that child welfare must develop more robust data systems, adding that businesses successfully use math to carry out predictive analysis and child welfare scholars and professionals could do the same if they had more precise data.

Richardson predicted that the solutions will be found across systems and will require funding that supports a newer, more flexible structure, as the education, child welfare, behavioral health, and health fields work together to ensure children's safety and well-being. His organization has looked to another 21st-century disruptive force, advances in neuroscience that are changing how we understand human behavior and therefore changing human services. As the field leaps forward, newer ways of understanding human behavior and the brain will have greater applicability to child welfare work. For example, Richardson has relied on findings about how an enriched environment affects children to inform the programs and services Hillside chooses. He said that the science exists; the challenge is to sustain any investment over time, not go in and provide services, then leave.

Alliance members describe a strong shift from a crisis-driven approach to a holistic approach that involves empowering families and communities. Jim Mason, president and chief executive officer of Beech Acres Parenting Center in Cincinnati, Ohio, cited his agency's parent mentoring program as an example of an approach that empowers families. He said at the turn of the 20th century, the emphasis was on charity, but now it is on building strengths in families and communities. According to Mason, the line is blurring between services and supports.

Dona Booe is president and chief executive officer of Kansas Children's Services League, which is creating a movement to promote healthy development and environments. According to Booe, it's not just about professionals determining what a service array should be, but that the best way to address maltreatment is to start with the strengths and resources that exist in a community and build on them so that communities can provide the healthiest environment for their children. Advances in technology and science will help us create cutting-edge programs. Ultimately, we will be guided by those we serve. The solutions will be found in the strengths of families and communities.

Enhancing Professionalism in Child Welfare Services (NASW)

NASW, since its creation in 1955, has worked closely with the Children's Bureau and has been an important advocate for programs and policies to ensure the safety, permanence, and well-being of children and families in the child welfare system and those at risk of becoming involved with the system. Although child welfare has been a focus of social work since its beginning, a 1982 CWLA monograph specifically defined it as a field of social work practice. This strong connection continues to be advanced as social work competencies now underpin child welfare practice (Children's Bureau, 2011; Rittner & Wodarski, 1999; Zlotnik, 2000; Zlotnik, Rome, & DePanfilis, 1998), social work education programs play a major role in the education and training of child welfare staff, social work researchers serve as a core of the child welfare scientific workforce, and social work leadership is strong in the development of child welfare policies and advocacy for their implementation (Zlotnik, 2002).

Not surprisingly, in the child welfare arena, a major focus for NASW is on enhancing the child welfare workforce. The NASW presidential initiative in the late 1980s to Promote Professional Social Work Practice in Public Child Welfare served as an impetus, and NASW has worked on this agenda continually—helping to create partnerships and collaboration among social work education programs, NASW chapters, and child welfare agencies, and advocating for the use of funding under Title IV-E of the Social Security Act created as part of the Adoption Assistance and Child Welfare Act of 1980 (P. L. 96-272), to provide BSW and MSW education to professionalize the child welfare workforce. This agenda continues to be articulated through one of the 12 imperatives from the 2005 Social Work Congress, "to assure a qualified social work labor force to serve children" (Clark et al., 2005, p. 4).

To reinforce its policy statements and standards, NASW developed information on the value of hiring professionally educated social workers in child welfare. Two key studies document this value: *If You Are Right for the Job, It Is the Best Job in the World* (NASW, 2004), a report on a survey of members of NASW's child welfare section, and *Assuring the Sufficiency of the Front-Line Workforce* (Whitaker, Weismiller, & Clark, 2006), the report of a benchmark national survey of licensed social workers.

The first study explored how the perspective of NASW members who work in child welfare may be similar to, or different from, the general trend of dissatisfaction and high turnover in the child welfare workforce (ACF, American Public Human Services Association, & CWLA, 2001; American Public Human Services Association, 2005; General Accounting Office, 2003). The study found that professional social workers in child welfare are more satisfied with their jobs than the general population of child welfare workers; that they have higher satisfaction with their supervisors and the frequency of supervision; that issues confronting children and families are the most challenging aspect of the job, not workplace issues; that their average tenure is 9.5 years in child welfare and 6.1 years at their current agency; and that the single most satisfying aspect of the work is success with children and families (NASW, 2004).

Results of the second study, the national survey of licensed social workers providing services to children and families, suggest that the social work profession maintains its commitment as a frontline service provider to the country's most vulnerable children and their families, but that the organizations serving these children and families are experiencing stressors that hinder their ability to retain licensed social work professionals and that the supply of licensed social workers is insufficient to meet the needs of these organizations, especially as baby boomers begin to retire (Whitaker et al., 2006).

The imperatives that emerged from the 2010 Social Work Congress related to influence, recruitment, retention, and leadership are congruent with much of the work that needs to take place to enhance child welfare service delivery (Clark et al., 2010). The Children's Bureau's National Child Welfare Workforce Institute and its collaborators focus on recruitment, retention, and leadership development, as do many of the Title IV-E educational partnerships between schools of social work and public agencies.

Elements of the Children's Bureau's training and technical assistance network focus on implementation of evidence-based programs, quality improvement, enhancing worker supervision, and improving the organizational culture and climate in child welfare agencies. NASW partnered with the National Child Welfare Workforce Institute on the 2010 symposium Supervision: The Safety Net for Front-Line Child Welfare Practice (Social Work Policy Institute, 2011), developing an agenda for action to focus on further workforce improvements. These efforts engage social workers and the social work community and will help to create and identify the child welfare leaders for the rest of this century. In addition, since social workers are employed in many systems, NASW is well positioned to help lead efforts that enhance understanding of how mental health, health, and child welfare can be better linked to ensure that the children in child welfare have better outcomes. One step was NASW's hosting of the 2011 think tank symposium Children at Risk: Optimizing Health in an Era of Reform (Social Work Policy Institute, 2012).

Advocating service improvements to achieve safety, permanence, and well-being must go hand in hand with addressing the challenges of the child welfare workforce. As agencies seek to incorporate implementation of evidence-based practices and trauma-informed care, organizations like NASW will continue their role in professional development through conferences and education programs, and through state- and federal-level advocacy, not only to promote the value of professional social work to improve child welfare outcomes, but also to advocate for service improvements that better integrate culturally competent care, support prevention, and promote permanence, safety, and well-being for our nation's most vulnerable children.

Collaboration—the Key to Capacity Building (CSWE)

Child welfare has long been a signature domain of social work education and the social work profession. Evolving from primarily voluntary status at the beginning of the 20th century, services were viewed as saving children from harsh realities encountered in contemporary life. However, after the establishment of the U.S. Children's Bureau in 1912, child welfare services increasingly came under the purview of the U.S. government, especially in the second half of the 20th century. Major funding, and expectations about services and outcomes reflected in funding formulae, were directed by the federal government to the states. Funds to the states under Title IV-E have been particularly instrumental in reimbursing states for a significant portion of foster care and adoption as well as independent living services as means-tested entitlements designed to protect vulnerable children and youths (Courtney, 2008; Pecora, 2008).

The priority of high-quality service provision to vulnerable children and families coupled with the pervasive deprofessionalization of the workforce led to a concentration of new initiatives to educate and train the workforce, particularly under Title IV-E. This priority quickly became a movement characterized by innovative partnerships between education and practice that were supported and nurtured over the years by CSWE and its accredited social work programs across the country (Hooper-Briar & Lawson, 1996a).

In addition to improving services to vulnerable children and families through workforce development, schools of social work developed strong partnerships with communities that strengthened their research capacities, enhanced knowledge building, and improved outcomes in child welfare. In addition, the partnerships sought to increase educational access and success for underrepresented student populations, nurture intellectual leadership in child welfare, and develop unique collaborations between town and gown. These partnerships have not only served child welfare but have also emerged as models for workforce development initiatives in other fields such as gerontological social work (Harris, 1994; Hooper-Briar & Lawson, 1996b; Zlotnik, 1993).

CSWE participated in these endeavors, along with the Children's Bureau, through several seminal projects that focused on workforce development for the public social services sector and innovative partnerships in the delivery of educational curricula (Harris, 1994; Hooper-Briar & Lawson, 1996a). Such projects underscored the importance of competency development in knowledge, values, and skills as an essential precursor to quality attainment in the workforce.

Building on the early successes in education and agency–community partnerships for workforce development, CSWE also established specialized sessions and practice focused clusters in child welfare at its annual program meeting and published books and monographs (Harris, 1994; Hooper-Briar & Lawson, 1996a; Zlotnik, 1993) that expanded the knowledge base and inspired further commitment to partnership, collaboration, and innovation.

With the themes of access, partnership, knowledge building, and research capacity development dominating the social work education agenda, a more recent emphasis has been the development of competencies for social work practice. CSWE has provided the framework for schools of social work to identify and evaluate achievement of specific practice competencies and behaviors in their curriculum. At the advanced practice level, core competencies serve as an educational underpinning while also advancing practice behaviors within fields of practice such as child welfare, gerontology, military social work, trauma-informed practice, substance abuse, and behavioral health reinforce the structure. Nowhere is the discourse on disproportionalities, for example, more intense than in social work, particularly in child welfare practice (Pecora, 2008).

Given the increasing dynamism in the service and educational sectors, CSWE envisions a future involving more close collaboration and partnerships with organizations, such as CWLA and the Council on Accreditation, that work to enhance postsecondary and professional education. Efforts of different organizations, practice specialties, and disciplinary boundaries are likely to intersect in complex ways. This suggests a primary role for social work education in the promotion of broad-based accountability—through its accreditation function and in the preparation of social work faculty and the recruitment and retention of diverse students. This is particularly pertinent in new or refashioned practice settings such as the military, behavioral health, consumer protection, gerontology, and innovative models of health care delivery, as well as the traditional and central domains of social work practice—child welfare, school social work, policy, and community practice. The educational continuum and the intersection of practice specializations are particularly relevant to the person-in-environment construct of social work and its ongoing commitment to enhancing the quality of life of children and families whose well-being requires services that transcend disciplinary boundaries.

The education of social work practitioners will take place online, in blended educational contexts, and within groundbreaking educational environments. For example, a public institution may partner with a for-profit entity to deliver its accredited program to students around the globe. Such formats and structures were hardly imaginable two or three decades ago, and with highly sophisticated technology, rapid momentum is inevitable. More important from an educational perspective, however, will be efforts to maximize accountability to a range of constituents and stakeholders—students, institutions of higher education, the public, government and nongovernment funders of higher education, and recipients of and participants in the delivery of evidence-based practice interventions.

In the second decade of the 21st century and beyond, social work education will refine its competency-based approach to educational outcomes. The basis for accountability has moved from curriculum content to program goals and objectives to competencies for practice. The assessment of competencies provides evidence that programs are effective in achieving an end result that is consistent with and reflective of the behaviors of social workers in the practice setting (CSWE, 2008). The sharpened focus of the competency approach requires a closer dialogue with those institutions that define and regulate social work practice at the state or federal level as well as with those who work in practice settings that cross disciplines or professions, such as child welfare. Along with behavioral competencies, social work accreditation must continue to acknowledge the institutional (and program) mission and purpose in the design of any social work educational program. A greater diversity of institutions and delivery modes will challenge traditional thinking about quality, affordability, and accessibility. In this regard, CSWE will be part of the larger educational dialogue at the national level.

Summary

To deliver effective services in the 21st century and beyond, social work education must pay careful attention to the larger context and build strong partnerships with others who share its issues and visions. The groundbreaking effort of social work educators, with funding mandates from programs within the Children's Bureau, is a tradition to be continued with strength and commitment.

References

Alliance for Children and Families. (2011). *Disruptive forces: Driving a human services revolution.* Milwaukee: Authors.

Alliance for Children and Families, American Public Human Services Association, & Child Welfare League of America. (2001). *The child welfare workforce challenge: Results from a preliminary study.* Washington, DC: Authors.

American Public Human Services Association. (2005). *Report from the 2004 Child Welfare Workforce Survey: State agency findings*. Retrieved from http://www.napcwa.org/Youth/docs/WorkforceReport05.pdf

Children's Bureau, Administration for Children and Families. (2011). Title IV-E, Administrative Functions/Costs, Training (8.1H8). In *Child welfare policy manual*. Retrieved from http://www.acf.hhs.gov/cwpm/programs/cb/laws_policies/laws/cwpm/policy_dsp.jsp?citID=116#1620

Child Welfare League of America. (1982). *Child welfare as a field of social work practice* (2nd ed.). Washington, DC: Author.

Clark, E. J., Hoffler, E., Jackson, E., Loomis, R., Myers, R. S., Rothblum, M., et al. (Eds.). (2010). *2010 Social Work Congress—Final report*. Retrieved from http://www.socialworkers.org/2010congress/documents/FinalCongress-StudentReport.pdf

Clark, E. J., Weismiller, T., Whitaker, T., Waller, G. W., Zlotnik, J. L., & Corbett, B. (Eds.). (2005). *2005 Social Work Congress—Final report*. Retrieved from http://www.socialworkers.org/congress/CongressFinalReport.pdf

Council on Social Work Education. (2008). *Educational policy and accreditation standards*. Alexandria, VA: Author.

Courtney, M. E. (2008). Child welfare: History and policy framework. In T. Mizrahi & L. E. Davis (Eds.-in-Chief), *Encyclopedia of social work* (20th ed., Vol. 1, pp. 277–282). Washington, DC and New York: NASW Press and Oxford University Press.

General Accounting Office. (2003). *Child welfare: HHS could play a greater role in helping child welfare agencies recruit and retain staff* (GAO-03-357). Washington, DC: Author.

Harris, N. J. (1994). *Technical assistance document for social work programs developing school-agency partnerships for child welfare. Report on a Council on Social Work Education project*. Unpublished manuscript.

Hooper-Briar, K., & Lawson, H. A. (1996a). Agenda setting: First call for vulnerable children, youth, and families. In K. Hooper-Briar & H. A. Lawson (Eds.), *Expanding partnerships for vulnerable children, youth, and families* (pp. 11–14). Alexandria, VA: Council on Social Work Education.

Hooper-Briar, K., & Lawson, H. A. (1996b). New schools and expanded partnerships. In K. Hooper-Briar & H. A. Lawson (Eds.), *Expanding partnerships for vulnerable children, youth, and families* (pp. 78–82). Alexandria, VA: Council on Social Work Education.

National Association of Social Workers. (2004). *If you're right for the job, it is the best job in the world*. Washington, DC: Author.

National Association of Social Workers, Center for Workforce Studies. (2006). *Practice sector analysis—children and families—key findings*. Retrieved from http://workforce.socialworkers.org/studies/children/children_key.asp

Pecora, P. J. (2008). Child welfare: Overview. In T. Mizrahi & L. E. Davis (Eds.-in-Chief), *Encyclopedia of social work* (20th ed., Vol. 1, pp. 270–277). Washington, DC and New York: NASW Press and Oxford University Press.

Rittner, B., & Wodarski, J. S. (1999). Differential uses for BSW and MSW educated social workers in child welfare services. *Children and Youth Services Review, 21,* 217–238.

Social Work Policy Institute. (2011). *Supervision: The safety net for front-line child welfare practice.* Washington, DC: Author. Retrieved from http://www.socialworkpolicy.org/news-events/supervision-the-safety-net-for-front-line-child-welfare-practice.html

Social Work Policy Institute. (2012). *Children at risk: Optimizing health in an era of reform.* Washington, DC: Author. Retrieved from http://www.socialworkpolicy.org/wp-content/uploads/2012/06/childrenatrisk-report1.pdf

The Social Welfare History Project. (2013). *Carl Christian Carstens (April 2, 1865–July 4, 1939): Child welfare advocate and first executive director Child Welfare League of America.* Retrieved from http://www.socialwelfarehistory.com/people/carl-christian-carstens/

Whitaker, T., Weismiller, T., & Clark, E. (2006). *Assuring the sufficiency of a frontline workforce: A national study of licensed social workers. Special report: Social work services for children and families.* Washington, DC: National Association of Social Workers.

Zlotnik, J. L. (1993). *Social work education and public human services: Developing partnerships.* Alexandria, VA: Council on Social Work Education.

Zlotnik, J. L. (2000). What are the core competencies for practitioners in child welfare agencies. In H. Dubowitz & D. Depanfilis (Eds.), *Handbook for child protection practice* (pp. 571–576). Thousand Oaks, CA: Sage Publications.

Zlotnik, J. L. (2002). Preparing social workers for child welfare practice:Lessons from an historical review of the literature. *Journal of Health & Social Policy, 15*(3/4), 5–22.

Zlotnik, J. L., Rome, S. H., & DePanfilis, D. (Eds.). (1998). *Educating for child welfare practice: A compendium of model syllabi.* Alexandria, VA: Council on Social Work Education.

Chapter 17

CHILD WELFARE FOR THE 21ST CENTURY: ORGANIZATIONAL AND PRACTICE IMPERATIVES

Mary McCarthy, Katharine Briar-Lawson, and Nancy Dickinson

I dentifying and implementing organizational and practice imperatives for the next century of child welfare services requires both vision and perspective. The word *perspective* has multiple meanings, two of which are especially relevant here: "representation in a drawing or painting of parallel lines as converging in order to give the illusion of depth and distance" and "the capacity to view things in their true relations or relative importance" ("Perspective," 1993). The authors of these chapters have provided many different perspectives on multiple dimensions of child welfare practice. Each has examined their practice or policy area historically, with a particular focus on the history of the Children's Bureau, and currently, with a focus on best practice or evidence-based practice as a platform for recommendations for the future.

Each chapter can be viewed as a part of the child welfare painting, with multiple parallel lines of practices and programs that make up the whole picture. Each line is critical for creating the depth needed to more effectively serve families and children and build healthier communities. The recommendations of the authors, coming from their various points of view, interact in a way that shows the strategic relationship and importance of multiple practices and programs. Child welfare is not a single practice or program, but a complex interaction of individual, family, and community needs, front-line services, local and national laws and policies, and programmatic responses developed and implemented by a workforce that seeks to provide safety and permanence for children in support of lifelong well-being.

This summary chapter provides a bridge between the principles of the early Children's Bureau and its current focus. It then highlights some of the important recommendations made by the authors of these chapters. These provide guidance for building a more integrated, family-focused, and evidence-informed 21st-century child welfare system. Although the recommendations are compelling and wide ranging, they do not cover all the issues. Ongoing challenges include bringing a corps of new recruits to the workforce from a wide array of backgrounds, moving evidence-based practices into full implementation, integrating collective impact strategies into a national approach to ending child abuse, and removing politics as a factor in selecting child welfare leaders.

Bridge from the Past to the Future

Authors have highlighted particular segments of the history of the Children's Bureau that most illustrate its work related to each chapter's focus. Julia Lathrop, the bureau's first chief, and her staff employed three first principles to guide all aspects of their work: using data, focusing on children and families, and applying an advocacy approach to practice. Data-rich reports informed the Children's Bureau's advocacy efforts, which influenced early legislation and policy. These data-informed advocacy approaches established practices and programs and resulted in more resources and services becoming available over time.

What was the cost of this change? Societal priorities changed from a protective system of services for vulnerable children and a public health approach for maternal and child health to "cost effectiveness and the dispensary model of providing for human services" (Lipsky, 1980, p. 80). Social service practice emphasized a deficit orientation to understanding problems that focused on personal deficiencies rather than using needs to guide allocation of resources and decision making. Child welfare also began to compete for scarce resources with other professionals such as mental health providers and the health care professions. As social norms changed, the values guiding programs became at various times conflicting or ambiguous. Social science research was often too under-funded to support much-needed studies of worker performance and client outcomes. The workforce increasingly comprised people whose life experiences were considerably different from those of the families being served (Lipsky, 1980).

These tensions and ambiguities are highlighted across the various chapters, painting a picture of the developmental nature and competing values of child welfare work, identifying strong programs and practices as well as ineffective and even misguided ones. What is inspirational about this 100-year journey is the current return to first principles. Recent laws and policies have again recognized the critical role of data, the voices of the child and family, the importance of the context that surrounds families, the need for funding flexibility, and advocacy as a driver for change.

This return to first principles is most clearly articulated in three memoranda released by the Children's Bureau in April, May, and August 2012 on well-being and trauma, waiver demonstration projects, and continuous quality improvement (U.S. Department of Health and Human Services, 2012a, 2012b, 2012c). While each memo provides in-depth guidance on a particular topic, together they form a coherent body of work that highlights organizational, programmatic, and workforce practices necessary for achieving the goals of safety, permanence, and well-being. All three memoranda stress the importance of practice guided by evidence, attention to agency structures and funding streams to accomplish improved practice, and continued attention to racial disparities. Also emphasized are inclusive family-focused practice, attending to the workforce and ensuring staff achievement of competencies and skills to deliver services, and improving the connection between safety, permanency, and well-being.

Recommendations

How will these first principles guide practice for the 21st century? Each of the authors of this book provides frameworks or recommendations for our work going forward. These recommendations call attention to workforce and leadership, professional preparation, evidence-based practices, family and youth voices, tribal sovereignty and tribally focused services, interprofessional and cross-systems work, poverty, and well-being. These recommendations are summarized below, organized around five themes: practice with children, youth, families, and communities; interprofessional and cross-systems practices; organizational development and change; programs and policies; and universities, schools of social work, and university–agency partnerships.

Practice with Children, Youths, Families, and Communities

Family empowerment

- Practitioners need to promote capacity building and empowerment of families, including by providing parent mentors (chapters 4, 5, and 16).
- Practice needs to move from an expert-oriented or compliance model to a model based on collaboration and cooperation with families and youths (chapters 2, 3, 4, and 5). Parents must be seen as experts in their own lives; knowing their worldview is essential to competent practice (chapters 2 and 4).
- Engaging families and youths, including fathers and paternal relatives, requires family-centered practices and organizational, service, and policy supports along with relevant training and evaluation (chapter 5).
- Family and youth voices are needed in the design of case plans, and in decision making about services, supports, policy, training, evaluation, and other systems issues (chapters 3, 4, and 5).
- Families must be treated with dignity and respect and empowered to make decisions about goals, priorities, and needs; the onus is on the practitioner to co-create case plans (chapters 3, 4, and 5); parents must be given equal power (chapter 2).

- Practitioners must remember that it is the service, not the client, that is involuntary (chapter 4); clients must not be labeled uncooperative, as their involuntary status implies resistance (chapter 2).

Resources

- Authentic engagement of families and youths helps increase resources and placement options, quality and focus of visits, placement stability and time in placement, timeliness of permanency decisions, family decision-making skills, and services; this ultimately reduces disproportionalities and disparities (chapter 5).
- Prevention and early intervention services need to be provided to families and children along with sustainable supports such as aftercare (chapters 4 and 16).
- Diverse families need to be matched with appropriate resources, supports, and services (chapters 3, 4, 13, and 16), building on strengths and addressing their needs (chapter 4).
- Child welfare agencies must address foster youths' educational, financial, and housing needs (chapter 6).

Strategies

- Interventions must be holistic, taking into account the interconnectedness of the child, family, and community and addressing all three (chapters 2, 4, and 16).
- Practitioners need to demonstrate culturally competent practices (chapters 2, 3, 12, and 16).
- Practitioners must acknowledge diversity of family structure, traditional beliefs, behavioral experiences, dimensions of culture and race, ethnicity, social class, age, gender, gender identity, religion, and national origin (chapter 4).
- Practitioners can reduce disproportionality with support systems for families (chapter 4).
- Understanding historical trauma is central to understanding disproportionality and disparity in child welfare (chapters 9 and 12).
- Families require an array of services that can include crisis intervention, brief solution-focused therapy, and cognitive–behavioral therapy; to maximize effectiveness, family-centered practice can use Homebuilders family preservation standards (chapter 4).
- Practitioners' interventions need to be based on assessments of adults (including the birth parents) including any emotional, behavioral, cognitive, and physical disregulation affecting their parenting. Assessments must address the child, who may be dealing with traumatic exposure (chapter 9).
- Assessment practices need to be ongoing to ensure that early perceptions can be modified when appropriate and to provide the fullest opportunity for families to have continuous input as partners in service delivery (chapter 10).

- Child protective workers could be more effective by using a partnering rather than an authoritative approach with families and providing psychoeducation about the impact of trauma on children (chapter 9).
- Trauma-informed practice is needed in child protective, preventive, foster care, and adoption services; trauma-informed interventions should include phase- or stage-oriented trauma treatment (chapter 9).
- Prospective adoptive parents should be assessed for their readiness to adopt a traumatized child and, whether they are kin or unrelated, should be trained in parenting traumatized children and adolescents (chapter 9).
- Communities should be helped to take ownership of the safety and well-being of the children in the community and to design and tailor services to their needs (chapter 2).
- Alternative services such as those in differential response systems require skills in family assessment and engagement (chapter 7).
- Practitioners must demonstrate understanding of the potential trauma of poverty (chapters 3 and 4).

Evidence-based practices

- Child welfare practice should be evidence based (chapters 1, 4, 10, and 16).
- Social workers have an important role in research, development, and implementation of evidence-based interventions (chapters 1 and 10).
- Many families involved with child welfare services who face co-occurring challenges are not receiving services with demonstrated effectiveness (chapter 10).
- In addition to increasing the availability of evidence-based, high-quality services in routine settings, further investigation is required of informal supports and the impact of community contexts on service need, service receipt, and service outcomes (chapter 10).
- Implementing evidence-based practices requires expert practitioners, skilled supervisors, leadership, an organizational climate that fosters innovation, and adequate financial resources to build the infrastructure necessary for implementing best practices (chapter 1).

Interprofessional and Cross-Systems Practices

Family engagement

- All agencies working with child welfare families must be family-centered and interprofessional collaborators (chapters 2, 3, 4, 7, and 10).
- Family and youth engagement is emerging as a powerful resource in policy, programs, and practice in numerous service delivery systems (chapter 5).

- The best assessments of family needs and challenges may come from families themselves rather than professionals (chapter 10).

Integrated funding streams, data systems, and services

- Because of co-occurring challenges, evidence-based service integration is essential for improved outcomes for child welfare families (chapters 2, 3, and 10).
- If services are ineffective, even the most well-coordinated system of care will be unable to help families (chapter 10).
- Collaborative mechanisms must be in place for linking case records across agencies to form integrated data systems; in addition to improving practices, such shared information may help prevent child fatalities (chapters 8 and 10). A growing number of states link birth records, child welfare services data, and mortality records in an effort to develop a clearer picture of child mortality risk related to maltreatment (chapter 1).
- Flexible or braided funding mechanisms may help overcome the funding "silos" that often characterize human service systems (chapter 10).
- Agencies need to optimize resources through collaboration (chapters 3, 4, and 6).
- Coalitions of support and cross-systems resource mobilization are required to support foster youths in transition to adulthood (chapter 6).

Community and other institutions

- Practitioners need to use both civil and criminal courts for ensuring child protection (chapter 8).
- Child welfare practice needs to take into account the connections between community contexts and family members' health and mental health (chapter 10).
- Temporary Assistance for Needy Families' practitioners need to see themselves as preventing child abuse and neglect (chapter 3).
- Temporary Assistance for Needy Families and related agencies should see sanctions on clients, and clients losing services due to time limits, as a systems failure rather than a client failure and should hold themselves accountable (chapter 3).
- Public and nonprofit agencies need to join forces to meet the economic, housing, transportation, health, child care, employment, and education needs of foster care youths in transition to adulthood (chapter 6).
- Child welfare practices must include the development of financial and other forms of support for youths and families who partner with agencies as youth leaders and parent mentors (chapter 5). Creating occupational, educational, and

income ladders for low-income parents and youths in child welfare is a best practice strategy (chapter 3).

Leadership

- Leadership needs to be understood from a cultural standpoint; in traditional tribal cultures a leader is one who is a servant to others and is willing to take on any task to benefit the community (chapter 12).

Organizational Development and Change

Capacity building

- Child welfare agencies must build community capacity to address unmet needs and not impose themselves upon the community (chapter 2).
- Child welfare agencies must provide expertise and assistance while yielding decision-making power to the community (chapter 2).
- Organizational and workforce development, along with leadership capacity building, lead to more positive outcomes for children and families (chapter 13).

Cultural proficiency

- Disproportionality must be addressed by communities in their redesign of services and supports for families (chapter 2).
- Child welfare agencies need to demonstrate cultural proficiency by honoring traditional cultural practices and engaging community elders and leaders to guide them in what resources are available within the community as well as what issues the community is facing (chapters 2 and 4).
- Managers and supervisors are key to culturally responsive practices and alliances and culturally proficient workforce development (chapters 2 and 13).
- The redesign of child welfare systems and community programs requires diverse and inclusive leadership groups with power equally distributed (see chapter 2).

Systems reform and quality improvement

- Child welfare agencies need to move beyond episodic and crisis-driven responses to undertake systems reform (chapter 2).
- Continuous quality improvement must be central to all child welfare agencies (chapter 16).
- Organizational climate and culture are key to retention of staff, especially those of color (chapter 13).

- Organizational effectiveness depends on data-driven decision-making (chapter 13).
- Data-driven, outcome-oriented systems will produce better outcomes for children (chapter 13).
- The organizational change process is just as important as change itself, requiring parallel processes of improved casework with clients, agency leadership with staff, and agency staff with community providers (chapter 14).
- For change to occur, thoughtful and purposeful activities need to be directed toward implementation processes (chapter 14).
- Workforce development in states, counties, and tribes requires progress-tracking systems that inform outcome evaluation and impacts on workforce stability and competence (chapter 13).
- Agencies need to have research capacity (chapter 16).
- Agency leaders must be committed to using programs as incubators of innovation (chapter 16).

Workforce recruitment and selection

- Workforce development requires systemic, agency-wide recruitment plans, including internships, and increasing outreach to increase diversity (chapter 13).
- Selection processes need to include entry-level caseworker competency requirements consistent with the agency's job requirements and practice model, realistic job previews, competency-based screening, and attention to how these affect recruitment among diverse cultural, ethnic, and linguistic groups (chapter 13).
- The impending retirement of large numbers of social workers puts even greater demands on the child welfare system to examine the supply and demand of child welfare workers and the pipeline to child welfare practice (chapter 15).

Education and training for the workforce

- Training and professional development need to move from individual to systems and holistic frameworks (chapter 13).
- There is a need for more training and supervision in family-centered practice for all protective service workers (chapter 7).
- Preservice training for all child welfare staff should include the impact of trauma on children, birth and foster parents, and workers serving traumatized populations (chapter 9).
- Staff training is required on the impact of trauma, evidence-based trauma treatments available in their communities, and the fit of different treatments for populations at different points in the child welfare service trajectory (chapter 9).

- Child welfare organizations need to address barriers to becoming trauma sensitive and trauma informed, emphasizing physical and psychological safety for staff (chapter 9).
- Vicarious and secondary traumatic stress can result in behavioral change in workers, specifically the emergence of symptoms similar to those seen in posttraumatic stress disorder (chapter 9).
- Supervisory training should include coaching for practice effectiveness and building supportive, "pro-retention" unit cultures (chapter 13).
- A comprehensive package of training and technical assistance improves supervisors' selection and retention skills (chapter 13).
- The National Child Welfare Workforce Institute leadership and related competency model offers a conceptual framework for leadership training and education for supervisors (chapter 13).
- Child welfare systems need financial incentives for staff members to participate in continuing education and earn a professional degree (chapter 13).

Supervision and leadership

- Strong supervision and staff support is the key to workforce development, the link between worker competence, satisfaction, and retention, organizational climate, and positive outcomes for children and youths (chapter 13).
- Staff require ongoing support to cope with home visits in violent neighborhoods, hostile clients, and reoccurring exposure to trauma, including child fatalities (chapter 9).
- Supervision must be more client centered and worker supportive to counter the emphasis on accountability (chapter 9).
- Leadership is critical to organizational culture, vision, participatory management, and outcome effectiveness (chapter 13).
- Leaders need to excel at relationship building and working in partnership with tribal and cultural stakeholders (chapters 2, 12, and 13).
- Organizational culture must be developed to establish a climate that promotes both physical and psychological safety for staff (chapter 9).

Programs and Policies

Trauma-informed practices

- The social work profession needs to create and sustain trauma-informed agencies, organizations, and services (chapter 9).
- Understanding historical trauma is central to understanding disproportionality and disparity in child welfare, which can result in guardedness, resistance

to accepting services, and poor communication between the population being served and child welfare staff, especially those representing the dominant culture (chapter 9).

Differential response and family group conferencing

- Differential response systems and practices retain both the investigation and family preservation paradigms for child protective services; they can greatly reduce the number of children who are unnecessarily placed in foster care (chapter 7).
- Unless there is adequate funding for services, it will be very difficult for child protective workers to feel safe referring families to those services rather than investigating them for child neglect (chapter 7).
- Family group conferencing and differential response are promising models that adhere to family-centered practice (chapter 4).

Preventing child fatalities

- Child welfare and related systems need to undertake systematic and comprehensive fatality reviews (chapter 8).
- National systems need to be in place to ensure better reporting on child fatalities (chapter 8).
- There is a need for children's advocacy centers and groups (chapter 8).
- Prevention of maltreatment and child fatalities requires a full range of targeted prevention interventions, including expanding current strategies that work, funding research to develop new prevention strategies, and developing strategic partnerships for collective impact across communities (chapter 1).

Valuing native peoples and family partners

- Many U.S. institutions and policies have been inconsistent and disruptive to Native people as they have not incorporated the practices, values, and beliefs of Native cultures (chapter 12).
- Youths and families require adequate compensation for their partner roles in reform efforts (chapter 5).

Universities, Schools of Social Work, and University–Agency Partnerships

Advanced education

- Postsecondary education can give youths new opportunities to belong and build long-term relationships while preparing for their future (chapter 6).

- Advanced education is a pathway to a better life for older youths in foster care, but no single agency has all the resources necessary to support youths' higher educational needs, such as tuition, books, housing, and health care (see chapter 6).
- Social work education is linked with higher worker retention rates, intention to stay in a child welfare position, and improved permanency outcomes (chapter 11).
- Social work programs and the Children's Bureau must make a commitment to meet the field's need for expert child welfare professionals by funding doctoral and postdoctoral child welfare research and supporting social work faculty in developing evidence-based child welfare interventions (chapter 1).

Communitywide supports

- Through partnerships with child welfare and youth-serving agencies, universities, colleges, and vocational schools can connect students to foster care alumni organizations (chapter 6).
- Foster care youths in transition to adulthood need college-based alumni associations, peer supports, community engagement, and leadership opportunities (chapter 6).

Curricular reform

- Schools of social work need to move from problem- or issue-focused educational preparation to a systemic focus on organizational development and practice implementation (chapter 13).
- Social work education must prepare students to be leaders, agents of organizational change, agents of the family, critical thinkers, and problem solvers; to see families as partners; and to create therapeutic alliances with families (chapter 4).
- Social work education needs to address child welfare leadership, systems of care, diversity, and organizational culture (chapter 11).
- Social work traineeships need to foster peer networks, incorporating a range of innovations to prepare students for the child welfare workforce and future programmatic leadership (chapter 11).
- Educational programs in social work need to address workforce development, leadership, and supervision and how these are linked to client outcomes (chapter 13).
- Social work educators must foster the skills needed to work in complex, collaborative, diverse contexts (chapter 13).
- Educational practices, including those in schools of social work, must incorporate theories, practices, and skills addressing a different way of knowing, hearing the

stories of child welfare challenges and remedies in Native communities (chapter 12).

- Schools of social work must ensure greater instruction in and exploration of youth and family engagement models and approaches, both in the classroom and through field education and supervision (chapter 5).
- Traineeship programs ensure that a social work education addresses the foundational knowledge and specialized preparation needed to work in child welfare, reinforced by courses covering such topics as substance abuse, mental health, rural practice, leadership, systems of care, and disparities in communities of color including Native Americans, in a way that is aligned with public agency preservice training requirements (chapter 11).
- Schools of social work can take the lead in offering training and encouraging public child welfare workers, as well as other students, to balance the goals of child protection and family preservation (chapter 7).
- Schools of social work need to incorporate the concept of historical trauma into analyses of oppression, social injustice, and human rights (chapter 9).
- There needs to be more attention to trauma and neuroscience in research (chapters 4, 9, and 16).

Recruitment

- Schools of social work need to attract, educate, and graduate social workers with experience in communities of color. Stronger partnerships with community colleges and high schools may create pathways to higher education (chapter 13).

Attributes of successful traineeship programs

- Traineeships can enhance recruitment, retention, and postgraduation supports, drawing on peer networks and an array of innovations (chapter 11).
- Traineeship programs are effective in developing leadership and addressing systems of care, diversity, and organizational culture (chapter 11).
- Bridging the gap between universities and tribal communities is an essential first step in developing child welfare traineeships with Native Americans (chapter 12).
- Effectively, ethically, and respectfully building bridges between universities and tribal communities requires an investment of time for all involved (chapter 12).
- Building diversity in traineeships involves having relationships with diverse populations, faculty and staff of color, a history of educating students of color with a diverse student body at both the BSW and MSW level, and the ability to recruit from a diverse community (chapter 11).

- Successful social work education focuses on building a sense of community for tribal students. Core to American Indian and Alaska Native identity is the experience of being part of a whole and being located in and attentive to a network of reciprocal connections, support, and community (chapter 12).
- Social work education programs should take into account students' familial and tribal obligations as well as the financial challenges faced by some American Indian and Alaska Native students, providing program flexibility (chapter 12).
- In recruiting and providing supports for students, schools of social work need to recognize that American Indian and Alaska Native students are more likely to come from backgrounds of poverty and may be the source of support for many family members (chapter 12).

Cross-disciplinary collaboration
- Improved outcomes for children and families will not be achieved by one discipline or one agency alone. Strategies are required for interprofessional education and training of physicians, social workers, lawyers, nurses, and psychologists (chapter 15).

Knowledge development and transfer

- Fieldwork sites can test innovative, promising, and evidence-informed practices; partnerships with agencies should involve field placements where students are exposed to evidence-informed intervention and treatment (chapters 9 and 14).
- Partnerships between schools of social work, child welfare agencies, and the Children's Bureau offer flexibility in funding and resources to implement innovations; the resultant knowledge can then be infused in curricula and reflected in laws, polices, and improved practices of child welfare agencies (chapter 14).
- Partnerships between schools of social work and child welfare agencies promote the integration of science into a real-world setting, testing the efficacy, feasibility, and sustainability of evidence-based practices, in turn promoting knowledge development and transfer across the field of child welfare (chapter 14).
- Schools of social work and agencies can better address the social-emotional needs of children by developing, implementing, testing, and replicating effective interventions that focus on well-being, safety, and permanence and target children in foster and kin care as well as in their own homes (chapter 15).
- Social work faculty working with tribal communities and traineeships may need to coach other faculty to understand the needs and learning styles of tribal and urban Native students (chapter 12).
- A continuum of support to attain a social work education (BSW, MSW, and postgraduate), as well as ongoing professional development and competency-based

training, will elevate the knowledge and practice skills of the child welfare work-force (chapter 14).

- Strengthening connections to agencies and extending relationships after train-ees graduate are ways to build on the curriculum and programmatic features of traineeship programs (chapter 11).

Policy advocacy

- Social work practitioners, policymakers, and researchers must be aware of the need for programs and social reforms that prevent family problems as well as respond to them (chapter 10).
- In the future, the Children's Bureau should propose, fund, and evaluate federal policies and programs relating to the "whole child" in all areas involving health and mental health; social, emotional, and economic welfare; and education (chapter 1).

Expanding collaborations

- Authentic relationship building in tribal and urban Indian settings by social work educators must include not just program planning but also cultural and rela-tional activities such as powwows, traditional honor ceremonies, and other tribal community events (chapter 12).
- Members of effective university–agency partnerships understand each other's culture and context, create an information exchange process, and develop trust (chapter 15).
- Universities participating in training collaborations can likely also explore research collaborations, and vice versa (chapter 15).
- University–agency partnerships must be supported by diverse funding sources, so that when one funding stream decreases or disappears, the partnership remains sustainable (chapter 15).
- The National Association of Social Workers, National Association of Public Child Welfare Administrators, Child Welfare League of America, Council on Social Work Education, and other organizations can play important roles in promoting uni-versity–agency partnerships in child welfare (chapter 15).
- University–agency collaborations can provide agencies access to the resources of the university, including libraries, research infrastructure, and the technologi-cal and analytic expertise to address practice improvements (chapter 15).
- Deans and directors of schools of social work, national social work and child wel-fare organizations, and the Children's Bureau must work together to address the need for staff to meet the emotional needs of children and families (chapter 15).

New Agendas

The recommendations that emerge from the authors help to inform the work ahead, but other challenges remain. How do we recruit enough qualified applicants for a strong workforce? How will states, tribes, and districts scale up evidence-based practices to full implementation? What are the models for implementation that result in effective program development? How can state-level leadership engage governors and legislators in a child welfare partnership? How do the early practices of the Children's Bureau offer guidance for the work ahead?

The historical overview of the Children's Bureau provided in chapter 1 illustrates the importance of social work practice and education. Although there is strong evidence that social work education provides necessary educational preparation for child welfare work, insufficient numbers of BSW and MSW graduates are entering the child welfare field. How do we build capacity to engage young people with degrees in human services to enter a career in child welfare?

The Children's Corps is one example of an approach to recruiting graduates from across the human service disciplines for child welfare work. The Corps, inspired by the Teach for America model, is now operating in New York City (Fostering Change for Children, n.d.). It recruits students from colleges and universities across the country, has a competency-based approach to selecting potential candidates, uses behavioral interviewing to select Corps members, and provides preservice training and ongoing support after placement, consisting of monthly group check-ins and training and individually assigned mentors (personal communication with V. De Milly, program director, Children's Corps, Fostering Change for Children, May 23, 2012). At the time of publication, the Corps was in its second year of operation, with early indications that this very structured approach to recruitment, selection, and continuous support of people from diverse educational backgrounds was showing positive results.

Another area that requires further exploration is how to move evidence-based and informed programs into full-scale implementation and do so with consistent and positive outcomes across the country. The practices emerging from the collective impact literature present important guidance for this work. As the name implies, collective impact is action taken by a group of people from different sectors around a common agenda to solve a complex social problem (FSG, 2012). By coordinating efforts in an organized and directed way, with committed resources, collective impact practices have achieved large-scale changes that were unachievable without collaboration.

Every author in this book has described the complex, multidimensional challenges that confront the child welfare system in the United States. These challenges are not technical in nature but call for adaptive solutions, at multiple points in the system, involving many providers, policies, and programs. One of the premises of collective impact is that the challenges presented by a social problem such as child abuse cannot be addressed by replicating or scaling a single program or policy: "Large-scale social change comes from better cross-sector coordination rather than from the isolated intervention of individual organizations" (Kania & Kramer, 2011, p. 38). Are we ready as a national system to agree to see whether a collective impact approach can support efforts to end seemingly intractable social problems such as child abuse and poverty?

Another challenge not covered in these chapters concerns the paralysis that often occurs when organizations attempt to attend to multiple priorities all at once. It would be difficult to dispute the value of the recommendations put forward by the authors in this book, but how can they be implemented? What models for systems reform support developmental approaches to incremental change? Business practices provide some models for new product development and roll-out that can be applied to child welfare systems. While profit margins provide businesses with the markers that determine the success of new initiatives, the Information Memorandum on Continuous Quality Improvement offers tenets for measuring the effectiveness of new practices (U.S. Department of Health and Human Services [HHS], 2012c, Attachment A). These tenets are consistent with recommendations throughout this book: set the focus for the work; parent and youth voices are critical; the whole workforce must be part of the team designing and implementing the work; clear outcomes must be identified and measured and used to guide program design and development; leadership with focus is crucial; work processes must include cooperation across subunits.

Funding protocols often hamper the ability of tribes and states to scale up evidence-based practices. The Children's Bureau is funding waiver demonstration projects under the Child and Family Services Improvement and Innovation Act of 2011 (P. L. 112-34) for up to 10 states a year (HHS, 2012b). The priorities are designed to test and implement approaches to child welfare practice that are consistent with all that is known about supporting positive well-being for children, youths, and families while contributing to new knowledge development and cross-systems investment within states (HHS, 2012b). The challenge for states and tribes is to develop thoughtful, integrated proposals that are cost neutral.

What would it take to engage governors and tribal chiefs as partners in this 21st-century agenda? State child welfare directors serve at the pleasure of the governor. In county-based systems, local commissioners serve at the pleasure of the county executive, mayor, or board of supervisors. In tribal child welfare systems, the commissioner or director serves at the pleasure of the tribal council, chiefs, and elders. Leaders serving in these positions focus the work of the state, county, or tribe on the mission and vision of the agency and guide all aspects of practice and policy implementation.

Middle managers, supervisors, and frontline workers move into a waiting state when there is a leadership change. Staff members sometimes refer to a new idea as the "flavor of the week," implying that if they just wait, the new idea will go away when the director or commissioner leaves and something else will take its place. The ability to implement evidence-based practices, and the many ideas put forward by the authors of this volume, would be enhanced by stable leadership with expertise in child welfare. Important change has often taken root and thrived under consistent leadership, and withered and died when leadership is inconsistent. What would it take to engage governors, tribal council members, elders, and chiefs as partners in maintaining stable, competent, experienced child welfare leaders across changes in administration? What would it take to engage them as partners in a collective impact strategy with a clear agenda and mutually reinforcing activities to achieve the goal of ending child abuse in the United States?

Conclusion

At the dawn of this second century of child welfare services, families and youths are at center stage, technology is providing the tools needed to capture and use data more deliberatively and effectively, and the need for workforce and leadership development is receiving increasing attention. We know what it takes to develop and implement programs that result in improved well-being for children and families, but the wealth of knowledge from pilot programs has not translated into broad-based systems reform (Schorr, Schorr, & Wilson, 1989). We need the will, focus, and resources to move the work forward. The authors have identified a clear blueprint for effective programs and services for the coming century, all of which are strongly aligned with recent publications by the Children's Bureau. It comes down to policy, people, and funding, which make up the platform that the next century of work will be built on (Mitchell et al., 2012).

References

Child and Family Services Improvement and Innovation Act, P.L. 112-34, 125 Stat. 369. Sec. 1130 [42 U.S.C. 1320a-9], P 8-11 (September 30, 2011).

Fostering Change for Children. (n.d.). *Children's Corps.* Retrieved from http://www.fosteringchangeforchildren.org/whatwedo/childrenscorps.html

Kania, J., & Kramer, M. (2011). Collective impact. *Stanford Social Innovation Review, Winter,* 36–41.

Lipsky, M. (1980). *Street-level bureaucracy: Dilemmas of the individual in public services.* New York: Russell Sage Foundation.

Mitchell, L., Walters, R., Thomas, M. L., Denniston, J., McIntosh, H., & Brodowski, M. (2012). The Children's Bureau's vision for the future of child welfare. *Journal of Public Child Welfare, 6,* 550–567.

Perspective. (1993). In *Merriam-Webster's collegiate dictionary* (10th ed.). Springfield, MA: Merriam-Webster, Inc.

Schorr, L., Schorr, D., & Wilson, W. J. (1989). *Within our reach: Breaking the cycle of disadvantage.* New York: Anchor Books.

U.S. Department of Health and Human Services, Administration for Children and Families, Administration on Children, Youth and Families, Children's Bureau. (2012a). *Promoting social and emotional well-being for children and youth receiving child welfare services* (ACYF-CB-IM-12-04). Washington, DC: Author.

U.S. Department of Health and Human Services, Administration for Children and Families, Administration on Children, Youth and Families, Children's Bureau. (2012b). *Child Welfare Waiver Demonstration Projects* (ACYF-CB-IM-12-05). Washington, DC: Author.

U.S. Department of Health and Human Services, Administration for Children and Families, Administration on Children, Youth and Families, Children's Bureau. (2012c). *Establishing and maintaining continuous quality improvement (CQI) systems in state child welfare agencies* (ACYF-CB-IM-12-07). Washington, DC: Author.

ABOUT THE EDITORS

Katharine Briar-Lawson PhD, LMSW, is dean, professor, and co-principal investigator, national Child Welfare Workforce Institute, School of Social Welfare, University at Albany, State University of New York.

Nancy S. Dickinson, **MSSW, PhD,** is clinical professor and director, National Child Welfare Workforce Institute, School of Social Work, University of Maryland, Baltimore.

Mary McCarthy, PhD, LMSW, is director, Social Work Education Consortium and co-principal investigator, National Child Welfare Workforce Institute, School of Social Welfare, University at Albany, State University of New York.

ABOUT THE CONTRIBUTORS

Gary R. Anderson, PhD, Michigan licensed clinical and macro social worker, is director and professor, Michigan State University School of Social Work, East Lansing, Michigan

Richard P. Barth, PhD, MSW, is dean and professor, University of Maryland School of Social Work, Baltimore.

William C. Bell, PhD, is president and chief executive officer of Casey Family Programs in Seattle, and currently resides in Sammamish, WA.

Freda Bernotavicz, MS, is senior research associate, Muskie School of Public Service, University of Southern Maine, Portland, ME.

David A. Berns, MSW, LCSW, MPH, is director of the District of Columbia Department of Human Services, Washington, DC.

Nicole Bossard, PhD, is president of TGC Consulting, Inc. and a senior consultant at the National Resource Center for Permanency and Family Connections.

Angela Braxton is a consultant and parent partner at the National Resource Center for Permanency and Family Connections.

Charmaine Brittain, PhD, is senior associate, Butler Institute for Families, University of Denver.

Katharine Cahn, PhD, MSW, is executive director, Child Welfare Partnership, Portland State University School of Social Work, Portland, OR.

James C. Caringi, PhD, MSW, is MSW program director and associate professor, University of Montana School of Social Work, coordinator of Qualitative Research National Native Children's Trauma Center Institute for Educational Research and Service, Missoula, MT.

Elizabeth J. Clark, **PhD, ACSW, MPH**, is former chief executive director, National Association of Social Workers, Washington, DC.

Debra Conway is a child welfare consultant specializing in parent and community partnerships. She can be reached by email at parentpartnerprogram@yahoo.com.

Theresa M. Covington, MPH, is executive director, National Center for the Review and Prevention of Child Deaths, Michigan Public Health Institute, Okmemos, MI and Washington, DC.

Heather Craig-Oldsen, MSW, CSW, is associate professor, program director, and chair of the Social Work Department and principal investigator of the Siouxland Indian Child Welfare Traineeship Project, Briar Cliff University, Sioux City, IA.

Nancy S. Dickinson, **MSSW, PhD,** is clinical professor and director, National Child Welfare Workforce Institute, University of Maryland School of Social Work, Baltimore.

Kathleen Coulborn Faller, PhD, ACSW, Michigan licensed clinical and macro social worker, DCSW, is Marion Elizabeth Blue endowed Professor of Children and Families, director, Family Assessment Clinic, University of Michigan School of Social Work, Ann Arbor.

Cecilia Fiermonte, JD, is child welfare policy director, Alliance for Children and Families, Washington, DC.

Christine James-Brown is president and chief executive officer of the Child Welfare League of America, Washington, DC.

Won Hee Kim, MSSW, is a doctoral student at Case Western Reserve University, Mandel School of Applied Science, Cleveland.

Miriam J. Landsman, PhD, is associate professor of Social Work and executive director of the National Resource Center for Family Centered Practice at the University of Iowa, Iowa City.

Robin Leake, PhD, is director, Research and Evaluation, Butler Institute for Families, University of Denver.

Anita Light, CAE, is deputy executive director, National Association of Public Child Welfare Administrators, Washington, DC.

Gerald P. Mallon, DSW, is the Julia Lathrop Professor of Child Welfare and executive director of the National Resource Center for Permanency and Family Connections at the Silberman School of Social Work at Hunter College in New York City.

Nancy McDaniel, MPA, is director, of Consultation and Capacity Building, Butler Institute for Families, University of Denver.

Brenda G. McGowan, PhD, LMSW, is professor, James Dumpson Chair of Child Welfare Studies, Fordham University Graduate School of Social Service, New York.

Roxana Torrico Meruvia is senior practice associate, National Association of Social Workers, Washington, DC. Meruvia conducts research and develops written products on issues related to children, youths and families. She has authored several publications related to child welfare specifically on the topic of youths aging out of foster care. She also has several years of experience working with diverse, low-income youths and families in the nonprofit and public systems.

Benjamin Muhammad is a former foster care youth and a staff member at the National Resource Center for Permanency and Family Connections.

Sara Munson, MSW, is the national dissemination coordinator for the National Child Welfare Workforce Institute at the University at Albany School of Social Welfare.

Michael Petit, MSW, is president and founder, Every Child Matters Education Fund, Washington, DC.

Cathryn Potter, PhD, is executive director, Butler Institute for Families, Graduate School of Social Work, University of Denver.

David Sanders, PhD, is executive vice president of Systems Improvement at Casey Family Programs in Seattle.

Brenda D. Smith, PhD, is associate professor, University of Alabama School of Social Work, Tuscaloosa.

Virginia C. Strand, DSW, is professor and codirector, National Center for Social Work Trauma Education and Workforce Development,, Graduate School of Social Service, Fordham University, New York.

Virginia Whitekiller, EdD, MSW, BSW, is associate professor, Northeastern State University, Department of Social Work, Tahlequah, OK.

Julia M. Watkins, PhD, is past executive director, Council on Social Work Education, Alexandria, VA.

Joan Levy Zlotnik, PhD, ACSW, is director, Social Work Policy Institute, National Association of Social Workers, Washington, DC.

INDEX

Motivational interviewing, 95
Mullen, J., 64
Multidimensional family therapy, 70
Multisystemic therapy, 70–71

N

National Adoption Information Clearinghouse,
    262
National Association of Deans and Directors
    of Schools of Social Work (NADD),
    278–279
National Association of Public Child Welfare
    Administrators (NAPCWA), 278–279,
    293–295
National Association of Social Workers (NASW),
    288
    Code of Ethics, 167
    foster care policies and, 120–121
    future directions of, 268–270
    goals, 300–302
    increase of social work knowledge base,
        266–267
    Social Work Policy Institute, 289
National Blueprint, 297–298
National Center for Child Death Review
    (NCCDR), 149
National Center for Housing and Child Welfare,
    120
National Center for the Review and Prevention
    of Child Deaths, 144
National Center on Child Abuse and Neglect, 11,
    143, 262
National Children's Alliance, 158
National Child Welfare Evaluation Summits, 280,
    288
National Child Welfare Leadership Institute (U of
    Utah), 243
National Child Welfare Research Centers, 11
National Child Welfare Workforce Institute
    (NCWWI), 217, 288–289, 301
    innovations, 202, 208–209
    Leadership Academy for Supervisors, 138
    leadership model, 244–246
    traineeship program, 201, 202–203, 207–
        209
National Clearinghouse on Child Abuse and
    Neglect Information, 11
National Incidence Study of Child Abuse and
    Neglect, 11
National Indian Child Welfare Association, 225
National Institutes of Health, 12
National Native Children's Trauma Center, 221

National Resource Center(s), 238
    for Community-Based Child Abuse
        Prevention, 281
    for Family Based Services (U of Iowa), 62
    for Organizational Improvement, 238
    for Permanency and Family Connections,
        115
    on Youth Development, 115
National Study on Child and Adolescent Well-
    being, 281
National Survey of Child and Adolescent Well-
    Being, 12, 133, 188
National Technical Assistance and Evaluation
    Center for Systems of Care, 94
National Violent Death Case Reporting System,
    149
National Youth in Transition Database, 12
*A Nation's Shame: Fatal Child Abuse and Neglect
    in the United States,* 143–144, 146–147
Native Americans. *See also* Indian child welfare
    settings, social work education in
    in child welfare system, 23–24
    Indian Adoption Project, 24, 25
    Indian Child Welfare Act, 25
    poverty and, 43
    in traineeship programs, 318
Native cultures, 316
Nebraska university-agency partnerships, 286
Needs assessments, 12–13
Neglect and deprivation. *See also* Child abuse
    classification of, 145t
    maltreatment fatalities, 8
    poverty and, 43–45
Neonaticide, 150
Neuroscience, 299
Nevada death review process, 152
New Haven Department of Health, 5
New York
    Bridge Builders, 35
    Children's Village, 299
    Coalition for Hispanic Family Services, 35
    Family Assessment Response, 132
    Hillside Family of Agencies, 299
    university–agency partnerships, 283
New York Children's Aid Society, 22
New York School of Applied Philanthropy, 5, 6
New York Society for the Prevention of Cruelty
    to Children, 23, 125, 134–135
North Carolina training and technical assistance
    studies, 242
Northeastern State University (Oklahoma),
    221–223

in Indian child welfare settings, 217–235
peer learning approaches and coaching, 250–251
professionalism and, 300–301
strengths-based family approach, 38
student family and cultural obligations, consideration of, 319
traineeship programs, 134, 201–215
trauma-informed practices, 179–180
Society for the Prevention of Cruelty to Children (SPCC), 125, 134–135
Solution-based casework, 67–68, 95
Specialized Native American Project (Native Unit), 219
Stark County study (Ohio), 191
Starting Early Starting Smart, 191
Steinberg, Lisa, 143
Stipend Student Inventory, 212–213
Strength-based perspective, 60
Strengthening Families and Communities, 136
Strengthening University/Agency Research Partnerships to Enhance Child Welfare Outcomes, 286
Structured psychotherapy for adolescents responding to chronic stress, 176
Substance abuse, 70, 189
family treatment drug courts, 192
recovery coach, 192
service co-location, 192–193
Substance Abuse and Mental Health Services Administration, 15
Supervision: The Safety Net for Front-Line Child Welfare Practice, 134
Supporting Success framework, 116, 117t–118t
Supreme Court Commission on Children and the Courts, 286
"Systems of care" delivery model, 185
Systems-of-care practice, 86, 190, 194

T

Temporary Assistance for Needy Families (TANF), 15, 45, 50–51, 312
family-centered approach to, 52–53
as primary prevention arm of child welfare, 53
Traineeship programs, 201–215, 217–218, 276
attributes of successful, 318–319
building a diverse workforce through, 209–211
challenges of, 204–207
Comprehensive Workforce Projects, 208
cross-site evaluation, 213
design of, 202–207

evaluative evidence for experience/outcomes of, 211–214
features of, 203–204
field placements, 206–207
future of social work education/practice and, 214–215
historical development of, 202
National Child Welfare Workforce Institute program, 207–209
payback/repayment period, 203, 205–206
recruitment strategies, 205
requirements for, 203
Title IV-E training, 277–278
Transformational leadership model, 264
Trauma-focused cognitive-behavioral therapy, 176
Trauma-informed practices, 60–61, 167–180, 310, 315–316
achieving trauma-informed systems, 178
adoption services, 176
disparity, 178
disproportionality, 178–179
emotional safety/security, 172–173
evidence-informed trauma principles, 170–178
foster care services, 175
future directions/practice implications, 178–180
historical antecedents, 168–169
historical trauma, 178
impact of trauma on children, 169, 170–171
impact of trauma on staff, 169, 177–178
intervention approaches, 171–172
parent training, 175
phase-oriented trauma treatment, 171–172
preventive services, 174
recognizing trauma triggers, 170
social work education, 179–180
social work practice, 179
stabilization, 172–176
trauma-specific services, 176
Trauma theory, 167–168
Trends, 298
Triage procedures, 132, 136
Tribal Stars (U of California-San Diego), 248
Tribal youth, 248
TRIO programs, 114

U

UNICEF (United Nations International Children's Emergency Fund), 6